PART 4 THE MAJOR ECONOMIC CHALLENGES

Understanding Macroeconomics

ROBERT L.
HEILBRONER

LESTER C.
THUROW

Seventh
Edition

PRENTICE-HALL, INC., Englewood Cliffs, NJ 07632

Library of Congress Cataloging in Publication Data

Heilbroner, Robert L
  Understanding macroeconomics

  Includes index.
  1. Macroeconomics. I. Thurow, Lester C.,
joint author. II. Title.
HB172.5H44   1981   339   80-22509
ISBN 0-13-936559-1

UNDERSTANDING MACROECONOMICS, 7th edition
by Robert L. Heilbroner and Lester C. Thurow

10 9 8 7 6 5 4 3 2 1

This is a Special Projects book.
Maurine Lewis, director
Susan Adkins, editor
Ray Keating, manufacturing buyer

Cover design by Olympia Shahbaz from drawings by Bernarda Bryson.
Front cover drawing from ''Economic Psychology'' by George Katona,
© 1954 by Scientific American, Inc. All rights reserved.
Illustrations by Don Martinetti.

Prentice-Hall International, Inc., *London*
Prentice-Hall of Australia Pty. Limited, *Sydney*
Prentice-Hall of Canada, Ltd., *Toronto*
Prentice-Hall of India Private Limited, *New Delhi*
Prentice-Hall of Japan, Inc., *Tokyo*
Prentice-Hall of Southeast Asia Pte. Ltd., *Singapore*
Whitehall Books Limited, *Wellington, New Zealand*

CONTENTS

PART 3 MACROECONOMICS:
THE ANALYSIS OF PROSPERITY AND RECESSION

Part

1 The Economic Background

Chapter

1 **WHAT THIS BOOK IS ALL ABOUT**

A LOOK AHEAD

This is the chapter in which to get your bearings. As you read, keep in mind these objectives:

(1) to get a feel for what is to come;

(2) to learn how the book is organized; and

(3) most important of all, to pick up a few study hints—you really want to pay attention to these.

This is a book about macroeconomics, and naturally you wonder what "macro" means. The word comes from the Greek, meaning large, and indeed macroeconomics is about giant sized things such as inflation and unemployment and economic growth. Yet microeconomics, its twin brother, is also about vast problems, like pollution and industrial power and wealth and poverty. So the difference between macro and micro isn't really one of scale. It is one of approach, of perspective. Macro looks at problems from above, as if we were flying over the economy and looking down on its vast rivers of production or its parched areas of unemployment. Microeconomics brings us to a different perspective, a kind of worm's eye view from which we examine what is going on in the economy from the vantage point of an individual consumer or working person or business firm.

Why two perspectives? The answer is that certain kinds of problems, such as those that we will study in this book, are best examined from a macro perspective,others from a micro perspective. Economic growth, for example, inflation or national unemployment, are issues that it is very hard to perceive, much less grasp, from a micro view. Other issues, like the shortages or surpluses we encounter in various markets, or the differences between individuals' incomes, or the effect of various kinds of taxes on people, are much easier to handle from a micro view, and very difficult to put into focus from an Olympian macro perch.

To be an economist, therefore, you really have to study both macro- and microeconomics. If this is your first introduction to economics, it follows that you will be only half an economist when you have finished this book. To complete your education, you should have a look into a text on micro to fill in the missing places.

WHAT THIS BOOK IS ABOUT

Macroeconomics is our subject, but we are not going to jump directly into the water. Macroeconomics is about the trajectory our economic system describes as it moves into the future, and about certain problems it generates in the course of its movement. Before we begin to investigate those difficulties, or even to describe that trajectory, we need to have some feel for what the economy looks like, and some general comprehension of what it means to have it move like a great vehicle through time.

That is what Part 1 is about. Chapter 2, "The Great Economists," is your first glance at the macro system itself (and at parts of the micro system, too), gained from a look at the thought of Adam Smith, Karl Marx, and John Maynard Keynes, the three most influential economists of our discipline. Chapter 3, "The Trend of Things," will then flesh out their large-scale conceptions by examining actual trends in the American economy over the past fifty years or so. As you watch the shape and size of the economic structure change, you will not only get a chance to judge how accurately Smith, Marx, and Keynes foresaw the future, but you will also gain a first acquaintance with the workings of the system itself.

Part 2 is a switch from a study of history and of actual institutions to a study of theory. Here in three chapters we learn the way that economists think about their subject, whether macro or micro. Chapter 5, "Supply and Demand," is probably the most important chapter of Part 2: it repays *thinking about,* as well as reading. Chapter 6 is a brief rundown of a few techniques of graphing and simple mathematics that you should be familiar with.

MACRO ITSELF

Now we are ready for the main subject. Part 3 is macroeconomics proper, from Chapter 7 through Chapter 18. You'll notice that we have cut this long part into three subsections to make it easier to master. The first subsection, Chapters 7 through 10, introduces you to the vocabulary and definitions of gross national product (GNP) and to the fundamental process of economic growth itself. Of these chapters, Chapter 10, "Saving and Investment," is crucial. Once you have learned that, you will already have unlocked one of the central mysteries of how the macrosystem works.

The next section takes up the different parts of GNP. In Chapters 11 through 13 we examine the flow of our national buying for consumption, the nature of the vital activity of investment, and the controversial issues surrounding government spending. Then, in Chapter 14, we combine the flows of consumption, investment and government spending to discover how the level of GNP is determined.

The third section of macro takes us to the most mystifying part of economics: money. In Chapters 15 through 18 we will discover what money consists of, how it is controlled, and the effects that it exerts on the flow of production and the level of prices.

These step-by-step chapters have now readied us for Part 4, the most important part of the book in so far as our future is concerned. Here we examine three major problems: inflation, unemployment, and defending the dollar. The first two issues need no explanation. But defending the dollar? Usually this is kept for a separate course on international economics. We think that it is no longer possible to pretend that the United States' economy proceeds along its trajectory solely under the influence of its domestic activities. We are inextricably part of a world economy and Chapter 21 discusses some of the ways in which our system is entangled with other capitalist systems. We think you will find it interesting and perfectly understandable.

Finally we end on a note of history, similar to that on which we began. The macroeconomic system whose trajectory and problems we have studied is that of the United States; and with some institutional changes, might be that of any advanced capitalist economy. Does our study also apply to India or Africa or South America? We shall use our final chapter to reflect on the differences between the advanced and the backward economic systems of the world.

STUDYING ECONOMICS

Now a word about getting ready to learn the subject. Many students begin economics with mixed feelings. On the one hand, they know it is terribly important; on the other hand, they are sure it will be terribly difficult.

Is economics difficult? Certainly it has its areas of rough sledding—what subject does not? But by and large, economics has acquired its reputation for difficulty for reasons that vanish when we examine them.

VOCABULARY

The first of these reasons is that economics requires a special vocabulary. **To become economists, you will have to learn at least a dozen words and phrases that have meanings somewhat different from those of everyday usage:** *capital, investment, demand,* **for example.** You will have to master another dozen phrases that come awkwardly to the tongue (and sometimes not at all to the mind): *marginal propensity to consume* is a good example.

In economics, as in French, some people acquire new words and phrases easily, some do not; and in economics, as in French, until you can say things correctly, you are apt to say them very wrongly. So when the text says *gross private domestic investment* those are the words to be learned, not just any combination of three of them because they seem to mean the same thing. Fortunately, the necessary economic vocabulary has far fewer words than French has, and the long and awkward phrases seem shorter and easier after you've said them a few times.

DIAGRAMS

Associated with learning the vocabulary of economics is learning how to draw a few diagrams. **Diagrams are an immensely powerful way of presenting many economic ideas.** Far from complicating things, they simplify them enormously. A supply and demand diagram makes things immediately clear in a way that a dozen pages could not.

So you must learn to draw a few diagrams. There is a great temptation to do so hastily, without thinking about the problem that the diagram is trying to make clear. A little care in labeling your axes (how else can anyone know what the diagram is about?) or in making lines tangent where they are supposed to touch, or cross where they are supposed to intersect, will not only make the difference between a poor grade and a better one, but will demonstrate that you truly understand the matter being illustrated.

You will also note that throughout the book, under each figure and most tables, there is a sentence or a paragraph which highlights the point being made. This should help you in reviewing the material.

KEY IDEAS

Studying a vast subject requires organization. This means putting first things first and keeping details and secondary material in the background.

We've tried to simplify the task of learning by putting a highly abbreviated and goal-oriented "A Look Ahead" and "Looking Back" at the beginning and at the end of each chapter. These sections do not necessarily embrace all the vocabulary or ideas in each chapter; instead they try to give you objectives to bear in mind before starting, and summaries to collect your thoughts when you're done.

At the end of each chapter, first read over the general review. Then look only at "Key Concepts" to see if you can yourself reproduce that review. Lastly, a glance at "Economic Vocabulary" will serve as a final vocabulary test. Page numbers follow each word for easy reference.

QUESTIONS AND EXTRA WORDS

Next, take time to answer all the questions at the ends of chapters. We have tried to make them few and central. If your instructor assigns the Student Guide that accompanies this text, do those problems too. There is no substitute for working out an example or for jotting down three reasons for this, four reasons for that. Learning is a process about which we know very little, but we do know that the physical and intellectual act of writing (or mumbling to yourself) is much more effective than merely thinking. Practice, as they say, makes perfect. You might reflect on the story of the sailor on a sinking ship. When asked if he knew how to swim, he answered, "Well, I understand the theory of it. . . ."

Economics has to be learned by arguing about it. Therefore after many chapters you will find a few additional pages—sometimes to add to your historical, statistical, or analytic knowledge, more often to open for your consideration problems of public policy that are related to the issues we have studied. The policy issues are often controversial. We hope you will worry about them—not just read them. They are there to open debate, not close it.

ANALYSIS AND ABSTRACTION

The idea of arguing brings us to our last word of counsel. Economics, as we have been at pains to say, is really not a hard language to learn. The key words and concepts are not too many or too demanding; the diagrams are no more difficult than those of elementary geometry. It is economic *thinking* that is hard, in a way that may have something to do with the aura of mystery we are out to dispel.

The hardness is not the sheer mental ability that is required. The reason lies, rather, in a **special attribute of economic thought:** *its abstract, analytic character.* Abstractness does not mean an indifference to the problems of the real world. Economics is about things as real as being without work. Nevertheless, as economists we do not study unemployment to learn firsthand about the miseries and sufferings that joblessness inflicts. We study unemployment to understand and analyze the causes of this malfunction of the economic system. Similarly, we do not study monopoly to fulminate against the profiteering of greedy capitalists, or labor unions to deplore the abuse of power by labor leaders, or government spending to declaim against politicians. We study these matters to shed light on their mechanisms, their reasons for being, their consequences.

There is nothing unusual in this abstract, analytic approach. All disciplines necessarily abstract from the immediate realities of their subject matters so that they may make broader generalizations or develop theories. What makes abstraction so difficult in economics is that the problems of the discipline are things that bother and affect us deeply in our lives. It is difficult, even unnatural, to suppress our feelings of approval or anger when we study the operations of the economic system and the main actors in it. The necessary act of analysis thus becomes mixed up with feelings of economic concern or even partisanship. Yet, unless **we make an effort to think analytically and abstractly in a detached way, we can be no more than slaves to our unexamined emotions.** Someone who *knows* that corporations or labor unions or governments are "good" or "bad" does not have to study economics, for the subject has nothing to teach such a person.

You must, therefore, make an effort to put aside your natural partisanship and prejudice while you study the problems of economics from its abstract, analytic, detached perspective. After you are done, your feelings will assuredly come back to you. No one has ever lost a sense of social outrage or social justice by taking a course in economics. But many students have changed or modified their preconceived judgments in one way or another. There is no escape, after all, from living in the world as economic citizens. But there is the option of living in it as intelligent and effective economic citizens. That is the prize we hope you carry away from this course.

ADAM SMITH

Chapter

THE GREAT ECONOMISTS

A LOOK AHEAD

In this chapter we shall learn something about the background of our economic system by reviewing the ideas of three great economists: Adam Smith, the father of our discipline: Karl Marx, its most revolutionary thinker; and John Maynard Keynes, who developed the special perspective that has come to be called "macroeconomics."

As we study the works of these great economists, a few questions ought to be kept in mind:

(1) What holds the system together and gives it "micro" order?

(2) Where is the system headed, giving it "macro" motion?

(3) What should we do to improve the system's operations, or what policies should we pursue?

THE INVENTION OF ECONOMICS

Our modern economic system emerged over turbulent centuries of change. Within the relatively static economic world of feudalism, a dynamic pulse began to stir as early as the eleventh century. The rise of powerful nation-states in the sixteenth century provided a great boost. But a fully capitalist system, knit together by a web of transactions embracing all of society's production and distribution, did not emerge until early modern times when the American colonies were being formed.

MERCANTILISM

Capitalism needed a philosophy—a reasoned explanation of how it worked. During the seventeenth and eighteenth centuries the understanding of market society was very imperfect. The Mercantilists, a group of British pamphleteers, tried to explain its workings in terms of a struggle among nations to gather "treasure"—gold and silver bullion. In this struggle, the Mercantilists saw merchants (hence *Mercant*ilism) playing a central role because they exported goods that were paid for in treasure.

Mercantilist policy was therefore very simple: Let England sell as much and buy as little abroad as possible. In that way, its national wealth would steadily pile up. No mercantilist seems to have been concerned about the impossibility of applying this philosophy to *all* nations. Can you see why it is impossible?

PHYSIOCRACY

In France during the eighteenth century an entirely different and equally inadequate explanation was called Physiocracy. In many ways the French school of ideas was the opposite of the British school. Physiocracy taught that the real wealth of economic life was production, not gold—an important step in the right direction. But the Physiocrats believed that production was essentially a gift of nature (*physiocracy* means the order of nature), and that therefore only labor working with nature was truly productive. Thus, whereas the Mercantilists extolled the merchants as active agents in creating national wealth, the Physiocrats regarded them as a "sterile" class that did no more than handle the wealth produced by the agriculturalist.

Mercantilism and Physiocracy are both indispensable stepping stones on the road to modern economics. Each yielded useful insights into the still unfinished economic revolution. But neither made the crucial breakthrough of seeing that the market was a system. That is, neither the Mercantilists nor the Physiocrats saw that the market network possessed an internal guidance mechanism to keep it on a steady course and that a society powered by the market was headed toward a visible destination.

These crucial insights came with Adam Smith, patron saint of our discipline and a figure of towering intellectual stature.

ADAM SMITH (1723-1790)

Adam Smith's fame resides in his masterpiece, *The Wealth of Nations*, published in 1776, the year of the Declaration of Independence. All things considered, it

PORTRAIT OF AN ABSENT-MINDED PROFESSOR

"I am a beau in nothing but my books" was the way that Adam Smith once described himself. Indeed, the famous medallion profile shows us a homely face. In addition, Smith had a curious stumbling gait that one friend called vermicular and was given to notorious fits of absent-mindedness. On one occasion, absorbed in discussion, he fell into a tanning pit.

Few other adventures befell Smith in the course of his scholarly, rather retiring, life. Perhaps the high point was reached at age four when he was kidnapped by a band of gypsies passing near Kirkaldy, his native hamlet in Scotland. His captors held him only a few hours; they may have sensed what a biographer later wrote: "He would have made, I fear, a poor gypsy."

Marked out early as a student of promise, at 16 Smith won a scholarship that sent him to Oxford. But Oxford was not then the center of learning that it is today. Little or no systematic teaching took place, the students being free to educate themselves, provided they did not read dangerous books. Smith was nearly expelled for owning a copy of David Hume's *Treatise of Human Nature,* a work we now regard as one of the philosophic masterpieces of the eighteenth century.

After Oxford, Smith returned to Scotland, where he obtained an appointment as Professor of Moral Philosophy at the University of Glasgow. Moral philosophy covered a large territory in Smith's time: We have notes of his lectures in which he talked about jurisprudence, military organization, taxation, and "police"—the last word meaning the administration of domestic affairs that we would call economic policy.

In 1759 Smith published *The Theory of Moral Sentiments,* a remarkable inquiry into morality and psychology. The book attracted widespread attention and brought Smith to the notice of Lord Townshend, one day to be the Chancellor of the Exchequer, responsible for the notorious tax on American tea. Townshend engaged Smith to serve as tutor to his stepson, and Smith resigned his professorial post to set off on the Grand Tour with his charge. In France he met Voltaire, Rousseau, and François Quesnay, the brilliant doctor who had originated the ideas of physiocracy. Smith would have dedicated *The Wealth of Nations* to him, had Quesnay not died.

Returning to Scotland in 1766, Smith lived out the remainder of his life largely in scholarly retirement. It was during these years that the *Wealth* was slowly and carefully composed. When it was done, Smith sent a copy to David Hume, by then his dear friend. Hume wrote: "Euge!* Belle! Dear Mr. Smith: I am much pleased with your Performance. . . ." Hume knew, as did virtually everyone who read the book, that Smith had written a work that would permanently change society's understanding of itself.

*Greek for "Well done!"

is not easy to say which document is of greater historic importance. The Declaration sounded a new call for a society dedicated to "Life, Liberty, and the pursuit of Happiness." The *Wealth* explained how such a society worked.

THE ROLE OF COMPETITION

Smith set himself two main problems, one on the micro, and one on the macro level (although you will not find these terms used in his great, rambling, discursive tract). The first problem was to elucidate how a market-run economic system was articulated, how it achieved what we would call micro-order.

Here Smith begins by resolving a perplexing question. The actors in the market, as we know, are all driven by the desire to make money for themselves—to "better their condition," as Smith puts it. The question is obvious: How does a market society prevent self-interested, profit-hungry individuals from holding up their fellow citizens for ransom? How can a socially workable arrangement arise from such a dangerously unsocial motivation as self-betterment?

The answer introduces us to a central mechanism of a market system, the mechanism of competition. For each person, out for self-betterment, with no thought of others, is faced with a host of similarly motivated persons. As a result, each market actor is forced to meet the prices offered by competitors.

In the kind of competition that Smith assumes, a manufacturer who tries to charge more than other manufacturers will not be able to find any buyers. A job seeker who asks more than the going wage will not be able to find work. And an employer who tries to pay *less* than competitors pay will not find anyone to fill the jobs.

In this way, the market mechanism imposes a discipline on its participants—buyers must bid against other buyers and therefore cannot gang up against sellers. Sellers must contend against other sellers and therefore cannot impose their will on buyers.

THE INVISIBLE HAND

But the market has a second, equally important function. Smith shows that the market will arrange for the production of the goods that society wants, in the quantities society wants—without anyone ever issuing an order of any kind! Suppose that consumers want more pots and fewer pans than are being turned out. The public will buy up the existing stock of pots, and as a result the price of pots will rise. Contrariwise, the pan business will be dull; as pan-makers try to get rid of their inventories, pan prices will fall.

Now a restorative force comes into play. As pot prices rise, so will profits in the pot business; and as pan prices fall, so will profits in that business. Once again, the drive for self-betterment will go to work. Employers in the favored pot business will seek to expand, hiring more factors of production—more workers, more space, more capital equipment; and employers in the disfavored pan business will reduce their use of the factors of production, letting workers go, giving up leases on space, cutting down on their capital investment.

Hence the output of pots will rise and that of pans will fall. And this is what the public wanted in the first place. Thus the pressures of the marketplace direct the selfish activities of individuals as if by an Invisible Hand (to use Smith's wonderful phrase) into socially responsible paths. The Invisible Hand transmutes private, self-regarding motives into public, socially oriented behavior. The market becomes a mechanism for the allocation of resources into the channels desired by society.

THE SELF-REGULATING SYSTEM

Smith's demonstration of how a market performs its social functions has never ceased to be of interest. Much of microeconomics, it is useful to know, consists of learning again, or of examining more closely, how the Invisible Hand works. Not that it always does work. There are areas of economic life where the

Invisible Hand does not exert its influence at all. In every market system, for instance, tradition continues to play a role in nonmarket methods of remuneration such as tipping. So, too, command is always in evidence *within* organizations or in the exercise of government powers such as taxation. Further, the market system has no way of providing certain public goods—goods that cannot be privately marketed, such as national defense or public law and order. Smith knew about these and recognized that such goods would have to be supplied by the government, not by the market. Then, too, the market does not always meet the ethical or aesthetic criteria of society, or it may produce goods that are profitable to make, but harmful to consume. These problems are of unquestionable importance. At this juncture, however, we had better stand in considerable awe of Smith's basic insight, for he showed his generation and all succeeding ones that a market system is a responsive and reliable force for basic social provisioning.

He also showed that it was self-regulating. The beautiful consequence of the market is that it is its own guardian. If anyone's prices, wages, or profits stray from levels that are set for everyone, the force of competition will drive them back. Thus a curious paradox exists. The market, which is the acme of economic freedom, turns out to be the strictest of economic taskmasters.

SMITH'S PHILOSOPHY

Because the market is its own regulator, Smith is vehemently opposed to government intervention that will interfere with the workings of self-interest and competition. Therefore, laissez-faire becomes his fundamental philosophy—not because Smith is opposed to the idea of social responsibility, but because he thinks it will be most effectively provided by the Invisible Hand, not by the efforts of government.

His commitment to laissez-faire does not make Smith a conventional conservative. The *Wealth of Nations* is shot through with biting remarks about the "mean and rapacious" ways of the manufacturing class (Smith does not use the word *capitalist*), and the book is openly sympathetic with, and concerned about, the lot of the workingman, hardly a popular position in Smith's day. If Smith is passionately in favor of the "system of natural liberty"—the system founded on economic freedom—the reason is that he believed it would benefit the general public, not the narrow interests of any single class.

ECONOMIC GROWTH

Smith's discovery of the self-regulating properties of a market system was his great "micro" insight (remember that is our phrase, not his). But his vision of an internally coherent market system was matched in importance by a second, "macro" vision. Smith saw that the market system, left entirely to its own devices, would grow, that the wealth of a nation under a system of "natural liberty" would steadily increase.

What brought about this growth? As before, the motive force was the drive for self-betterment, the thirst for profits, the wish to make money. This meant that every employer was constantly seeking to accumulate more capital, to expand the wealth of the enterprise; in turn, this led each employer to seek to increase sales in the hope of gaining a larger profit.

THE DIVISION OF LABOR AGAIN

But how to enlarge sales in a day long before advertising existed as we know it? Smith's answer was to improve productivity: Increase the output of the work force. And the road to increasing productivity was very clear: *Improve the division of labor.*

In Smith's conception of the growing *wealth* (we would say the growing *production*) *of nations,* the division of labor therefore plays a central role, as this famous description of a pin factory makes unforgettably clear:

> One man draws out the wire, another straits it, a third cuts it, a fourth points it, a fifth grinds it at the top for receiving the head; to make the head requires two or three distinct operations; to put it on is a peculiar business; to whiten it another; it is even a trade by itself to put them into paper.
> . . . I have seen a small manufactory of this kind where ten men only were employed and where some of them consequently performed two or three distinct operations. But though they were poor, and therefore but indifferently accommodated with the necessary machinery, they could when they exerted themselves make among them about twelve pounds of pins in a day. There are in a pound upwards of four thousand pins of middling size. These ten persons, therefore, could make among them upward of forty-eight thousand pins in a day. . . . But if they had all wrought separately and independently . . . they could certainly not each of them make twenty, perhaps not one pin in a day.[1]

CAPITAL AND GROWTH

But how is the division of labor to be enhanced? Smith places principal importance on the manner already announced in his description of the process of making pins: *Machinery is the key.* The division of labor—and therefore the productivity of labor—is increased when the tasks of production can be taken over, or aided and assisted, by the capacities of machinery. In this way each firm seeking to expand, is naturally led to introduce more machinery as a way of improving the productivity of its workers. **Thereby the market system becomes an immense force for the accumulation of capital, mainly in the form of machinery and equipment.** Moreover, Smith showed something remarkable about the self-regulating properties of the market system as a growth-producing institution. We recall that growth occurred because employers installed machinery that improved the division of labor. But as they thereupon added to their work force, would it not follow that wages would rise as all employers competed to hire labor? And would that not squeeze profits and dry up the funds by which machinery could be bought?

Once again, however, the market was its own regulator. For Smith showed that the increased demand for labor would be matched by an increased supply of labor, so that wages would not rise or would rise only moderately. The reason was plausible. In Smith's day, infant and child mortality rates were horrendous: "It is not uncommon," wrote Smith, ". . . in the Highlands of Scotland for a mother who has borne twenty children not to have two alive." As wages rose and better food was provided for the household, infant and child mortality would decline. Soon there would be a larger work force available for hire: Ten was the working age in Smith's day. The larger work force would hold back the rise in wages—and so the accumulation of capital could go on. Just as the system assured internal micro order, it also provided an overall macro dependability.

[1]Adam Smith, *The Wealth of Nations* (New York: Modern Library, 1937), pp. 4, 5.

SMITH TODAY

Of course, Smith wrote about a world that is long since vanished—a world in which a factory of ten people, although small, was still significant enough to mention; in which remnants of mercantilist, and even feudal, restrictions determined how many apprentices an employer could hire in many trades; in which labor unions were largely illegal; in which almost no social legislation existed; and above all, where the great majority of people were very poor.

Yet Smith saw two essential attributes in the economic system that was not yet fully born in this time.

1. A society of competitive profit-seeking individuals can assure its orderly material provisioning through the self-regulating market mechanism.
2. Such a society tends to accumulate capital, and in so doing enhances its productivity and wealth.

These insights are not the last word. We have already mentioned that the market mechanism does not always work successfully, and our next two economists will demonstrate that the growth process is not without serious defects. But the insights themselves are still germane. Micro- and macroeconomics are about internal order and growth, even though we may come to different conclusions than those of Smith. What is surprising after two centuries is not how mistaken Smith was, but how deeply he saw. In a real sense, as economists we are still his pupils.

KARL MARX (1818–1883)

Every economist is roughly familiar with the ideas and influence of Adam Smith. Not so many recognize the degree to which economics also owes a debt to Karl Marx—not as the founder of a political movement that has troubled the world ever since, but as an economist whose dissection of capitalism has much to teach us.

CLASS STRUGGLE

Adam Smith was the architect of capitalism's orderliness and progress; Marx the diagnostician of its disorders and eventual demise. Their differences are rooted in the fundamentally opposite way that each saw history. In Smith's view, history was a succession of stages through which humankind traveled, climbing from the "early and rude" society of hunters and fisherfolk to the final stage of commercial society. **Marx saw history as a continuing struggle among social classes, ruling classes contending with ruled classes in every era.**

Moreover, Smith believed that commercial society would bring about a harmonious, mutually acceptable solution to the problem of individual interest in a social setting that would go on forever—or at least for a very long time. Marx saw tension and antagonism as the outcome of the class struggle, and the setting of capitalist society as anything but permanent. Indeed, the class struggle itself, expressed as the contest over wages and profits, would be the main force for changing capitalism and eventually undoing it.

PROFILE OF A REVOLUTIONARY

A great, bearded, dark-skinned man, Karl Marx was the picture of a revolutionary. And he was one—engaged, mind and heart, in the effort to overthrow the system of capitalism that he spent his whole life studying. As a political revolutionary, Marx was not very successful, although with his lifelong friend Friedrich Engels, he formed an international working class "movement" that frightened a good many conservative governments. But as an intellectual revolutionary Marx was probably the most successful disturber of thought who ever lived. The only persons who rival his influence are the great religious leaders, Christ, Mohammed, and Buddha.

Marx led as turbulent and active a life as Smith's was secluded and academic. Born to middle-class parents in Trier, Germany, Marx was early marked as a student of prodigious abilities but not temperamentally cut out to be a professor. Soon after getting his doctoral degree (in philosophy) Marx became editor of a crusading, but not communist, newspaper, which rapidly earned the distrust of the reactionary Prussian government. It closed down the paper. Typically, Marx printed the last edition in red. With his wife Jenny (and Jenny's family maid, Lenchen, who remained with them, unpaid, all her life), Marx thereupon began life as a political exile in Paris, Brussels, and finally in London. There, in 1848, together with Engels, he published the pamphlet that was to become his best known, but certainly not most important work: *The Communist Manifesto.*

The remainder of Marx's life was lived in London. Terribly poor, largely as a consequence of his hopeless inability to manage his own finances, Marx's life was spent in the reading room of the British Museum, laboriously composing the great, never finished opus, *Capital.* No economist has ever read so widely or so deeply as Marx. Before even beginning *Capital,* he wrote a profound three-volume commentary on all the existing economists, eventually published as *Theories of Surplus Value,* and filled 37 notebooks on subjects that would be included in *Capital*—these notes, published as the *Grundrisse* (Foundations) did not appear in print until 1953! *Capital* itself was written backwards, first Volumes II and III, in very rough draft form, then Volume I, the only part of the great opus that appeared in Marx's lifetime, in 1867.

Marx was assuredly a genius, a man who altered every aspect of thinking about society—historical and sociological as well as economic—as decisively as Plato altered the cast of philosophic thought, or Freud that of psychology. Very few economists today work their way through the immense body of Marx's work; but in one way or another his influence affects most of us, even if we are unaware of it. We owe to Marx the basic idea that capitalism is an *evolving* system, deriving from a specific historic past and moving slowly and irregularly toward a dimly discernible, different form of society. That is an idea accepted by many social scientists who may or may not approve of socialism, and who are on the whole vehemently "anti-Marxist"!

1. CAPITALIST GROWTH: USING M

A great deal of interest in Marx's work focuses on that revolutionary perspective and purpose. But Marx the economist interests us for a different reason: Marx also saw the market as a powerful force in the accumulation of capital and wealth. From his conflict-laden point of view, however, he traces out the process —mainly in Volume II of *Capital*—quite differently than Smith does. As we have seen, Smith's conception of the growth process stressed its self-regulatory nature, its steady, hitch-free path. Marx's conception is just the opposite. To him, growth

Courtesy of the Library of Congress

KARL MARX

is a process full of pitfalls, a process in which crisis or malfunction lurks at every turn.

Marx starts with a view of the accumulation process that is much like that of a businessman. The problem is how to make a given sum of capital—money sitting in a bank or invested in a firm—yield a profit. **As Marx puts it, how does M (a sum of money) become M', a** *larger* **sum?**

Marx's answer begins with capitalists using their money to buy commodities and labor power. Thereby they ready the process of production, obtaining needed raw or semi-finished materials, and hiring the working capabilities of a labor force. Here the possibility for crisis lies in the difficulty that capitalists may have in getting their materials or their labor force at the right price. If that should happen—if labor is too expensive, for instance—M stays put and the accumulation process never gets started at all.

2. THE LABOR PROCESS

But suppose the first stage of accumulation takes place smoothly. Now money capital, M, has been transformed into a hired work force and a stock of physical goods. These have next to be combined in the labor process; that is, actual work must be expended on the materials and the raw or semi-finished goods transformed into their next stage of production.

It is here, on the factory floor, that Marx sees the genesis of profit. In his view, profit lies in the ability of capitalists to pay less for labor power—for the working abilities of their work force—than the actual value workers will impart to the commodities they help to produce. This theory of *surplus value* as the source of profit is very important in Marx's analysis of capitalism, but it is not central to our purpose here. Instead, we stop only to note that the labor process is another place where accumulation can be disrupted. If there is a strike, or if production encounters snags, the M that is invested in goods and labor power will not move along toward its objective, M'.

3. COMPLETING THE CIRCUIT

But once again suppose that all goes well and workers transform steel sheets, rubber casings, and bolts of cloth into automobiles. The automobiles are not yet money. They have to be sold—and here, of course, lie the familiar problems of the marketplace: bad guesses as to the public's taste; mismatches between supply and demand; recessions that diminish the spending power of society.

If all goes well, the commodities *will* be sold—and sold for M', which is bigger than M. In that case, the circuit of accumulation is complete, and the capitalists will have a new sum M', which they will want to send on another round, hoping to win M''. But unlike Adam Smith's smooth growth model, we can see that Marx's conception of accumulation is riddled with pitfalls and dangers. Crisis is possible at every stage. Indeed, in the complex theory that Marx unfolds in *Capital*, the inherent tendency of the system is to generate crisis, not to avoid it.

We will not trace Marx's theory of capitalism further except to note that at its core lies a complicated analysis of the manner in which surplus value (the unpaid labor that is the source of profit) is squeezed out through mechanization. A student who wants to learn about Marx's analysis must turn to other books, of which there are many.°

INSTABILITY AND BREAKDOWN

Our interest lies in Marx as the first theorist to stress the instability of capitalism. Adam Smith originated the idea that growth is an inherent characteristic of capitalism; but to Marx we owe the idea that that growth is wavering and uncertain, far from the mechanically assured process Smith described. Marx makes it clear that capital accumulation must overcome the uncertainty inherent in the market system and the tension of the opposing demands of labor and capital. The accumulation of wealth, although certainly the objective of business, may not always be within its power to achieve.

In *Capital*, Marx sees instability increasing until finally the system comes tumbling down. His reasoning involves two further, very important prognoses for the system. The first is that the size of business firms will steadily increase as the consequence of the recurrent crises that wrack the economy. With each crisis,

---

*At the risk of appearing self-serving, a good first reader is R. L. Heilbroner, *The Worldly Philosophers* (New York: Simon & Schuster, 6th ed., 1980), Chapter V. The bibliography suggests a number of other books about Marx.

small firms go bankrupt and their assets are bought up by surviving firms. Thus a trend toward big business is an integral part of capitalism.

Second, Marx expects an intensification of the class struggle as the result of the "proletarianization" of the labor force. More and more small business-people and independent artisans will be squeezed out in the crisis-ridden process of growth. Thus the social structure will be reduced to two classes—a small group of capitalist magnates and a large mass of proletarianized, embittered workers.

In the end, this situation proves impossible to maintain. In Marx's words:

> Along with the constant decrease in the number of capitalist magnates, who usurp and monopolize all the advantages of this process of transformation, the mass of misery, oppression, slavery, degradation and exploitation grows; but with this there also grows the revolt of the working class, a class constantly increasing in numbers, and trained, united and organized by the very mechanism of the capitalist process of production. The monopoly of capital becomes a fetter upon the mode of production which has flourished alongside and under it. The centralization of the means of production and the socialization of labour reach a point at which they become incompatible with their capitalist integument. This integument is burst asunder. The knell of capitalist private property sounds. The expropriators are expropriated.[2]

WAS MARX RIGHT?

Much of the economic controversy that Marx generated has been focused on the questions: Will capitalism ultimately undo itself? Will its internal tensions, its "contradictions," as Marx calls them, finally become too much for its market mechanism to handle?

There are no simple answers to these questions. Critics of Marx vehemently insist that capitalism has *not* collapsed, that the working class has *not* become more and more "miserable," and that a number of predictions that Marx made, such as that the rate of profit would tend to decline, have not been verified.

Supporters of Marx argue the opposite case. They stress that capitalism almost did collapse in the 1930s. They note that more and more people have been reduced to a "proletarian" status, working for a capitalist firm rather than for themselves; in 1800, for example, 80 percent of Americans were self-employed; today the figure is 10 percent. They stress that the size of businesses has constantly grown, and that Marx did correctly foresee that the capitalist system itself would expand, pushing into noncapitalist areas such as Asia, South America, and Africa.

MARX'S SOCIOANALYSIS

It is doubtful that Marx's contribution as a social analyst will ultimately be determined by this kind of score card. Certainly he made many remarkably penetrating statements, and equally certainly, he said things about the prospects for capitalism that seem to have been wrong. What Marx's reputation rests on is something else. It rests on his vision of capitalism as a system under tension, and in a process of continuous evolution as a consequence of that tension. Many economists do not accept Marx's diagnosis of class struggle as the great motor of change in capitalist and precapitalist societies or his prognosis of the inevitable arrival of socialism, but few would deny the validity of that vision.

[2]Karl Marx, *Capital,* Vol. I (New York: Vintage, 1977), p. 929.

There is much more to Marx than the few economic ideas sketched here suggest. Indeed, Marx should not be thought of primarily as an economist, but as a pioneer in a new kind of critical social thought: It is significant that the subtitle of *Capital* is *A Critique of Political Economy*.

In the gallery of the world's great thinkers, where Marx certainly belongs, his proper place is with historians, rather than economists. Most appropriately, his statue would be centrally placed, overlooking many corridors of thought—sociological analysis, philosophic inquiry, and of course, economics.

For Marx's lasting contribution was a penetration of the *appearances* of our social system and of the ways in which we think about that system, in an effort to arrive at buried essences deep below the surface. That most searching aspect of Marx's work is not one that we will pursue here; but bear it in mind, because it accounts for the persisting interest of Marx's thought.*

JOHN MAYNARD KEYNES (1883–1946)

Marx was the intellectual prophet of capitalism as a self-destructive system; John Maynard Keynes (the name should be pronounced "canes," not "keens") was the engineer of capitalism repaired. Today, that is not an uncontested statement. To some people, Keynes's doctrines are as dangerous and subversive as those of Marx—a curious irony, since Keynes himself was totally opposed to Marxist thought and wholly in favor of sustaining and improving the capitalist system.

The reason for the continuing distrust of Keynes is that more than any other economist he is the father of the idea of a "mixed economy" in which the government plays a crucial role. To many people these days, all government activities are suspicious at best and downright injurious at worst. Thus, in some quarters Keynes's name is under a cloud. Nonetheless, he remains one of the great innovators of our discipline, a mind to be ranked with Smith and Marx as one of the most influential our profession has brought forth. As Nobelist Milton Friedman, a famous conservative economist, has declared: "We are all Keynesians now."

THE GREAT DEPRESSION

The great economists were all products of their times: Smith, the voice of optimistic, nascent capitalism; Marx, the spokesman for the victims of its bleakest industrial period; Keynes, the product of a still later time, the Great Depression.

The depression hit America like a typhoon. One half the value of all production simply disappeared. One quarter of the working force lost its jobs. Over a million urban families found their mortgages foreclosed, their houses lost to them. Nine million savings accounts went down the drain when banks closed, never to reopen.

Against this terrible reality of joblessness and loss of income, the economics profession, like the business world or government advisers, had nothing to offer.

---

*What about the relation of Marx to present-day communism? That is a subject for a book about the politics, not the economics, of Marxism. Marx himself was a fervid democrat—but also a very intolerant man. Perhaps his system of ideas has encouraged intolerance in revolutionary parties that have based their ideas on his thought. Marx himself died long before present-day communism came into being. We cannot know what he would have made of it—probably he would have been horrified at its excesses but still hopeful for its future.

Fundamentally, economists were as perplexed at the behavior of the economy as were the American people themselves. In many ways the situation reminds us of the uncertainty that the public and the economics profession share in the face of inflation today.

It was against this setting of dismay and near-panic that Keynes's great book appeared: *The General Theory of Employment Interest and Money.* A complicated book—much more technical than the *Wealth of Nations* or *Capital*—the *General Theory* nevertheless had a central message that was simple enough to

21
CHAPTER 2
THE GREAT
ECONOMISTS

PORTRAIT OF A MANY-SIDED MAN

Keynes was certainly a man of many talents. Unlike Smith or Marx, he was at home in the world of business affairs, a shrewd dealer and financier. Every morning, abed, he would scan the newspaper and make his commitments for the day on the most treacherous of all markets, foreign exchange. An hour or so a day sufficed to make him a very rich man; only the great English economist David Ricardo (1772–1823) could match him in financial acumen. Like Ricardo, Keynes was a speculator by temperament. During World War I, when he was at the Treasury office running England's foreign currency operations, he reported with glee to his chief that he had got together a fair amount of Spanish pesetas. The chief was relieved that England had a supply of *that* currency for a while. "Oh no," said Keynes. "I've sold them all. I'm going to break the market." And he did. Later during the war, when the Germans were shelling Paris, he went to France to negotiate for the English government; on the side, be bought some marvelous French masterpieces at much reduced prices for the National Gallery—along with a Cezanne for himself!

More than an economist and speculator, he was a brilliant mathematician; a businessman who very successfully ran a great investment trust; a ballet lover who married a famous ballerina; a superb stylist and an editor of consummate skill; a man of huge kindness when he wanted to exert it, and of ferocious wit when (more often) he chose to exert

that. On one occasion, banker Sir Harry Goshen criticized Keynes for not "letting things take their natural course." "Is it more appropriate to smile or rage at these artless sentiments?" wrote Keynes. "Best, perhaps, to let Sir Harry take *his* natural course."

Keynes's greatest fame lay in his economic inventiveness. He came by this talent naturally enough as the son of a distinguished economist, John Neville Keynes. As an undergraduate, Keynes had already attracted the attention of Alfred Marshall, the commanding figure at Cambridge University for three decades. After graduation, Keynes soon won notice with a brilliant little book on Indian finance; he then became an adviser to the English government in the negotiations at the end of World War I. Dismayed and disheartened by the vengeful terms of the Versailles Treaty, Keynes wrote a brilliant polemic, *The Economic Consequences of the Peace,* that won him international renown.

Almost thirty years later, Keynes would himself be a chief negotiator for the English government, first in securing the necessary loans during World War II, then as one of the architects of the Bretton Woods agreement that opened a new system of international currency relations after that war. On his return from one trip to Washington, reporters crowded around to ask if England had been sold out and would soon be another American state. Keynes's reply was succinct: "No such luck."

The Bettmann Archive, Inc.

JOHN MAYNARD KEYNES

grasp. The overall level of economic activity in a capitalist system, said Keynes (and Marx and Adam Smith would have agreed with him) was determined by the willingness of its entrepreneurs to make capital investments. From time to time, this willingness was blocked by considerations that made capital accumulation difficult or impossible: In Smith's model we saw the possibility of wages rising too fast, and Marx's theory pointed out difficulties at every stage of the process.

But all the previous economists, even Marx to a certain extent, believed that a failure to accumulate capital would be a temporary, self-curing setback. In Smith's scheme, the rising supply of young workers would keep wages in check. In Marx's conception, each crisis (up to the last) would present the surviving entrepreneurs with fresh opportunities to resume their quest for profits. For Keynes, however, the diagnosis was more severe. He showed that a market system could reach a position of "underemployment equilibrium"—a kind of steady, stagnant state—despite the presence of unemployed workers and unused industrial equipment. The revolutionary import of Keynes's theory was that there was no self-righting property in the market system to keep capitalism growing.

We will better understand the nature of Keynes's diagnosis as we learn macroeconomics, but we can easily see the conclusion to which his diagnosis drove him. If there was nothing that would automatically provide for capital accumulation, a badly depressed economy could remain in the doldrums—unless some substitute were found for business capital spending. And there was only one such possible source of stimulation. This was the government. **The crux of Keynes's message was therefore that government spending might be an essential economic policy for a depressed capitalism trying to recover its vitality.**

Whether or not Keynes's remedy works and what consequences government spending may have for a market system have become major topics for contemporary economics—topics we will deal with later at length. But we can see the significance of Keynes's work in changing the very conception of the economic system in which we live. Adam Smith's view of the market system led to the philosophy of laissez-faire, allowing the system to generate its own natural propensity for growth and internal order. Marx had stressed a very different view in which instability and crisis lurked at every stage, but of course Marx was not interested in policies to maintain capitalism. Keynes propounded a philosophy as far removed from Marx as from Smith. For if Keynes was right, laissez-faire was not the appropriate policy for capitalism—certainly not for capitalism in depression. And if Keynes was right about his remedy, the gloomy prognostications of Marx were also incorrect—or at least could be rendered incorrect.

But was Keynes right? Was Smith right? Was Marx right? To a very large degree these questions frame the subject matter of economics today. That is why, even if their theories are part of our history, the "worldly philosophers" are also contemporary. A young writer once remarked impatiently to T. S. Eliot that it seemed so pointless to study the thinkers of the past, because we knew so much more than they. "Yes," replied Eliot. "They are what we know."

KEY CONCEPTS

Mercantilists and physiocrats extolled treasure and land

Adam Smith's Invisible Hand—competition plus self-interest

LOOKING BACK

This chapter has tried to give us a conception of capitalism as seen by the three greatest economists—conceptions that still powerfully affect our understanding of the system. Let us go over the main ideas that have emerged from this survey:

1. Economics itself is a modern intellectual invention that awaited the advent of market society. Prior to Adam Smith, the main attempts to understand and explain the system were those of the Mercantilists, who stressed the importance of foreign trade as a means of gaining gold or treasure; and those of the French Physiocrats, who extolled the wealth-generating powers of the land and who dismissed the merchant class as sterile.

2. Adam Smith contributed two immensely important ideas to economic understanding. The first was the idea of an Invisible Hand by which the market system converted the selfish drives of individuals to a

coordinated mechanism for social provisioning. Smith showed how this fortunate outcome arose from the workings of competition, which prevented the drive for profits or selfish interest from simply gouging the consumer or the worker.

Capital accumulation and division of labor bring growth

3. Smith was also the first economist to explain how the market provided a powerful mechanism for accumulating capital. Smith's theory of economic growth hinged on the steady improvement in productivity that occurred when machinery was added to production, making possible a finer division of labor.

Class struggle

4. Marx was the great prophet of capitalism's doom. The essential cause of its demise would be the class struggle between workers and capitalists.

The unstable process of production

5. Marx also saw the market mechanism as inherently unstable—as tending toward crisis or disruption in the accumulation of capital. He analyzed this instability by tracing the obstacles faced by a firm as it sought to convert M, a sum of capital, into M', a larger sum. This was done in three stages: first by using M to buy labor power and materials, then by combining labor power with materials, and finally by selling the finished goods. At each stage, the accumulation process was subject to disruption of various sorts.

Growth of monopolies and proletarians lead to revolution

6. In Marx's view the process of capitalist accumulation lead to the growth of big business and an "immiserated" proletariat. As successive crises wracked the system, the working class would eventually revolt, and a transition would be made from capitalism to socialism.

Marxism as a system of thought

7. Marx's system of thought was much larger than an effort to analyze the economic tensions of capitalism. Essentially it embraced a mixture of philosophy, historical analysis, and a critique of economic beliefs and forms.

Keynes's *General Theory* with its idea of underemployment equilibrium, ushered in the mixed economy

8. John Maynard Keynes's *General Theory* (as it is widely called) was an attempt to explain how capitalism could have a *lasting* depression. In technical terms, Keynes's breakthrough was the explanation of underemployment equilibrium.

9. Equally important was Keynes's work in paving the way for the mixed economy in which government plays a crucial role in maintaining the economic growth of capitalism. Mixed economies are found in every capitalist system today; we shall be studying them in depth in the pages to come.

ECONOMIC VOCABULARY

Mercantilism 10	Invisible hand 12	Marx's circuit of production: *M*-into-*M'* 17
Physiocracy 10	Self-regulation 12	Underemployment equilibrium 22
Competition 11	Growth 13, 14	

QUESTIONS

1. Why does Smith's model of the economy require *two* elements—the motivation of self-betterment and the restraining institution of competition? Explain why the system would not work with only one of the two.

2. From your own experience, think of how the division of labor can increase productivity. Choose one example from agriculture, one from manufacturing, and one from a service industry such as hotel management, transportation, or retailing.

3. Is the accumulation of capital needed for the improvement of productivity today? In what ways could additional capital—more machines, buildings, roads, etc.—improve the amount of production that a typical farmer or worker could create.

4. Take any business you know about and see if you think that Marx's description of the circuit *M*-into-*M'* describes the way in which that business tries to accumulate capital. Which of Marx's three phases of the accumulation process is most likely to lead to trouble, in your opinion?

5. How do you feel about the idea of a mixed economy? Do you think it means an economy in which the government does a lot of interfering? Could a government simply spend money—for example, for Social Security—and not interfere in the market system at all? Could it interfere extensively, but not spend much money? Which of the two functions—interfering (regulating) or spending—is basic to Keynes's theory? Is it possible, do you think, to have a basically laissez-faire policy with respect to the market, and yet have government spending to cure a depression?

AN EXTRA WORD ABOUT
PARADIGMS

How does science advance? The prevailing view used to be that it grew by accretion, gradually adding new knowledge and better established hypotheses while shedding error and disproved hypotheses. That view has now been seriously challenged by the influential book, *The Structure of Scientific Revolutions,* by Thomas Kuhn, published in 1962.

Kuhn's view is that the growth of science is not a continuous, seamless extension of knowledge. Rather, science grows in discontinuous leaps, in which one prevailing paradigm is displaced by another. *A paradigm is a set of premises, views, rules, conventions, and beliefs that form the kinds of questions that a science asks.* For example, the Ptolemaic paradigm, with its view of the earth as the center of the universe, was replaced by the Copernican paradigm, which based its questions on the premise that the planets revolve around the sun. In cosmology the Newtonian paradigm was displaced by the Einsteinian, in biology the biblical paradigm by the Darwinian.

Paradigms change, says Kuhn, when the puzzles encountered by scientists become more and more difficult to answer within the existing set of ground rules. Then, usually in a short space of time, a new view of things comes to the fore, explaining the puzzles of the earlier paradigm and reorienting the questions for scientists who will work within the new rules.

PRECLASSICAL AND CLASSICAL ECONOMICS

Kuhn's short, provocative book is worth reading by anyone interested in science or social science. The question it raises for us is whether economics also has paradigms. The answer seems to be both yes and no.

First the yes answer. We can easily separate the history of economic thought into paradigm-like divisions that resemble the bounded inquiries of science. One of the first such paradigms was the economics of the medieval schoolmen, who argued and worried about the moral problems raised by the emerging market process. For example, one of their main concerns was whether lending money at interest (usury) was in fact a sin (remember, in the early Middle Ages it had been considered a *mortal* sin); and they endlessly discussed the criteria for the "just" prices at which commodities should sell.

That view of the economic world was displaced by the Classical economists, whose most brilliant achievements were expressed in the works of Adam Smith and David Ricardo (1772–1823). The Classical economists had no interest whatever in "just" prices or in the sinfulness of usury. For them the great question was *how to understand, not evaluate, economic processes, in particular the accumulation and distribution of national wealth.* Smith, as we have seen, wrote an extraordinary exposition of how the members of society, although engaged in a search for their individual betterment, were nonetheless guided by an Invisible Hand (the market) to expand the wealth of nations. Ricardo wrote with equal force about the course of national economic growth, arguing that a growing population, pressing against limited fertile acreage, would drive up crop prices and divert the wealth of the country into the hands of the landlords.

MARGINALIST ECONOMICS

The Classical paradigm concerned large issues of national growth and dealt boldly with the fate of social classes. The Marxian paradigm, in turn, grew out of the Classical, differing from it in its much more critical approach to society and to thinking about society. Then, around the 1870s, a new angle of vision abruptly displaced the older one. The new view had numerous European originators, preeminent among them W. Stanley Jevons and Leon Walras. As a group they are referred to as the Marginalists, for *they turned the focus of economic inquiry away from growth and class conflict into a study of the interactions of individuals.*

The new paradigm explained many things that the older one did not, above all the finer workings of the price system. But just as the Classical or Marxian paradigms had dropped all interest in the just prices of the medievalists, so the Marginalists paid little attention to the questions of growth and class fortune that had so preoccupied the Classicists and Marxists.

KEYNESIAN ECONOMICS

Inherent in the Marginalist view of the world, with its extreme emphasis on interacting individuals rather than on classes, was a micro approach to economic problems. The next radical shift in view came from the work of John Maynard Keynes, whose perception of the economic system brought into focus a macro perspective on *total* income, *total* employment, *total* output. The most striking result of Keynes's shift from a micro to a macro perspective was his discovery that an economy that worked well at the micro level did not necessarily work well at the macro level. From the perspective of the Marginalists, such an economic state of affairs could hardly be envisioned.

PARADIGMS OR NOT?

Hence we can certainly discern sharp changes in the views and visions of economics. The very definition of the economic problem itself alters as we go from the medieval schoolmen to the Keynesians.

Why, then, should we not call this a series of paradigmatic shifts, similar to those in science? *The main reason is that the new economic paradigms do not explain the questions of the older views they displace. Unlike the new paradigms of natural science, which embrace the problems of their predecessors, the shifts in economics are characterized by the fact that they ignore or dismiss the very questions that disturbed their predecessors.* Classical economists, as we have said, forgot about economic justice; Marginalist economists, about growth or classes; Keynesian economists, about the inner working of the market.

Hence the shifts in economics are not quite like those in science, although the concept of a change of perspectives, bringing new problems into view, is as applicable to one as to the other. We can relate these shifts in perspective to the changing backdrop of social organization. Each paradigm of economic thought reflects to some degree the historical characteristics and problems of its time. This reflection of social issues and problems in economic thought differs, too, from the nature of scientific paradigms. Change in social structures generally plays a small role in causing one scientific perspective to replace another.

What paradigm rules economics today? A mixture of Marginalist and Keynesian thought lies behind most contemporary micro- and macroeconomics. A Marxian view underlies much of the radical critique of our time. Perhaps it is fair to say that no paradigm is firmly ensconced today. We live in a period in which much of the conventional wisdom of the past has been tried and found wanting. Economics is in a state of self-scrutiny, dissatisfied with its established paradigms, not yet ready to formulate a new one. Indeed, perhaps the search for such a new paradigm, a perspective that will highlight new elements of reality and suggest new modes of analysis, is the most pressing economic task of our time.

Chapter

3 THE TREND OF THINGS

A LOOK AHEAD

The last chapter was a whirlwind tour through intellectual history. Now we want to turn to the living edge of history, to our own society. What does modern capitalism look like? A good way to gain a first impression is to take a series of pictures over time, showing us how the American economy has developed during the last decades. This will also give us a chance to test the ideas of Smith, Marx and Keynes in action.

In particular we are going to examine four major trends of modern times:

(1) the growth of production measured by GNP—gross national product;
(2) trends in income distribution;
(3) the drift toward big business; and
(4) the rapid rise in government.

Warning before you begin: Don't get bogged down in facts and figures. Keep your eye out for trends and for explanations of trends. The facts are there to illustrate these trends and to test explanations, not to be learned for themselves.

THE PROCESS OF GROWTH

Imagine that we have had a camera trained on the U.S. economy over the last 80 years or so. What would be the most striking changes to meet our eye?

There is no doubt about the first impression: It would be a sense of growth. Everything would be getting larger. Business firms would be growing in size. Labor unions would be bigger. There would be many more households, and each household would be richer. Government would be much larger. And underlying all of this, the extent of the market system itself—the great circular flow of inputs and outputs—would be steadily increasing in size.

Growth is not, of course, the only thing we would notice. Businesses are different as well as bigger when we compare 1980 and 1900: There are far more corporations now than in the old days, far more diversified businesses, fewer family firms. Households are different because more women work outside the home. Labor unions today are no longer mainly craft unions, limited to one occupation. Government is not only bigger but has a different philosophy.

TOTAL OUTPUT

Nonetheless, it is growth that first commands our attention. The camera vision of the economy gives us a picture that keeps widening. It *has* to widen to encompass the increase in the sheer mass of output. Hence the first institution

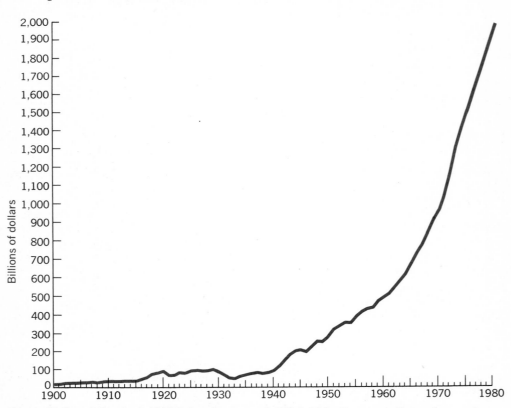

FIGURE 3.1
VALUE OF GNP
1900–1980

Gross National Product (GNP) has increased 100 fold in three quarters of a century, measured in the prices of each year's production.

VOLUME AND VALUE

You should be warned that there is no entirely satisfactory way of wringing price increases out of the hodgepodge of goods and services called GNP, because different items in this collection of goods rise or fall in price in different degrees. There is always a certain element of arbitrariness in correcting GNP for price changes. Different methods, each perfectly defensible, will yield somewhat different measures of "corrected" GNP.

Isn't there some way of getting around the problem of dollar values when we compare GNPs? One way is to measure actual physical volumes. When certain kinds of outputs, such as foodstuffs, bulk very large in GNP as they do in India or China, we sometimes measure growth just by adding up the tonnages of food production. The problem, of course, is that the composition of these tonnages may change—more wheat one year, more rice another—which gets us into another comparison problem. And then such a measure ignores entirely the outputs of nonagricultural goods. (We meet the same problem if we try to measure growth by tonnages of freight, metal production, etc.)

A more defensible way might be to consider GNP as a sum total of labor time, the embodiment of so many million hours of work. Even this does not get us around the measurement and comparison problem, for we use different kinds of labor as time goes on. Therefore, we have to make the difficult assumption that all kinds of labor, skilled and unskilled, trained and untrained, can be "reduced" to multiples of one "basic" kind. That basic labor, in turn, would have to boil down to some constant unit of "effort." But does the unit of "effort"—of human energy—remain constant over time?

In the end, the task of measuring an aggregate of different things can never be solved to our complete satisfaction. Any concept of GNP always has an element of unmeasureableness about it. Growth is a concept that we constantly use, but that remains tantalizingly beyond precise definition.

whose growth we must examine is that of the market system itself.

More specifically, we must trace the tremendous growth in our total output. The technical name for this flow of output is gross national product (GNP), a term we will use many times in the future and which we will later define more carefully. Here we only note that it is the dollar value of our annual flow of final output. Figure 3.1 gives us a graphic representation of this increase in yearly output.

CORRECTING FOR INFLATION

As we can see, the dollar value of all output from 1900 to 1980 has grown by a factor of about 100. But perhaps a cautionary thought will have already struck you. If we measure the growth of output by comparing the dollar value of production over time, what seems to be growth in actual economic activity may be no more than a rise in prices. If the economy in 1980 produced no more actual tons of grain than the economy in 1900, but if grain prices today were double those of 1900, our GNP figures would show growth where there was really nothing but inflation.

To arrive at a measure of real growth, we have to correct for changes in prices. To do so, we take one year as a *base* and use the prices of that year to evaluate output in all succeeding years.

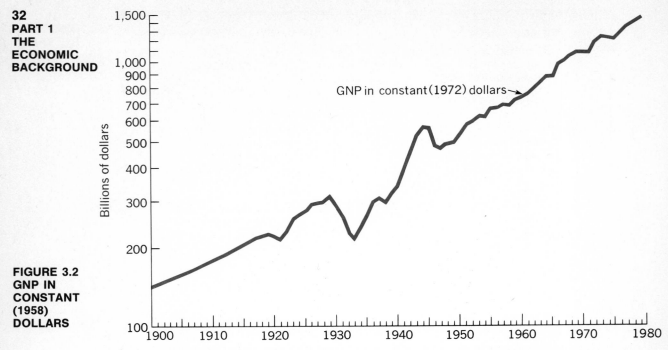

**FIGURE 3.2
GNP IN
CONSTANT
(1958)
DOLLARS**

Measured in real terms, GNP has increased only 8 times, not 100 times. In this graph we use a semi log scale because it shows more clearly the *rate of growth* rather than the absolute dollar growth of GNP.

Here is an elementary example. Suppose that our grain economy produces 1 million tons in 1900 and 2 million tons in 1980, but wheat sells for $1 in 1900 and $2 in 1980. Our GNP in the current prices of 1900 and 1980 is $1 million for 1900 and $4 million 80 years later. But if we evaluate the GNP using only the 1900 prices (i.e., $1 per bushel), our GNP is reduced to $2 million in 1980. This constant dollar GNP is often referred to as the **real GNP**, while the current dollar GNP is called the **nominal GNP**. We can use the prices of any year as the base. The important thing is that all outputs must be evaluated with only one set of prices.

Figure 3.2 shows us the much reduced growth of output when output is measured in 1972 dollars.

PER CAPITA GROWTH

As we can see, growth in real (or constant dollar) terms is much less dramatic than growth in current dollars that make no allowance for rising prices. Nonetheless, the value of 1980 output, compared to that of 1900, with price changes eliminated as best we can, still shows a growth factor of almost ten.

But there still remains one last adjustment to be made. The growth of output is a massive assemblage of goods and services to be distributed among the nation's households, and the number of those households has increased. In 1900,

United States population was 76 million; in 1980 it was about 222 million. To bring our constant GNP down to life size, we have to divide it by population, to get GNP per person, or per capita.

HISTORICAL RECORD

In Figure 3.3 we see the American experience from the middle of the nineteenth century in terms of real per capita GNP this time in 1929 prices.* Viewed from the long perspective of history, our average rate of growth has been astonishingly consistent. This holds true for an average over the past thirty-odd years since the Great Depression or back to the 1870s (or even 1830s). As the chart shows, the swings are almost all contained within a range of 10 percent above or below the trend. The trend itself comes to about 3.5 percent a year in real terms, or a little over 1.5 percent a year per capita. Although 1.5 percent a year may not sound like much, remember that this figure allows us to double our real per capita living standards every 47 years. This is Adam Smith's growth model come to life!

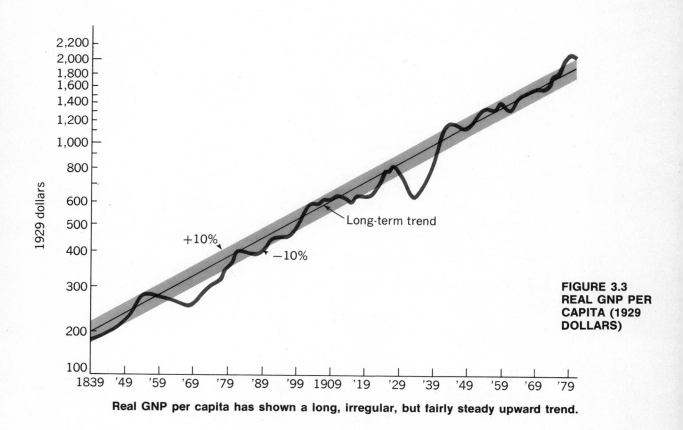

Real GNP per capita has shown a long, irregular, but fairly steady upward trend.

**FIGURE 3.3
REAL GNP PER
CAPITA (1929
DOLLARS)**

*Why do we use 1929 as a base here and 1972 as a base in Figure 3.2? We do it to accustom you to the idea that different years can serve as the basis for comparison.

THE DIFFERENCE THAT GROWTH RATES MAKE

The normal range in growth rates for capitalist economies does not seem to be very great. How much difference does it make, after all, if output grows at 1.7 or 2.7 percent?

The answer is: an amazing difference. This is because growth is an *exponential* phenomenon involving a percentage rate of growth on a steadily rising base. At 1.7 percent, per-capita real income will double in about 40 years. At 2.7 percent, it will double in 26 years.

Professor Kenneth Boulding has pointed out that before World War II no country sustained more than 2.3 percent per-capita growth of GNP. Since World War II, Japan has achieved a per-capita growth rate of 8 percent. Boulding writes: "The difference between 2.3 and 8 percent may be dramatically illustrated by pointing out that [at 2.3 percent] children are twice as rich as their parents—i.e., per capita income approximately doubles every generation—while at 8 percent per annum, children are six times as rich as their parents."

SOURCES OF GROWTH

How do we explain this long upward trend? Here we can give only a brief summary of the causes that we will study more systematically in Part 3. Essentially, we grew for two reasons:

1.   The quantity of inputs going into the economic process increased

In 1900 our labor force was 27 million. In 1980 it was almost 110 million. Obviously, larger inputs of labor produce larger outputs of goods and services. (Whether they may even produce *proportionally* larger outputs is another question that we will investigate later.)

Our inputs of capital increased as well. In 1900 the total horsepower energy delivered by "prime movers"—engines of all kinds, work animals, ships, trains, etc.—was 65 million horsepower. In 1980 it was around 30 *billion*.

Land in use also increased. In 1900, there were 839 million acres of land used for cultivation, and over 1,000 million acres for other purposes such as grazing. By 1980, land in cultivation had increased to over 1,000 million acres, and land in grazing use had also increased: We had reclaimed virgin land and made it economically productive.

2.   The quality of inputs improved

The population working in 1980 was not only more numerous than in 1900, it was better trained and better schooled. The best overall gauge of this is the amount of education stored up in the work force. In 1900, when only 6.4 percent of the working population had gone beyond grade school, there were 223 million man-years of schooling embodied in the population. In 1980, when over two-thirds of the population had finished high school, the stock of education embodied in the population had grown to over a billion man-years.

The quality of capital has also increased, along with its quantity. As an indication of the importance of the changing quality of capital, consider the contribution made to our output by the availability of surfaced roads. In 1900 there were about 150,000 miles of such roads. In 1980, there were almost 4 million miles. That is an increase in the quantity of roads of over 25 times. But that increase does not begin to measure the difference in the transport capability of the two road systems, one of them gravelled, narrow, built for traffic that averaged 10 to 20 miles per hour; the other, concrete or asphalt, multilane, fast-paced.

PRODUCTIVITY

There are still other sources of growth, such as shifts in occupations and efficiencies of large-scale operation, but the main ones are the increase in the quantity and the quality of inputs. Of the two, **improvements in the quality of inputs—in human skills, in improved designs of capital equipment—have been far more important than mere increases in quantity.** Better skills and technology enable the labor force to increase its productivity, the amount of goods and services it can turn out in a given time.

Figure 3.4 shows the trend in productivity during recent years. As you can see, the growth has been fairly steady up to the early 1970s, despite occasional dips. After 1972 the trend seems to shift downward. We will look into the reasons for this later. Here we want to emphasize the contribution made to long term growth by our normal steady improvement in our ability to grow and extract and handle and shape and transport goods.

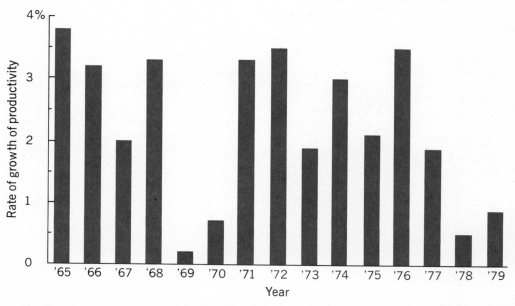

**FIGURE 3.4
THE
PRODUCTIV-
ITY PICTURE**

These data show that our increases in productivity have been steadily falling in recent years. The causes for this productivity decline will interest us later in our book.

CHANGES IN DISTRIBUTION

We have seen how striking was the increase in output in the twentieth century, but what happened to the division of this output among the various classes of society? Have the rich gotten richer and the poor poorer? Has the trend been in the direction of greater equality?

CHANGES IN DOLLAR INCOMES VS. CHANGES IN SHARES

The question is not easy to answer. Remember, we are interested in the changes in shares going to different groups, not just in absolute amounts. There has certainly been a tremendous change in the dollar amounts that we have used to define different social classes, as Figure 3.5 shows.

The figures show that growth has helped boost all income classes, but has the *proportion* of income going to the various classes also changed? That is not what we find. Figure 3.6 shows that sharing-out of incomes among social groups has been remarkably steady.

Thus the distribution of total income among those at the top, in the middle, and on the bottom has not shifted very much. The poor have a little larger share of the income cake; the well-to-do, a little smaller. Only if we go back to the 1920s do we see a marked change. In those days, the share of the top 5 percent

POVERTY

What are the characteristics of poverty? Here is a chance to take a systematic look. Below we put all households—families and individuals—into various categories to show us the chance that someone in a given category will be a member of a low-income (poor) household.

But we must always be very careful before we impute poverty to any single source. One of the authors, sitting in a Ph.D. exam, was questioning a candidate about a dissertation on poverty. It seemed there were many causes for poverty, all impressively substantiated with evidence.

"But if you had to single out one cause as the *most* important," asked the examiner, "which would it be?"

The candidate hemmed and hawed. There was skill. There was health. There was culture. There was native ability. But if he *had* to choose, he would say that education—or rather, the lack of it—was the greatest contributory factor in poverty. Most poor people simply didn't have the knowledge to enable them to get high-paying jobs.

"And why didn't they have the education?" asked the examiner.

That was easy. Education was expensive. Poor people couldn't afford private schools. The need for income was so great that they dropped out of school early to earn money.

"I see," said the examiner. "People are poor because they are uneducated. They are uneducated because they haven't the money to buy education. So *poverty causes poverty.*"

All families	11.4
Single persons	22.1
White families	9.1
Black and other nonwhite families	27.5
Families headed by females	
White	23.5
Black, other	50.6

CHANCES OF BEING POOR (1978)

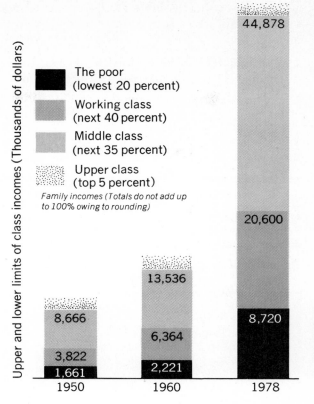

The poor
(lowest 20 percent)

Working class
(next 40 percent)

Middle class
(next 35 percent)

Upper class
(top 5 percent)

Family incomes (Totals do not add up to 100% owing to rounding)

The dollar incomes of all social classes have increased markedly.

**FIGURE 3.5
CHANGES IN
DOLLAR
LIMITS OF
SOCIAL
CLASSES**

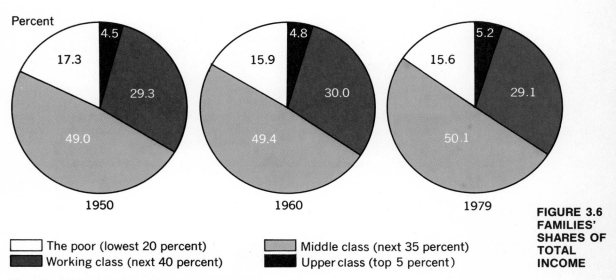

Percent

The poor (lowest 20 percent)

Working class (next 40 percent)

Middle class (next 35 percent)

Upper class (top 5 percent)

**FIGURE 3.6
FAMILIES'
SHARES OF
TOTAL
INCOME**

The distribution of income among different social classes has shown very little change.

was perhaps twice as large as it is today. In addition, various social programs, such as Medicare or state-supported higher education, have probably raised the the real income of the poorest 20 percent somewhat more than Figure 5.6 shows. °

THE ELIMINATION OF POVERTY?

Does this mean that poverty is being eliminated from the United States? Without a question the number of persons below the designated low-income level has been dropping, both absolutely and relative to the larger population, even though the threshold of a poverty income has been steadily adjusted upward to allow for inflation. We can see this gradual shrinkage in Table 3.1, where we should note the reversal of the trend in the 1975 recession.

**TABLE 3.1
PERSONS
BELOW LOW-
INCOME
LEVEL**

	1959	1965	1969	1975	1979
All persons (millions)	39.5	33.2	24.1	25.9	24.5
Percent of population	22.4	17.3	12.1	12.3	11.4

There has been a steady fall in measured poverty.

HOW BIG IS BIG?

Just to get an idea of scale, the 100th largest industrial corporation in 1978 ranked by sales was P.P.G. Industries. Its sales that year were $2.8 billion. It was not the 100th largest in terms of assets, which just topped $1 billion. The 100th biggest firm in assets was Pennzoil, with $2.1 billion. Its sales were $1.7 billion.

Thus it makes a difference whether we rank companies in size by sales or assets. At the very top of the heap, 8 of the first 10 firms in sales are also among the top 10 in assets, but this coincidence is no longer true once we get part way down the list. Examples: Esmark was 38th in sales, 98th in assets; Greyhound 55th in sales, 129th in assets; Burroughs 64th in assets, 118th in sales.

Which is more important, sales or assets? Sales measure the dominance of a company within its field; assets measure its overall financial strength. Actually both sales and assets measure size, but what counts in the marketplace is profitability. Here the correct measure is the net rate of return: the rate of profit earned per dollar of capital. The average big business earns twice to three times the return of the average small business, but really spectacular rates of return are usually found in smaller businesses on their way to stardom.

Rule of thumb: To make it into the Fortune 500 list at the end of the 1970s, you had to have about a half billion in sales and about $50 million in assets.

*A more detailed study of changes in income distribution would have to take into account some facts that are not included in the figures above. For technical reasons, the Census Bureau does not include most forms of capital income (such as capital gains on stocks or real estate) in its computation of incomes. If it did, the share of the top 1 percent would be larger. The Census Bureau also does not fully take into account cash and noncash payments to the poor, such as food stamps or welfare aid. This would add to the share of the poor. In other words, the Census figures are mainly derived from earnings, not returns on capital or "transfers" that may benefit high- or low-income groups. It is extremely difficult to net out the effects of all these flows of money. The result is probably more favorable to lower income groups, but it is not possible to say by exactly how much. In all likelihood, the net change is not very great.

These figures do not tell us, however, whether poverty simply melts away as a result of overall growth or whether we eliminate certain kinds of poverty (eg. poverty from low wages), while leaving other kinds relatively untouched. During the past 20 years, the conditions of life in the slums of many big cities have worsened. This makes it difficult to say that we have less of a poverty problem in the nation as a whole. Possibly we have a greater one.

Such considerations make it difficult to pass judgment on Marx's expectations of "increasing misery." Many people have argued that this is the least justified of Marx's expectations about capitalism. Others have claimed that by "misery" Marx did not mean money income, but the quality of life. Perhaps a fair judgment is that misery measured in money has probably decreased much more than Marx ever imagined, but that misery measured in the experience of social life may not have disappeared nearly as much as Marx's critics expected.*

TRENDS IN BUSINESS

We have examined the main trends in personal income. Now let us turn to business. Here one change immediately strikes the eye. There is a marked decline of the independent, small business—with its self-employed worker—as a main form of enterprise.

In 1900 there were about 8 million independent enterprises, including 5.7 million farms. By 1980, the number of proprietorships had grown to over 10 million, a figure that included some 2.8 million farms. Meanwhile, the labor force itself more than tripled. Thus as a percentage of all persons working, the proportion of self-employed has fallen from about 30 percent in 1900 to under 10 percent today.

RISE OF BIG BUSINESS

With the decline of the self-employed worker has come the rise of the giant firm. Back in 1900, the giant corporation was just arriving on the scene. In 1901, financier J. P. Morgan created the first billion-dollar company when he formed the United States Steel Corporation out of a dozen smaller enterprises. In that year, the total capitalization of all corporations valued at more than $1 million was $5 billion. By 1904 it was $20 billion. In 1980 it was over about $5 trillion.

It hardly comes as a surprise that the main trend of the past 80 years has been the emergence of big business. More interesting is the question of whether big business is continuing to grow. This is a more difficult question to answer, for it depends on what we mean by "growth."

Certainly the place of the biggest companies within the world of corporations has been rising, at least during the years up to the early 1970s, as Table 3.2 shows. Marx was also indubitably right in predicting this trend. Indeed, as

---

*It is worth remarking that Adam Smith also expected "misery" to increase, despite a rise in income, because commercial society (as he called it) exposed the working population to the dulling influence of monotonous work. A capitalist society, Smith believed, was rich but its working classes were likely to be made less alert and intelligent, because of the labor they performed. See *Wealth of Nations*, p. 734.

TABLE 3.2 LARGEST MANUFAC- TURERS SHARE OF ASSETS (%)	1948	1960	1970	1975	The share of the big- gest corporations grew rapidly during the fifties and sixties, but may now have stabilized.
100 largest corporations	40.2	46.4	48.5	46.5	
200 largest corporations	48.2	56.3	60.4	58.5	

Table 3.2 shows, the top 100 companies in the 1970s held approximately as large a share of total corporate wealth as the top 200 companies in 1948.

SALES VS. ASSETS

This growing concentration of assets in the hands of the mightiest corporations is not the same thing, however, as a growing predominance of those companies in *each marketplace*. The share of the biggest companies in various markets has tended to remain about the same—up in a few industries, down in others. This is a matter we will look into much more carefully in Chapter 18, but it is important to have the general conclusion now. Over the last quarter-century, concentration of business has continued to increase if we measure assets, not if we measure sales.

EXPLAINING THE TREND TO BUSINESS SIZE

Can we explain the long-term trend toward the concentration of business assets, as we did the trend toward growth in GNP? By and large, economists would stress three main reasons for the appearance of giant enterprise.

1. Advances in technology have made possible the mass production of goods or services at falling costs

The rise of bigness in business is very much a result of technology. Without the steam engine, the lathe, the railroad, it is difficult to imagine how big business would have emerged.

But technology went on to do more than make large-scale production possible. Typically it also brought an economic effect that we call **economies of scale**. That is, technology not only enlarged, it also cheapened the process of production. Costs per unit fell as output rose. The process is perfectly exemplified in the huge reduction of cost in producing automobiles on an assembly line rather than one car at a time (see box).

Economies of scale provided further powerful impetus toward a growth in size. The firm that pioneered in the introduction of mass production technology usually secured a competitive selling advantage over its competitors, enabling it to grow in size and thereby to increase its advantage still further. These cost-reducing advantages were important causes of the initial emergence of giant companies in many industries. Similarly, the absence of such technologies explains why corporate giants did not emerge in all fields.

2. Concentration is also a result of corporate mergers

Ever since J. P. Morgan assembled U.S. Steel, mergers have been a major source of corporate growth. At the very end of the nineteenth century there was the first great merger "wave," out of which came the first huge companies, including U.S. Steel. In 1890 most industries were competitive, without a single company dominating the field. By 1904 one or two giant firms, usually created by mergers, had arisen to control at least half the output in 78 different industries.

Again, between 1951 and 1960 one-fifth of the top 1,000 corporations disappeared—not because they failed, but because they were bought up by other corporations. In all, mergers have accounted for about two-fifths of the increase in concentration between 1950 and 1970; internal growth accounts for the rest.

3.   Depressions or recessions plunge many smaller firms into bankruptcy and make it possible for larger, more financially secure firms to buy them up very cheaply

This is once more as Marx anticipated. Certainly the process of concentration is abetted by economic distress. When industries are threatened, the weak producers go under; the stronger ones emerge relatively stronger than before. Consider, for example, that three once-prominent American automobile producers succumbed to the mild recessions of the 1950s and 1960s, and to the pressure of foreign competition: Studebaker, Packard, Kaiser Motors. And Chrysler is currently threatened with bankruptcy.

FROM PIN FACTORY TO ASSEMBLY LINE

Adam Smith showed the power of the division of labor in a tiny pin factory. Here is how it looked 150 years later in a giant automobile factory:

Just how were the main assembly lines and lines of component production and supply kept in harmony? For the chassis alone, from 1,000 to 4,000 pieces of each component had to be furnished each day at just the right point and right minute: a single failure, and the whole mechanism would come to a jarring standstill. . . . Superintendents had to know every hour just how many components were being produced and how many were in stock. Whenever danger of shortage appeared, the shortage chaser—a familiar figure in all automobile factories—flung himself into the breach. Counters and checkers reported to him. Verifying in person any ominous news, he mobilized the foreman concerned to repair deficiencies. Three times a day he made typed reports in manifold to the factory clearing-house, at the same time chalking on blackboards in the clearing-house office a statement of results in each factory-production department and each assembling department.[1]

Such systematizing in itself resulted in astonishing increases in productivity. With each operation analyzed and subdivided into its simplest components, with a steady stream of work passing before stationary men, with a relentless but manageable pace of work, the total time required to assemble a car dropped astonishingly. Within a single year, the time required to assemble a motor fell from 600 minutes to 226 minutes: to build a chassis, from 12 hours and 28 minutes to 1 hour and 33 minutes. A stopwatch man was told to observe a 3-minute assembly in which men assembled rods and pistons, a simple operation. The job was divided into three jobs, and half the men turned out the same output as before.

As the example of the assembly line illustrates, the technology behind economies of scale often reduced the act of labor to robot-like movements. A brilliant account of this fragmentation of work will be found in Harry Braverman's *Labor and Monopoly Capital* (New York: Monthly Review Press, 1974).

[1]Allan Nevins, *Ford, the Times, the Man, the Company* (New York: Scribner's, 1954), 1,507.

A CONTINUING TREND TO BIGNESS?

Recent statistics suggest that the trend to bigness may have levelled off, as we can see if we compare the figures for 1970 and 1975 in Table 3.2. On the other hand, there is evidence that a new merger wave may have broken out in the late 1970s. We will not have data on this for a few years. It seems doubtful, however, that we have heard the last of the problem of business concentration. This is because the main forces making for concentration—technical advances, mergers, and business cycles—are still very much with us.

LABOR UNIONS

What about labor unions? Have they also shown trends comparable to the big corporation? Their history is parallel in many ways. Over the last 75 years, the percent of the labor force belonging to a union has increased from 3.2 to 22.6. Thus, the twentieth century has seen the emergence of big labor alongside big business. Yet, as Table 3.3 shows, the percent of unionized nonagricultural workers has actually declined in recent years.

This does not mean, of course, that all unions today are diminishing. The last two decades have brought a boom in unions for white-collar workers, such as teachers or office workers; in unions for municipal employees, such as police, firemen, transit workers; in diversified union organization, such as the powerful Teamsters. The declines have come where industries are declining, such as amongst railwaymen or clothing trades workers. Unions are certain to remain a major force in crucial areas of the economy.

	1940	1950	1960	1970	1979
TABLE 3.3 **LABOR FORCE** **IN UNIONS** — Percent unionized	27.2	31.9	31.4	30.1	22.0

The importance of unions in the labor force has been falling, although unions remain powerful in key sectors.

FROM SMALL TO LARGE GOVERNMENT

We pass now to the last great trend of the economy, a trend whose end result has been the emergence of that large government apparatus which commands so much public attention.

RISE OF THE PUBLIC SECTOR

There are three quite different ways of measuring the rise of the public sector. The first is to examine the proportion of GNP that government directly produces or purchases. This might be regarded as a rough indication of the degree to which we have become a "statist" economy.

A second way is to inquire into the extent to which the government reallocates incomes by taxing some persons and giving others "transfer payments" such as Social Security benefits or welfare or unemployment insurance. This might be regarded as an index of the degree to which we have become a welfare state.

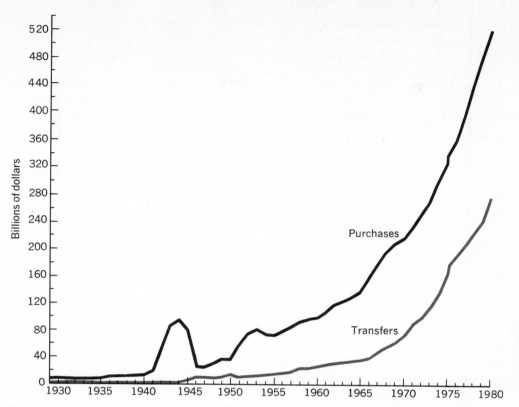

**FIGURE 3.7
ALL
GOVERNMENT
BUYING OR
SPENDING**

Government trends are sharply up both in purchases and in income payments for transfer purposes. This is traceable mainly to defense buying and to social security and other welfare payments.

Last is the extent to which government interferes in the working of the economy by regulating various aspects of economic life or by exercising its economic powers in other ways. This, by far the most difficult to measure exactly, might be thought of as an indication of the extent to which we have moved in the direction of a guided or controlled capitalism.

1. Purchases Figure 3.7 shows the first two measurements: public purchases and income reallocation. Let us begin by examining the trend of production or purchases. As we can see, a steadily rising fraction of GNP is produced or bought by government. **Today about a fifth of all output is produced to fill government demand. What the graph does not show, however, is that increased state and local buying, even more than federal buying, causes the rise.**

Federal purchases have increased mainly with our growing role in world affairs. In 1900, total U.S. military purchases came to $300 million; in 1980, to over $115 billion. But nonfederal purchasing—for education, roads, police, and similar functions—accounts for the major portion of total government buying. In 1980 the states and localities bought over $325 billion worth of GNP; the federal government (including defense) bought only some $175 billion.

2. *Transfers* Next, we notice the rapid rise in the amount of GNP reallocated by government. Here is where the expansion of the federal sector has played the leading role. In 1929, only .9 percent of GNP was redistributed by government. In 1980, transfer payments amounted to 10 percent of GNP, and the great bulk of this originated with the federal government. If we add both the goods produced or purchased by the federal government and the various transfer payments it has made, a total of over $800 billion passed through its hands, or about one-third of GNP.

3. *Intervention* What reasons lay behind this swelling volume of government buying or spending? Let us defer the answer until we examine the last indication of the growing presence of government, the widening role of government as a supervisor or regulator of the economy.

Because of its varied nature, and because the importance of government intervention is not always shown by the amount of money that an agency spends or the number of personnel it employs, this is a trend that defies easy quantification or graphic representation. Much of the spending that we have noted, for example, is carried out through established departments of the executive branch of government, especially Health, Education, and Welfare, from which Social Security checks flow, and the Defense Department, source of military spending.

But we ought to have at least some indication, however impressionistic and incomplete, of the widening reach of government concern within various areas of the economic system. The following list gives us some inkling of the variety and importance of these functions:

Agency	Function
Civil Aeronautics Board	Regulates air routes and fares
Environmental Protection Agency	Administers antipollution legislation
Federal Reserve Board	Regulates supply of money
Federal Communications Commission	Assigns airwave frequencies to stations
Federal Trade Commission	Polices business activities in restraint of trade
Interstate Commerce Commission	Regulates rail, canal, and truck industry
National Labor Relations Board	Supervises union elections
National Science Foundation	Supports scientific research
Tariff Commission	Holds hearings on tariff matters
Office of Economic Opportunity	Oversees employment practices

BEHIND THE RISE IN GOVERNMENT

How shall we account for all these trends of government: more buying, more transfer payments, more regulation and intervention? Among the many causes are these developments:

•**The growing size of business has evoked a need for government supervision.** As business firms have increased in size, private decisions have become fraught with social consequences. It is impossible for a big company to make an important decision that does not have widespread repercussions. Building or not building a plant may spell prosperity or decline for a town, even a state. Cutthroat competition can spell ruin for an industry. Polluting a river can ruin a region. Much government effort, at the local and state as well as federal level, represents attempts to prevent big business from creating social or economic problems, or to cope with problems it has created.

•**Technology brings a need for public supervision.** An impressive amount of government effort goes into the regulation of problem-creating technologies. Examples: the network of state and local highway and police authorities that deal with the automobile; the panoply of agencies designed to cope with airplanes, television and radio, atomic energy, new drugs, and weaponry. As long as technology increases its power to affect our social and natural environment, it is likely that public supervision will also increase.

•**Urbanization brings a need for centralized administration.** City life has its appeals, but it also has its perils. Men and women cannot live in crowded quarters without police, public health, traffic, sanitation, and educational facilities far more complex than those needed in a rural setting. Government is, and always has been, concentrated in cities. As a nation urbanizes, it requires more government.

•**Unification of the economy creates additional problems.** Industrialization knits an economy together into a kind of vast, interlocked machinery. An unindustrialized, localized economy is like a pile of sand: if you poke a finger into one side of it, some businesses and individuals will be affected, but those on the other side of the pile will remain undisturbed. The growing scale and specialization of industrial operations unifies the sandpile. You poke one side of it, and the entire pile shakes. Problems can no longer be localized. The difficulties of the economy grow in extent: there is a need for a national, not a local, energy program, for national transportation, urban and educational programs. Government—largely federal government—is the principal means by which such problems are handled.

•**Economic malfunction has brought public intervention.** Fifty or seventy-five years ago, the prevailing attitude toward the economy was a kind of awed respect. People felt that the economy was best left alone, that it was fruitless as well as ill-advised to try to change its normal workings. That attitude changed once and for all with the advent of the Great Depression. In the ensuing collapse, the role of government greatly enlarged, to restore the economy to working order. The trauma of the Depression and the determination to prevent its recurrence were a watershed in the trend of government spending and government intervention. Keynes's thinking played a very important part in this transition to a mixed economy.

•A new philosophy of "entitlement" has replaced the older one of "rugged individualism." Largely, but not wholly as a consequence of the experience of the Depression, a profound change has been registered in public attitudes toward the appropriate role of government. We no longer live in a society in which old-age retirement, medical expenses, and income during periods of unemployment are felt to be properly the responsibility of the individuals concerned. For better or worse, these and similar responsibilities have been gradually assumed by governments in all capitalist nations. In fact, the United States is a laggard in these matters compared with many European capitalist states. Here lie crucial reasons for the swelling volume of state, local, and federal production and purchase that have steadily enlarged the place of government within the economy.

No doubt there are other causes that could be added to this list. Bureaucracies have ways of feeding on themselves. But the overall conclusion is already evident. In modern capitalism, government is a major factor in the economic system. How well it fulfills its functions and to what extent it realizes the hopes that have been thrust upon it are themes that will constantly occupy us as we continue with our studies.

KEY CONCEPTS

LOOKING BACK

This chapter has been concerned with the economy in movement —not in quick, month-to-month fluctuations of the kind that will concern us when we study macroeconomics, but in longer-run, year to year, or decade to decade changes. Here are the most important of them.

Real vs. nominal growth

More inputs and more productive inputs

1. There is a long-term growth pattern to GNP—a pattern that is much more striking in nominal GNP than in real GNP (that is, in figures uncorrected for inflation than in corrected figures), but remarkable even with all adjustments for rising prices. The source of this growth can be attributed mainly to two factors: an increase in the quantity of inputs as our labor force and our stock of wealth grows, and an increase in the quality and effectiveness of inputs as our productivity grows. Here is Adam Smith's growth projection in reality.

Rise in incomes but little change in distribution

2. A second main trend is directly connected with the rise in output. It is the rise in dollar incomes for all levels of households—a rise that is, of course, much greater before we adjust for inflation than after. The distribution of income among classes changes only very slowly, however. Poverty is gradually being eroded, but remains a stubborn problem.

Big business share of assets has grown, but not its share of individual markets

3. The share of total assets belonging to the biggest corporations has shown a startling increase in the decades of the 1950s and 1960s. However, the increase in the share of sales in different markets going to the biggest firms has shown no significant change. Big firms get bigger by absorbing assets of companies in *different* branches of business, so that their degree of monopoly control within markets shows little change. The main sources of business growth have been technology and mergers. Marx's view of business expansion seems to have been correct.

4. The fourth main trend has been the striking rise in the size of the government sector. Here we have to make careful distinctions between different meanings of the expansion of government. Government buying of goods has increased within the economy mainly because of much greater federal defense expenditure, and swollen state and local spending for education, roads, and the like. Government income payments have increased largely as a result of larger federal transfer payments, like Social Security.

Increased government
spending is mainly transfer
payments like Social Security

Reasons for growing public
regulation are linked to the
attributes of evolving
capitalism

5. There are many reasons for the rise of regulatory government. Here is a list of the most important causes:

the growing size of business,
the disruptive effects of technology,
urbanization,
the unification of the economy,
a Keynesian remedy for economic malfunction,
a new philosophy of entitlement

Thinking about these background elements, what do you believe is likely to be the direction of future change in government's place in the economy? How would you seek to alter things, if you could?

ECONOMIC VOCABULARY

Gross national product 31	**Per capita growth** 32	**Economies of scale** 40
Real and nominal GNP 32	**Productivity** 35	

QUESTIONS

1. Here are some raw data:

	(current $billions)	Price index	Population (millions)
1965	$ 688	100	194
1970	982	123	204
1975	1,498	170	214

What is real GNP per capita in 1970 and 1975 in 1965 dollars? In 1975 dollars? Hint: You will need a new price index with 1975 = 100.

2. If there were no change whatsoever in technology, do you think that a larger quantity of labor might result in GNP growing faster or slower than the sheer increase of man-hour input? Hint: Can people organize their activities better as their numbers change? Does this continue indefinitely?

3. Do you think it might be possible to construct a theory to explain why the pretax, pretransfer shares of income are so fixed? Could there be a kind of pecking order

in society? Could different income groups establish economic distances that satisfy them? Would they then strive only to retain, not to increase, those differences?

4. Can you imagine an invention that would result in rapid concentration in a very unconcentrated industry, say the restaurant business? Or the laundry business? Can you imagine an invention that could radically deconcentrate an industry? How might a watch-sized CB radio affect A.T.&T.? What invention could do the same for Exxon? U.S. Steel?

5. Do you think the rise of government within the economy is "socialistic"? "Capitalistic"? What do you mean by either term?

Part

2 A Kit of
Economic Tools

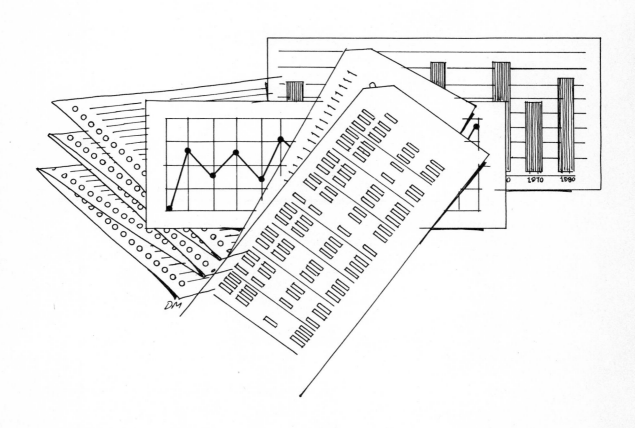

Chapter

4 ECONOMIC SCIENCE

A LOOK AHEAD

Now that we have some background in the field, we are ready to take the next step toward becoming economists by learning something of the ways economists think. Here we are dealing with the abstract and analytic aspects of the field that we mentioned in Chapter 1.

Essentially this short chapter tells you that economic theory is about maximizing behavior that takes place against constraints. Acquisitiveness is a good first approximation of the meaning of "maximizing," and "constraints" implies limits, boundaries, or costs. Economic reasoning consists of puzzling out what happens when rational acquisitors face constraints imposed by nature or society. Keep that in mind and the chapter will unfold step by step.

What it is that we are trying to reason about as economists? Certainly it is not the economic attributes of *all* societies. Our last chapter focused on the United States not merely because we are naturally interested in the economic aspects of our own country, but also because the United States is a kind of society that lends itself to economic analysis. Economic reasoning, we should note at the outset, applies most cogently to societies that are built on the foundations of economic individualism. These are market societies, capitalisms.

Equally to be noted, economic reasoning will not try to come to grips with all of society. Our earlier survey paid no attention to vast areas of social life that we call sociological or political, much less religious or artistic. Economics is concerned with the facts that bear on only one aspect of our social life: our efforts to produce and to distribute wealth. Boom and bust, inflation and depression, poverty and riches, growth or no growth—all can be described in terms of the production of wealth and its distribution.

MAXIMIZING VS. CONSTRAINTS

Our task, then, is to find some way of explaining production and distribution in scientific terms. Therefore, economists observe the *human* universe, just as natural scientists observe the physical universe, in search of data and orderly relationships that may permit them to construct hypotheses.

What do economists see when they scrutinize the world of economic activity? Two attributes of a market society attract their attention:

1. Individuals in such a society display a particular behavior pattern when they participate in economic activities, as consumers or business people. They behave in acquisitive, money-searching, "maximizing" ways. (See box, p. 52.)

2. A series of obstacles or constraints stands between the acquisitive drive of marketers and their realization of economic gain. Some are the constraints of nature; some are the obstacles of social institutions.

Thus an extraordinary conclusion begins to dawn. A great deal of the activity of a market society can be explained as the outcome of two interacting forces. One is the force of maximizing behavior—a force that we have described in terms of the acquisitive behavior of men and women in a market society. The other is the constraining counterforce of nature or of social institutions—a series of obstacles that holds back or channels or directs the acquisitive drive. This suggests the daring scientific task that economics sets for itself. It is to explain the events of economic reality—even to predict some of the events of future economic reality—by reasoning based on fundamental hypotheses about maximizing behavior and its constraints.

HYPOTHESES ABOUT BEHAVIOR

Obviously we must investigate these hypotheses with a great deal of care. Let us start with the economist's assumption about behavior. We can sum it up in a sentence: *Man is a maximizer.*

MAXIMIZING UTILITIES

What does that hypothesis mean? Essentially, it means that people in market societies seek to gain as much pleasurable wealth from their economic activity as they can. We call this pleasurable wealth "utility." Thus we hypothesize that men and women are utility-maximizers.

Note that we define utility as *pleasurable* wealth. Economists do not argue that people try to accumulate the largest amount of wealth possible, regardless of its pleasures. We all know that after a certain point, wealth-producing work brings fatigue or even pain. Therefore we assume that as people work to maximize their wealth, they take into account the pains (or disutilities) of achieving it.

It is impossible to *prove* that people maximize in this fashion. But it seems plausible that most of us do seek wealth both as wage-earners or as businessmen, and that we take account of the nuisances and difficulties of achieving it.

SATIABLE AND INSATIABLE WANTS

Economics not only assumes that men and women are maximizers, but it also has a hypothesis about why they behave so acquisitively. The hypothesis is that peoples' wants are insatiable; that human desires for utility can never be filled.

Are our wants, in fact, insatiable? Does human nature keep us on a treadmill of striving that can never bring us to a point of contentment? As with maximizing, there is a prima facie plausibility about the assumption. For if we include among our aims leisure as well as goods, more time to enjoy ourselves as well as more income to be enjoyed, it seems true enough that something very much like insatiability afflicts most people. At least this seems true in societies that encourage striving for status and success and that set high value on consumption and recreation.

For example, surveys regularly show that men and women at all economic levels express a desire for more income (usually about 10 percent more than they actually have), and *this drive for more does not seem to diminish as we move up the economic scale.* If it did, we would be hard put to explain why people who are generally in the upper echelons of the distribution of wealth and income work just as hard as, or even harder than, those on the lower rungs of the economic ladder.

There is, however, a very important qualification to the assumption that wants are insatiable for all wealth, including leisure. The qualification is that economists assume that human wants for particular kinds of wealth, including

ACQUISITIVENESS

Remember that we are talking about the kind of behavior that we find in a market society. Perhaps in a different society of the future, another hypothesis about behavior would have to serve as our starting point. People might then be driven by the desire to better the condition of others rather than of themselves.

A story about heaven and hell is to the point. Hell has been described as a place where people sit at tables laden with sumptuous food, unable to eat because they have three-foot long forks and spoons strapped to their hands. Heaven is described as the very same place. There, people feed one another.

leisure, **are indeed capable of being satiated.** This idea of the satiability of particular wants will play a key role in our next chapter, when we shall see how we can derive the concept of demand and demand "curves" from our hypotheses concerning behavior.

RATIONALITY

Equally important is an assumption about the way that individuals think and act as they go about striving to fulfill their insatiable wants-in-general or their satiable wants-in-particular. **This assumption is that man is a** *rational* **maximizer.** By this economists mean that people in a market milieu stop to consider the various courses of action open to them and to calculate in some fashion the means that will best suit their maximizing aims. There may be two different ways of producing a good. As rational maximizers, people will choose the method that will yield them the good for the smallest effort or cost.

This concept of rational maximizing does not mean that human beings may not wish, on some occasions, to go to more trouble than necessary. After all, people could worship God in very simple buildings or out-of-doors, but they go to extraordinary lengths to erect magnificent churches and decorate them with sculpture and paintings. It is meaningless to apply the word *rational* to pursuits such as these, which may have vast importance for society.

But when people are engaged in producing the goods and services of ordinary life, seeking to achieve the largest possible incomes or the most satisfaction-yielding patterns of consumption, the economist assumes that they *will* stop to think about the differing ways of attaining a given end and will then choose the way that is least costly.

THE ECONOMIST'S VIEW OF MAN

Of course, economists do not believe that men and women are solely rational, acquisitive creatures. They are fully aware that a hundred motivations impel people: aesthetic, political, religious. If they concentrate on the rational and acquisitive elements in people, it is because they believe these to be decisive for economic behavior; that is, for the explanation of our productive and distributive activities.

Economic theory is therefore a study of the effects of one aspect of human behavior as it motivates people to undertake their worldly activities. Very often, as economists well know, other aspects will override or blunt the acquisitive, maximizing orientation. To the extent that this is so, economic theory loses its clarity or may even suggest outcomes different from those that we find in fact. **But economists think that rational maximizing—the calculated pursuit of pleasurable wealth—is universal and strong enough to serve as a good working hypothesis on which to build their complicated theories.** To put it differently, economists do *not* think that political or religious or other such motives regularly overwhelm maximizing behavior. If that were so, economic theory would be of little avail.

A final point. Economists regard maximizing as a potentially useful mode of behavior. Of course economists understand that there is a lot more to life than making as much money as possible. But economics allows us to see that maximizing can be a beneficial activity. Business schools exist, in part, to teach people to be better maximizers—that is, more efficient, productive, socially useful managers.

HYPOTHESES ABOUT CONSTRAINTS

So far, we have traced the basic assumptions of economic reasoning about behavior. What about constraints? As we have seen, people do not maximize in a vacuum or, to speak in more economic terms, in a world where all goods are free, available effortlessly in infinite amounts. Instead, people exert their maximizing efforts in a world where nature, technical limitations, and social institutions oppose those efforts. Goods and services are not free but must be won by working with the elements of the physical world. Land, resources, man-made artifacts inherited from past generations are not boundlessly abundant. Laws and social organizations constantly impede our maximizing impulses.

Another way of putting it is that maximizing describes what we *want* to do while constraints describe what we *cannot* do. Economics thus studies the problems, and sometimes the impossibility, of achieving what we want. That is why economics is often characterized as maximizing subject to constraints.

CONSTRAINTS OF NATURE

Constraints are obviously very important. But we cannot sum them up as simply as we can sum up the idea of maximizing.

Let us first think about some constraints on our maximizing desires that are imposed by nature. There are three of them. Later we will study these constraints in greater detail, but this is a good time to become generally familiar with them.

1.   Diminishing Returns

It's quite apparent that we cannot grow all the world's food requirements in a flowerpot. But why not? Why can't we go on adding seeds and getting more and more output?

The answer has to do with the physical and chemical properties of nature. If you go on adding more and more of any single input to a fixed amount of other inputs, after a time you will run up against obstacles imposed by the structure of things. Add more and more labor to a factory, and after a time it will be so crowded that output will fall. Add more and more ships to the earth's fishing fleet, and after a time the catch will diminish; in fact, as Figure 4.1 shows, that seems to be exactly what is happening today.

Thus nature imposes limits or constraints because we have to expect, and allow for, diminishing returns. **We can't always count on twice as much output just by doubling one input.**

2.   Returns to Scale

A second constraint has to do with sheer size, or scale. **It describes the fact that size matters—also a consequence of the physical world.** You can't mass produce automobiles in a garage. Why not? Because mass production requires giant presses and an organized flow of assembly, and those require a big scale of production.

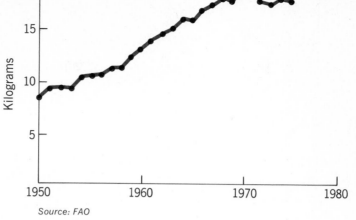

**FIGURE 4.1
WORLD FISH
CATCH PER
CAPITA,
1950–75**

Source: FAO

**Despite steadily increasing inputs of
capital (ships), the output of fish has dwindled.**

This constraint means that small might be more beautiful, but big is often more economical. It means that we can expect that production will become more efficient, and that each additional unit will become cheaper, as we move from small scale to large scale production—at least up to a point.

3. **Increasing Cost**

The last constraint is the least familiar. It looks like diminishing returns, but it is different. It has to do with the fact that not all land or labor or resources are alike, so that **as we move from one kind of production to another, we are likely to find it more and more costly to produce more and more of the new output.**

Here a diagram can help us visualize the problem. In Figure 4.2 we see a community that can produce two kinds of output—milk and grain. If it puts all its labor and all its land into milk production, it can produce an amount of milk that we'll represent by the distance *OA* on the milk axis. If it puts all its land and labor into grain, it will produce *OB* of grain, as represented on that axis.

Now suppose that our community is producing nothing but milk and that it decides to balance its output. It cuts its milk production in half (to *OX*), moving land and labor into grain. We can see that it thereby gains *OY* amount of grain. Now notice what happens if the community moves the remaining half of its land and labor into grain. Output rises only a small amount, *YB*. Why is the second half of the community investment in land and labor less productive than the first half? Because we have already plowed the best fields and availed ourselves of the most skilled farmers. The last bushels of grain are much harder to win than the first. And of course the same result would take place in reverse if we started from all grain, at *B*, and switched over into milk. **The constraint means that the more of any one product that we want, the more of some other product we have to give up to get it.**

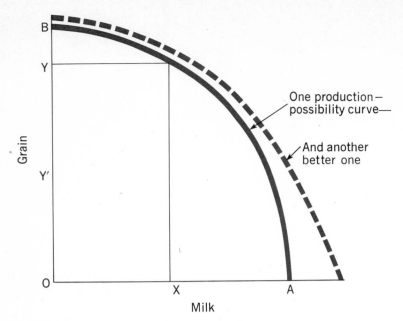

FIGURE 4.2
INCREASING
COST

The curve *AB* is called a production possibility curve. The dotted line shows how better technology, for instance, could move such a curve out. What would an earthquake do to it? Draw in such a reduced production possibility curve. The curve bows because of the law of increasing cost—that is, because it becomes less and less efficient to move labor and resources from one use to another. Compare how much grain we get (*OY*) as we cut milk production in half (moving from *OA* to *OX*), with how little we get (*BY*) as we move the remaining half (*OX*). Use a pencil to see if it works the other way round. Start from all grain (*OB*) and zero milk. First chart how much milk you get if you move the economy out of grain (from *OB* to *OY'*). Now eliminate all grain production. How much *additional* milk do you get?

How much of one thing do we have to surrender to get something else? That depends on a host of things—the resources available, the skills we can call on, the energy we can muster. The curve in Figure 4.2 shows us the grain-milk trade-off in our hypothetical community on some imaginary date, but a new invention, a change in climate, even a new economic system could change the efficiency with which we use our wealth. Thus the curve in Figure 4.2, which we call a **production-possibilities curve**, can move—loosening our constraints, as the dotted line shows, or possibly tightening them. We will come back to study this when we take up the subject of economic growth in Chapter 7.

OPPORTUNITY COST

Here is a good place to make a very important point about the constraint of cost. Cost constrains us because it means that we have to give something up to gain wealth: The cost of the grain in Figure 4.2 is the milk we had to give up to get it, and the cost of the milk is the grain we had to forego. That is why economists say "There is no such thing as a free lunch." Even if you did not pay money for it, someone had to produce that lunch, and the labor and materials in it are locked up forever and ever, and can never be retrieved to make something else.

All costs, to economists, are opportunity costs. They are the utilities we must do without because we have chosen to devote our energies and wealth to creating the utilities we have. Later on, we will be talking about costs in dollars and cents, which is the way we usually think of cost. But when we say that something costs $10, what we really mean is that it costs us whatever utilities we might have enjoyed if we had spent the $10 on something else. Have you ever hesitated over whether to buy this *or* that? Then you know what opportunity cost means.

CONSTRAINTS AND COSTS

All these properties of nature set the stage for maximizing behavior. People seek wealth through the production and exchange of goods and services, but they do not maximize in a world where goods can be limitlessly and effortlessly obtained. Nature and our given technology offer us their services easily or reluctantly, depending on whether we are trying to maximize output by adding more and more of one kind of input (when we encounter diminishing returns); whether we are seeking to organize our production in accordance with the technological characteristics of the agencies of production (economies of scale); or whether we are trying to increase the output of one good or service at the expense of others (when the law of increasing cost comes into play).

Thus constraints will play a basic role in establishing costs or supplies. We shall return to these considerations in our next chapter, where we encounter a supply curve, the counterpart of the demand curve, about which we heard our first words on page 53.

CONSTRAINTS OF SOCIETY

Perhaps we can already see the makings of a powerful analytic device in the interplay of maximizing drives and constraining influences. Before we move on, however, it is necessary to recognize that nature is not the only constraint on the maximizing force of behavior.

Society's constraints on our behavior are just as effective as nature's. The *law* is a major constraining factor on our acquisitive propensities. *Competition* also limits freedom of action, preventing us from charging as much as we would like for goods or services. The banking system, labor unions, the legal underpinnings of private property are all *institutions* that operate like the constraints of nature in curbing the unhampered exercise of our maximizing impulse. So is the constraint of our available resources, our *budget*. Like technology, this is partly a constraint imposed by nature, partly one that is the consequence of man. Different societies enjoy different settings in nature—rich or poor soils, cold or warm climates, easily available or scarce mineral deposits. These gifts of nature help establish the limits of our productive activities, our national budget of annual output. We shall spend a lot of time later investigating how all these various constraints affect individual behavior.

BASIC HYPOTHESES

Let us briefly review the basic propositions in this first look into economic analysis. They can be summed up very simply.

Because economics generalizes about human behavior and the behavior of nature, it can theorize about, and predict, the operations of a market society. If we were not able to make such generalizations, if we could not begin with the plausible hypothesis that people are maximizers and that nature (and social institutions) constrain their behavior in clearly defined ways, we could not hazard the simplest predictive statement about economic society. We could not explain why a store that wants to sell more goods marks its prices down rather than up or why copper costs will probably rise if we try to double copper production in a short period of time.

ECONOMICS AS A SOCIAL SCIENCE

Perhaps these simple generalizations about behavior and nature do not seem to be an impressive foundation for a social science. Ask yourself, though, whether we can match these economic generalizations when we think in political or sociological terms. Are there political or social laws of behavior that we can count on with the same degree of certainty we find in laws of economics? Are there constraints of nature, comparable to the laws of production, discoverable in the political and social areas of life? There are not. That is why we are so much less able to predict political or sociological events than to predict economic events.

Although economic prediction has sharp limitations, its underlying structure of behavioral and natural laws gives it unique strength. Its capabilities we must now explore. The place to begin must be obvious from our look into economic reality and our first acquaintance with supply and demand. It is the market mechanism.

KEY CONCEPTS

LOOKING BACK

This chapter covers quite a few technical ideas, such as diminishing returns or increasing costs. Don't try to master them yet. Instead, be sure that you have the following simple conception of economic reasoning firmly in mind.

Economics is about production and distribution

1. Economic reasoning is about production and distribution of wealth, and only about those things. Economics has nothing to say about politics, religion, or anything other than material wealth.

Economics theorizes from two premises: utility maximizing and constraints

2. Economics erects hypotheses—or, much the same thing, economics theorizes—about the production and distribution of wealth. In doing so, it begins from two premises: (a) Men and women are maximizers of utility, and (b) they maximize in the face of well-defined obstacles or constraints.

Maximizing means insatiable desire for utility in general, not for any one kind of utility

3. Maximizing behavior means that individuals seek as much pleasurable wealth as possible. This pleasurable wealth is called utility. Economists believe that in a market society such as ours, there is an insatiable desire for pleasurable wealth in general, although not for each

particular kind of pleasurable wealth; after a certain point, more food makes us sick, more leisure is a bore.

Maximizing is guided by rational choice

4. Economists also assume that individuals pursue their maximizing goals rationally—not in a haphazard, thoughtless way, but by making the best choices they can. Maximizing can therefore be socially useful.

Nature's constraints:

5. Maximizing behavior has to contend with the obstacles set by nature and by society. Nature and technology together establish three important kinds of constraints:

law of diminishing returns

The law of diminishing returns puts limits on the amount of output we can get from adding any one input—we can't grow all the world's food in a flowerpot.

law of increasing costs

The law of increasing costs limits our attempts to maximize because not all resources can be applied efficiently to any given purpose: We can't raise dairy cattle in Nevada. We can graph this in a production possibility curve.

law of scale

Returns to scale inhibit maximizing, because it is not efficient to produce all kinds of goods on a very small (or a very large) scale. Small may be beautiful, but it is also very expensive if you are thinking about making steel.

Institutional and budget constraints

6. Society also imposes constraints on maximizing—laws, institutional barriers, competition, and the like. Another important limit is imposed by budget considerations.

7. A powerful social science has been derived from the idea of interplay between maximizing and constraining forces. We shall see a demonstration of this power as we enter into a discussion of supply and demand in the next chapter.

Costs are missed opportunities

8. Finally, remember that costs are basically missed opportunities. The phrase "opportunity cost" makes it clear that costs are not just sums of money, but possibilities for making wealth of various kinds that are forever missed because we have chosen to make wealth of one kind.

ECONOMIC VOCABULARY

Maximizing 51	Constraints 54	Increasing cost 55
Utilities 51	Diminishing returns 54	Production possibility curve 56
Rationality 53	Scale 54	Opportunity cost 56

QUESTIONS

1. Do you feel like a maximizer? Are you content with your income? If you are not, do you expect that some day you will be satisfied?

2. Do you act rationally when you spend money? Do you consciously try to weigh the various advantages of buying this instead of that, and to spend your money for the item that will give you the greatest pleasure? Consciously or not, do you generally act as a rational maximizer?

3. How valid do you think the laws of economic behavior are? If they are *not* valid, why does economic society function and not collapse? If they *are* valid, why can't economists predict more accurately?

4. In what way is competition an institution? Are people naturally competitive? Would there be competition in a society that denied spatial or social mobility to labor, as under feudalism?

5. Can you think of any political activities or limits comparable to economic maximizing or constraints? Are there constraints of national size? Might it be possible to devise an economics of politics?

6. Suppose that you had a very large flowerpot and extraordinary chemicals and seeds. Could you conceivably grow all the world's food in it? Why would you still get diminishing returns?

7. Describe the economies of scale that might be anticipated if you were opening a department store. What economies might be expected as the store grew larger? Do you think you would eventually reach a ceiling on these economies?

8. What is the opportunity cost of undertaking a program such as the NASA space exploration? Of mounting a vast slum clearance program? Suppose the two cost the same amount of money? Does that mean the opportunity cost is the same?

Chapter

SUPPLY AND DEMAND

A LOOK AHEAD

Here is your first real encounter with economics. In it you come to grips with the most important and powerful tool that economic reasoning gives us. The tool is an understanding of supply and demand and how they drive the market system.

It will help you to go through this chapter if you keep the following three steps in mind:

(1) You are going to learn exactly what the word "demand" means, and what a "demand curve" represents.

(2) You will learn the same thing about supply—what the word "supply" means and what a "supply curve" represents.

(3) You will put the two together and see how demand and supply give rise to the idea of an equilibrium price.

Our look at the great economists has given us a general understanding of the market system. The next step in understanding the fundamental concepts of economics is to learn much more about that system.

What impresses us first when we study the market as a solution to the economic problem? The striking fact is that the market uses only one means of persuasion to induce people to engage in production or to undertake the tasks of distribution. It is neither time-honored tradition nor the edict of any authority that tells the members of a market society what to do. *It is price.*

PRICES AND BEHAVIOR

Thus the first attribute of a market system that we must examine is how prices take the place of tradition or command to become the guide to economic behavior.

The key lies in maximization. Through prices, acquisitive individuals learn what course of action will maximize their incomes or minimize their expenditures. This means that in the word *price* we include prices of labor or capital or resources that we call wages, profits, interest, or rent. Of course, within the category of prices we also include those ordinary prices that we pay for the goods and services we consume and the materials we purchase in order to build a home or to operate a store or factory. In each case, the only way that we can tell how to maximize our receipts and minimize our costs is by reading the signals of price that the market gives us.*

Therefore, if we are to understand how the market works as a mechanism— that is, how it acts as a guide to the solution of the economic problem—we must first understand how the market sets prices. When we say "the market," we mean the activity of buying and selling, or in more precise economic language, *demand and supply.* Let us discover how demand and supply interact to establish prices.

DEMAND

TASTE AND INCOME

When you enter the market for goods and services (almost every time you walk along a shopping street), two factors determine whether or not you will actually become a buyer and not just a window-shopper. The first factor is your taste for the good. It is your taste that determines in large degree whether a good offers you pleasure or utility, and if so, how much. The windows of shops are crammed with things you could afford to buy but which you simply do not wish to own, because they do not offer you sufficient utility. Perhaps if some of these were cheaper, you might wish to own them; but some goods you would not want even if they were free. For such goods, for which your tastes are too weak to motivate you, your demand is zero. **Thus taste determines your willingness to buy.**

---

*In the real world, reading prices can be very complicated, for it involves not only how much we know about the market, but how much we *think* we know about it. Here we simplify matters and assume, to begin with, that we all have perfect knowledge.

On the other hand, taste is by no means the only component of demand. Shop windows are also full of goods that you might very much like to own but cannot afford to buy. Your demand for Rolls Royces is also apt to be zero. **In other words, demand also hinges on your ability to buy—on your possession of sufficient wealth or income as well as on your taste.** If demand did not hinge on ability as well as willingness to buy, the poor, whose wants are always very large, would constitute a great source of demand.

BUDGETS

Note that your demand for goods depends on your willingness and ability to buy goods or services *at their going price.* From this it follows that the amounts of goods you demand will change as their prices change, just as it also follows that the amounts you will demand change as your wealth or income changes. There is no difficulty understanding why changing prices should change our ability to buy: Our wealth simply stretches further or less far. **In economic language, our budget constraint is loosened when prices fall and tightened when they rise.**

DIMINISHING MARGINAL UTILITY

Why should our *willingness* to buy be related to price? The answer lies in the nature of utility. People are maximizing creatures, but they do not want ever more of the *same* commodity. On the contrary, as we saw, economists take as a plausible generalization that additional increments of the same good or service, within some stated period of time, will yield smaller and smaller increments of pleasure. **These increments of pleasure are called marginal utility, and the gen-**

UTILITIES AND DEMAND

Does diminishing marginal utility really determine how much we buy? The idea seems far removed from common sense, but is it? Suppose we decide to buy a cake of fancy soap. In common-sense language, we'll do so only "if it's not too expensive." In the language of the economist this means we'll only do so *if the utilities we expect from the soap are greater than the utilities we derive from the money we have to spend to get the soap.*

If we buy one or two cakes, doesn't this demonstrate that the pleasure of the soap is greater than the pleasure of holding onto the money or spending it for something else? In that case, why don't we buy a year's supply of the soap? The commonsense answer is that we don't want *that much* soap. It would be a nuisance. We wouldn't use it all for months and months, etc. *In the language of the economist, the utilities of the cakes of* *soap after the first few would be less than the utilities of the money they would cost.*

In the accompanying diagram we show these diminishing marginal utilities of successive cakes. The price of soap represents the utility of the money we have to pay. As you can see, if soap costs *OA,* we'll buy three cakes; no more.

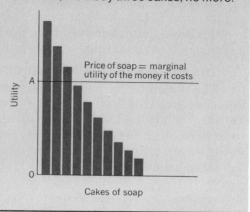

Price of soap = marginal utility of the money it costs

Utility

Cakes of soap

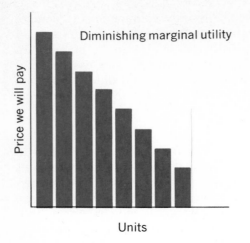

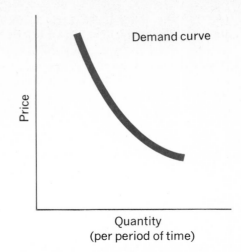

FIGURE 5.1 DIMINISHING MARGINAL UTILITY AND A DEMAND CURVE

Notice, on the left, how the marginal utility of each additional unit of a good diminishes. The curve on the right simply generalizes the fact that each additional unit yields less pleasure than the one before it, and will therefore command a smaller price.

eral tendency of marginal utility to diminish is called the law of *diminishing marginal utility*. Remember: Diminishing marginal utility refers strictly to behavior and not to nature. The units of goods we continue to buy are not smaller —it is the pleasure associated with each additional unit that is smaller.

DEMAND CURVES*

In the bar chart on the left of Figure 5.1, we show the ever smaller amounts of money we are willing to pay for additional units of some good or service, simply because each additional unit gives us less utility than its predecessor. In the graph on the right, we have drawn a *demand curve* to generalize this basic relationship between the quantity of a good we are interested in acquiring and the price we are willing to pay for it.

Figure 5.1 deserves a careful look. Note that each *additional* unit affords us less utility, so we are not willing to pay as much for the next unit as for the one we just bought. This does not mean that the *total utility* we derive from all 3 or 4 units is less than that derived from the first. Far from it. It is the *addition* to our utility from the last unit that is much lower than the *addition* of the first or second.

THE PUZZLE OF BREAD AND DIAMONDS

The notion of diminishing marginal utility also clears up an old puzzle of economic life. This is why we are willing to pay so little for bread, which is a necessity for life, and so much for diamonds, which are not. The answer is that we have so much bread that the marginal utility of any loaf we are thinking of buying is very little, whereas we have so few diamonds that each carat has a very high marginal utility. If we were locked inside Tiffany's over a long holiday, the

---

*Anyone unfamiliar with graphs should turn right now to page 78 and learn how to read them and use them. Look as well into the Extra Word on graphs at the end of Chapter 6.

prices we would pay for bread and diamonds, after a few days, would be very different from those we would have paid when we entered.

SUPPLY

What about the supply side? Here, too, willingness and ability enter into the seller's actions. As we would expect, they bring about reactions different from those in the case of demand.

At high prices, sellers are much more *willing* to supply goods and services because they will take in more money. They will also be much more easily *able* to offer more goods because higher prices will enable less efficient suppliers to enter the market, or will cover the higher costs of production that may result from increasing their outputs.

Therefore, we depict normal supply curves as rising. These rising curves present a contrast to the falling curves of demanders: sellers eagerly respond to high prices; buyers respond negatively. Figure 5.2 shows such a typical supply curve.

SUPPLY AND DEMAND

The idea that buyers welcome low prices and sellers welcome high prices is hardly apt to come as a surprise. What is surprising is that the meaning of the words *supply* and *demand* differs from the one we ordinarily carry about in our heads. It is very important to understand that when we speak of demand as economists, we do not refer to a single purchase at a given price. **Demand in its proper economic sense refers to the various quantities of goods or services that we are willing and able to buy at different prices at a given time. That relationship is shown by our demand curve.**

The same relationship between price and quantity enters into the word *supply.* When we say *supply,* we do not mean the amount a seller puts on the market at a given price. We mean the various amounts offered at different prices. Thus our supply curves, like our demand curves, portray the relationship between willingness and ability to enter into transactions at different prices.

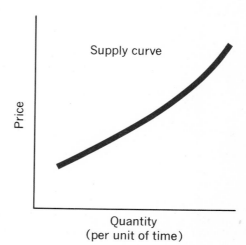

A typical supply curve slopes upward because each additional unit tends to be more difficult or expensive to make, at least in the short run.

FIGURE 5.2 THE SHORT-RUN SUPPLY CURVE

INDIVIDUAL AND COLLECTIVE SUPPLY AND DEMAND

We must add one last word before we investigate the market at work. Thus far we have considered only the factors that make an *individual* more willing and able to buy or less willing and able to sell as prices fall. Generally when we speak of supply and demand we refer to markets composed of *many* suppliers and demanders. That gives us an additional reason for relating price and behavior. If we assume that most individuals have somewhat different willingnesses and abilities to buy, because their incomes and their tastes are different, or they have unequal willingnesses or abilities to sell, then we can see that *a change in price will bring into the market new buyers or sellers:* As price falls, it will tempt or permit one person after another to buy, thereby adding to the quantity of the good that will be purchased at that price. Conversely, as prices rise, the number of sellers drawn into the market will increase, and the quantity of goods they offer will rise accordingly.

We can see this graphically in Figure 5.3. Here we show three individuals' demand curves. At the going market price of $2, A is either not willing or not able to buy any of the commodity. B is both willing and able to buy 1 unit. C buys 3 units. If we add up their demands, we get a *collective or market demand curve.* At the indicated market price of $2, the quantity demanded is 4 units. What would it be (approximately) for each buyer, and for the group, at a price of $1?

The same, of course, applies to supply. In Figure 5.4 we show individual supply curves and a collective or market supply curve that is 7 units at $2 market supply. What would total supply be at a price of $1? What would seller A's supply be at $1?

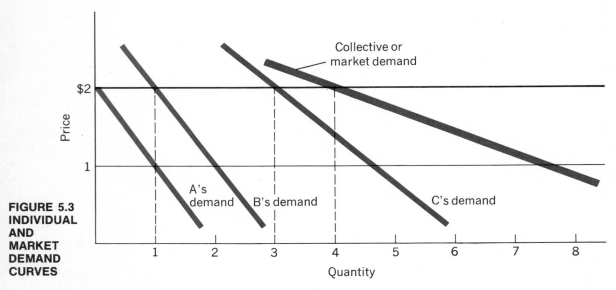

FIGURE 5.3 INDIVIDUAL AND MARKET DEMAND CURVES

The demand curves for a product on a market are nothing but the sum of the individual demand curves for it.

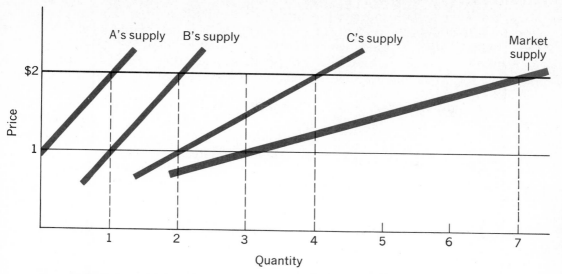

Price

$2

1

1   2   3   4   5   6   7

Quantity

**FIGURE 5.4
INDIVIDUAL
AND
MARKET
SUPPLY
CURVES**

**Like market demand curves, market supply curves sum up the
willingness and ability of individuals into a market total.**

BALANCING SUPPLY AND DEMAND

We are now ready to see how the market mechanism works. Undoubtedly you have already grasped the crucial point on which the mechanism depends. This is the opposing behavior that a change in prices brings about for buyers and sellers. Rising prices will be matched by an increase in the willingness and ability of sellers to offer goods, but in a decrease in the willingness and ability of buyers to take goods.

It is through these opposing reactions that the market mechanism works. Let us examine the process in an imaginary market for shoes in a small city. In Table 5.1 we show the price-quantity relationships of buyers and of sellers: how many thousand pairs will be offered for sale or sought for purchase at a range of prices from $50 to $5. We call such an array of price-quantity relationships a schedule of supply and demand.

Price	Quantity demanded (1,000 prs.)	Quantity supplied (1,000 prs.)
$50	1	125
$45	5	90
$40	10	70
$35	20	50
$30	25	35
$25	30	30
$20	40	20
$15	50	10
$10	75	5
$ 5	100	0

Go down the price schedule and notice that quantities demanded do not equal quantities supplied —until you get to $25. Below $25 they are also unequal. $25 is the equilibrium price.

**TABLE 5.1
DEMAND
AND SUPPLY
SCHEDULES**

As before, the schedules tell us that buyers and sellers react differently to prices. At high prices, buyers are either not willing or unable to purchase more than small quantities of shoes, whereas sellers would be only too willing and able to flood the city with them. At very low prices, the quantity of shoes demanded would be very great, but few shoe manufacturers would be willing or able to gratify buyers at such low prices.

If we now look at *both* schedules at *each* price level, we discover an interesting thing. *There is one price—$25 in our example—at which the quantity demanded is exactly the same as the quantity supplied.* At every other price, one schedule or the other is larger, but as $25 the amounts in both columns are the same: 30,000 pairs of shoes. We call this balancing price the *equilibrium price.* We shall soon see that it *is* the price that emerges spontaneously in an actual market where supply and demand contend.°

EMERGENCE OF THE EQUILIBRIUM PRICE

How do we know that an equilibrium price will be brought about by the interaction of supply and demand? The process is one of the most important in all of economics, so we should understand it very clearly.

INTERPLAY OF SUPPLY AND DEMAND

Suppose in our example above that for some reason or other the shoe retailers put a price tag on their shoes not of $25 but of $45. What would happen? Our schedules show us that at this price shoe manufacturers will be pouring out shoes at the rate of 90,000 pairs a year, whereas customers would be buying them at the rate of only 5,000 pairs a year. Shortly, the shoe factories would be bulging with unsold merchandise. It is plain what the outcome of this situation must be. In order to realize some revenue, shoe manufacturers will begin to unload their stocks at lower prices. *They do so because this is their rational course as competitive maximizers.*

As they reduce the price, the situation will begin to improve. At $40, demand picks up from 5,000 pairs to 10,000, while at the same time the slightly lower price discourages some producers, so that output falls from 90,000 pairs to 70,000. Shoe manufacturers are still turning out more shoes than the market can absorb at the going prices, although the difference between the quantities supplied and the quantities demanded is smaller than it was before.

Let us suppose that the competitive pressure continues to reduce prices so that shoes soon sell at $30. Now a much more satisfactory state of affairs exists. Producers will be turning out 35,000 pairs of shoes. Consumers will be buying them at a rate of 25,000 a year. Still there is an imbalance. Some shoes will still be piling up, unsold, at the factory. Prices will therefore continue to fall, eventually to $25. At this point, the quantity of shoes supplied by the manufacturers— 30,000 pairs—is exactly that demanded by customers. There is no longer a surplus of unsold shoes hanging over the market and acting to press prices down.

---

*Of course we have made up our schedules so that the quantities demanded and supplied would be equal at $25. The price that actually brought about such a balancing of supply and demand might be some odd number such as $24.98.

THE MARKET CLEARS

Now let us quickly trace the interplay of supply and demand from the other direction. Suppose that prices were originally $5. Our schedules tell us that customers would be standing in line at the shoe stores, but producers would be largely shut down, unwilling or unable to make shoes at those prices. We can easily imagine that customers, many of whom would gladly pay more than $5, let it be known that they would welcome a supply of shoes at $10 or even more. They, too, are trying to maximize their utilities. If enough customers bid $10, a trickle of shoe output begins. Nevertheless, the quantity of shoes demanded at $10 far exceeds the available supply. Customers snap up the few pairs around and tell shoe stores they would gladly pay $20 a pair. Prices rise accordingly. Now we are getting closer to a balance of quantities offered and bid for. At $20 there will be a demand for 40,000 pairs of shoes, and output will have risen to 20,000 pairs. Still the pressure of unsatisfied demand raises prices further. Finally a price of $25 is tried. Now, once again, the quantities supplied and demanded are exactly in balance. There is no further pressure from unsatisfied customers to force the price up further, because at $25 no customer who can afford the going price will remain unsatisfied. The market "clears."

CHARACTERISTICS OF EQUILIBRIUM PRICES

Thus we can see how the interaction of supply and demand brings about the establishment of a price at which both suppliers and demanders are willing and able to sell or buy the same quantity of goods. We can visualize the equilibrating process more easily if we now transfer our supply and demand schedules to graph paper. Figure 5.5 is the representation of the shoe market we have been dealing with.

The graph shows us at a glance the situation we have analyzed in detail. At the price of $25, the quantities demanded and supplied are equal: 30,000 pairs of shoes. The graph also shows more vividly than the schedules why this is an *equilibrium* price.

Suppose that the price were temporarily lifted above $25. If you will draw a horizontal pencil line from any point on the vertical axis above the $25 mark to represent this price, you will find that it intersects the demand curve before it

Demand and supply curves only show what the schedule has already revealed: There is one price at which the two quantities are equal. This is the equilibrium price.

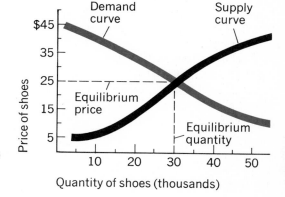

**FIGURE 5.5
DETERMINA-
TION OF AN
EQUILIBRIUM
PRICE**

reaches the supply curve. In other words, *the quantity demanded is less than the quantity supplied at any price above the equilibrium price, and the excess of the quantity supplied means that there will be a downward pressure on prices, back toward the equilibrium point.*

The situation is exactly reversed if prices should fall below the equilibrium point. Now the quantity demanded is greater than that supplied, and the pressure of buyers will push the price up to the equilibrium point.

Thus equilibrium prices have two important characteristics:

1. They are the prices that will spontaneously establish themselves through the free play of the forces of supply and demand.

2. Once established, they will persist unless the forces of supply and demand themselves change.

DOES "DEMAND EQUAL SUPPLY"?

There is one last thing to be noted carefully about equilibrium prices. They are the prices that bring about an equality in the *quantities demanded* and the *quantities supplied.* They are not the prices that bring about an equality of "supply and demand."

Probably the most common beginning mistake in economics is to say that supply and demand are equal when prices are in equilibrium. If we remember that both supply and demand mean the *relationships* between quantities and prices, we can see that an equality of supply and demand would mean that the demand schedule and the supply schedule for a commodity were alike, so that the curves would lie one on top of the other. In turn, this would mean that at a price of $50, buyers of shoes would be willing and able to buy the same number of shoes that suppliers would be willing to offer at that price, and the same for buyers at $5. If such were the case, prices would be wholly indeterminate and could race high and low with no tension of opposing interests to bring them to a stable resting place.

Hence we must take care to use the words *supply* or *demand* to refer only to relationships or schedules. When we want to speak of the effect of a particular price on our willingness or ability either to buy or sell, we use the longer phrase *quantity demanded* or *quantity supplied.*

THE ROLE OF COMPETITION

We have seen how stable, lasting prices may spontaneously emerge from the flux of the marketplace, but we have silently passed over a basic condition for the formation of these prices. This is the role played by competition in the operation of the market mechanism.

Competition is often discussed as a somewhat unpleasant attribute of economic man. Now, however, we can see that it is an attribute that is indispensable if we are to have socially acceptable outcomes for a market process.

Competition is the regulator that "supervises" the orderly working of the market. But economic competition (unlike the competition for prizes outside economic life) is not a single contest. It is a *continuing process.* It monitors a race that no one ever wins, a race where all must go on endlessly trying to stay in front, to avoid the economic penalties of falling behind.

SUPPLY AND DEMAND, AGAIN

Here is one of the oldest "puzzles" in economics. Suppose that the price of A.T.&T. stock rises. Because the price rises, the demand for the stock falls. Therefore the price of A.T.&T. must decline. It follows that the price of A.T.&T. should never vary or at least should quickly return to the starting point.

Tell that to your broker. Better, tell it to your instructor and show him—and yourself—with a graph of supply and demand, where the fallacy of this puzzle lies. Hint: When the price rises, does the *demand* for A.T.&T. stock fall or does the *quantity demanded* fall? Will the price fall again?

Moreover, unlike the contests of ordinary life, economic *competition involves not just a single struggle among rivals, but two struggles.* One is between the two sides of the markets; the other is among the marketers on each side. The competitive marketplace is not only where the clash of interest between buyer and seller is worked out by the opposition of supply and demand, but also where buyers contend against buyers and sellers against sellers.

TWO NECESSARY ASPECTS OF COMPETITION

It is this double aspect of the competitive process that accounts for its usefulness. A market in which buyers and sellers had no conflict of interest would not be competitive, for prices could then be arranged at some level convenient for both sides, instead of representing a compromise between the divergent interests of the two. Conversely, a market that was no more than a place where opposing forces contended would be only a tug of war, a bargaining contest with an unpredictable outcome, unless we knew the respective strengths and cunning of the two sides.

Competition drives buyers and sellers to a meeting point because each side of the price contest is also contesting against itself. Vying takes place not merely *between* those who want high prices and those who want low ones. On each side of this divide, vying takes place *among* marketers whose self-interest urges them to meet the demands of the other side. If some unsatisfied shoe buyers, although preferring low prices to high ones, did not want shoes enough to offer a little higher price than the prevailing one, and if some unsatisfied sellers, although hoping for high prices, were not driven by self-interest to offer a price a little below that of their rivals, the price would not move to the balancing point where the two sides arrived at the best possible settlement.

Thus, whereas buyers as a group want low prices, each individual buyer has to pay as high a price as he can to get into the market. Whereas sellers as a group want high prices, each individual seller has to trim his prices if he is to be able to meet the competition.

MAXIMIZING SUBJECT TO CONSTRAINTS

Does the extraordinary market mechanism bear a relation to the general notion of maximizing? Indeed it does. Buyers and sellers both are *willing* to respond to price signals because they wish to maximize their incomes or utilities. But neither can maximize at will. Buyers are *constrained* by their budgets, and sellers are *constrained* by their costs. Thus the *ability* of buyers or sellers to respond to price signals is limited by obstacles of budgets or cost.

In addition, buyers and sellers are both constrained by the operation of the market. A seller might like to sell his goods above the market price, and a buyer might like to buy goods below the market price; but the presence of competitors means that a seller who quotes a price above the market will be unable to find a buyer, and a buyer who makes a bid below the market will be unable to find a seller.

Thus the market mechanism is a very important example of what economists call "maximizing subject to constraints." Furthermore, we can see that it is the very interaction of the maximizing drives and the constraining obstacles that leads the market to the establishment of equilibrium prices. We can also see that if we could know these maximizing forces and constraints beforehand, we would know the supply and demand curves of a market and could actually predict what its equilibrium price would be! In actual fact, our knowledge falls far short of such omniscience, but the imaginary example nonetheless begins to open up for us the analytical possibilities of economics.

KEY CONCEPTS

LOOKING BACK

You can now see that the purpose of this chapter is to show how maximizing subject to constraints works in terms of demand and supply. Here are the main points that you should carry away from what you have read:

Demand is the willingness and ability to buy at a given price

1. Demand is a central idea of economics. It means the willingness and ability of any person or group of persons to buy a good or service at a particular price. Your demand schedule reflects your desire to maximize your utilities for that good, within the constraint of your budget.

Marginal utility typically falls

2. Our willingness or ability to buy more of any kind of wealth reflects the marginal utility that another unit of that wealth will yield. The marginal utility means the additional utility—the pleasures of the *next* movie, the *next* pair of shoes, the *next* dollar of income—within a given period of time. A basic assumption of economic reasoning is that the marginal utility of any one thing diminishes: The second movie, pair of shoes, or dollar will not give as much pleasure as the first one.

Therefore typical demand curves fall

3. This gives rise to normal, downward-sloping demand curves, showing that we are only willing to buy more units of the same goods at cheaper prices. These curves represent our schedules in simplified form.

Supply curves typically rise

4. Supply curves typically rise, because suppliers are not able (or willing) to offer more and more goods within a given period of time, except at higher prices.

Supply and demand vs. quantities supplied or demanded

5. Supply and demand refer to the range of goods or services that sellers or buyers will offer at differing prices. At any given price we should refer to the *quantity supplied* or the *quantity demanded*. When we say supply or demand, we mean the whole schedule or the curve that represents that schedule.

The idea of equilibrium where quantities offered are equal to quantities demanded

6. When we compare schedules or plot two supply and demand curves, we can find out if there is an equilibrium price. This is a price where the quantities offered or supplied are equal to the quantities demanded. Economists are often careless and say that at an equilibrium price "supply equals demand," but students should watch their language! In an equilibrium price, the *quantities demanded* equal the *quantities supplied,* and the market clears.

How equilibrium prices emerge and persist

7. Equilibrium prices spontaneously establish themselves through the interplay of supply and demand, and they will persist unless the willingness or abilities of buyers and sellers change.

There is a two-sided aspect of competition

8. There is a double-edged aspect to competition. Competition not only means that buyers oppose sellers, each trying to get the better of the other, but also that buyers have to win out against other buyers and that sellers have to outdo—or do as well as—other sellers.

The price system

9. Lastly, bear in mind that you are learning the remarkable way in which an economic mechanism coordinates the very different objectives and activities of buyers and sellers through only one means—the signal of price. Prices inform people how to maximize rationally. The Invisible Hand does the rest!

ECONOMIC VOCABULARY

QUESTIONS

1. Fill out the schedule below by supplying reasonable numbers to show the quantities demanded and supplied for T-shirts in a small town, at prices ranging from $1.00 to $10.00, over a period of, say, one year. (You might assume that there are about 10,000 potential buyers in your market.) Now graph the schedule in the graph space provided. Be sure to indicate the quantities on the horizontal axis.

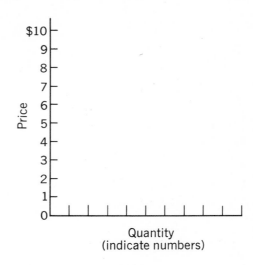

Schedule of supply and demand for T-shirts, per year.		
Price of T-shirts	Quantity demanded	Quantity supplied
$10		
9		
8		
7		
6		
5		
4		
3		
2		
1		

2. Choose any arbitrary price above equilibrium. How will maximizing behavior lead this higher price back toward equilibrium? Does it require a contest among buyers? Sellers? Both? Either?

3. Now do the same thing with a price below the equilibrium.

4. Subtract the quantities in your supply schedule from those in your demand schedule. There will be a plus or minus at all prices except one. Why is that? Does that help explain why an equilibrium price clears a market?

5. Whatever quantity is sold must be bought; whatever is bought must be sold. Then how can we say that only one price will clear the market? Hint: Look again at your answer to question 2.

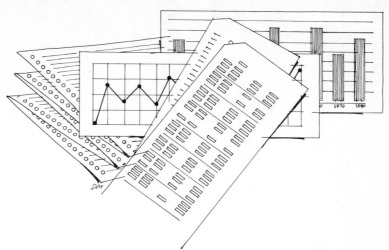

Chapter

6 SIX TOOLS YOU SHOULD KNOW HOW TO HANDLE

A LOOK AHEAD

This is a chapter about concepts and techniques. It isn't about "economics," but about some ideas, simple statistical devices, and other tools with which every economist must be familiar. There is no single, large idea to keep in mind as you go through this chapter. We suspect that for most students it will be very easy; easy or hard, it has to be mastered. Keep a list of the six ideas as they come, and check them off against the review in "Looking Back" after you have finished.

This chapter will give us a series of concepts and techniques that we shall use in thinking clearly about economics. Some of them seem very simple but are more subtle than they appear at first. Others look demanding at first, even though they are actually very simple. There are six of these intellectual tools. Try to master them, for we will be using them continuously from now on.

1. CETERIS PARIBUS

The first concept is the need to eliminate outside influences that might invalidate our efforts to make scientific statements about economic behavior. If we were physicists trying to arrive at the formula for gravitation, for instance, we would have to make allowances for wind or air resistance in calculating the force that gravity really exerts. So, too, in economics we have to eliminate disturbing influences from our observations. We do so by making the assumption that "other things" remain constant while we focus on the particular relationships we're interested in.

This assumption of holding "other things equal" is called by its Latin name, *ceteris paribus.* It is extremely easy to apply in theory and extremely difficult to apply in practice. In our examination of the demand curve, for example, we assume that the *income* and *tastes* of the person (or of the collection of persons) are unchanged while we examine the influence of price on the quantities of shoes they are willing and able to buy. The reason is obvious. If we allowed their incomes or tastes to change, both their willingness *and* their ability would also change. If prices doubled but a fad for shoes developed, or if prices tripled but income quadrupled, we would not find that demand decreased as prices rose.

Ceteris paribus is applied every time we speak of supply and demand and on many other occasions as well. Since we know that in reality prices, tastes, incomes, population size, technology, moods, and many other elements of society are continually changing, we can see why this is a heroic assumption. It is one

---

STATICS AND DYNAMICS: THE IMPORTANCE OF TIME

Of all the sources of difficulty that creep into economic analysis, none is more vexing than *time.* The reason is that time changes all manner of things and makes it virtually impossible to apply *ceteris paribus.* That is why, for example, we always mean "within a fixed period of time" when we speak of something like diminishing marginal utility. There is no reason for the marginal utility of a meal tomorrow to be less than one today, but good reason to think that a second lunch on top of the first will bring a sharp decline in utilities.

So, too, supply and demand curves presumably describe activities that take place within a short period of time, ideally within an instant. The longer the time period covered, the less is *ceteris* apt to be *paribus.*

This poses many difficult problems for economic analysis, because it means that we must use a "static" (or timeless) set of theoretical ideas to solve "dynamic" (or time-consuming) questions. The method we will use to cope with this problem is called comparative statics. We compare an economic situation at one period with an economic situation at a later period, without investigating in much detail the path we travel from the first situation to the second. To inquire into the path requires calculus and advanced economic analysis. We'll leave that for another course.

that is almost impossible to trace in actual life or to correct for fully by special statistical techniques.

Yet we can also see that unless we apply *ceteris paribus*, at least in our minds, we cannot isolate the particular interactions and causal sequences that we want to investigate. The economic world then becomes a vast Chinese puzzle. Every piece interlocks with every other, and no one can tell what the effect of any one thing is on any other. If economics is to be useful, it must be able to tell us something about the effect of changing *only* price or *only* income or *only* taste or any *one* of a number of other things. We can do so only by assuming that other things are equal and by holding them unchanged in our minds while we perform the intellectual experiment in whose outcome we are interested.

2. FUNCTIONAL RELATIONSHIPS

Economics, it is already very clear, is about relationships—relationships of mankind and nature, and relationships of individuals to one another. The laws of diminishing marginal utility or diminishing returns or supply and demand are all statements of those relationships, which we can use to explain or predict economic matters.

We call relationships that portray the effect of one thing on another *functional relationships*. Functional relationships may relate the effect of price on the quantities offered or bought, or the effect of successive inputs of the same factor on outputs of a given product, or the effect of population growth on economic growth, or whatever.

One important point: Functional relationships are not logical relationships of the kind we find in geometry or arithmetic, such as the square of the hypotenuse of a right triangle being equal to the sum of the squares of the other two sides, or the number 6 being the product of 2 times 3 or 3 times 2. Functional relationships cannot be discovered by deductive reasoning. They are descriptions of real events that we can discover only by empirical investigation. We then search for ways of expressing these relationships in graphs or mathematical terms. In economics, the technique used for discovering these relationships is called *econometrics*.

3. IDENTITIES

Before going on, we must clarify an important distinction between functional relationships and another kind of relationship called an *identity*. We need this distinction because both relationships use the word *equals*, although the word has different meanings in the two cases.

A few pages ahead we shall meet the expression

$$Q_d = f(P)$$

which we read "Quantity demanded (Q_d) *equals* or *is* a function of price $(= f(P))$." This refers to the kind of relationship we have been talking about. We shall also find another kind of "equals," typified by the statement $P \equiv S$ or purchases equals sales. $P \equiv S$ is *not* a functional relationship, because purchases do not "depend" on sales. They are *the same thing* as sales, viewed from the vantage point of the buyer instead of the seller. *P* and *S* are identities: *Q* and *P* are not. The identity sign is $\equiv$.

Identities are true by definition. They cannot be "proved" true or false, because there is nothing to be proved. On the other hand, when we say that the quantity purchased will depend on price, there is a great deal to be proved. Empirical investigation may disclose that the suggested relationship is not true. It may show that a relationship exists but that the nature of the relationship is not always the same. Identities are changeless as well as true. They are logical statements that require no investigations of human action. The signs $\equiv$ and $=$ do not mean the same things.

Sometimes identities and behavioral equations are written in the same manner with an equal sign ($=$). Technically, identities should be written with an identity sign ($\equiv$). Unfortunately, the sign also reads "equals." Since it is important to know the difference between definitions, which do not need proof, and hypotheses, which *always* need demonstration or proof, we shall carefully differentiate between the equal sign ($=$) and the identity sign ($\equiv$). Whenever you see an equal sign, you will know that a behavioral relationship is being hypothesized. When you see the identity sign, you will know that a definition is being offered, not a statement about behavior.

Identities, being definitions, deserve our attention because they are the way we establish a precise working language. Learning this language, with its special vocabulary, is essential to being able to speak economics accurately.

4. SCHEDULES

We are familiar with the next item in our kit of intellectual tools. It is one of the techniques used to establish functional relationships: the technique of drawing up *schedules* or lists of the different values of elements.

We met such schedules in Chapter 5, in our lists of the quantities of shoes supplied or demanded at various prices. **Schedules are thus the empirical or hypothetical data whose functional interconnection we wish to investigate.** As working economists we would experience many problems in drawing up such schedules in real life. We often use them, however, in economic analysis, as examples of typical economic behaviour.

5. GRAPHS

The depiction of functional relationships through schedules is simple enough, but economists usually prefer to represent these relationships by graphs or equations. This is so because schedules show the relationship only between *specific* quantities and prices or specific data of any kind. **Graphs and equations show** *generalized* **relationships, relationships that cover all quantities and prices or all values of any two things we are interested in.**

The simplest and most intuitively obvious method of showing a functional relationship in its general form is through a graph. Everyone is familiar with graphs of one kind or another, but not all graphs show functional relationships. A graph of stock prices over time, as in Figure 6.1, shows us the level of prices in different periods. It does not show a behavioral connection between a date and

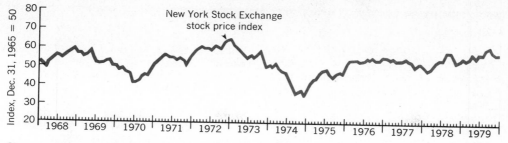

FIGURE 6.1
STOCK
MARKET
PRICES

Some graphs, like this one, just show how a given variable behaves over time.

a price. Such a graph merely describes and summarizes history. No one would maintain that such and such a date *caused* stock market prices to take such and such a level.

On the other hand, a graph that related the price of a stock and the quantities that we are willing and able to buy *at that price, ceteris paribus,* is indeed a graphic depiction of a functional relation. If we look at the hypothetical graph below, we can note the dots that show us the particular price/quantity relationships. Now we can tell the quantity that would be demanded at any price, simply by going up the price axis, over to the demand curve, and down to the quantity axis. In Figure 6.2, for example, at a price of $50 the quantity demanded is 5,000 shares per day. *

Other graphs, like this one, depict relationships. There is more about this in the extra word following this chapter.

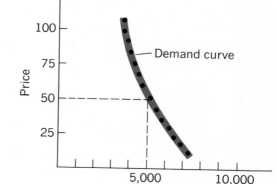

FIGURE 6.2
PRICE/
QUANTITY
RELATION-
SHIP OF A
GIVEN SHARE

*Technically we would need a schedule of survey results showing the quantities demanded for every conceivable price in order to draw a graph. In fact, we obtain results for a variety of prices and assume that the relationship between the unmeasured points is like that of the measured points. The process of sketching in unmeasured points is called *interpolation.*

UPWARD SLOPING DEMAND CURVES

Although most demand curves slope downward, in three interesting cases they don't. The first concerns certain *luxury goods* in which the price itself becomes part of the "utility" of the good. The perfume Joy is extensively advertised as "the world's most expensive perfume." Do you think its sales would increase if the price were lowered and the advertisement changed to read "the world's second-most expensive perfume"?

The other case affects just the opposite kind of good: certain basic staples. Here the classic case is potatoes. In nineteenth-century Ireland, potatoes formed the main diet for very poor farmers. As potato prices rose, Irish peasants were forced to cut back on their purchases of other foods, to devote more of their incomes to buying this necessity of life. More potatoes were purchased, even though their prices were rising, because potatoes were the cheapest thing to eat.

Such goods have upward sloping demand curves. The higher the price, the more you (are forced to) buy. Of course, when potatoes reach price levels that compete with, say wheat, any further price rises will result in a fall in the quantity demanded, since buyers will shift to wheat.

Finally, there is a very important upward sloping curve that relates quantities demanded and *incomes:* the higher our incomes, the more we buy. We will use this special demand relationship a great deal in macroeconomics. However, in microeconomics, the functional relation is mainly between *price* and quantities demanded, not income and quantities demanded. Still, it is useful to remember that the functional relationships involving demand do not all slope in the same direction.

6. EQUATIONS

A third way of representing functional relationships is often used for its simplicity and brevity. **Equations are very convenient means of expressing functional relationships, since they allow us to consider the impact of more than one factor at a time.** A typical equation for demand might look like this:

$$Q_d = f(P)$$

Most of us are familiar with equations but may have forgotten their vocabulary. There are three terms in the equation above: Q_d, f, and P. Each has a name. We are interested in seeing how our quantity demanded (Q_d) is affected by changes in prices (P). In other words, our "demand" is dependent on changes in price. Therefore the term Q_d is called the **dependent variable:** "variable" because it changes; "dependent" because it is the result of changes in P. As we would imagine, the name for P is the **independent variable.**

Now for the term f. The definition of f is simply **"function"** or "function of," so that we read $Q_d = f(P)$ as "quantity demanded is a function of price." If we knew that the quantity demanded was a function of both price *and* income (Y) we would write $Q_d = f(P, Y)$. Such equations tell us what independent variables affect what dependent variables, but they do not tell us *how* Q_d changes with changes in P or Y.

The "how" depends on our actual analysis of actual market behavior. Let us take a very simple case for illustrative purposes. Suppose that a survey of consumer purchasing intentions tells us that consumers would take 100 units of a product if its price were zero—that is, if it were given away free—and that they would buy one-half unit less each time the price went up by $1. The demand equation would then be:

$$Q_d = 100 - .5(P)$$

Thus, if price were $10, buyers would take $100 - .5 \times 10$, or 95 units.*

We should stop to note one important property of ordinary price/quantity demand or supply functions. It is that they have opposite "signs." A normal demand function is negative, showing that quantities demanded *fall* as prices rise. A supply function is usually positive, showing that quantities supplied *rise* as prices rise. A survey of producers might tell us that the quantity supplied would go up by 2 units for every $1 increase in price, or

$$Q_s = 2(P)$$

Note that the sign of the function 2 is positive, whereas the sign of the demand function was negative, $-.5$.

ECONOMIC TECHNIQUES REVIEWED

The basic assumptions that economics makes regarding economic society can be summed up in two sets of general propositions or laws—laws about be-

---

EQUILIBRIUM IN EQUATIONS

It is very easy to see the equilibrium point when we have a supply curve and a demand curve that cross. But since equations are only another way of representing the information that curves show, we must be able to demonstrate equilibrium in equations. Here is a simple example:

Suppose the demand function, as before, is:
$$Q_d = 100 - .5 (P),$$ and that the supply function is:
$$Q_s = 2(P)$$

The question is, then, what value for P will make Q_d equal to Q_s? The answer follows:

If $Q_d = Q_s$, then
$100 - .5(P) = 2(P)$.
Putting all the P's on one side
$2(P) + .5 (P) = 100$, or $2.5p = 100$. Solving, $P = 40$.

Substituting a price of 40 into the demand equation we get a quantity of 80. In the supply equation we also get 80. Thus 40 must be the equilibrium price.

---

*Suppose we wanted an equation that would measure the effect on quantity demanded of both price and income (see box). Such an equation might be:

$$Q_d = 100 - .5(P) + .1(Y)$$

where Y = income

In this equation the quantity demanded goes *up* by 100 units whenever incomes rise by $1,000. As before, it goes *down* by ½ unit as prices rise by $1. If incomes were $2,000 and P were $10, the quantity demanded would be $(100 - .5 \times 10 + .1 \times 2,000) = 295$ units.

havior and laws about production. What we have been learning in this chapter are the *techniques* of economic analysis—the ways in which economics uses its basic premises.

These techniques, as we have seen, revolve around the central idea of functional relationships. Because behavior or production is sufficiently regular, functions enable us to explain or predict economic activity. Their relationships are presented in the form of graphs or equations derived from the underlying schedules of data.

As we have seen, the ability to establish functional relationships depends critically on the *ceteris paribus* assumption. Unless we hold other things equal, either by econometric means or simply in our heads, we cannot isolate the effect of one variable on another.

ECONOMIC FALLACIES

No chapter on the mode of economic thought would be complete without reference to *economic fallacies*. **Actually there is no special class of fallacies that is called economic. The mistakes we find in economic thought are only examples of a larger class of mistaken ways of thinking that we call fallacies.** But they are serious enough to justify a warning in general and some attention to one fallacy in particular.

The general warning can do no more than ask us to be on guard against the sloppy thinking that can make fools of us in any area. It is easy to fall into errors of false syllogisms,° of trying to prove an argument *post hoc, ergo propter hoc* ("after the fact, therefore the cause of the fact"). An example would be "proving" that government spending must be inflationary by pointing out that the government spent large sums during periods when inflation was present, ignoring other factors that may have been at work.

The gallery of such mistaken conclusions is all too large in all fields. One fallacy that has a special relevance to economics is called the **fallacy of composition.** Suppose we had an island community in which all farmers sold their produce to one another. Suppose further that one farmer was able to get rich by cheating: selling his produce at the same price as everyone else, but putting fewer vegetables into his bushel baskets. Does it not follow that all farmers could get rich if all cheated?

We can see that there is a fallacy here. Where does it arise? In the first example, when our cheating farmer got rich, we ignored a small side effect of his action. The side effect was that a loss in real income was inflicted on the community. To ignore that side effect was proper so long as our focus of attention was what happened to the one farmer. When we broaden our inquiry to the entire community, the loss of income becomes a consideration. Everyone loses as much by being shortchanged as he gains by shortchanging. The side effects have become central effects. What was true for one turns out not to be true for all. Later on, we will find a very important example of exactly such a fallacy when we encounter what is called the Paradox of Thrift.

---

*See the questions at the end of this chapter.

LOOKING BACK

This is a chapter about the concepts and techniques of economic analysis, not about the basic assumptions underlying economic theory. We should become familiar with a few of these ideas, or tools.

1. *Ceteris paribus* is the assumption that everything other than the two variables whose relationship is being investigated is kept equal. Without *ceteris paribus* we cannot discern functional relationships.

2. Functional relationships showing that *X* depends on *Y* lie at the very center of economic analysis. They are not logical or deductive relationships but relationships that we discover by *empirical investigation*.

3. Identities are purely definitional, therefore not subject to proof or to empirical investigation. Such definitions can, however, be very important.

4. The three techniques used to represent functional relationships are:
   a. schedules, or lists of data;
   b. graphs, or visual representations;
   c. equations.

5. You should know the meaning of three equational terms: the *independent variable,* the causative element that interests us; the *dependent variable,* the element whose behavior is affected by the independent variable; and the *function,* a mathematical statement of the relation between the two. Read the sentence $x = f(y)$ as "*x* is a function of *y*." Here, *x* is the dependent variable; *y* is the independent variable.

6. Finally, learn to be on guard against economic fallacies, especially against the fallacy of composition.

ECONOMIC VOCABULARY

QUESTIONS

1. Suppose you would acquire 52 books a year if books were free, but that your acquisitions would drop by 5 books for every dollar that you had to pay. Can you write a demand function for books?

2. Can you write a hypothetical function that might relate your demand for food and the price of food, assuming *ceteris paribus?*

3. "The quantity of food bought equals the quantity sold." Is this statement a functional relationship? If not, why not? Is it an identity?

4. Here is a schedule of supply and demand:

Price	Units supplied	Units demanded
$1	0	50
2	5	40
3	10	30
4	20	25
5	30	20
6	50	10

Does the schedule show an equilibrium price? Can you draw a graph and approximate the equilibrium price? What is it?

5. How do we read aloud the following? $C = f(Y)$ where C = consumption and Y = income. Which is the independent variable? The dependent?

6. Which of the following statements is a fallacy?

> All X is Y
> Z is Y
> Therefore Z is X

> All X is Y
> Z is X
> Therefore Z is Y

Try substituting classes of objects for the X's and Y, and individual objects for the Z's. Example: All planets (X's) are heavenly bodies (Y). The sun (Z) is a heavenly body (Y). Therefore the sun (Z) is a planet (X). Clearly, a false syllogism. Since Z is Y, however, the sun is a heavenly body.
Other fallacies:
If I can move to the head of the line, all individuals can move to the head of the line.
If I can save more by spending less, all individuals should be able to save more by spending less. Hint: If all spend less, what will happen to our incomes?
The fact that Lenin called inflation a major weapon that could destroy the bourgeoisie indicates that inflations are part of the communist strategy for the overthrow of capitalism.

AN EXTRA WORD ABOUT
GRAPHS AND ECONOMIC CAUSATION

Many students worry a great deal about drawing graphs and worry very little about what graphs show. They are wrong on both counts. The technique of graphing is essentially simple. What graphs show is not.

USES OF GRAPHS

As we have seen on p. 113 some graphs show the movement of a variable over time—for example, stock market prices. No one is perplexed by graphs of this kind. But other graphs show relationships. These are the graphs that worry students. Here are some hints to help you to draw these kinds of graphs.

1. *Always begin by labeling the axes of a graph.* Even the most common supply and demand type of graph should have one label identified as Price (or *P*) and another as Quantity (or *Q*). No mistake is as frequent as omitting *P*'s and

Q's or whatever identifying symbols are called for on a graph.

2. *Each point on a graph represents* two *variables.* Each point shows what value of *X* is related to a given value of *Y*—e.g., what quantity is offered (or bought) at a given price. Therefore every point must always be referred to *both* axes. In the figure below for example, point *H* shows *five* units of quantity offered at a price of *six* dollars. Five units and six dollars are called the *coordinates* of point *H*.

3. *Curves show how relationships vary.* A given dot shows the relation of only one pair of coordinates, such as five units and six dollars. A curve shows the relationship of many pairs of coordinates for the function we are interested in. The upward curve *FGH* shows how *P* and *Q* vary for sellers, for instance. An-

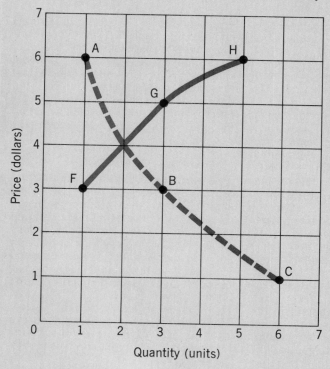

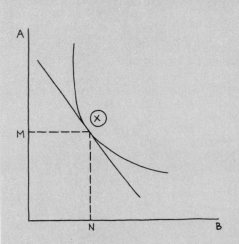

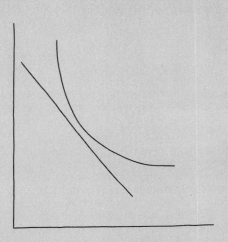

Note that axes are labeled. This graph shows that there is one point (*X*), where there is a common pair of co-ordinates, *M* and *N,* for two functions or curves.

Note axes are not labeled. The graph shows that there is no point where one pair of coordinates relates to both curves. Is that what you want to show?

other curve, *ABC*, shows a relationship with a downward slope, perhaps for buyers. What are the actual values of *P* and *Q* at points *A*, *B*, and *C*? What, if any, coordinates are shared by both curves?

4. *Graphs should be carefully drawn.* Very often a graph represents visually an important idea. It may show that a pair of coordinates lies on *two* curves, as does the equilibrium point in the standard supply/demand graph. Or it may show that one curve touches another at just one point, which also means that the two curves have one pair of coordinates in common. When you draw a curve, you are *describing* a relationship: Be sure you describe it right. Above are two freehand examples for you to study.

5. In his excellent text *Basic Economics,* Professor Edwin Dolan writes: "When you come to a chapter in this book that is full of graphs, how should you study it? The first and most important rule is do *not ever memorize graphs.*"

Professor Dolan is so right! Graphs come last, to capsulize what you know. They never come first, to tell you what you *should* know. Graphs are a pictorial shorthand for ideas, usually ideas about functional relationships (curves) and their interconnections. Learn the economics and the graphs will follow. Learn the graphs—and you will know only geometry.

CORRELATION

That was the easy part of understanding graphs. Now for the hard part. Most students think that graphs "explain" things. They look at a graph of a demand curve and say "The lower price *causes* us to buy more." They look at a graph showing a nice regular pattern between variable *A* and variable *B,* and they assume that this pattern of "correlation" implies an explanation.

Here's an example. On the left, next page, we have plotted the shoe size and the IQs of a group of seniors. No pattern—no "correlation"—is visible.

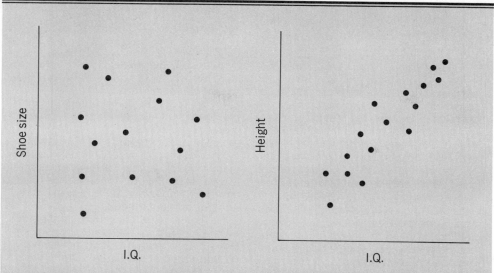

No pattern or correlation exists here.

A clear pattern or correlation is visible.

Hence no one assumes that large shoe sizes cause high IQs. In the graph on the right, we correlate a sample of the heights and the IQs of a number of individuals. There is a clearly visible pattern or correlation.

Does this mean that height causes IQ to increase? Certainly not. Height is associated with age. Our graph happens to cover a population that includes both infants and adults, and so of course there is a correlation, but it is not a causal one. Height does not *cause* IQ. It is associated with IQ through the mediating factor of age and maturity. Lesson: Be very, very careful of jumping to conclusions about causes just from the evidence of associations, or correlations.

Here are a few examples for you to think about.

1. *Wrong-way causation.* It is a statistical fact that there is a positive correlation between the number of babies born in various cities of northwestern Europe and the number of storks'

nests in those cities. Is this evidence that storks really do bring babies? The answer is that we are using a correlation to establish a causal connection the wrong way. The true line of causation lies in the opposite direction. Cities that have more children tend to have more houses, which offer storks more chimneys to build their nests in!

2. *Spurious causation.* Suppose there was a positive correlation all during the 1970s between the cost of living in Paris and the numbers of Americans visiting there. Does that imply that American visitors are the cause of price increases in that city?

Here at least there is little danger of getting the causal links back to front. Few people would argue that more Americans visit Paris *because* its prices are going up. It would be equally difficult to argue that American tourists are the cause of rising Parisian prices, simply because the total amount of American spending is small in relation to the total amount of expenditure in Paris.

The answer, then, is that the correlation is spurious in terms of causality, although it is real in terms of sheer statistics. The true explanation for the correlation is that the rising numbers of American visitors and the rising costs of living in Paris are both aspects of a worldwide expansion in incomes and prices. Neither is the "cause" of the other. Both are the results of more fundamental, broader-ranging phenomena.

3. *The problem of* ceteris paribus. Finally, we must consider again the now familiar problem of *ceteris paribus,* the necessity of other things being equal. Suppose we correlate prices and sales, in order to test the hypothesis that lower prices "cause" us to increase the quantities we buy. Now suppose that the correlation turns out to be very poor. Does that disprove the hypothesis? Not necessarily. First we have to find out what happened to income during this period. We also have to find out what, if anything, happened to our tastes. We might also have to consider changes in the prices of other, competitive goods.

As we know, this problem affects all scientific tests, not just those of economics. Scientists cannot test the law of gravitation unless "other things" are equal, such as an absence of air that would cause a feather to fall much more slowly than Galileo predicted. The trouble with the social sciences is that the "other things" are often more difficult to spot—or just to think of—than they are in the laboratory.

WHAT CAN CORRELATION TELL US?
These (and still other) pitfalls make economists extremely cautious about using correlations to "prove" causal hypotheses. *Even the closest correlation may not show in which direction the causal influences are working.*

So, too, *the interconnectedness of the economic process often causes many series of data to move together.* In inflationary periods, for example, most prices tend to rise, or in depression many indexes tend to fall, without establishing that any of these series was directly responsible for a movement in another particular series.

Finally, economists are constantly on the lookout for factors that have not been held constant during correlation, so that *ceteris paribus conditions were not in fact maintained.*

Is there an answer to such puzzling problems of correlation and causation? There is a partial answer. We cannot claim that a correlation is proof that a causal relationship exists. But every valid hypothesis—economic or other—*must* show a high and "significant" correlation coefficient between "cause" and "effect," provided that we are reasonably certain that our statistical test has rigorously excluded spurious correlations and unsuspected "other things."

This exclusion is often very difficult, sometimes impossible to achieve with real data. A physicist can hold "other things equal" in his laboratory, but the world will not stand still just so an economist can test his theories. *The net result is that correlations are a more powerful device for* disproving *hypotheses than for proving them.* All we can say on the positive side is that a causal relationship is likely to exist (or at least has not been shown *not* to exist) when we can demonstrate a strong correlation backed by solid reasoning.

Part

3 Macroeconomics:

The Analysis of
Prosperity and Recession

SECTION 1: The Basic Elements of Growth

Chapter 7
GNP— THE NATION'S OUTPUT

A LOOK AHEAD

This chapter introduces us to the subject of gross national product, or GNP—the value of the annual final output of the economic system. Much of macroeconomics focuses on this strategic figure in an effort to discover

(1) how it is determined,

(2) what makes it change, and

(3) how we can help its growth.

Two main ideas run through the pages ahead. First, we learn the very important vocabulary by which we identify the components of GNP. Be sure you grasp the difference between final and intermediate goods, and between consumption and investment goods. Second, we learn the difficulties associated with GNP as a measure of output. GNP is the single most important device for counting overall activity that economics has, but as we will see, it is far from a reliable measure of welfare.

What is "macroeconomics"? The word derives from the Greek *macro* meaning "big," and the implication is therefore that it is concerned with bigger problems than is microeconomics (*micro* = small). Yet microeconomics wrestles with problems that are quite as large as those of macroeconomics. The difference is really not one of scale. It is one of approach, of original angle of incidence. **Macroeconomics begins from a viewpoint that initially draws our attention to aggregate economic phenomena and processes, such as the growth of total output.** Microeconomics begins from a vantage point that first directs our analysis to the workings of the marketplace. Both views are needed to comprehend the economy as a whole, just as it takes two different lenses to make a stereophoto jump into the round. Since we can learn only one view at a time, we now turn to the spectacle of the entire national economy as it unfolds to the macroscopic gaze.

THE MACRO PERSPECTIVE

What does the economy look like from the macro perspective? The view is not unlike that from a plane. What we see first is the fundamental tableau of nature—fields and forests, lakes and seas, with their inherent riches; then the diverse artifacts of humankind—cities and towns, road and rail networks, factories and machines, stocks of half-completed or unsold goods; finally the human actors themselves with all their skills and talents, their energies, their social organization.

Thus our perspective shows us a vast panorama from which we single out for special attention one process that we can see taking place in every corner of the economy. **This process is a vast river of output, a ceaseless flow of production that emerges from the nation's economic activity.**

OUTPUT

How does this flow of production arise? In microeconomics, we investigate motives that lead factors of production to offer their services to business firms, and motives that lead entrepreneurs to hire factors. A macro perspective, however, studies the market process from a somewhat different standpoint, one that focuses on the stream of output as a whole, rather than tracing it back to its individual springs and rivulets.

It may help us picture the flow as a whole if we imagine that each and every good and service that is produced—each loaf of bread, each nut and bolt, each doctor's service, each theatrical performance, each car, ship, lathe, or bolt of cloth—can be identified and followed as a radioactive isotope allows us to follow the circulation of certain kinds of cells through the body. Then if we look down on the economic panorama, we can see the continuous combination of land, labor, and capital giving off a continuous flow of "lights" as goods and services emerge in their saleable form.

INTERMEDIATE GOODS

Where do these lights go? Many are soon extinguished. **The goods or services they represent are *intermediate goods* that are incorporated into other products to form more fully finished items of output.** Thus, from our aerial perspective we can follow a product such as cotton from the fields to the spinning mill, where its light is extinguished, for there the cotton disappears into a new product: yarn. In turn, the light of the yarn traces a path as it leaves the spinning mill by way of sale to the textile mill, there to be doused as the yarn disappears into a new good: cloth. Again, cloth leaving the textile mill lights a way to the factory where it will become part of an article of clothing.

FINAL GOODS: CONSUMPTION

And what of the clothing? Here at last we have what the economist calls a *final* good. Why "final"? Because once in the possession of its ultimate owner, the clothing passes out of the active economic flow. As a good in the hands of a consumer, it is no longer an object on the marketplace. Its light is now extinguished permanently; or if we wish to complete our image, we can imagine it fading gradually as the clothing disappears into the utility of the consumer. In the case of consumer goods like food or of consumer services like recreation, the light goes out faster, for these items are "consumed" as soon as they reach their final destination.*

We shall have a good deal to learn in later chapters about the macroeconomic behavior of consumers. What we should notice in this first view is the supreme importance of this flow of production into consumers' hands. By this vital process, the population replenishes or increases its energies and ministers to its wants and needs. If the process were halted very long, society would perish. That is why we speak of *consumption* as the ultimate end and aim of all economic activity.

A SECOND FINAL GOOD: INVESTMENT

Nevertheless, for all the importance of consumption, if we look down on the illuminated flow of output we see a surprising thing. Whereas the greater portion of the final goods and services of the economy is bought by the human agents of production for their consumption, we also find that a lesser but still considerable flow of final products is not. What happens to it?

If we follow an appropriate good, we may find out. Watch the destination of steel leaving a Pittsburgh mill. Some of it, like our cotton cloth, will become incorporated into consumers' goods, ending up as cans, automobiles, or household articles. But some will not find its way to a consumer at all. Instead, it will end up as part of a machine or an office building or a railroad track.

Now in a way, these goods are not "final," for they are used to produce still further goods or services. The machine produces output of some kind; the building produces office space, the rail track produces transportation. Yet there is a difference between such goods, used for production, and consumer goods, like clothing. The difference is that the machine, the office building, and the track are goods that are used by business enterprises as part of their permanent productive equipment. In terms of our image, these goods slowly lose their light-giving powers as their services pass into flows of production, but usually they are replaced with new goods before their light is totally extinguished.

That is why we call them *capital goods* or *investment goods*, as distinguished from consumers' goods. As part of our capital, they will be preserved, maintained,

---

*In fact, of course, they are not *really* consumed but remain behind as garbage, junk, wastes, and so on. Economics used to ignore these residuals, but it does so no longer.

and renewed, perhaps indefinitely. Hence the stock of capital, like consumers, constitutes a final destination for output.

GROSS AND NET INVESTMENT

We call the great stream of output that goes to capital **gross investment.** The very word *gross* suggests that it conceals a finer breakdown; and looking more closely, we can see that the flow of output going to capital does indeed serve two distinct purposes. Part of it is used to replace the capital—machines, buildings, track, or whatever—that has been used up in the process of production. Just as the human agents of production have to be replenished by a flow of consumption goods, so the material agents of production need to be maintained and renewed if their contribution to output is to remain undiminished. **We call the part of gross investment whose purpose is to keep society's stock of capital intact, replacement investment, or simply replacement.**

Sometimes the total flow of output going to capital is not large enough to maintain the existing stock, as for example when we allow inventories (a form of capital) to become depleted, or when we simply fail to replace wornout equipment or plant. This running-down of capital we call **disinvestment,** meaning the very opposite of investment. Instead of maintaining or building up capital, we are literally consuming it.

Not all gross investment is used for replacement purposes, however. Some of the flow may *increase* the stock of capital by adding buildings, machines, track, inventory, and so on.° If the total output consigned to capital is sufficiently great not only to make up for wear and tear but to increase the capital stock, we say there has been new or net investment, or net capital formation.

CONSUMPTION AND INVESTMENT

A simple diagram may help us picture the flow of final output that we have been discussing. Figure 7.1 calls our attention to these paramount attributes of the output process:

1. **The flow of output is circular, self-renewing, self-feeding.** This circularity is one of the dominant elements in the macroeconomic processes we will study. Consumption output returns to restore or increase our human capital—our ability to work. Investment output restores or increases our material capital.

2. **Societies must make a choice between consumption and investment.** At any given level of output, consumption and investment uses are rivals for the current output of society. Furthermore, we can see that society can add to its capital only the output that it refrains from consuming. Even if it increases its output, it cannot invest the increase except by not consuming it.

3. **Both consumption and investment flows are split between public and private use.** Like consumption and investment, these are also rival uses for output. A society can devote whatever portion of output it pleases to public consumption or public investment, but only by refraining from using that portion for private consumption or investment.

4. **Output is the nation's budget constraint.** Our output is the total quantity of goods and services available for all public and private uses (unless we want to

*Note carefully that increased inventory is a form of investment. Later this will receive special attention.

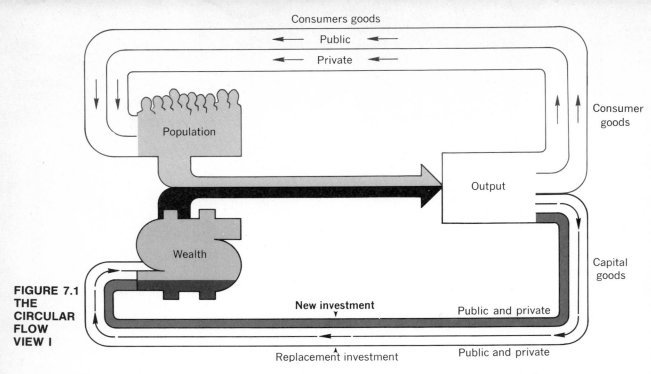

Consumers goods

Public

Private

Population

Output

Consumer goods

Wealth

FIGURE 7.1 THE CIRCULAR FLOW VIEW I

New investment

Public and private

Capital goods

Replacement investment

Public and private

The first view of the circular flow shows that output divides into two main streams, consumption and investment—consumption replenishing our human capital, investment replenishing our material capital. Note that there are public and private flows in both consumption and investment output.

use up our past wealth). More goods and services may be desired, but if output is not large enough, they cannot be had.

GROSS NATIONAL PRODUCT

We have had a first view of the overall flow of national output that will play so large a role in our macroeconomic studies. Now we want to look into the flow more closely. Here we can begin by defining gross national product, a term that is already familiar to us from Chapter 3. **We call the dollar value of the total annual output of final goods and services in the nation its gross national product.** The gross national product (or GNP as it is usually abbreviated) is thus nothing but the dollar value of the total output of all consumption goods and of all investment goods produced in a year. We are already familiar with this general meaning, and now we must move on to a more precise definition.

GNP MEASURES FINAL GOODS

We are interested, through the concept of GNP, in measuring the value of the *ultimate* production of the economic system; that is, the total value of all goods and services enjoyed by its consumers or accumulated as new or replacement captial.

Hence we do not count the intermediate goods we have already noted in our economic panorama. We do not add up the value of the cotton *and* the yarn *and* the cloth *and* the final clothing when we compute the value of GNP. That kind of multiple counting might be very useful if we wanted certain information about our total economic activity, but it would not tell us accurately about the final value of output. When we buy a shirt, the price we pay includes the cost of the cloth to the shirtmaker. In turn, the amount the shirtmaker paid for his cloth included the cost of the yarn. In turn, again, the seller of yarn included in his price the amount he paid for raw cotton. Embodied in the price of the shirt, therefore, is the value of all the intermediate products that went into it.

Thus in figuring the value for GNP, we add only the values of all final goods, both for consumption and for investment purposes. Note as well that GNP includes only a given year's production of goods and services. Therefore sales of used car dealers, antique dealers, etc., are not included, because the value of these goods was picked up in GNP the year they were produced.

FURTHER KINDS OF OUTPUT

In our first view of macroeconomic activity we divided the flow of output into two great streams: consumption and gross investment. Now, for purposes of a closer analysis, we must impose a few refinements on this basic scheme.

First we must pay heed to a small flow of production that has previously escaped our notice. That is the net flow of goods or services that leaves this country; that is, the total flow going abroad minus the flow that enters. This international branch of our economy will play a relatively minor role in our analysis for quite a while. We will largely ignore it until Chapters 12 and 21, but we must give it its proper name *net exports*. Because these net exports are a kind of investment (they are goods we produce but do not consume), we must now rename the great bulk of investment that remains in this country. We will henceforth call it **gross private domestic investment.**

By convention, gross private domestic investment refers only to investments in physical assets such as factories, inventories, homes. Personal expenditures on acquiring human skills, as well as expenditures for regular use, are considered **personal consumption expenditures**—the technical accounting term for *consumption*. As these accounting terms indicate, *public* consumption and investment are included in neither personal consumption expenditures nor gross private domestic investment. Here is our last flow of final output: All public buying of final goods and services is kept in a separate category called **government purchases of goods and services.**

FOUR STREAMS OF FINAL OUTPUT

We now have four streams of final output, each going to a final purchaser of economic output. **Therefore we can speak of gross national product as being the sum of personal consumption expenditure (C), gross private domestic investment (I), government purchases (G), and net exports (X), or (to abbreviate a long sentence) we can write that**

$$GNP \equiv C + I + G + X$$

This is a descriptive identity that should be remembered.

It helps, at this juncture, to look at GNP over the past decades. In Figure 7.2 we show the long irregular upward flow of GNP from 1929 to the present,

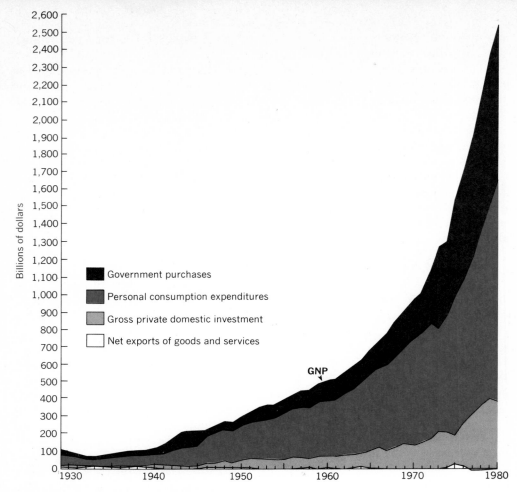

FIGURE 7.2 GNP AND COMPONENTS, 1929—1980
Here we see the historical record of GNP (a graph we have already met) this time with its component parts added.

with the four component streams of expenditure visible. Later we will be talking at length about the behavior of each stream, but first we need to be introduced to the overall flow itself.

GNP AS A MEASURE

GNP is an indispensable concept in dealing with the performance of our economy, but it is well to understand the weaknesses as well as the strengths of this most important single economic indicator.

1.   GNP deals in dollar values, not in physical units; we have to correct it for inflation

Trouble arises when we compare the GNP of one year with that of another to determine whether or not the nation is better off. If prices in the second year are higher, GNP will appear higher, even though the actual volume of output is unchanged or even lower!

We could correct for this price change easily if all prices moved in the same direction or proportion. We would then choose any year as a "base year," and we could easily establish an index to show whether GNP in another year was really higher or lower than in the base year, and by how much.

Problems arise, however, when there are changes in relative prices, with some prices rising more rapidly than others. Then the choice of a base year will affect our calculations. There is no correct way of choosing a base year. We just have to be aware that our choice affects our results. In Figure 7.3 we have used 1972 as our base.

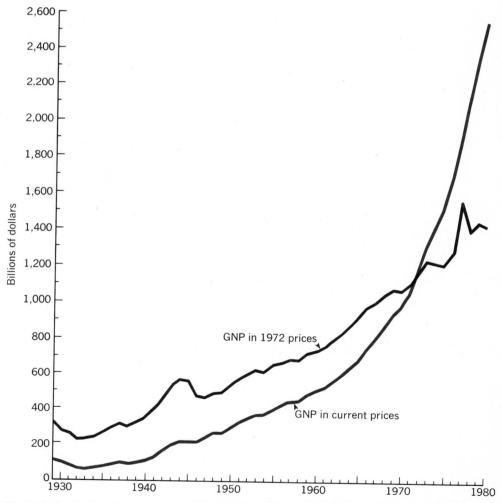

**FIGURE 7.3
GNP IN
CONSTANT
AND
CURRENT
PRICES
1929–1980**

We reduce nominal or current GNP—output measured at existing prices—to real GNP by using a price index. Because relative prices change, it matters which year we use as our base. There is no correct year, but our choice affects our results. Here we use 1972 as our base.

REAL AND CURRENT GNP

It's worth a moment to review the ideas on p. 97.

How do we arrive at a figure for "real" GNP? *The answer is that we "correct" the value of GNP (or any other magnitude measured in dollars) for the price changes that affect the value of our dollars but not the real quantities of goods and services our dollars buy.*

We make this correction by applying a *price index.* Such an index is a series of numbers showing the variation in prices, year to year, from a starting or *base year* for which the price level is set at 100. Thus if prices go up 5 percent a year, a price index starting in year one will read 105 for year two, 110.25+ for year three (105 × 1.05), 115.8 for year four, and so on.

In correcting GNP we use a very complex price index called a GNP *price deflator.* This index, constructed by the Department of Commerce, allows for the fact that different parts of GNP, such as consumer goods and investment goods may change in price at different rates. The present price deflator uses GNP price levels in 1972 as a base. In 1975, the value of the deflator was 126.37. That is, the price index was up 26.37% from 1972.

Now let us work out an actual example. *To arrive at a corrected GNP, we divide the current GNP by the deflator and then multiply by 100.* For example, GNP in current figures was $1,702 billion for 1976; $1,900 billion for 1977; and $2,128 billion for 1978. The deflators for those years were 134, 142, and 152. Here are the results:

$$\frac{\$1702}{134} = 12.70 \times 100 = 1270 \text{ billion}$$

$$\frac{\$1900}{142} = 13.38 \times 100 = 1338 \text{ billion}$$

$$\frac{\$2128}{152} = 14.00 \times 100 = 1400 \text{ billion}$$

Thus the "real value" of GNP in 1978 was $1400 billion, *in terms of 1972 prices,* rather than the $2128 billion of its current value. Two things should be noted in this process of correction. First, the real value of any series will differ, depending on the base year that is chosen. For instance, if we started a series in 1976, the real value of GNP for that year would be $1702, the same as its money value.

Second, the process of constructing a GNP deflator is enormously difficult. In fact there is no single, accurate way of constructing an index that will reflect all the variations of prices of the goods within GNP. To put it differently, we can construct different kinds of indexes, with different weights for different sectors, and these will give us differing results. The point then is to be cautious in using corrected figures. Be sure you know what the base year is. And remember that complex indexes, such as the GNP deflator, are only approximations of a change that defies wholly accurate measurement.

2.   Changes in quality of output will not show in GNP

The second weakness of GNP also involves its inaccuracy as an indicator of "real" trends over time. The difficulty revolves around changes in the utility of goods and services. In a technologically advancing society, goods are usually improved from one decade to the next or even more rapidly, and new goods are constantly being introduced. In an urbanizing, increasingly high-density society, the utility of other goods may be lessened over time. An airplane trip today, for example, is certainly preferable to one 30 years ago; a subway ride is not. This year's car costs more than last year's car, but it also gets better gas mileage. How much of the increase in price reflects that improvement in quality and how much of the increase is simply an increase in price? It is difficult for anyone to know, but government statisticians try to adjust GNP statistics for just such changes in quality. Generally speaking, the longer the time period over which comparisons of real GNP are being made, the larger is the quality factor, and therefore the more tentative the results become.

3.   GNP does not reflect the purpose of production

A third difficulty with GNP lies in its blindness to the ultimate use of production. If in one year GNP rises by a billion dollars, owing to an increase in expenditure on education, and in another year it rises by the same amount because of a rise in cigarette production, the figures in each case show the same amount of growth of GNP. Even output that turns out to be wide of the mark or totally wasteful—such as the famous Edsel car that no one wanted or military weapons that are obsolete from the moment they appear—all are counted as part of GNP.

The problem of environmental deterioration adds another difficulty. Some types of GNP growth directly contribute to pollution—cars, paper or steel production, for example. Other types of GNP growth are necessary to stop pollution—sewage disposal plants or the production of a clean internal combustion engine. Still other types of GNP have little direct impact on the environment. Most personal services fall into this category.

Our conventional measure of GNP makes no distinction among such outputs. For instance, the cleaning bills we pay to undo damage caused by smoke from the neighborhood factory become part of GNP, although cleaning our clothes does not increase our well-being. It only brings it back to what it was in the first place.

4.   GNP does not include most goods and services that are not for sale

Presumably GNP tells us how large our final output is. Yet it does not include one of the most useful kinds of work and chief sources of consumer pleasure—the labor of women in maintaining their households. Yet, curiously, if this labor were paid for—that is, if we engaged cooks and maids and babysitters instead of depending on wives for these services, GNP *would* include their services as final output, since they would be purchased on the market. The labor of wives being unpaid, it is excluded from GNP.*

A related problem is that some parts of GNP are paid for by some members of the population and not by others. Rent, for example, measures the services of landlords for homeowners and is therefore included in GNP, but what of the homeowner who pays no rent? Similarly, what of the family that grows part of its food at home and therefore does not pay for it?

There is no entirely satisfactory solution to such problems. Because no one has devised a way of valuing housewives' services in a manner that appears fair and objective, we just leave the value of these services out of GNP. On the other hand, when it is possible to impute a value to unpaid services, statisticians at the

---

*An added difficulty here is that we are constantly moving toward purchasing "outside" services in place of home services. Laundries, bakeries, restaurants, etc., all perform work that used to be performed at home. Thus the process of *monetizing* activity gives an upward trend to GNP statistics that is not fully mirrored in actual output.

Department of Commerce do so. For instance, they include in GNP an estimate of the value of the rentals of owner-occupied homes and of food grown at home.

5. GNP does not indicate anything about the distribution of goods and services among the population

Societies differ widely in how they allocate their production of purchasable goods and services among their populations. A pure egalitarian society might allocate everyone the same quantity of goods and services. Many societies establish minimum consumption standards for individuals and families. Few deliberately decide to let someone starve if they have the economic resources to prevent such a possibility. *Yet to know a nation's GNP, or even to know its average (per capita) GNP, is to know nothing about how broadly or how narrowly this output is shared. A wealthy country can have many poor families. A poor country can have some very wealthy families.*

GNP AND WELFARE
All these doubts and reservations should instill in us a permanent caution against using GNP as if it were a clear-cut measure of social contentment or happiness. Economist Edward Denison once remarked that perhaps nothing affects national economic welfare so much as the weather, which certainly does not get into the GNP accounts! Hence, because the U.S. may have a GNP per capita that is higher than that of say, Holland, it does not mean that life is better here. It may be worse. In fact, by the indices of health care or quality of environment, it probably *is* worse.

Yet, with all its shortcomings, GNP is still the simplest way we possess of summarizing the overall level of market activity of the economy. If we want to examine its welfare, we had better turn to specific social indicators of how long we live, how healthy we are, how cheaply we provide good medical care, how varied and abundant is our diet, etc.—none of which we can tell from GNP figures alone. But we are not always interested in welfare, partly because it is too complex to be summed up in a single measure. For better or worse, therefore, GNP has become the yardstick used by most nations in the world. Although other yardsticks are sure to become more important, GNP will be a central term in the economic lexicon for a long time to come.

KEY CONCEPTS

The macro
perspective

Intermediate vs. final goods:
consumption and investment

Gross investment comprises
net investment and
replacement

LOOKING BACK

1. Our introduction to macroeconomics involves a special perspective on the economy, one that emphasizes total output rather than behavior in the marketplace.

2. Observing the flow of total output, we discover that it can be divided into intermediate goods and final goods. Intermediate goods go *into* final goods. Final goods are those used for consumption or for investment.

3. Investment can be further divided into gross and net investment. Gross investment is the sum of output not used for consumption. Part of it is for replacement of worn out capital goods. The remainder is net investment.

Output is a circular flow

4. The flow of output has four major characteristics: It is circular, replenishing our human or material wealth; it is used for consumption or investment, but the same item cannot be used for both simultaneously; it has public and private uses, both as consumption and as investment; and it constitutes the budget constraint of the nation.

Gross national product is the value of final output

5. The annual flow of final output, valued at its market price, is called the gross national product, or GNP. Note that it includes only final, not intermediate output.

GNP ≡ C + I + G + X

6. The annual output can be described as comprising four distinct flows:

a consumption flow,
an export flow,
a flow of domestic gross investment,
a public flow.

Together they give us the identity GNP $= C + I + G + X$.

GNP is a widely used measure of performance. But GNP does not show quality, usefulness, or nonmarket output, and it ignores income distribution

7. Gross national product is widely used as a measure of economic performance. However, it suffers a number of deficiencies as such a measure. It has even more difficulty as an indicator of welfare or well-being because:

Real GNP is not easy to calculate from nominal GNP; different base years give different results.
GNP gives a very imperfect indication of the quality of output.
The size of GNP does not inform us of its purpose or usefulness.
GNP does not include (or imprecisely includes) any output that is not sold.
GNP gives us no clue as to the distribution of income.

ECONOMIC VOCABULARY

Macroeconomics 91	Gross and net investment 93	GNP 94
Intermediate goods 91	Disinvestment 93	Gross private domestic investment 95
Final goods 92	Capital formation 93	Personal consumption expenditures 95
Consumption goods 92	Circular flow 93	Government purchases 95

QUESTIONS

1. Explain how the circularity of the economic process means that the outputs of the system are returned as fresh inputs.

2. What is meant by net investment? How is it different from gross investment? Does the idea of "net consumption" mean anything? (Suppose there is a minimum amount of consumption needed to keep body and soul together?)

3. Why are investment goods considered final goods and not intermediate ones?

4. Write the basic definitional formula for GNP.

5. Do you think we should develop measures other than GNP to measure our performance? What sorts of measures? After thinking about this, look at the "Extra Word" in this chapter.

AN EXTRA WORD ABOUT
SOCIAL INDICATORS

Many people object to the gross national product on the grounds that it focuses our attention on too narrow a band of human activity. Many of the things that improve or degrade our society are left out. Worse still, because they are left out they are ignored. These are not the previously mentioned items, such as imputed income for housewives or negative economic outputs in the form of pollution, that might be added to the GNP to make it a more comprehensive measure of economic *output*. These omissions are measurements of life expectancy, morbidity, mental illness, crime, social unrest and other areas of human activity.

The Social Indicators movement is an effort to expand our system of social accounts to measure progress (or the lack of progress) in these other dimensions. The GNP would not be eliminated but would be just one of a number of measurements in an expanded set of social accounts, some of them listed in Table 9.1.

First, there are many aspects of human existence that are important to welfare but *unmeasurable*. Consider friendship. Without doubt, social relationships influence our welfare; but could we measure whether the average American has more or fewer friends, better or less helpful friends? Clearly we cannot. Unfortunately, the Social Indicators movement has been so closely linked to the idea of measurement that such problems have led to less and less political interest in the idea.

Second, there is the aggregation problem. We have seen that dollar values are used as the common denominator to aggregate different economic goods and services. What is to be the common denominator used to aggregate life expectancy, crime, and mental illness? Nothing obvious suggests itself. Although there is nothing wrong in presenting three dozen different indices of social progress, one cannot easily say, if indicators point in different directions, whether society is improving.

**TABLE 7.1
SOME SOCIAL
INDICATORS**

Life expectancy at birth	72.8 years (1976)
Days of disability	18 days per year per person (1976)
Violent crimes	467 per 100,000 (1977)
Property crimes	4,588 per 100,000 (1977)
High school graduate rate	75.4 percent (1977)
Job satisfaction	3.44 on a scale of 1 to 4 (1973)
Substandard housing units	7.4 percent (1970)

Ideally, such a wide-ranging set of social accounts would give us a better indication of the trend of general welfare than that provided by simple GNP measurements. Yet, although the federal government now issues a social report every other year, the Social Indicators movement has never had the impact that was imagined when it started in the mid 1960s. There are two fundamental reasons for its weakness.

Lacking an aggregate measure of general welfare, social indicators have had very little impact on public opinion. A declining GNP is front-page news. General welfare may also be declining, but no one social indicator is able to show us this. The net result is that the GNP, for all its shortcomings, is not about to be eclipsed by a more general indicator of social welfare in the near future.

Chapter

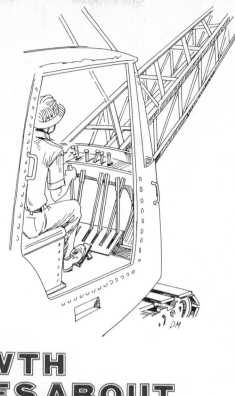

8 HOW GROWTH COMES ABOUT

A LOOK AHEAD

We learned some essential macroeconomic vocabulary in our last chapter. Now we are about to learn some essential macroeconomics.

(1) The center of our focus is economic growth, the principal issue with which macroeconomics is concerned. We already know from Chapter 3 that growth comes from increases in the quantity and quality of labor and capital inputs. Here we are going to look into these inputs more closely. We will discover that we cannot easily distinguish increases in the quantity of capital from changes in its quality.

(2) Our discussion will end with a second look at production possibility curves, this time as depictions of the constraints on economic growth.

Macroeconomics is essentially concerned with growth. Chapter 3 opened a discussion of the long upward trend of U.S. output and the reasons for this trend. Recall that our growth trend for nearly 100 years has resulted in an average annual increase in real GNP per capita of about 1.5 percent a year—enough to double per capita income every 47 years. In our last chapter we began to analyze this process by familiarizing ourselves with the way our stock of wealth interacts with our labor force to yield a flow of output that we call gross national product.

Now we are going to push forward by learning much more about the underlying trends and causes of growth in the American economy. That will set the stage for the work that still lies ahead, when we will narrow our focus down to the present and inquire into the reasons for the problems of our macrosystem —unemployment and inflation, booms and busts.

THE SOURCES OF GROWTH

What determines how fast we have grown in the past, and how rapidly we may grow in the future? We already know the basic answer from Chapter 3. Growth comes from increases in the quantity or in the quality of the two major inputs— labor and capital. Of course, it also depends mightily on the resources with which we are endowed and it is influenced by our sheer willingness to work hard. And that willingness in turn is affected by economic policies, such as how much of our incomes go in taxes. Therefore growth is anything but a cut and dried subject that can be disposed of by a simple analysis of the essential inputs of labor and capital. Nevertheless, by looking into these inputs we will learn a lot.

THE LABOR FORCE

Output depends on work and work depends on people working. Thus the first source of growth is the rise in the sheer number of people in the labor force.

Figure 8.1 gives us a picture of the population and the labor force over the past half century. As we would expect, the size of the force has been steadily rising as our population has increased.

But there is more here than quickly meets the eye. One might expect that as our society has grown richer and more affluent, fewer people would seek employment. But that is not the case. Looking back to 1890 or 1900, we find that only 52 out of every 100 persons over 14 sought paid work. Today about 60 out of every 100 persons of working age seek employment. Looking forward is more uncertain; but if we can extrapolate (extend) the trend of the past several decades to the year 2000, we can expect perhaps as may as 65 persons out of 100 to be in the labor market by that date.

PARTICIPATION IN THE LABOR FORCE

The overall trend toward a larger participation rate for the entire population masks a number of significant changes:

1. **Young males entering the labor force are older than were those who entered in the past.**

A larger number of young men remain in high school now or go on to college. Only a third of elementary school pupils now go on to college, but the ratio is steadily growing.

105
CHAPTER 8
HOW
GROWTH
COMES
ABOUT

2. Older males show a dramatic withdrawal from the labor force.

Almost 7 out of 10 older males used to work. Now only 2 or 3 out of ten work. The reason is the advent of Social Security and private pension plans. It is probable that the proportion of older males in the labor force will continue to fall as the retirement age is slowly reduced.

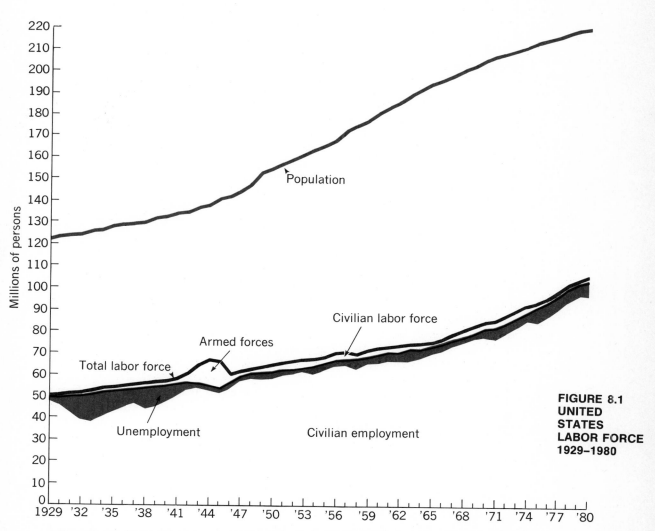

**FIGURE 8.1
UNITED
STATES
LABOR FORCE
1929–1980**

Although our eyes cannot easily make it out on the graph, the proportion of the total population seeking work has steadily risen. Today about two-thirds of the *working age* population is in the labor force—at work or looking for work.

3. Counterbalancing this fall in male participation is a spectacular rise in total female participation. Indeed, the overall trend toward an increasing search for work within the population at large is entirely the result of the mass entrance of women into the labor force.

This surge of women into the labor market reflects several changing factors in the American scene (many of these changes can be found abroad, as well). One factor is the growth of nonmanual, as contrasted with manual, jobs. Another is the widening cultural approval of working women and working wives. The average American girl who marries today in her early twenties and goes on to raise a family will nevertheless spend 25 *years* of her life in paid employment after her children are grown. Yet another reason for the influx of women is that technology has released them from household work. Finally there is the pressure to raise living standards by having two incomes within the household.

HOURS OF WORK

In addition to deciding whether to participate in the labor force, individuals decide how much labor they wish to contribute as members of the labor force. That is, they must decide how many hours of work they wish to offer during a week or how many weeks they wish to work in a year.

Had we asked this question in the days of Adam Smith, it would have been relatively simple to answer. Wages were so close to subsistence that someone in the labor force was obliged to work extremely long hours to keep body and soul together. Paid vacations were unknown to the employees of the cotton mills. Unpaid vacations would have been tantamount to starvation.

With the slow rise in productivity, working men and women gradually found their income rising above subsistence, and a new possibility came into being: the possibility of deliberately working less than their physical maximum, *using part of their increased productivity to buy leisure for themselves instead of wages.* Thus, beginning in the early nineteenth century we find that labor organizations (still very small and weak) sought to shorten the workweek. A signal victory was won in England in 1847 with the introduction of the Ten Hour Day as the legal maximum for women and children. In America, in the prosperity of the 1920s, the 48-hour week finally became standard. More recently, the two-day weekend has become the general practice. Now we hear of the coming of the three-day weekend.

Thus the total supply of labor-time has not risen as fast as the labor force, because a decline in average hours has offset the rise in participation rates and in population. On balance, the total supply of labor-hours has increased, but the supply of labor-hours *per employee,* male and female, has fallen.

QUANTITY VS. QUALITY

So far we have only looked at changes in the quantity of labor inputs. Now we must get some feeling for the importance of this rising quantity in bringing about economic growth.

We do so by comparing the increase in total hours of labor with the increase in total output. In 1900 our labor force was approximately 30 million men and

107
CHAPTER 8
HOW
GROWTH
COMES
ABOUT

women who worked approximately 60 hours a week. As a result they expended 94 billion hours of annual labor. By 1980 the total labor force had grown to almost 110 million. The average workweek was now 36 hours. Total man-hours of labor input therefore amounted to roughly 206 billion hours of annual labor.*

Total hours of labor input over this eighty-year period therefore increased by a little more than two-fold. But total economic output over the same period increased by almost ten-fold. Clearly the sheer physical increase in the hours of labor was not sufficient to account for more than a small part of our growth trajectory.

THE QUALITY OF LABOR INPUTS

Where shall we look for the remaining sources of growth? Our first move will be to examine changes in the quality of our labor hours. The 206 billion hours of labor expended in 1980 were in many cases more skillful, more knowledgable, more healthy, than the labor hours of 1900. These changes in the quality of our working abilities have come about in two ways.

1. Growth of human capital

By human capital, we mean the skills and knowledge possessed by the labor force. Even though the measurement of human capital is fraught with difficulties, we cannot ignore this vital contributory element in labor productivity. Ferenc Jánossy, a Hungarian economist, has suggested a vivid imaginary experiment to highlight the importance of skills and knowledge.

Suppose, he says, that the populations of two nations of the same size could be swapped overnight. Fifty million Englishmen would awake to find themselves in, say, Nepal, and 50 million Nepalese would find themselves in England. The newly transferred Englishmen would have to contend with all the poverty and difficulties of the Nepalese economy. The newly transferred Nepalese would confront the riches of England. But the Englishmen would bring with them an immense reservoir of literacy, skills, discipline, and training, whereas the Nepalese would bring the very low levels of human capital that are characteristic of underdeveloped countries. Is there any doubt, asks Jánossy, that growth rates in Nepal, with its new, skilled population, would soon rise dramatically, and that those of England would fall catastrophically?

One way of indicating in very general terms the rising amount of human capital is to trace the additions to the stock of education that the population embodies. Table 8.1 shows the change in the total number of years of schooling of the U.S. population over the past three-quarters of a century, as well as the rise in formal education per capita. While these measures of human capital are far from exact or all-inclusive, they give some dimensions to the importance of skills and knowledge in increasing productivity.

---

*This is a *very* rough calculation, intended for purposes of illustration. Our estimate makes no allowance for vacations, strikes, illnesses, or unemployment. But it will be legitimate enough to make the central point that soon follows; The *quantity* of labor input cannot possibly account for more than a small portion of our total growth.

**TABLE 8.1
STOCK OF
EDUCATION,
U.S.**

	1900	1980
Total man-years of schooling embodied in population (million)	228	2728
Percent of labor force with high-school education or more	6	68
Percent of high-school graduates entering college	17	46

Here are three indicators of the huge increase in the education embodied in the labor force.

2.   Shifts in the occupations of the labor force

A second source of added productivity results from shifts in employment from low productivity areas to high productivity areas. If workers move from occupations in which their productivity is low to other occupations in which output per man-hour is high, the productivity of the economy will rise even if there are no increases in productivity *within* the different sectors.

A glance at Table 8.2 shows that very profound and pervasive shifts in the location of labor have taken place. What have been the effects of this shift on our long-term ability to produce goods?

The answer is complex. In the early years of the twentieth century, the shift of labor out of agriculture into manufacturing and services probably increased the overall productivity of the economy, since manufacturing was then the most technologically advanced sector. In more recent years, however, we would have to arrive at a different conclusion. Agriculture, although highly productive, is now a very small sector in terms of employment. Moreover, the proportion of the labor force employed in manufacturing is roughly constant, up or down only a few percentage points year to year.

Today, growth in employment takes place mainly in the mixture of occupations we call the service sector: government, retail and wholesale trade, utilities and transportation, professions such as the law, accounting, and the like. The growth of output per capita is less evident in these occupations. Thus the drift of labor into the service sector means that average GNP per worker is growing more slowly today than if labor were moving into manufacturing or agriculture.

Why is this growth-lowering shift taking place? The reason has to do with the changing pattern of demand in an affluent society. There seems to be a natural sequence of wants as a society grows richer: first for food and basic clothing,

**TABLE 8.2
PERCENT
DISTRIBUTION
OF ALL
EMPLOYED
WORKERS**

	1900	1980
Agriculture, forests, and fisheries	38.1	3.3
Manufacturing, mining, transportation, construction, utilities	37.7	34.4
Trade, government, finance, professional and personal services	24.2	62.3

Notice the long-term shift out of agriculture, through manufacturing and other goods-related occupations, into services. This has had a dragging effect on national productivity.

then for the output of a wide range of industrial goods, then for recreation, professional advice, public administration, and the enjoyment of other services.

109
CHAPTER 8
HOW
GROWTH
COMES
ABOUT

OVERALL CONTRIBUTION OF LABOR

Can we sum up the overall contribution of changes in the inputs of labor to our economic growth? Clearly, changes in the quality of inputs—in our skills and capacities—far outweigh changes in our quantity of inputs—sheer man-hours of effort. When it comes to *measuring* the effect of changes in the quality of inputs, however, we are faced with difficult problems. Partly this is because we must balance the favorable effects of increases in human capital with the unfavorable effects of shifts in occupation. In part it is also because individuals are performing different tasks within each sector, as well as moving from one sector to another.

In the end we are left with little more than the recognition that knowledge and know-how, energy and initiative, enthusiasm and intelligence are powerful motors of economic growth. Indeed, economic growth expresses the gradual accumulation of these qualities of humankind much more than it expresses the increase in its sheer volume of exertion.

CAPITAL

What about capital? It must be apparent that without increases in the quantity of capital we could never achieve much growth. The rising labor force would then have to work with the same amount of machines, buildings, transportation equipment and the like, and diminishing returns would soon lower productivity severely. Therefore we have to **widen capital**—to keep the amount of capital per worker at least abreast of increases in the labor force—if we are to have any significant growth at all.

Actually, a vigorous economy does better than that. It also **deepens capital**, adding to its stock of capital wealth faster than to its labor force, so that each worker has more capital equipment than his or her predecessor, thereby experiencing the same increase in productivity that Adam Smith's workers experienced when new machinery was added to their pin factory.

THE MEASUREMENT PROBLEM

By how much has our stock of capital grown? Right away we come across a problem that we did not have to face when we considered the labor force. When we seek to measure the effects of changing labor inputs, we can at least count heads, or hours, in comparing past and present. But there is no such convenient unit of measurement when we come to capital. Is a power crane comparable to a shovel? Can we measure the amount of capital used by a bookkeeper today and in 1900 by comparing a computer (or even a desk calculator) to a pencil?

Such considerations make it plain that we cannot easily distinguish changes in the size of our capital stock from changes in its quality. Occasionally we can directly measure changes in the amount of capital; for instance we can compare miles of railroad trackage over time. But even here there are changes in quality embodied in the "same" capital—modern rails are welded not riveted, roadbeds are different, trackage is electrified.

Structures	$2,555	
farm		$ 20.9
residential		952.9
public		745.2
institutional		125.6
other priv. non-res.		710.5
Equipment	1,041.3	
priv. business and public		543.7
consumer durables		496.6
Inventories	707.2	
Land	1,284.8	
Total	5,587.6	

Our total national capital is usually broken down as the table shows. Why do we not include the value of stocks and bonds, or money? The answer is that these are claims on our real wealth; in themselves they are not wealth.

TOTAL CAPITAL STOCK

How large is our modern capital stock? Table 8.3 gives us an overall view.

As we can see, our total national capital amounts to $5.5 trillion dollars, an unimaginably vast sum. If we take only the total for structures and equipment, the figure is $3.5 trillion—about $41,000 worth of capital for every person in the labor force.

This total capital stock is about five or six times as large as the capital stock at the beginning of the century. (Remember: To some extent we are comparing apples and pears here. The smaller sum was not only less capital of the same kind—fewer miles of railroad trackage, if you will—but also very different capital: pencils instead of computers.) **But one thing is indubitable from this general overview. The increase in the quantity and the quality of capital is of critical importance in explaining our national growth. More and better capital are essential elements in increasing our productivity capacity.**

INVESTING AND INVENTING

How do we augment the amount of capital or improve its quality? Actually the two processes generally go hand in hand, for the very act of adding to our capital stock is usually accompanied by an improvement. But it is useful, nonetheless, to separate the two processes in our minds.

We increase the quantity of capital by withholding resources from consumption—saving them—and by using those resources to build capital goods. This is the process of investment that we studied in our last chapter. A great deal of our macroeconomic studies in the chapters immediately ahead will be about this central, vital process.

We improve the quality of our capital by a process for which there is no simple name. Let us call it technology. Technology includes inventing and applying new products and processes, and achieving economies of scale—improvements that arise from sheer size.

SOURCES OF TECHNOLOGY

Technology is probably the single most important factor in determining how fast we grow. One instance of the astonishing power of technology is to compare the period of time it has taken various economies to recover from the devastation of war. In ancient times it could take centuries for a city painfully to rebuild itself: Think of Rome after the "fall"! After the Civil War it required

Very few economies actually operate on their efficiency frontiers. Most economies have at least *some* unemployed inputs or are not using their inputs with all possible efficiency. Perhaps only in wartime do we reach the frontiers of our production-possibility map. Nonetheless, we can see that a major job of economic policy makers is to move the economy as close to its frontiers as possible, under normal conditions and to move the frontier out as fast as possible.

113
CHAPTER 8
HOW
GROWTH
COMES
ABOUT

KEY CONCEPTS

Growth is the central trend at 1.5 percent a year, per capita

Increases in labor inputs reflect population growth and changes in participation rates

Total labor hours have roughly doubled 1900–1980

Labor hours embody more education, but the labor force works in less productive occupations

Total real output is up 10 times, 1900–1980. Much of this comes from capital but we cannot measure increases in quantity vs. quality

Investment is the process by which we add to the quantity of capital; technology adds to its quality

R & D is a key activity, recently declining as a percent of GNP

Changes in labor and capital inputs move out the production-possibility frontier

LOOKING BACK

1. Growth is the central concern of macroeconomics and it is a central trend of the economy. In Chapter 5 we saw that our real per capita growth has increased at about 1.5 percent a year, plus or minus 10 percent. This doubles real per capita living standards every 47 years.

2. Growth comes from increases in the quantity or quality of our main inputs, labor and capital. Increases in the quantity of labor have resulted from growth in population and a gradual rise in the over-all participation rate, especially the entrance of women into the labor force.

3. Weekly hours have decreased since the turn of the century. Overall, it is likely that total labor hours (labor force times working hours) have slightly more than doubled, 1900–1980.

4. Changes in the quality of labor are more difficult to measure. They include increases in the amount of education embodied in the labor force and adding to the value of our human capital, and also changes in the kinds of work we do. There has been a long-term shift into service occupations which have lower than average productivity.

5. Total real output between 1900 and 1980 has increased some ten-fold. A major portion of this growth must come from capital inputs. However it is almost impossible to separate changes in the quantity and quality of capital, because capital is always changing.

6. Although quantity and quality are almost impossible to separate, we speak of increases in the quantity of capital as arising through investment, and increases in its quality as arising through technology. In fact, an act of saving and investment is the means by which invention or innovation takes place.

7. The sources of technology are not clearly understood. Research and development activities are likely a very important source of technological improvement; recently R&D has been declining in the U.S.

8. Production-possibility curves can now be seen as describing the constraints on growth. We can move the frontiers out by the changes in labor and capital inputs that we have been describing.

ECONOMIC VOCABULARY

QUESTIONS

1. Set up a production-possibilities curve for an economy producing food and steel. Show how some combinations of food and steel cannot be produced, even though each of the goods lies within the limit of production on its own axis. Explain why the P-P curve is bowed.

2. Think about ways in which education can improve productivity—and ways in which it cannot. Would you think that going or not going to elementary school would have a greater or lesser effect on output per hour than going to college? In what line of work?

3. Try to think of some kinds of capital that have remained essentially unchanged over the last 50 years. How about ordinary tools, such as those that a carpenter uses? Can you picture in your mind's eye the effect of widening this kind of capital to match a growing force of carpenters, as against equipping the force with new kinds of tools such as power saws?

4. Is it possible for an economy that failed to invest to continue to grow? Suppose it worked harder? Are there limits to such kinds of growth? Are there limits to the growth that new and better capital will bring?

Chapter

9 HOW PRODUCTION IS SUSTAINED

A LOOK AHEAD

Here we move from considerations of long-term growth to a closer understanding of how the economy works. This will involve us in a step-by-step analysis of one central question: How can an economy sustain itself? Or in other words, how can it buy back all its own production?

We will attack the problem by seeing how every item of cost incurred in production becomes someone's income. That is a key part of the answer: Costs are also incomes. But it is not the whole answer. Incomes must thereafter be spent if they are to become demand. And if they are not spent? Then we have trouble, recession, slowdowns in production.

We end with a few definitions that you should be sure to learn. When you finish this chapter you will be ready for the all-important next one on saving and investment. So read this one carefully!

So far, we have talked about GNP from the supply point of view. First we familiarized ourselves with the actual process of production itself—the interaction of the factors of production and the accumulated wealth of the past as they cooperated to bring a flow of output into being. Next we examined the forces that swelled that volume of output over time, mainly the increase in skills and capital equipment and technology that are responsible for our long-term trend of growth.

But we cannot pursue the problem of growth much further before we have understood something about the operation of the economy that is both very simple and surprisingly complex. **How do we know that there will be enough purchasing power to buy the amount of production that the economy creates?** Until we understand how an economy can sustain itself, we will not be able to understand how it can pull itself up by its own bootstraps—that is, how it can grow.

OUTPUT AND DEMAND

The question leads us to understand a fundamental linkage between demand and output. How does output actually come into existence? Anyone in business will give you the answer. The crucial factor in running a business is *demand* or *purchasing power;* that is, the presence of buyers who are willing and able to buy some good or service at a price the seller is willing to accept.

But how does demand or purchasing power come into existence? Any buyer will tell us that dollars come in as part of *income* or cash receipts. But where, in turn, do the dollar receipts or incomes of buyers come from? If we inquire again, most buyers will tell us that they have money in their pockets because in one fashion or another they have contributed to the process of production; that is, because they have helped to make the output that is now being sold.

Thus output is generated by demand—and demand is generated by output! Our quest for the motive force behind the flow of production therefore leads us to discover a great *circular flow* within the economy.

THE CIRCULAR FLOW

At the top of the circle in Figure 9.1 we see payments flowing from households to firms or government units (cities, states, federal agencies, etc.), thereby creating the demand that brings forth production. At the bottom of the circle, we see more payments, this time flowing from firms or governments back to households, as businesses hire the services of the various factors in order to carry out production. **Thus we can see that there is a constant regeneration of demand as money is first spent by the public on the output of firms and governments, and then in turn spent by firms and governments for the services of the public. That is how an economy that has produced a given GNP is able to buy it back.**

This is by no means a self-evident matter. Indeed, one of the most common misconceptions about the flow of economic activity is that there will not be enough purchasing power to buy everything we have produced—that somehow we are unable to buy enough to keep up with the output of our factories. So it is well to understand once and for all how an economy can sustain a given level of production through its purchases on the market.

We start, then, with an imaginary economy in full operation. We can, if we

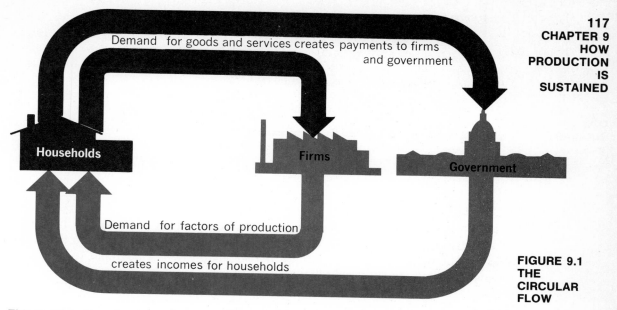

Demand for goods and services creates payments to firms and government

Households

Firms

Government

Demand for factors of production

creates incomes for households

FIGURE 9.1
THE
CIRCULAR
FLOW

This is the same circular flow concept that we encountered in Figure 7.1. Here we use it to emphasize that the demand for output is itself generated by output.

wish, imagine ourselves as having collected a year's output, which is now sitting on the economic front doorstep looking for a buyer. What we must now see is whether it will be possible to *sell* this gross national product to the people who have been engaged in producing it. We must ask whether enough income or receipts have been generated in the process of production to buy back all the products themselves.

COSTS AND INCOMES

How does production create income? Business people do not think about "incomes" when they assemble the factors of production to meet the demand for their product. They worry about *cost*. All the money they pay out during the production process is paid under the heading of *cost*, whether it be wage or salary cost, cost of materials, depreciation cost, tax cost, or whatever. Thus it seems that the concept of cost may offer us a useful point of entry into the economic chain. If we can show how all costs become incomes, we will have taken a major step toward understanding whether our gross national product can in fact be sold to those who produced it.

It may help us if we begin by looking at the kinds of costs incurred by business firms in real life. Since governments also produce goods and services, this hypothetical firm should be taken to represent government agencies as well as business firms. Both incur the same kinds of costs; only the labels differ.

Table 9.1, a hypothetical expense summary of General Output Company, will serve as an example typical of all business firms, large or small, and all

TABLE 9.1 **GENERAL** **OUTPUT** **COMPANY** **COST** **SUMMARY**	Wages, salaries, and employee benefits	$100,000,000
	Rental, interest, and profits payments	5,000,000
	Materials, supplies, etc.	60,000,000
	Taxes other than income	25,000,000
	Depreciation	20,000,000
	Total	$210,000,000

government agencies. (If you examine the year-end statements of any business, you will find that costs all fall into one or more of the cost categories shown.)

FACTOR COSTS

Some of these costs we recognize immediately as payments to factors of production. The item for wages and salaries is obviously a payment to the factor *labor.* The item for interest (perhaps not so obviously) is a payment to the factor *capital;* that is, to those who have lent the company money in order to help it carry on its productive operation. The item for rent is, of course, a payment for the rental of *land* or natural resources from their owners.

Note that we have included profits with rent and interest. In actual accounting practice, profits are not shown as an expense. For our purposes, however, it will be quite legitimate and very helpful to regard profits as a special kind of factor cost going to business people for their risk-taking function. Later we shall go more thoroughly into the matter of profits.

FACTOR COSTS AND VALUE OF OUTPUT

Two things strike us about these factor costs. *First, it is clear that they represent payments that have been made to secure production.* In more technical language, they are payments for factor inputs that result in commodity outputs. All the production actually carried on within the company or government agency, all the value it has added to the economy has been compensated by the payments the company or the agency has made to land, labor, and capital. To be sure, there are other costs, for materials and taxes and depreciation, and we shall soon turn to these. But whatever production or assembly or distribution the company or agency has carried out during the course of the year has required the use of land, labor, or capital. **Thus the total of its factor costs represents the value of the total new output that General Output by itself has given to the economy.**

From here it is a simple step to add up *all* the factor costs paid out by *all* the companies and government agencies in the economy, in order to measure the total new *value added* by all productive efforts in the year. This measure is called **national income.** As we can see, it is less than gross national product, for it does not include other costs of output, namely certain taxes and depreciation.

FACTOR COSTS AND HOUSEHOLD INCOMES

A second fact that strikes us is that *all factor costs are income payments.* **The wages, salaries, interest, rents, etc., that were costs to the company or agency were income to its recipients. So are any profits, which will accrue as income to the owners of the business.**

118

Thus, just as it sounds, national income means the total amount of earnings of the factors of production within the nation. If we think of these factors as constituting the households of the economy, we can see that *factor costs result directly in incomes to the household sector.* If factor costs were the only costs involved in production, the problem of buying back the gross national product would be a very simple one. We should simply be paying out to households, as the cost of production, the very sum needed to buy GNP when we turned around to sell it. A glance at the General Output expense summary shows that this is not the case. There are other costs besides factor costs. How shall we deal with them?

COSTS OF MATERIALS

The next item of the expense summary is puzzling. Called payments for "materials, supplies, etc.," it represents all the money General Output has paid, not to its own factors, but to other companies for other products it has needed. We may even recognize these costs as payments for those *intermediate products* that lose their identity in a later stage of production. How do such payments become part of the income available to buy GNP on the marketplace?

Perhaps the answer is already intuitively clear. When General Output sends its checks to, let us say, U.S. Steel or General Electric or to a local supplier of stationery, each of these recipient firms now uses the proceeds of General Output's checks to pay its own costs.

And what are those costs? What must U.S. Steel or all the other suppliers now do with their checks? The answer is obvious. They must reimburse their own factors and then pay any other costs that remain.

Figure 9.2 may make the matter plain. It shows us, looking back down the chain of intermediate payments, that what constitutes material costs to one

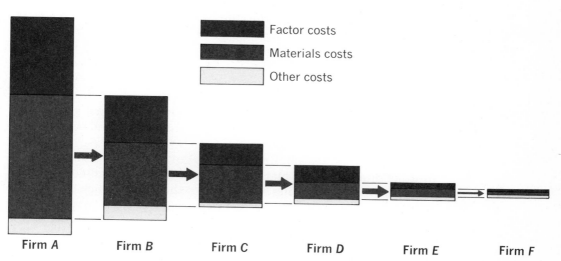

Factor costs

Materials costs

Other costs

Firm A   Firm B   Firm C   Firm D   Firm E   Firm F

FIGURE 9.2 HOW MATERIALS COSTS BECOME OTHER COSTS
The cost of materials to Firm A consists of Firm B's payments to its factors and other costs, just as Firm B's materials cost is made up of Firm C's factor and other costs. Eventually all costs of materials reduce to payments to labor, capital and land. After all, what other ultimate costs are there?

firm is made up of factor and other costs to another. Indeed, as we unravel the chain from company to company, it is clear that all the contribution to new output must have come from the contribution of factors somewhere down the line. **All the costs of new output—all the value added—must ultimately be resolvable into payments to the owners of land (or natural resources), labor, and capital.**

Another way of picturing the same thing is to imagine that all firms or agencies in the country were bought up by a single gigantic corporation. The various production units of the new supercorporation would then ship components and semifinished items back and forth to one another, but there would not have to be any payment from one division to another. The only payments that would be necessary would be those required to buy the services of factors—that is, various kinds of labor or the use of property or capital—so that at the end of the year, the supercorporation would show on its expense summary only items for wages and salaries, rent, and interest (and as we shall see, taxes and depreciation), but it would have no item for materials cost.

We have come a bit further toward seeing how our gross national product can be sold. **To the extent that GNP represents new output made during the course of the year, the income to buy back this output has already been handed out as factor costs, either paid at the last stage of production or carried along in the guise of material costs.**

But a glance at the General Output expense summary shows that entrepreneurs incur two kinds of costs that we have still not taken into account: taxes and depreciation. Here are costs employers have incurred that have not been accounted for on the income side. What can we say about them?

TAX COSTS

Let us begin by tracing the taxes that General Output pays, just as we have traced its material payments.* In the first instance, its taxes will go to government units—federal, state, and local. But we need not stop there. Just as we saw that General Output's checks to supplier firms paid for the suppliers' factor costs and for still further interfirm transactions, so we can see that its checks to government agencies pay for goods and services that these agencies have produced—goods such as roads, buildings, or defense equipment; or services such as teaching, police protection, and the administration of justice. General Output's tax checks are thus used to help pay for factors of production—land, labor, and capital—that are used in the *public sector.*

In many ways, General Output's payments to government units resemble its payments to other firms for raw material. Indeed, if the government *sold* its services to General Output, charging for the use of the roads, police services, or defense protection it affords the company, there would be *no* difference whatsoever. The reason we differentiate between a company's payment to the public sector and its payments for intermediate products is important, however, and worth looking into.

---

*For simplicity, we also show government agencies as taxpayers. In fact, most government units do *not* pay taxes. Yet there will be hidden tax costs in the prices of many materials they buy. No harm is done by treating government agencies like taxpaying firms in this model.

The first reason is clearly that with few exceptions, the government does *not* sell its output. This is partly because the community has decided that certain things the government produces (education, justice, or the use of public parks, for instance) should not be for sale but should be supplied to all citizens without direct charge. In part, it is also because some things the government produces, such as defense or law and order, cannot be equitably charged to individual buyers since it is impossible to say to what degree anyone benefits from—or even uses—these communal facilities. Hence General Output, like every other producer, is billed, justly or otherwise, for a share of the cost of government.

There is also a second reason why we consider the cost of taxes as a new kind of cost, distinct from factor payments. It is this. **When business firms have finished paying the factors, they have not yet paid all the sums that employers must lay out. Some taxes, in other words, are an addition to the cost of production.**

INDIRECT VS. DIRECT TAXES

These taxes—so-called *indirect taxes*—are levied on the productive enterprise itself or on its actual physical output. Taxes on real estate, for instance, or taxes that are levied on each unit of output (such as excise taxes on cigarettes) or taxes levied on goods sold at retail (sales taxes) are all payments that entrepreneurs must make as part of their costs of doing business.

This does not mean that all taxes collected by the government are costs of production. Many taxes will be paid, not by the entrepreneurs as an expense of doing business, but by the *factors* themselves. These so-called *direct* taxes (such as income taxes) are *not* part of the cost of production. When General Output adds up its total cost of production, it naturally includes the wages and salaries it has paid, but it does not include the taxes its workers or executives have paid out of their incomes. Such direct taxes transfer income from earners to government, but they are not a cost to the company itself.

In the same way, the income taxes on the profits of a company do *not* constitute a cost of production. General Output does not pay income taxes as a regular charge on its operations but waits until a year's production has taken place and then pays income taxes on the profits it makes *after* paying its costs. If it finds that it has lost money over the year, it will not pay any income taxes—although it will have paid other costs, including indirect taxes. **Thus direct taxes, such as income taxes, are not a cost paid out in the course of production that must be recouped, but a payment made by factors (including owners of the business) from the incomes they have earned through the process of production.**

TAXES AS COST

Now we can see two reasons why taxes are handled as a separate item in GNP and are not telescoped into factor costs, the way materials costs are. One reason is that taxes are a payment to a sector different from that of business and thus indicate a separate stream of economic activity.

The second reason, and the one that interests us more at this moment, is that *certain taxes*—indirect taxes—*are an entirely new kind of cost of production, not previously picked up.* As an expense paid out by entrepreneurs, over and above factor costs (or material costs), these tax costs must be part of the total selling price of GNP.

Will there be enough incomes handed out in the process of production to cover this item of cost? We can see that there will be. The indirect tax costs paid out by firms will be received by government agencies who will use these tax receipts to pay income to factors working for the government. Any direct taxes (income taxes) paid by General Output or by its factors will also wind up in the hands of a government. **Thus all tax payments result in the transfer of purchasing power from the private to the public sector, and when spent by the public sector, they will again become demand on the marketplace.**

DEPRECIATION

But there is still one last item of cost. At the end of the year, when the company is totting up its expenses to see if it has made a profit for the period, its accountants do not stop with factor costs, material costs, and indirect taxes. If they did, the company would soon be in serious straits. In producing its goods, General Output has also used up a certain amount of its assets—its buildings and equipment—and a cost must now be charged for this wear and tear if the company is to be able to preserve the value of its physical plant intact. If it did not make this cost allowance, it would have failed to include all the resources that were used up in the process of production, and it would therefore be overstating its profits.

Yet this cost has something about it clearly different from other costs that General Output has paid. Unlike factor costs or taxes or material costs, depreciation is not paid for by check. When the company's accountants make an allowance for depreciation, all they do is make an entry on the company's book, stating that plant and equipment are now worth a certain amount less than in the beginning of the year.

At the same time, however, General Output *includes* the amount of depreciation in the price it intends to charge for its goods. As we have seen, one of the resources used up in production was its own capital equipment, and it is certainly entitled to consider the depreciation as a cost. Yet it has not paid anyone a sum of money equal to this cost! How, then, will there be enough income in the marketplace to buy back its product?

REPLACEMENT EXPENDITURE

The answer is that in essence it has paid depreciation charges to itself. Depreciation is thus part of its gross income. Together with after-tax profits, these depreciation charges are called a business's *cash flow*.

A business does not *have* to spend its depreciation accruals, but normally it will, to maintain and replace its capital stock. To be sure, an individual firm may not replace its worn-out capital exactly on schedule. But when we consider the economy as a whole, with its vast assemblage of firms, that problem tends to disappear. Suppose we have 1,000 firms, each with machines worth $1,000 and each depreciating its machines at $100 per year. Provided that all the machines were bought in different years, this means that in any given year, about 10 percent of the capital stock will wear out and have to be replaced. It's reasonable to assume that among them, the 1,000 firms will spend $100,000 to replace their old equipment over a ten-year span.*

This enables us to see that insofar as there is a steady stream of replacement expenditures going to firms that make capital goods, there will be payments just large enough to balance the addition to costs due to depreciation. As with all other payments to firms, these replacement expenditures will become incomes to factors, etc., and thus can reappear on the marketplace.

THE THREE STREAMS OF EXPENDITURE

Our analysis is now complete. Item by item, we have traced each element of cost into an income payment, so that we now know there is enough income paid out to buy back our GNP at a price that represents its full cost. Perhaps this was a conclusion we anticipated all along. After all, ours would be an impossibly difficult economy to manage if somewhere along the line purchasing power dropped out of existence, so that we were always faced with a shortage of income to buy back the product we made. But our analysis has also shown us something more unexpected. We are accustomed to thinking that all the purchasing power in the economy is received and spent through the hands of people—usually meaning households. Now we can see that this is not true. There is not only one, but there are *three* streams of incomes and costs, all quite distinct from one another (although linked by direct taxes).

1. Factor costs → Households → Consumers goods

   Direct Taxes

2. Indirect taxes → Government agencies → Government goods

   Direct Taxes

3. Depreciation → Business firms → Replacement investment

The one major crossover in the three streams is the direct taxes of households and business firms that go to governments. This flow permits governments to buy more goods and services than could be purchased with indirect taxes alone.

There is a simple way of explaining this seemingly complex triple flow. Each stream indicates the existence of a *final taker* of gross national product: the consumer, government, and business itself.† Since output has final claimants

---

*What if the machines *were* all bought in one year or over a small number of years? Then replacement expenditures will *not* be evenly distributed over time, and we may indeed have problems. This takes us into the dynamics of prosperity and recession, to which we will turn in due course. For the purpose of our explanatory model, we will stick with our (not too unrealistic) assumption that machines wear out on a steady schedule and that aggregate replacement expenditures therefore also display a steady, relatively unfluctuating pattern.

†We continue to forget about net exports until the "Extra Word" on page 217. They are taken care of quite satisfactorily as a component of gross private investment.

other than consumers, we can obviously have a flow of purchasing power that does not enter consumers' or factors' hands.

THE COMPLETED CIRCUIT OF DEMAND

The realization that factor owners do not get paid incomes equal to the total gross value of output brings us back to the central question of this chapter: Can we be certain that we will be able to sell our GNP at its full cost? Has there surely been generated enough purchasing power to buy back our total output?

We have thus far carefully analyzed and answered half the question. We know that all costs will become incomes to factors or receipts of government agencies or of firms making replacement items. To sum up again, factor costs become the incomes of workers, managements, owners of natural resources and of capital; and all these incomes together can be thought of as comprising the receipts of the household sector. Tax costs are paid to government agencies and become receipts of the government sector. Depreciation costs are initially accrued within business firms, and these accruals belong to the business sector. As long as worn-out capital is regularly replaced, these accruals will be matched by equivalent new receipts of firms that make capital goods.

CRUCIAL ROLE OF EXPENDITURES

What we have not yet established, however, is that these sector receipts will become sector expenditures. That is, we have not demonstrated that all households will now *spend* all their incomes on goods and services, or that government units will necessarily *spend* all their tax receipts on public goods and services, or that all firms will assuredly *spend* their depreciation accruals for new replacement equipment.

What happens if some receipts are not spent? The answer is of key importance in understanding the operation of the economy. A failure of the sectors to spend as much money as they have received means that some of the costs that have been laid out will *not* come back to the original entrepreneurs. As a result, they will suffer losses. If, for instance, our gross national product costs $1 trillion to produce but the various sectors spend only $900 billion in all, then some entrepreneurs will find themselves failing to sell all their output. Inventories of unsold goods will begin piling up, and business people will soon be worried about overproducing. The natural thing to do when you can't sell all your output is to stop making so much of it, so businesses will begin cutting back on production. As they do so, they will also cut back on the number of people they employ. As a result, business costs will go down; but so will factor incomes, for we have seen that costs and incomes are but opposite sides of one coin. As incomes fall, the expenditures of the sectors might very well fall further, bringing about another twist in the spiral of recession.

This is not yet the place to go into the mechanics of such a downward spiral of business. But the point is clear. **A failure of the sectors to bring all their receipts back to the marketplace as demand can initiate profound economic problems. In the contrast between an unshakable equality of costs and incomes on**

THE THREE FLOWS

To help visualize these three flows, imagine for an instant that our money comes in colors (all of equal value): black, gray, and red. Now suppose that firms always pay their factors in red money, their taxes in gray money, and their replacement expenditures in black money. In point of fact, of course, the colors would soon be mixed. A factor that is paid in red bills will be paying some of his red income for taxes; or a government agency will be paying out gray money as factor incomes; or firms will be using black dollars to pay taxes or factors, and gray or red dollars to pay for replacement capital.

But at least in our minds, we can picture the streams being kept separate. A gray tax dollar paid by General Output to the Internal Revenue Service for taxes could go from the government to another firm, let us say in payment for office supplies, and we can think of the office supply firm keeping these gray dollars apart from its other receipts to pay its taxes with. Such a gray dollar could circulate indefinitely from government agencies to firms and back again, helping to bring about production but never entering a consumer's pocket! In the same way, a black replacement expenditure dollar going from General Output to, let us say, U.S. Steel could be set aside by U.S. Steel to pay for *its* replacement needs; and the firm that received this black dollar might, in turn, set it aside for its own use as replacement expenditure. We can imagine a circuit of expenditures in which black dollars went from firm to firm to pay for replacement investment and never ended up in a pay envelope or as a tax payment.

the one hand, and the uncertain connection between incomes and expenditures on the other, we have come to grips with one of the most important problems in macroeconomics.

FROM RECESSION TO INFLATION

We have concentrated on the problem of buying back GNP because that is the best way to understand the circular flow properties of production. But most of us these days are worried about inflation. How does that tie into our analysis?

The answer should be clear enough. If recession arises because there is too little expenditure to cover the costs of producing GNP, inflation arises because there is too much expenditure. We have all heard inflation described as "too much money chasing too little goods"; as a description that is entirely correct, although it fails to explain where "too much money" comes from.

We have something of a problem in going further into an explanation of inflation at this point. We have not yet learned about money, nor have we studied the motivation of expenditure. So we will simply have to wait before we go deeply into the inflationary phenomenon. We will be back to the subject many times.

SOME IMPORTANT DEFINITIONS

We have completed the necessary economic analysis of this chapter, showing how the demand for GNP is generated. But we still need to improve and refine our economic vocabulary. Before we move on, therefore, we must learn some very useful and frequently encountered definitions.

The first of these concerns two ways of looking at GNP. One way is to think of GNP as measuring the value of a year's final output. As we know that value is a sum of costs: factor costs, indirect tax costs, the costs of depreciation. But we also know that these same costs are identical with the incomes or receipts of sectors. Therefore GNP measures total incomes as well as total costs.

GNP AND GNI

To express the equality with the conciseness and clarity of mathematics, we can write two equations. First, GNP as a sum of final outputs:

$$GNP \equiv C + G + I + X,$$

where C, I, G, and X (exports) are designations of the four categories into which we divide our flow of production.

Next, we write an equation that describes GNP not as a sum of outputs but as a sum of costs:

$$GNP \equiv F + T + D,$$

where F, T, and D are familiar to us as factor, indirect tax, and depreciation costs. *But we have also learned that all costs are identical with incomes.* It follows, therefore, that we can speak of the sum of these costs as Gross National Income, or GNI. Hence the last set of identities:

**Gross National Product ≡ Gross National Income
or GNP ≡ GNI,
or $C + G + I + X \equiv F + T + D$.**

It is important to remember that these are all accounting identities, true by definition. The National Income and Product Accounts, the official government accounts for the economy, are kept in such a manner as to make them true. As the name implies, these accounts are kept in two sets of books, one on the products produced in the economy and one on the costs of production, which we know to be identical with the incomes generated in the economy. Since both sets of accounts are measuring the same output, the two totals must be equal.

NNP AND NATIONAL INCOME

It is now easy to understand the meaning of two other measures of output. One of these is called **net national product** (NNP). As the name indicates, it is exactly equal to the gross national product minus depreciation. GNP is used much more than NNP, since the measures of depreciation are very unreliable. The other measure, national income, we have already met. It is *GNP minus both depreciation and indirect taxes.* This makes it equal to the sum of factor costs only. Figure 9.3 should make this relationship clear. The aim of this last measure is to identify the net income that actually reaches the hands of factors of production. Consequently, the measure is sometimes called the *national income at factor cost.* Its abbreviation is Y.

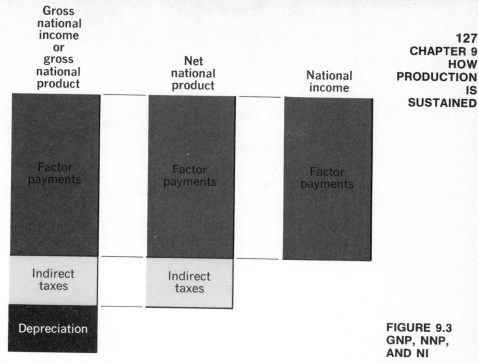

**FIGURE 9.3
GNP, NNP,
AND NI**

GNP, NNP, and NI (or Y) fit into one another like a nest of Chinese boxes. As you can see, the basic unit of measurement of output is national income; net and gross national products are derived by adding specific costs—indirect taxes for NNP and depreciation for GNP.

THE CIRCULAR FLOW AGAIN

The "self-reproducing" model economy we have now sketched out is obviously still very far from reality. Nevertheless, the particular kind of unreality that we have deliberately constructed serves a highly useful purpose. An economy that regularly and dependably buys back everything it produces gives us a kind of bench mark from which to begin our subsequent investigations. We call such an economy, whose internal relationships we have outlined, an economy in **stationary equilibrium,** and we denote the changeless flow of costs into business receipts, and receipts back into costs, a *circular flow.*

We shall return many times to the model of a circular flow economy for insights into a more complex and dynamic system. Hence it is well that we summarize briefly two of the salient characteristics of such a system.

1. **A circular flow economy will never experience a recession**

Year in and year out, its total output will remain unchanged. Indeed, the very concept of a circular flow is useful in showing us that an economic system can maintain a given level of activity *indefinitely,* so long as all the sectors convert all their receipts into expenditures.

2.   A circular flow economy will never know a boom

That is, it will not grow, and its standard of living will remain unchanged. That standard of living may be high or low, for we could have a circular flow economy of poverty or of abundance. But in either state, changelessness will be its essence.

THE GREAT PUZZLE

What we have demonstrated in this chapter is an exceedingly important idea. There *can* always be enough purchasing power generated by the process of output to buy back that output.

Yet we all know, from our most casual acquaintance with economics, that in fact there is not always enough purchasing power around, or that on occasions there is too much purchasing power. With too little, we have slumps and recessions; with too much, booms and inflation.

Hence the circular flow sets the stage for the next step in our study of macroeconomics. If there *can be* the right amount of purchasing power generated, why isn't there? Or to put the question more perplexingly: if there *can be* enough purchasing power to buy *any* size output, small or large, what determines how large purchasing power will actually be, and therefore how large output will actually be?

These questions point the way for the next stage of our investigation. We must study the workings of demand much more realistically than heretofore by removing some of the assumptions that were necessary to create a model of a circular flow system.

KEY CONCEPTS

The demand for GNP is generated in the act of production as firms hire factors

Factor costs are income to the factors of production

Indirect taxes are costs that become receipts of government agencies. (Note: Income taxes are not costs of production)

Depreciation costs accrue to firms and can be used for replacement investment

LOOKING BACK

1. The question to be grasped is how an economy can sustain itself, how it can generate enough demand to buy back its own output. This leads at once to the origin of demand for output, or purchasing power. In turn we see that purchasing power is generated by the act of production, as firms and government employers hire factors of production. Thus we begin with the concept of a circular flow.

2. When factors are hired, they create costs. It is important to see that all costs are necessarily also incomes. We group all costs—including material costs—into three categories. The first category, factor costs—wages, salaries, interest payments, and the like—are obviously incomes for the factors of production who receive them.

3. In the second category are the costs of indirect taxation. These are not direct income taxes which are borne by the factors out of their incomes and are not a cost of production. Indirect taxes are simply added onto factor costs as an expense of production. Such indirect taxes become part of the receipts of government agencies.

4. Depreciation costs are the final category of production cost. These costs are received by business firms, who use them to finance replacement investment.

5. Thus there are three streams of spending in the economy: (1) factor costs which go to the households who spend these "costs" (their incomes) for consumption; (2) indirect taxes which go to government for expenditure on public goods and services; and (3) depreciation costs that accrue to business firms for expenditure as replacement investment. It is important to see that the transition from "cost" to "income" is unbreakable—they are identities. This is not so for the transition from cost (or income) to expenditure. Here is a crucial area of potential malfunction.

GNP ≡ GNI

6. We can express GNP in two ways: as a sum of final outputs or as a sum of incomes. Thus there is an identity between gross national income and gross national product.

A circular flow economy has no growth

7. The model of a circular flow economy elucidates how such an economy can repurchase its own production. But a circular flow system has no vitality, no growth.

ECONOMIC VOCABULARY

Factor costs 118	Depreciation 122	Circular flow 127
National income 118	GNP and GNI 126	Stationary equilibrium 127
Direct and indirect taxes 121	Net national product 126	

QUESTIONS

1. What are factor costs? To what sector do they go? Do all factor costs become personal incomes? Do they become personal expenditures? (Careful about this last: Suppose that a household *saves* part of its income!)

2. What are direct taxes? What is "direct" about them? Why are they distinguished from "indirect" taxes? Why is an indirect tax, such as a sales tax, considered an addition to the value of GNP, whereas an income tax is not? Think: Does the value of the goods or services you personally create get bigger if you pay a larger income tax? Does it get larger if the sales tax is increased?

3. To whom are material costs paid? Why do we not count them as a separate part of GNP?

4. Exactly what is depreciation? Why is it a cost? Who pays it, and how? Who receives it? Is it possible that a firm can pay depreciation to itself? How else would you describe a business that made an allowance at the end of the year for the value of the machinery that had been used up in production?

5. Why is the link between an expenditure and a receipt an identity? Why is the link between a receipt and an expenditure not an identity? Can there be any expenditure ever without someone receiving it? Can someone receive a payment but not make an expenditure himself? Be sure you grasp the difference here.

Chapter

10 SAVING AND INVESTMENT

A LOOK AHEAD

This key chapter tells us about the process that injects growth into a circular flow economy—the process of saving and investment.

(1) It shows how the act of saving creates a gap in final demand, a gap that can only be offset by compensatory action from the other sectors. When this compensatory action is undertaken by business it is called investment, and it results in the creation of growth-promoting capital goods.

(2) We trace how savings move from the household sector to the business (or government) sector where they are spent.

(3) We note the effects of transfer payments on the flow of spending, and learn how profits can be returned to create new demand.

Our model of a circular flow economy which buys back all of its output by spending all of its receipts begins to explain how our economic system works—and why sometimes it does not work. Yet it leaves us in the dark with respect to the central question of growth, for an economy that merely bought back all its output by spending all its receipts would not grow. It would remain in place, reproducing itself from year to year. If we want to put growth into the picture we have to add something that has so far been lacking from our exposition.

Moreover, we know what is lacking from our circular flow model. It is the process of saving and investing by which we add more capital and better capital—the key to economic growth. Therefore, in this chapter we are going to connect the previous analysis of how the macrosystem works with our central concern with understanding growth.

THE MEANING OF SAVING

We begin by making sure that we understand a key word—*saving*. Saving, for an economist, cannot be defined just as putting money in the bank. Rather, it is refraining from spending *all or part of income for consumption goods or services*. It should be very clear then why saving is such a key term. In our discussion of the circular flow, it became apparent that expenditure was the critical link in the steady operation of the economy. If saving is not-spending, then it would seem that saving could be the cause of just that kind of downward spiral of which we caught a glimpse in our preceding chapter.

And yet this clearly is not the whole story. The act of investing—of spending money to direct factors into the production of capital goods—requires an act of saving. **We must save—that is, not use all our income for consumption—if we are to have the ability to hire factors to build capital goods. A society that did no saving would have no way of breaking out of a stationary circular flow.**

Hence, saving is clearly necessary for the process of investment. Now, how can one and the same act be necessary for economic expansion and a threat to its stability? This is a problem that will occupy us during much of the coming chapters.

THE DEMAND DIAGRAM

Let us use a diagram to show how saving can create both a "gap" in demand and an "opening" for investment.

In Figure 10.1 we trace the flow of expenditure through the economy from left to right. On the left we start with three blocks showing the factor, tax, and depreciation costs that have been incurred by businesses and government agencies as costs of production. Now we are going to follow those costs as they become incomes to different sectors, and thereafter as they get translated into new demand through the act of expenditure.

Look at the blocks for taxes and depreciation first. Here we see that an amount of taxes becomes the exact equivalent amount of government receipts; and thereafter an equal amount of government expenditure. (We could think of this as a sum of indirect taxes that becomes the income of a city government and thereafter is all paid out as salaries to city employees.) Clearly there is no gap in demand here. But neither is there an opening for investment.

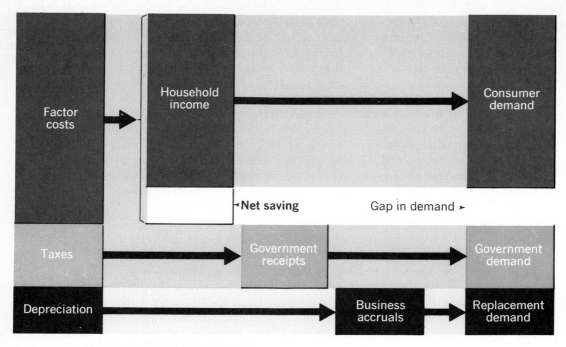

FIGURE 10.1 THE DEMAND GAP
We have used a circular flow type of diagram to show how a demand gap—and also an opening for investment—can arise. We assume that business and government spend all their receipts—of course that assumption may not be true. But it highlights the effects of saving in the household sector. This is the focus of our present investigation.

The same analysis applies to the bottom block. First we see the cost of depreciation, every penny of which becomes a receipt of the business sector, and all of which is spent as replacement investment. No gap here, and no net investment either.

THE GAP

But now look at the top block, representing factor costs. Every penny of those costs becomes factor income, as our diagram shows. This must be the case because all costs, as we know, are incomes. If households now spent all their income, there would be no gap here either, and we would have a stationary, circular flow economy. But our diagram shows that households save a part of their incomes. The result is precisely what we would expect. **There is a gap in demand introduced by the deficiency of consumer spending.** It begins to look as if we are approaching the cause of economic recession and unemployment. Yet whereas we have introduced net saving, we have forgotten about its counterpart, net investment. Cannot the investment activity of a growing economy in some way close the demand gap?

This is indeed, as we shall soon see, the way out of the dilemma. But before we trace the way investment compensates for saving, let us draw some important conclusions from the analysis we have made up to this point.

1. Any act of saving, in and by itself, creates a gap in demand, a shortage of spending. Unless this gap is closed, there will be trouble in the economic system, for employers will not be getting back as receipts all the sums they laid out.

2. The presence of a demand gap forces us to make a choice. If we want a dynamic, investing economy, we will have to be prepared to cope with the problems that net saving raises. If we want to avoid these problems, we can close the gap by urging consumers or corporations not to save. Then we would have a dependable circular flow, but we would no longer enjoy economic growth.

THE OFFSET TO SAVINGS

How, then, shall we manage to make our way out of the dilemma of saving? The diagram makes clear what must be done. If a gap in demand is due to the savings of households, then *that gap must be closed by the expanded spending of some other sector*. There are only two other such sectors: government and business. Thus in some fashion or other, the savings of one sector must be offset by the increased activity of another.

But how is this offset to take place? How are the resources that are relinquished by consumers to be made available to entrepreneurs in the business sector or to government officials? In a market economy there is only one way that resources or factors not being used in one place can be used in another. Someone must be willing and able to hire them.

Whether or not government and business *are* willing to employ the factors that are not needed in the consumer goods sector is a very critical matter, soon to command much of our attention. But suppose that they are willing. How will they be able to do so? How can they get the necessary funds to expand their activity?

INCREASING EXPENDITURE

There are six principal methods of accomplishing this essential increase in expenditure.

1. The business sector can increase its expenditures by *borrowing* the savings of the public through the sale of new corporate bonds.

2. The government sector can increase its expenditures by *borrowing* savings of the other sectors through the sale of new government bonds.

3. Both business and government sectors can increase expenditures by *borrowing* additional funds from commercial banks.*

4. The business sector can increase its expenditures by attracting household savings into partnerships, new stock, or other *ownership (or equity)*.

*Actually, they are borrowing from the public through the means of banks. We shall learn about this in Chapter 16.

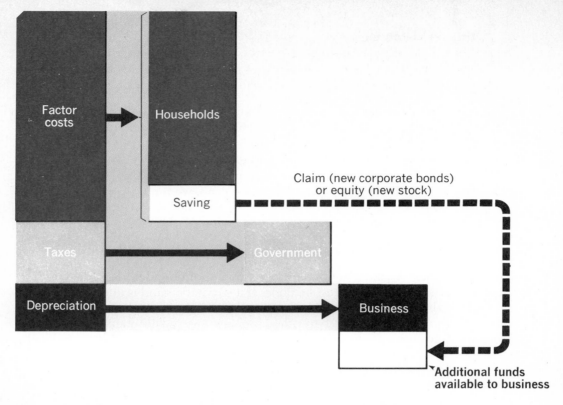

Claim (new corporate bonds)
or equity (new stock)

Additional funds
available to business

**FIGURE 10.2
TWO WAYS OF
TRANSFER-
RING SAVING
BETWEEN
SECTORS**

Here we depict the way a demand gap can be closed by transferring the savings of
one sector to another which will spend it. Our diagrams show how savings can go
into business, in exchange for claims (bonds or stock) or to government, in exchange
for government bonds.

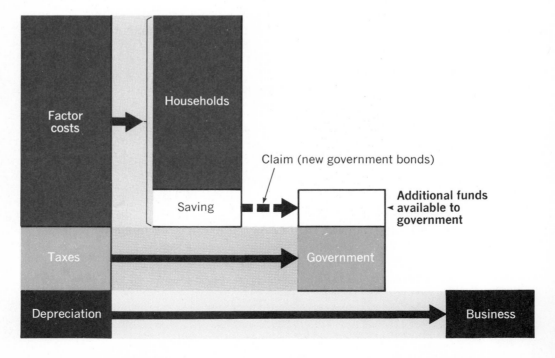

Claim (new government bonds)

Additional funds
available to
government

5. The government sector can increase its expenditures by *taxing* the other sectors. (We will see later why the increase in government spending is likely to be larger than the decreased spending caused by the taxes.)

6. Both business and government sectors can increase their expenditures by drawing on *accumulated past savings,* such as unexpended profits or tax receipts from previous years.

CLAIMS

The first four of these methods have one attribute that calls them especially to our attention. **They give rise to claims that reveal from whom the funds have been obtained and to whom they have been made available, as well as on what terms.** Bonds, corporate or government, show that savings have been borrowed from individuals, banks, or firms by business and government units. Shares of stock reveal that savings have been obtained on an equity (ownership) basis, as do new partnership agreements. Borrowing from banks gives rise to loans that also represent the claims of one part of the community against another.

PUBLIC AND PRIVATE BORROWING

Now let us look at the upper diagram in Figure 10.2. This shows what happens when savings are made available to the business sector by direct borrowing from households. Note the claim (or equity) that arises. If the government were doing the borrowing rather than the business sector, the diagram would look like the lower diagram in Figure 10.2. Notice that the claim is now a government bond.

We have not looked at a diagram showing business or government borrowing its funds from the banking system. (This process will be better understood when we take up the problem of money and banking, in Chapter 15.) The basic concept, however, although more complex, is much the same as above.

COMPLETED ACT OF OFFSETTING SAVINGS

There remains only a last step, which must now be fully anticipated. We have seen how it is possible to offset the savings in one sector, where they were going to cause an expenditure gap, by increasing the funds available to another sector. It remains only to *spend* those additional funds in the form of additional investment or, in the case of the government, for additional public goods and services. The two completed expenditure circuits now appear in Figure 10.3.

While Figure 10.3 is drawn so that the new investment demand or new government demand is exactly equal to net saving, it is important to understand that there is nothing in the economic system guaranteeing that these demands will exactly equal net saving. The desire for new investment or new government goods and services may be either higher or lower than new saving.

INFLATION AGAIN

This last point is absolutely essential. If the offsets of business plus government are not large enough to cover the gap, we will not succeed in buying back GNP at its actual cost and recession will ensue. It follows that if the offsets are larger than the gap, we will be spending more on GNP than it cost to produce and inflation may be the result, if the economy cannot expand its output.

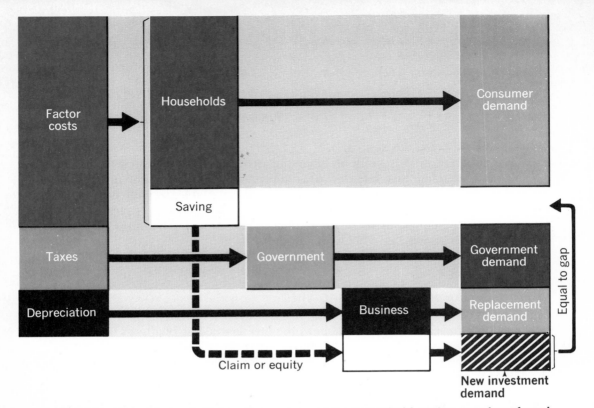

FIGURE 10.3 TWO WAYS OF CLOSING THE DEMAND GAP

There remains only to show how the savings of the household sector, now transferred to business or government, can be spent by these latter sectors to offset the gap in demand in consumption. Note: There is no guarantee that the offsets will just balance the savings. They may be too much, bringing us growth or inflation—or too little, bringing recession.

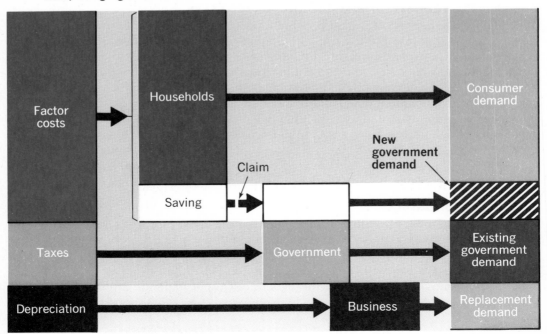

This is not yet a full explanation of either recession or inflation, because it does not explain why (or even how) offsets might be too large or too small. We need to understand more than we yet do about the money mechanism, especially in the case of inflation. But at least we are closer to seeing how the economy works—or fails to work—as a whole.

INTERSECTORAL OFFSETS

We would be getting a little ahead of ourselves if we stopped now to investigate recession or inflation. For we must first grasp the point that an economy which is working normally, in which saving takes place, *must* generate potential demand gaps, and that such an economy *must* offset those gaps if it is to function properly.

Once this simple but fundamental point is clearly understood, much of the mystery of macroeconomics disappears, for we can then begin to see that an economy in movement, as contrasted with one in a stationary circular flow, is one in which sectors must *cooperate* to maintain the closed circuit of income and output. In a dynamic economy, we no longer enjoy the steady translation of incomes into expenditure which, as we have seen, is the key to an uninterrupted flow of output. Rather, we are faced with the presence of net saving and the possibility of a gap in final demand. Difficult though the ensuing problems are, let us not forget that net saving is the necessary condition for the accumulation of capital. The price of economic growth, in other words, is the risk of economic decline.

TRANSFER PAYMENTS AND PROFITS

We have talked about the transfer of purchasing power from savers to investors, but we have not yet mentioned another kind of transfer, also of great importance in the overall operation of the economy. This is the transfer of incomes from sector to sector (and sometimes within sectors).

TRANSFERS

As we already know, income transfers, called *transfer payments,* are a very useful and important means of reallocating purchasing power in society. Through transfer payments, members of the community who do not participate in production are given an opportunity to enjoy incomes that would otherwise not be available to them. Thus Social Security transfer payments make it possible for the old or the handicapped to be given an income of their own (not, to be sure, a currently *earned* income), and unemployment benefits give purchasing power to those who cannot get it through employment.

Not all transfers are in the nature of welfare payments, however. The distribution of money *within* a household is a transfer payment. So is the payment of interest on the national debt.* So is the grant of a subsidy to a private enter-

---

*As we know, the payment of interest on corporate debt is not considered a transfer payment, but a payment to a factor of production. Actually, much government interest should also be thought of as a factor payment (for the loan of capital for purposes of public output); but by convention, all government interest is classified as a transfer payment.

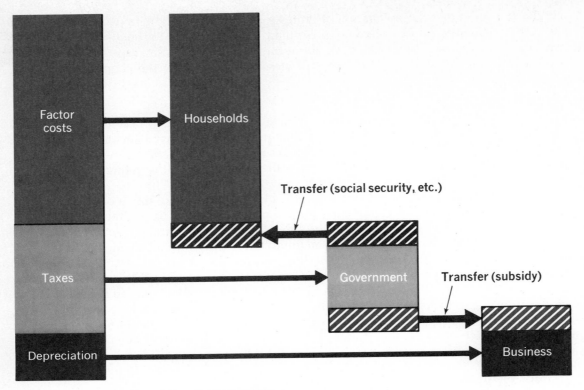

FIGURE 10.4 TRANSFER PAYMENTS
Transfer payments shift spending power from one sector (or group within a sector) to another. They do not increase production and therefore cannot increase incomes. But they can redistribute income, for reasons good and bad.

prise such as an airline, or of a scholarship to a college student. Any income payment that is not earned by selling one's productive services on the market falls in the transfer category.

It may help to understand this process if we visualize it in our flow diagram. Figure 10.4 shows two kinds of transfers. The upper one, from government to the household sector, shows a typical transfer of incomes, such as veterans' pensions or Social Security; the transfer below it reflects the flow of income that might be illustrated by a payment to agriculture for crop support. Transfers *within* sectors, such as household allowances, are not shown in the diagram.

One thing we may well note about transfers is that they can only rearrange the incomes created in the production process; they cannot increase those incomes. Income, as we learned in the last chapter, is inextricably tied to output—indeed, income is only the financial counterpart of output.

Transfer payments, on the other hand, are a way of arranging individual claims to production in some fashion that strikes the community as fairer or more efficient or more decorous than the way the market process allocates them through the production process. As such, transfer payments are an indispensable and often invaluable agency of social policy. But it is important to understand that no amount of transfers can, in themselves, increase the total that is to be shared. That can happen only by raising output itself.

TRANSFER PAYMENTS AND TAXES

We have mentioned, but only in passing, another means of transferring purchasing power from one sector to another: taxation. Heretofore we have often spoken as though all government tax receipts were derived from indirect taxes that were added onto the cost of production.

In fact, this is not the only source of government revenue. Indirect taxes are an important part of state and local revenues, but they are only a minor part of federal tax receipts. Most federal taxes are levied on the income of the factors of production or on the profit of business after the other factors have been paid.

Once again it is worth remembering that the government taxes the consumer (and business) because it is in the nature of much government output

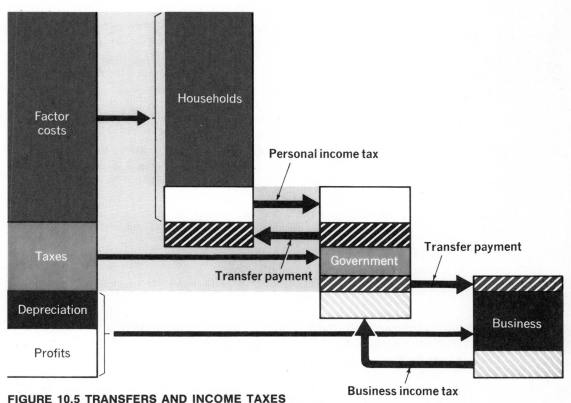

FIGURE 10.5 TRANSFERS AND INCOME TAXES
Direct (income) taxes are a kind of transfer—a redistribution from the private to the public sphere. The chart shows how complex the back-and-forth effect of taxes and transfers can be.

that it cannot be *sold.* Taxes are the way we are billed for our share—rightly or wrongly figured—of government production that has been collectively decided upon. As we can now see, taxes—both on business and on the household sector— also finance many transfer payments. That is, the government intervenes in the distribution process to make it conform to our politically expressed social purposes, taking away some income from certain individuals and groups and providing income to others. Figure 10.5 shows what this looks like in the flow of GNP. (Note that the business sector is drawn with profits, as our next section will explain.)

As we can see, the exchanges of income between the household and the government sector can be very complex. Income can flow from households to government units via taxation and return to the household sector via transfer payments; and the same two-way flows can take place between government and business.

PROFITS AND DEMAND

The last diagram has already introduced a new element of reality into our discussion. Taxes on business *income* presuppose that businesses make *profits.* Let us see how these profits fit into the savings-investment process.

During our discussion of the circular flow, we spoke of profits as a special kind of factor cost—a payment to the factor *capital.* Now we can think of profits not merely as a factor cost (although there is always a certain element of risk-remuneration in profits), but as a return to especially efficient or forward-thinking firms who have used the investment process to introduce new products or processes ahead of the run of their industries. We also know that profits accrue to powerful firms that exact a semimonopolistic return from their customers.

What matters in our analysis at this stage is not the precise explanation we give to the origin of profits, but a precise explanation of their role in maintaining a "closed-circuit" economy in which all costs are returned to the marketplace as demand. A commonly heard diagnosis for economic maladies is that profits are at the root of the trouble, in that they cause a withdrawal of spending power or income from the community. If profits are saved or retained within the firm, this can be true. In fact, however, profits are usually distributed in three ways. They may be

1. **Paid out as income to the household sector in the form of dividends or profit shares, to become part of household spending.**
2. **Directly spent by business firms for new plant and equipment.**
3. **Taxed by the government and spent in the public sector.**

All three methods of offsetting profits appear in Figure 10.6.

Thus, we can see that profits need not constitute a withdrawal from the income stream. Indeed, unless profits are adequate, business will very likely not invest enough to offset the savings of the household sector. They may, in fact, even fail to make normal replacement expenditures, aggravating the demand gap still further in this way.

Thus the existence of profits, far from being deflationary—that is, far from

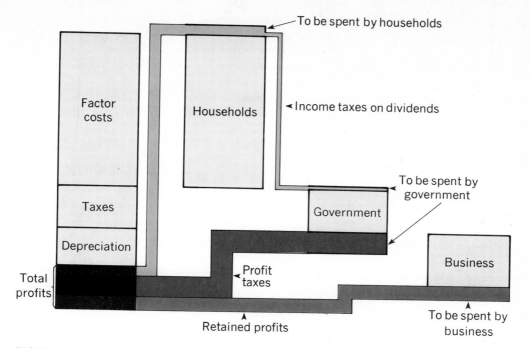

FIGURE 10.6 PROFITS IN THE CIRCULAR FLOW

There are three ways in which profits can be returned to GNP as expenditure: (1) by being distributed as dividends and spent by households; (2) by being taxed away and spent by government, and (3) by being directly spent by business for new investment.

---

causing a fall in income—is, in fact, essential for the maintenance of a given level of income or for an advance to a higher level. Nonetheless, there is a germ of truth in the contention of those who have maintained that profits can cause an insufficiency of purchasing power. For unless profits are returned to the flow of purchasing power as dividends that are spent by their recipients or as new capital expenditures made by business or as taxes that lead to additional public spending, there will be a gap in the community's demand. Unspent, hoarded profits are a drag on growth, but not invested profits.* Thus we can think of profits just as we think of saving—an indispensable source of economic growth or a potential source of economic decline.

SAVING, INVESTMENT, AND GROWTH

We are almost ready to leave our analysis of the circle of production and income to proceed to a much closer study of the individual dynamic elements

---

*Here we must distinguish between the individual firm and all firms together. An individual firm that saves its profits will usually put them in a bank and thereby make them available to other firms. But if all firms collectively hold onto their profits, trouble will result.

that create and close demand gaps. Before we do, however, it is well that we take note of one last fact of the greatest importance. In offsetting the savings of any sector by investment, we have closed the production and income circuit, much as in the stationary circular flow, but there is one crucial difference from the circular flow. Now we have closed the flow by diverting savings into the creation of *additional* capital. Unlike the stationary circular flow where the handing around of incomes did no more than maintain unchanged the original configuration of the system; in our new dynamic saving-and-investment model *each closing of the circuit results in a quantitative change—the addition of a new "layer" of capital.*

Hence, more and more physical wealth is being added to our system; and thinking back to our earlier chapters on the interaction of wealth and population, we would expect more and more productiveness from our human factors. Growth has entered our model.

LOOKING BACK

1. Saving is indispensable for investment. To save means to refrain from using all our income for consumption, thus freeing resources for use as capital wealth.

2. A circular flow economy has no gaps. But if we introduce the act of saving there will be some purchasing power that is not returned to the economy. Thus the act of saving, which is necessary for growth, creates the necessity to offset the gap it leaves in spending.

3. Demand gaps can only be offset if another sector increases its spending sufficiently to offset the gap. The second sector can do this by issuing claims or equities—such as bonds or stocks—that attract saving for its use.

4. Another form of intersectoral (and sometimes intrasectoral) transfer is a direct transfer payment—a redistribution of income from one group to another. Social Security is an example of such a transfer. So are welfare payments, subsidies to business, crop supports, and the like. Transfers may be very important in providing additional income for some persons, but cannot increase total income, because they are not payments that arise from production.

5. Profits can all return to the flow of demand, either as dividend payments, tax revenues, or as expeditures for investment. They are not, therefore, a source of insufficient purchasing power—unless they are not used. Hoarded, unspent profits lower demand; profits which are used do not.

6. The essential point is that intersectoral cooperation is necessary in any modern economy that has net saving. Saving creates the conditions for growth—and for decline. There must be offsets to demand gaps if GNP is not to decline. And needless to say, if the offsets are too large, inflation will follow.

ECONOMIC VOCABULARY

QUESTIONS

1. What do we mean by a demand gap? Show in a diagram. (And draw the diagram very, very carefully.)

2. In the same diagram show how this gap can be offset by business investment. Now show how the gap could have been filled by government spending.

3. Why is saving indispensable for investment? Can you think of any way in which a society could gather together the factors of production to undertake investment unless it had performed an act of saving? From this point of view, what does "saving" mean?

4. Can we have an act of saving without an act of investment?

5. Diagram the three ways in which business profits can be returned to the expenditure flow. What happens if they are not returned?

SECTION 2: The Determination of Income

Chapter

11 CONSUMPTION DEMAND

A LOOK AHEAD

With this chapter we begin to investigate the way in which the different sectors—household, business, and government—"work."

(1) There is one essential economic fact to be mastered in this chapter. It has to do with the basic passivity of consumption—the fact that consumption has generally followed income and has rarely been an independent economic force of its own.

(2) There is a new relationship, and its associated vocabulary, to learn: The propensity to consume describes how we divide our income between consumption and saving. The *average* propensity to consume describes the division of our total income; the *marginal* propensity to consume describes the division of any changes in our income.

(3) Putting together the propensity to consume and the idea of consumption's passivity we will arrive at a consumption function—a simple mathematical way of depicting how the nation's consumption relates to its income.

With a basic understanding of the crucial role of expenditure and of the complex relationship of saving and investment behind us, we are in a position to look more deeply into the question of the determination of gross national product. For what we have discovered so far is only the *mechanism* by which a market economy can sustain or fail to sustain a given level of output through a circuit of expenditure and receipt. Now we must try to discover the *forces* that dynamize the system, creating or closing gaps between income and outgo. What causes a demand for the goods and services measured in the GNP? Let us begin to answer that question by examining the flow of demand most familiar to us—consumption.

THE HOUSEHOLD SECTOR

Largest and in many respects most important of all the sectors in the economy is that of the nation's households—that is, its families and single-dwelling individuals (the two categories together called consumer units) considered as receivers of income and transfer payments* or as savers and spenders of money for consumption.

How big is this sector? In 1979 it comprised some 59 million families and some 21 million independent individuals who collectively gathered in $1920 billion in income and spent $1503 billion. As Figure 11.1 shows, the great bulk of receipts was from factor earnings, and transfer payments played only a relatively small role. **As we can also see, we must subtract personal tax payments from household income (or *personal income* as it is officially designated) before we get *disposable personal income*—income actually available for spending.** It is from disposable personal income that the crucial choice is made to spend or save. Notice the presence of savings in the bar on the right. This is the source of a demand gap that other sectors will have to fill.

SUBCOMPONENTS OF CONSUMPTION

Finally we see that consumer spending itself divides into three main streams. The largest of these is for **nondurable** goods, such as food and clothing or other items whose economic life is (or is assumed to be) short. Second largest is an assortment of expenditures we call consumer **services,** comprising things such as rent, doctors' or lawyers' or barbers' ministrations, theater or movie admissions, bus or taxi or plane transportation, and other purchases that are not a physical good but work performed by someone or some equipment. Last is a substream of expenditure for consumer **durable** goods, which, as the name suggests, include items such as cars or household appliances whose economic life is considerably greater than that of most nondurables. We can think of these goods as comprising consumers' physical capital.

There are complicated patterns and interrelations among these three major streams of consumer spending. As we would expect, consumer spending for durables is extremely volatile. In bad times, such as 1933, it has sunk to less than 8 percent of all consumer outlays; in the peak of good times in the early 1970s,

---

*Remember that the word "transfer" refers to payments made unilaterally—that is, without any service being performed by the recipient. Social Security (or any pension) is a transfer payment. So are unemployment insurance, or business subsidies, or allowances paid to children.

All figures in billions*

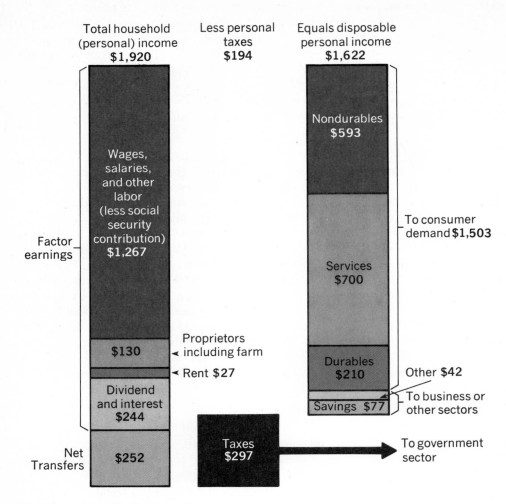

FIGURE 11.1
HOUSEHOLD
SECTOR,
1979

Totals do not always add, owing to rounding

Notice that the consumption flow chart shows that the sector is a net saver. Here is the source of a demand gap that other sectors must compensate for.

it came to nearly double that. Meanwhile, outlays for services have been a steadily swelling area for consumer spending in the postwar economy. As a consequence of the growth of consumer buying of durables and of services, the relative share of the consumer dollar going to soft goods has been slowly declining.

CONSUMPTION AND GNP

The internal dynamics of consumption are of great interest to someone who seeks to project consumer spending patterns into the future—perhaps as an aid to merchandising. But here we are interested in the larger phenomenon of the relationship of consumption as a whole to the flow of gross national product.

Figure 11.2 shows us this historic relationship since 1929. Certain things stand out.

1. **Consumption spending is by far the largest category of spending in GNP**

Total consumer expenditures—for durable goods such as automobiles or washing machines, for nondurables like food or clothing, and for services such as recreation or medical care—account for approximately two-thirds of all the final buying in the economy.

2. **Consumption is not only the biggest, but the most stable of all the streams of expenditure**

Consumption is *the* essential economic activity. Even if there is a total break-down in the social system, households will consume some bare minimum. Further, it is a fact of common experience that even in adverse circumstances, households seek to maintain their accustomed living standards. Thus consumption activities constitute a kind of floor for the level of overall economic activity. Investment and government spending, as we shall see, are capable of sudden reversals; but the streams of consumer spending tend to display a measure of stability over time.

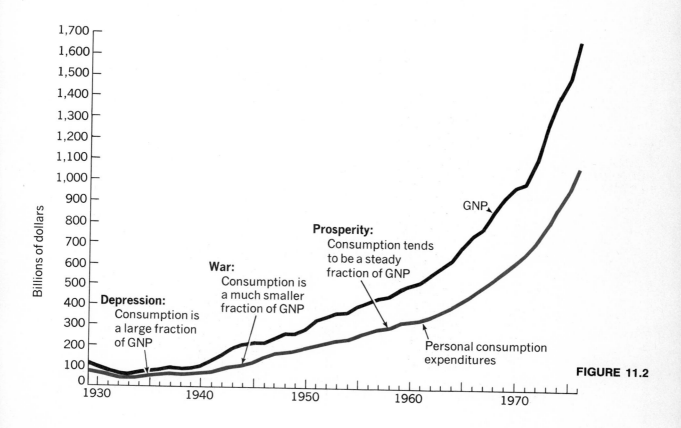

FIGURE 11.2

3. **Consumption is nonetheless capable of considerable fluctuation as a proportion of GNP**

Remembering our previous diagrams, we can see that this proportionate fluctuation must reflect changes in the relative importance of investment and government spending. And indeed this is the case. As investment spending declined in the Depression, consumption bulked relatively larger in GNP; as government spending increased during the war, consumption bulked relatively smaller. The changing *relative* size of consumption, in other words, reflects broad changes in *other* sectors rather than sharp changes in consuming habits.

To this broad generalization, we must make a partial exception for the behavior of consumption during inflation. As we shall see, consumption can take on a life of its own in periods when consumers buy in advance of their normal needs because they hope to beat expected price rises.

4. **Despite its importance, consumption alone will not "buy back" GNP**

It is well to recall that consumption, although the largest component of GNP, is still *only* two-thirds of GNP. Government buying and business buying of investment goods are essential if the income-expenditure circuit is to be closed. During our subsequent analysis it will help to remember that consumption expenditure by itself does not provide the only impetus of demand.

SAVING IN HISTORIC PERSPECTIVE

This first view of consumption activity sets the stage for our inquiry into the dynamic causes of fluctuations in GNP. We already know that the saving-investment relationship lies at the center of this problem and that much saving arises from the household sector. Hence, let us see what we can learn about the saving process in historic perspective.

SAVING AND INCOME

We begin with Figure 11.3 showing the relationship of household saving to disposable income—that is, to household sector incomes after the payment of taxes.

What we see here are two interesting facts. First, during the bottom of the Great Depression there were *no* savings in the household sector. In fact, under the duress of unemployment, millions of households were forced to dissave—to borrow or to draw on their old savings (hence the negative figure for the sector as a whole). By way of contrast, we notice the immense savings of the peak war years when consumers' goods were rationed and households were urged to save. Clearly, then, the *amount* of saving is capable of great fluctuation, falling to zero or to negative figures in periods of great economic distress and rising to as much as a quarter of income during periods of goods shortages.

In this graph we are struck by another fact. However variable the amounts, the savings *ratio* shows a considerable stability in normal years. This steadiness is particularly noteworthy in the postwar period. From 1950 to the mid 1970s, consumption has ranged between roughly 92 to 95 percent of disposable per-

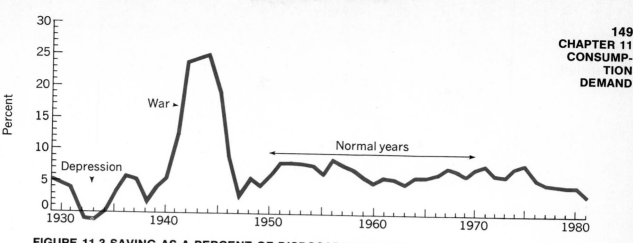

FIGURE 11.3 SAVING AS A PERCENT OF DISPOSABLE INCOME
The ratio of savings to disposable income is remarkably steady. This steadiness will become the basis of an important generalization about the macro behavior of the economy.

sonal income—which is, of course, the same as saying that savings have ranged roughly between 8 percent and 5 percent. If we take the postwar period as a whole, we can see that in an average year we have consumed a little more than 94 cents of each dollar of income and that this ratio has remained fairly constant even though our incomes have increased markedly.

SAVINGS AND INFLATION

You will notice, however, a drop in the savings rate starting in 1976. This is almost certainly the consequence of the worsening inflation rate of those years. As consumers came to anticipate rising prices, they tried to get ahead of the inflationary situation by buying in advance of normal needs, or by borrowing. After 1974, when we had our first taste of double-digit inflation, consumer credit rose precipitously, almost doubling from 1975 to 1980. The fall in savings, in other words, did not reflect a drop in real incomes but a shift in the propensity to consume. Whether this will be a permanent shift we will not know for some time.

LONG-RUN SAVINGS BEHAVIOR

The long-run stability of the savings ratio is an interesting, important phenomenon and something of a puzzling one, for we might easily imagine that the savings ratio would rise over time. Statistical investigations of cross sections of the nation show that rich families tend to save not only larger amounts, but larger *percentages* of their income, than poor families do. Thus as the entire nation has grown richer and as families have moved from lower income brackets to higher ones, it seems natural to suppose that they would also take on the higher savings characteristics that accompany upper incomes.

Were this so, the economy would face a very serious problem. In order to sustain its higher levels of aggregate income, it would have to invest an ever larger *proportion* of its income to offset its growing ratio of savings to income. As we shall see in our next chapter, investment is always a source of potential trouble because it is so much riskier than any other business function. If we had to keep on making proportionally larger investments each year to keep pace with our proportionally growing savings, we should live in an exceedingly vulnerable economic environment.

Fortunately, we are rescued from this dangerous situation, because our long-run savings ratio, as we have seen, displays a reassuring steadiness. In fact, there has been no significant upward trend in the savings ratio for the nation's households since the mid-1800s, and there may have been a slight downward trend. (See box.)

THE CONSUMPTION-INCOME RELATIONSHIP

What we have so far seen are some of the historical and empirical relationships of consumption and personal saving to income. We have taken the trouble to investigate these relationships in some detail, since they are among the most important causes of the gaps that have to be closed by investment. But the statistical facts in themselves are only a halfway stage in our macroeconomic inves-

SHORT-RUN VS. LONG-RUN SAVINGS BEHAVIOR

How do we reconcile the stability of the long-run savings ratio with the fact that statistical studies always reveal that rich families save a larger percentage of their incomes than do poor families? As the nation has moved en masse into higher income brackets, why has it not also saved proportionately more of its income?

The explanation for the long-run stability of savings behavior revolves around the importance of *relative* incomes, or "keeping up with the Joneses," in consumption decisions. If a family earned $20,000 in 1940, it was a wealthy family with an income far above the average. It could save a large fraction of its income and still have more than other families in the community had to spend on consumption. By 1980 the family with a $20,000 annual income was simply an average family. To keep up with consumption standards of other families in the community, it needed to spend a large fraction of its income. As a result, the savings rates for families with $20,000 gradually fell over time as the families changed from wealthy to average.

The same relative income effect is seen in the savings rates of black families. For any given income level, the average black family saves more than the average white family. Since black family incomes are lower than white family incomes, any given income has a higher relative position among blacks than it does among whites. To keep up with their peer group, whites must consequently spend more than blacks.

As a result of these and still other motivations, savings behavior in the long run differs considerably from that in the short run. Over the years, American households have shown a remarkable stability in their rate of overall savings. Its importance has already been mentioned. In a shorter period of time, however—over a few months or perhaps a year—households tend to save higher fractions of increases in their incomes than they do in the long run. The very great importance of this fact we shall subsequently note.

tigation. Now we want to go beyond the facts to a generalized understanding of the behavior that gives rise to them. Thus our next task is to extract from the facts certain behavioral *relationships* that are sufficiently regular and dependable for us to build into a new dynamic model of the economy.

If we think back over the data we have examined, one primary conclusion comes to mind. This is the indisputable fact that the *amount* of saving generated by the household sector depends in the first instance upon the income enjoyed by the household sector. Despite the stability of the savings ratio, we have seen that the dollar volume of saving in the economy is susceptible to great variation, from negative amounts in the Great Depression to very large amounts in boom times. Now we must see if we can find a systematic connection between the changing size of income and the changing size of saving.

PROPENSITY TO CONSUME

There is indeed such a relationship, lying at the heart of macroeconomic analysis. We call it the *consumption function* or, more formally, the *propensity to consume*, the name invented by John Maynard Keynes, the famous English economist who first formulated it in 1936* What is this "propensity" to consume? **It means that the relationship between consumption behavior and income is sufficiently dependable so that we can actually *predict* how much consumption (or how much saving) will be associated with a given level of income.**

We base such predictions on a *schedule* that enables us to see the income-consumption relationship over a considerable range of variation. Table 11.1 is such a schedule, a purely hypothetical one, for us to examine.

| | BILLIONS OF DOLLARS | |
Income	Consumption	Savings
$100	$80	$20
110	87	23
120	92	28
130	95	35
140	97	43

A typical propensity-to-consume schedule shows that savings and consumption both rise as income rises.

**TABLE 11.1
A
PROPENSITY-
TO-CONSUME
SCHEDULE**

One could imagine, of course, innumerable different consumption schedules; in one society a given income might be accompanied by a much higher propensity to consume (or propensity to save) than in another. But the basic hypothesis of Keynes—a hypothesis amply confirmed by research—was that the consumption schedule in all modern industrial societies had a particular basic configuration, despite these variations. **The propensity to consume, said Keynes, reflected the fact that on the average, people tended to increase their consumption as their incomes rose, but not by as much as their income increased. In other words, as the incomes of individuals rose, so did both their consumption** *and their savings.*

*See Chapter 2 for more on Keynes.

Note that Keynes did not say that the *proportion* of saving rose. We have seen how involved is the dynamic determination of savings ratios. Keynes merely suggested that in the short run, the *amount* of saving would rise as income rose—or to put it conversely again, that families would not use *all* their increases in income for consumption purposes alone. It is well to remember that these conclusions hold in going down the schedule as well as up. Keynes' basic law implies that when there is a decrease in income, there will be some decrease in the *amount of saving,* or that a family will not absorb a fall in its income entirely by contracting its consumption.

What does the consumption schedule look like in the United States? We will come to that shortly. First, however, let us fill in our understanding of the terms we will need for our generalized study.

AVERAGE PROPENSITY TO CONSUME

The consumption schedule gives us two ways of measuring the fundamental economic relationship of income and saving. One way is simply to take any given level of income and to compute the percentage relation of consumption to that income. This gives us the *average propensity to consume.* In Table 11.2, using the same hypothetical schedule as before, we make this computation.

The average propensity to consume, in other words, tells us how a society at any given moment divides its total income between consumption and saving. It is thus a kind of measure of long-run savings behavior, for households divide their incomes between saving and consuming in ratios that reflect established habits and, as we have seen, do not ordinarily change rapidly.

| BILLIONS OF DOLLARS | | Consumption ÷ Income (Av. propensity to consume) |
Income	Consumption	
$100	$80	.80
110	87	.79
120	92	.77
130	95	.73
140	97	.69

TABLE 11.2 CALCULATION OF THE AVERAGE PROPENSITY TO CONSUME

We calculate the average propensity to consume simply by dividing consumption by income.

MARGINAL PROPENSITY TO CONSUME

But we can also use our schedule to measure another very important aspect of saving behavior: the way households divide *increases* (or decreases) in income between consumption and saving. This *marginal propensity to consume* is quite different from the average propensity to consume, as the figures in Table 13.3 (still from our original hypothetical schedule) demonstrate.

Note carefully that the last column in Table 11.3 is designed to show us something quite different from the last column of the previous table. Take a given income level—say $110 billion. In Table 11.2 the average propensity to consume for that income level is .79, meaning that we will actually spend on consumption 79 percent of our income of $110 billion. But the corresponding figure opposite

BILLIONS OF DOLLARS				Marginal propensity to consume = Change in consumption ÷ change in income
Income	Consumption	Change in income	Change in consumption	
$100	$80	—	—	—
110	87	$10	$7	.70
120	92	10	5	.50
130	95	10	3	.30
140	97	10	2	.20

TABLE 11.3
CALCULATION
OF THE
MARGINAL
PROPENSITY
TO CONSUME

We calculate the marginal propensity to consume by dividing changes in our consumption by changes in our income.

$110 billion in the marginal propensity-to-consume table (11.3) is .70. This does *not* mean that out of our $110 billion income we somehow spend only 70 percent, instead of 79 percent, on consumption. It *does* mean that we spend on consumption only 70 percent *of the $10 billion increase* that lifted us from a previous income of $100 billion to the $110 billion level. The rest of that $10 billion increase we saved.

Much of economics, in micro- as well as macroanalysis, is concerned with studying the effects of *changes* in economic life. It is precisely here that marginal concepts take on their importance. When we speak of the average propensity to consume, we relate all consumption and all income from the bottom up, so to speak, and thus we call attention to behavior covering a great variety of situations and conditions. **But when we speak of the marginal propensity to consume, we are focusing only on our behavior toward** *changes* **in our incomes.** Thus the marginal approach is invaluable, as we shall see, in dealing with the effects of short-run fluctuations in GNP.

A SCATTER DIAGRAM

The essentially simple idea of a systematic, behavioral relationship between income and consumption will play an extremely important part in the model of the economy we shall soon construct. But the relationships we have thus far defined are too vague to be of much use. We want to know if we can extract from the facts of experience not only a general dependence of consumption on income, but a *fairly precise method of determining exactly how much saving will be associated with a given amount of income.*

Here we reach a place where it will help us to use diagrams and simple equations rather than words alone. So let us begin by transferring our conception of a propensity-to-consume schedule to a new kind of diagram directly showing the interrelation of income and consumption.

The *scatter diagram* (Figure 11.4) shows precisely that. Along the vertical axis on the left we have marked off intervals to measure total consumer expenditure in billions of dollars; along the horizontal axis on the bottom we measure disposable personal income, also in billions of dollars. The dots tell us, for the years enumerated, how large consumption and income were. For instance, if we take the dot for 1966 and look directly below it to the horizontal axis, we can

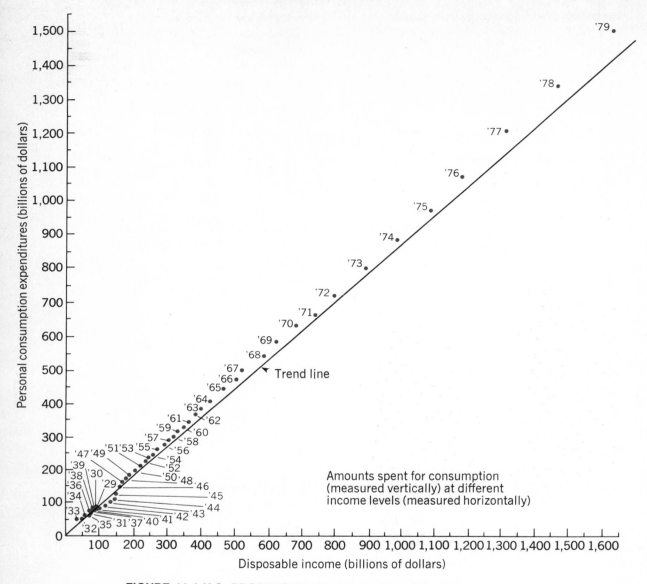

FIGURE 11.4 U.S. PROPENSITY TO CONSUME 1929–1979
A scatter diagram shows the functional relationship between two variables—in this case between consumption and income. The trend line is fitted by a statistical technique known as "the least squares method." The trend line shows us the average propensity to consume. We get a very rough (and not very accurate) idea of the marginal propensity to consume by noting the slope of the line between two consecutive years.

see that disposable personal income for that year was roughly $510 billion. The same dot measured against the vertical axis tells us that consumption for 1966 was a little more than $475 billion. If we now divide the figure for consumption by that for income, we get a value of 93.1 percent for our propensity to consume. If we subtact that from 100, our propensity to save must have been 6.9 percent.*

Returning to the diagram itself, we notice that the black line which fits the trend of the dots does not go evenly from corner to corner. If it did, it would mean that each amount of income was matched by an *equal* amount of consumption—in other words, that there was no saving. Instead, the line leans slightly downward, indicating that as income goes higher, consumption also increases, but not by quite as much.

Does the chart also show us marginal propensity to consume? Not really. As we know, our short-run savings propensities are higher than our long-run propensities. This chart shows our settled position from year to year, after the long-run, upward drift of spending has washed out our marginal (short-run) savings behavior.

Nevertheless, if we look at the movement from one dot to the next, we get some notion of the short-run forces at work. During the war years, for instance, as the result of a shortage of many consumer goods and a general exhortation to save, the average propensity to consume was unusually low. That is why the dots during those years form a bulge below the trend line. After the war, we can also see that the marginal propensity to consume must have been very high. As a matter of fact, for a few years consumption actually rose faster than income, as people used their wartime savings to buy things that were unavailable during the war. Between 1946 and 1947, for example, disposable income rose by some $9.8 billion, but personal outlays rose by almost $18 billion! By 1950, however, the consumption-income relationship was back to virtually the same ratio as during the 1930s.

THE CONSUMPTION FUNCTION IN SIMPLE MATH

There is another way of reducing to shorthand clarity the propensity to consume. Obviously, what we are looking for is a functional relationship between income (Y) the independent variable, and consumption (C), the dependent variable. In mathematical language we write

$$C = f(Y)$$

and we want to discover what f looks like.

Highly sophisticated and complex formulas have been tried to fit values of C and Y. Their economics and their mathematics are both beyond the scope of this book. But we can at least get a clearer idea of what it means to devise a *consumption function* by trying to make a very simple one ourselves. If we look at Figure 11.4 we can see that during the depression years, at very low levels of income, around $50 billion, consumption was just as large as income itself. (In some years it was actually bigger; as we have seen, there was net dissaving in

---

*It is difficult to read figures accurately from a graph. The actual values are: disposable income, $512 billion; consumption, $479 billion; average propensity to consume, 93.4 percent.

1933). Hence, we might hypothesize that a consumption function for the United States might have a fixed value representing this "bottom," plus some regular fraction designating the amount of income that would be saved for all income over that amount.

A GENERALIZED CONSUMPTION FUNCTION

This is a very important hypothesis. It enables us to describe the consumption function as an amount that represents rock-bottom consumption, to which we add additional consumption spending as income rises. If a is the bottom, and subsequent spending out of additional income is $b(Y)$, where b represents this spending propensity, we can now write the consumption function as a whole as:

$$C = a + b(Y)$$

We have seen that a is $50 billion, and we know that our actual spending propensity, b, is about 94 percent. Therefore, we can get a *very rough* approximation of consumption by taking $50 billion and adding to it 94 percent of our disposable income over $50 billion. In 1973 for example, disposable income was $883 billion. If we add $50 billion and .94 (883 − 50), we get $833. Actual consumption in 1973 was $828 billion.

Let the reader be warned, however, that devising a reliable consumption function is much more difficult than this simple formula would indicate. The process of translating economics into *econometrics*—that is, of finding ways to represent abstract theoretical relationships in terms of specific empirical relations—is a very difficult one. Nonetheless, even our simple example gives one an idea of what the economist and the econometrician hope to find: a precise way of expressing functional interrelations (like those between consumption and income), so that the relations will be useful in making predictions.

PASSIVITY OF CONSUMPTION

Throughout this chapter we have talked of the dynamics of consuming and saving. Now it is important that we recall the main conclusion of our analysis, the essential passivity of consumption as an economic process. Consumption spending, we will recall, is a function of income. This means it is a *dependent* variable in the economic process, a factor that is acted *on*, but that does not itself generate spontaneous action.

To be sure, it is well to qualify this assertion. For one thing, consumption is so large a fraction of total spending that small changes can bring large results. In 1974 and again in 1979 consumers held back on car purchases for fear of gasoline shortages, and the effect on automobile sales had considerable impact on GNP. And we have already called attention to the push exerted by inflation-induced consumption in the late 1970s.

Yet these are exceptions to the rule. During the normal course of things, no matter how intense wants may be, consumers ordinarily lack the spendable cash to translate their desires into effective demand. Brief swings in consumption—as for automobiles—may give rise to short-run fluctuations in saving, but these savings are short-lived and therefore cannot drive the economy upward or downward for any extended period of time. This is probably true for inflation-induced spending too.

CONSUMER CREDIT

What about consumer credit, someone will ask. Aren't many families in debt up to their ears? Doesn't the ability to buy "on time" enable consumers as a group to spend more than their incomes?

Consumer credit indeed enables families to spend a larger amount than they earn as incomes or receive as transfers, for short periods of time. During the late 1970s consumers have gone on a credit card binge, piling up unprecedented amounts of outstanding credit. Nonetheless, consumers do not use credit to spend more than their total receipts; some consumers do, but consumers as a group do not. We know this is true because the value of all consumption spending includes purchases that are made on credit, such as cars or many other kinds of items bought on household loans or on installment. But this total spending is still less than the total receipts of the consumer sector. Thus there continues to be net household saving, although the *rate* of saving has fallen.

Would there be more saving if there were no credit? In that situation, many families would put income aside until they had accumulated enough to buy cars, refrigerators, houses, and other big items. During the period that they were saving up to buy these goods, their savings rates would certainly be higher than if they had consumer credit at their disposal. But after they had bought their "lumpy" goods, their savings rates would again fall, perhaps below the level of a consumer credit economy, which tempts us to buy lumpy items and to perform our saving through installment payments.

As a result, we would expect to find high savings rates in an economy where desires for lumpy items were increasing but where consumer credit was not available. Economists cite this as one explanation of the fact that Japanese families have savings rates that are more than three times as high as American families, even though Japanese incomes are lower. In Japan you cannot "buy now, pay later"; so you save now and buy later.

This highlights an extremely important point. Wants and appetites *alone* do not drive the economy upward; if they did, we should experience a more impelling demand in depressions, when people are hungry, than in booms, when they are well off. Hence the futility of those who urge the cure of depressions by suggesting that consumers should buy more! There is nothing consumers would rather do than buy more, if only they could. Let us not forget, furthermore, that consumers are at all times being cajoled and exhorted to increase their expenditures by the multibillion dollar pressures exerted by the advertising industry.

The trouble is, however, that consumers cannot buy more unless they have more incomes to buy with. Of course, for short periods they can borrow or they may temporarily sharply reduce their rate of savings; but each household's borrowing capacity or accumulated savings are limited, so that once these bursts are over, the steady habitual ways of saving and spending are apt to reassert themselves.

Thus it is clear that in considering the consumer sector we study a part of the economy that, however ultimately important, is not in itself the source of major changes in activity. Consumption mirrors and, as we shall see, can magnify disturbances elsewhere in the economy, but it does not initiate the greater part of our long-run economic fortunes or misfortunes.

LOOKING BACK

1. The household sector is the largest of the components of GNP. Household income is called disposable personal income—it is factor earnings after taxes. Household expenditures are called consumption. The main categories of consumption are nondurables, durables, and services. Altogether consumption spending is the biggest and the steadiest of the GNP flows.

2. Despite its steadiness and size, however, consumption fluctuates and will not buy back GNP.

3. Savings behavior is very steady over the long run. We tend to save about 4 to 8 percent of our incomes, except for exceptional periods such as war, depression, or inflation. This long-run stability is probably attributable to the sociological factor known as "keeping up with the Joneses." Inflation may be changing these spending habits.

4. The relation between saving and income is called the propensity to consume. The words themselves simply mean the ratio into which we divide income between consumption and saving. But the behavior hypothesis of the propensity to consume is that _increases_ in income are never entirely spent or entirely saved, but are used for both spending and saving in regular, predictable ways.

5. The measure of the relation between any given level of income and its associated level of consumption is called the average propensity to consume. The relation between a change in income and the associated change in saving or consumption is called the marginal propensity to consume.

6. The generally accepted hypothesis about consumption behavior is that there is a "bottom"—a level of consumption that will be maintained (for a while) even if income falls below consumer spending by using up past saving to maintain a minimum standard of living. Additional income over this bottom will be divided in some regular way between consumption and saving. The bottom is designated _a_. The division of income (_Y_) between consumption and saving is designed _b_. Thus we write the consumption function as $C = a + b(Y)$.

7. Although changes in consumption can exert considerable effects on GNP because of the size of total consumption, consumption is usually a passive element in the flow. It is _Y_ that is the independent variable, not _C_.

ECONOMIC VOCABULARY

1. Why are some components of consumption more dynamic than others? Why, for instance, does the demand for durables fluctuate more widely than that for services? (Has *durability* something to do with it?)

2. "The reason we have depressions is that consumption isn't big enough to buy the output of our farms and factories." What is wrong about this statement? Is it *all* wrong?

3. Suppose a family has an income of $10,000 and saves $500. What is its average propensity to consume? Can you tell from this information what its marginal propensity to consume is?

4. Suppose the same family now increases its income to $12,000 and its saving to $750. What is its new propensity to consume? Now can you figure out its marginal propensity to consume?

5. Draw a scatter diagram to show the following:

Family income	Savings
$4,000	$ 0
5,000	50
6,000	150
7,000	300
8,000	500

From the figures above, calculate the average propensity to consume at each level of income. Can you calculate the marginal propensity to consume for each jump in income?

AN EXTRA WORD ABOUT
AID IN CASH OR KIND

Over the past 15 years there has been a gradual expansion in the public provision of *private* consumption goods —not roads, but actual consumers' goods. For example, food stamps have risen from $.03 billion in 1965 to $4.6 billion in the 1978 budget. Government medical expenditures rose from $7 billion to $34 billion from 1965 to 1978. Why is the government getting increasingly involved in the distribution of private goods?

Food stamps and medical expenditures can both be viewed as income redistribution measures. Both raise the real incomes of recipients, who are mainly poor. But what arguments can be mustered in favor of giving the poor food or medical aid, rather than cash? Cash, such as welfare payments, could always be used to buy food or medical treatment; and it might yield a much higher real income to the recipient, if he or she did not happen to need food or medical assistance, but something else, such as better housing. Why force the poor to consume things that they may not rank at the top of their lists of needs?

There are two classic arguments in favor of aid-in-kind, rather than aid-in-cash. One is that the poor cannot be trusted to buy what is best for them. They may actually *need* food or medical care, it is said, but if given the money they will spend it on luxuries or liquor. Thus, by "tying" their aid, we are really doing them a favor.

Is this a valid argument? We need hardly point out that it involves value judgments. Indeed, the argument has a patronizing ring to it. To be sure, there probably are people on welfare who *would* spend a cash bonus for luxuries or liquor instead of food or medical help, although the poor are not alone in spending their incomes in ways that maximize short-run pleasures rather than long-run benefits.

The second argument for aid-in-kind is more sophisticated. It revolves around the distinction between luxuries and necessaries. As a society we have quite egalitarian beliefs about how necessaries should be distributed, but we have no such beliefs about luxuries. We look with favor on rationing of a very scarce "necessity," such as a new vaccine, but we easily tolerate a high degree of inequality in the distribution of new Cadillacs. This distinction puts us on the horns of a dilemma. If we distribute welfare through equal amounts of cash, we are helping to bring about a more egalitarian distribution of luxuries, since the poor are free to spend their money on luxuries if they wish. On the other hand, if we distribute cash welfare unequally, we are possibly contributing to the unequal distribution of necessities, where we would like the poor to get a "fair share."

Aid-in-kind is an effort to get around this dilemma. When we distribute medical care equally, we are lending support to the equal sharing of medical care, which we consider a necessity. When we distribute food stamps, we are actually printing a different kind of money, usable only for food, and distributing this money in special ways. Thus aid-in-kind ties egalitarianism to "necessaries."

Does this justify aid-in-kind? Most economists, including ourselves, would prefer to give aid in cash, allowing each recipient to do with it as he or she wished. But to the extent that the preferences of the public are to be taken into account—and the tax-paying public far outnumbers the recipients of aid—the distribution of aid-in-kind may commend itself simply because it seems to accord with the political and social wishes of the public, the supreme arbiter in these matters.

Chapter

12 INVESTMENT DEMAND

A LOOK AHEAD

Warning! This is a chapter that ought to be read twice. It contains ideas that are both new and important. What is more, the vocabulary is one that most of us are not used to.

(1) The vocabulary: Investment, unlike consumption, is not an activity we are familiar with at first hand; we have to learn to think of it in real terms, not financial ones.

(2) There are two new ideas, both much used by economists: a) The idea of the multiplier; you will want to learn the formula for the multiplier and to understand why it is determined by the marginal propensity to save. b) The idea of marginal efficiency; here you need to know about discounting future income—the key to understanding expected profit and the decision-making process behind investment.

(3) Most important of all: Investment gives us the first real insight into why the macro system can be unstable. It is not only the key to growth, but the key to booms and busts. That's the idea that will unify the pages ahead.

In studying the behavior of the consumption sector, we have begun to understand how the demand for GNP arises. Now we must turn to a second source of demand —investment demand. This requires a shift in our vantage point. As experienced consumers, we know about consumption, but the activity of investing is foreign to most of us. Worse, we are apt to begin by confusing the meaning of investment, as a source of demand for GNP, with "investing" in the sense familiar to most of us when we think about buying stocks or bonds.

INVESTMENT: REAL AND FINANCIAL

We had best begin, then, by making certain that our vocabulary is correct. **Investing, or investment, as the economist uses the term in describing the demand for GNP, is an activity that uses the resources of the community to maintain or add to its stock of physical capital.** It is the counterpart of the real activity of saving we learned about in Chapter 10.

Investment may or may not coincide with the purchase of a security. When we buy an ordinary stock or bond, we usually buy it from someone who has previously owned it, and therefore our personal act of "investment" becomes, in the economic view of things, merely a *transfer* of claims without any direct bearing on the creation of new wealth. A pays B cash and takes his General Output stock; B takes A's cash and doubtless uses it to buy stock from C; but the transactions between A and B and C in no way alter the actual amount of real capital in the economy. Only when we buy *newly issued* shares or bonds, and then only when their proceeds are directly allocated to new equipment or plant, does our act of personal financial investment result in the addition of wealth to the community. In that case, A buys his stock directly (or through an investment banker) from General Output itself, and not from B. A's cash can now be spent by General Output for new capital goods, as presumably it will be.

Thus, much of investment, as economists see it, is a little-known form of activity for the majority of us. This is true not only because real investment is not the same as personal financial investment, but because the real investors of the nation usually act on behalf of an institution other than the familiar one of the household. **The unit of behavior in the world of investment is typically the business firm, just as in the world of consumption it is the household.** Boards of directors, chief executives, or small-business proprietors are the persons who decide whether or not to devote business cash to the construction of new facilities or to the addition of inventory; and this decision, as we shall see, is very different in character and motivation from the decisions familiar to us as members of the household sector.

THE INVESTMENT SECTOR IN PROFILE

Before we begin an investigation into the dynamics of investment decisions, however, let us gain a quick acquaintance with the sector as a whole, much as we did with the consumption sector.

Figure 12.1 gives a first general impression of the investment sector in a recent year. Note that the main source of gross private domestic investment expenditure is the retained earnings of business; that is, the expenditures come from depreciation accruals or from profits that have been kept in the business.

All figures in billions*

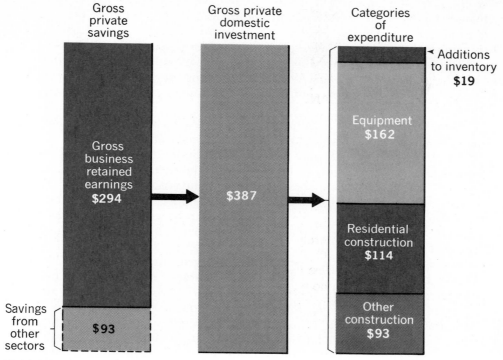

* Totals do not always add, owing to rounding

**FIGURE 12.1
BUSINESS
SECTOR
1979**

There is one essential difference between this flow chart and that for consumption. The consumption chart shows net saving—the source of a demand gap. Investment typically shows net spending—an excess of business expeditures over the retained earnings of business.

However, as the next bar shows, gross investment *expenditures* are considerably larger than retained earnings. The difference represents funds that business obtains in the various ways—mainly borrowing or issuing new equity—that we discussed on page 133.

Our chart enables us to see that most gross investment is financed by business itself from its *internal* sources—retained earnings plus depreciation accruals —and that external sources play only a secondary role. In particular, this is true of new stock issues, which, during most of the 1960s and early 1970s, raised only some 3 to 8 percent of the funds spent by the business sector for new plant and equipment.

CATEGORIES OF INVESTMENT

From the total funds at its disposal, the business sector now renews its worn-out capital and adds new capital. Investment, as we know, is one of the main vehicles for growth. Let us say a word concerning some of the main categories of investment expenditure.

1. **Inventories**

At the top of the expenditure bar in Figure 12.1 we note an item of $19 billion for *additions to inventory*. Note that this figure does not represent total inventories, but only *changes* in inventories, upwards or downwards. If there had been no change in inventory over the year, the item would have been zero, even if existing inventories were huge. Why? Because those huge inventories would have been included in the investment expenditure flow of *previous* years when they were built up.

Inventories are often visualized as completed TV sets sitting in some warehouse. While some inventories are completed goods sitting in storage, most are in the form of goods on display in stores, half-finished goods in the process of production, or raw materials to be used in production. When a steel company adds to its stock of iron ore, it is adding to its inventories.

Investments in inventory are particularly significant for one reason. Alone among the investment categories, inventories can be *rapidly* used up as well as increased. A positive figure for one year or even one calendar quarter can quickly turn into a negative figure the next. **This means that expenditures for inventory are usually the most volatile element of any in gross national product.** A glance at Figure 12.2 shows a particularly dramatic instance of how rapidly inventory spending can change. In the fourth quarter of 1973, we were investing in inventories at an annual rate of over $20 billion. Five quarters later, we were working off inventories—*disinvesting* in inventories—by roughly the same amount. Thus, within a span of a year and a half, there was a swing of almost $50 billion in spending. Rapid inventory swings, although not quite of this magnitude, are by no means uncommon. Look at the change from June 30 to December 31, 1979.

As we shall see more clearly later, this volatility of investment has much significance for business conditions. Note that while inventories are being built up, they serve as an offset to saving—that is, some of the resources released from

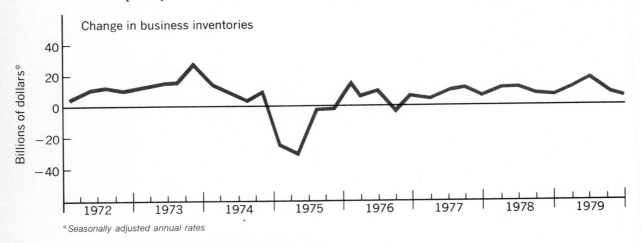

Seasonally adjusted annual rates

FIGURE 12.2 INVENTORY SWINGS
Inventories are a crucial portion of investment because they can change so rapidly
Compare 3Q (3rd quarter) 1973 with 2Q 1975!

consumption are used by business firms to build up stocks of inventory capital. But when inventories are being "worked off," we are actually making the demand gap bigger. As we would expect, this can give rise to serious economic troubles.

2. Equipment

The next item in the expenditure bar (Figure 12.1) is more familiar: $162 billion for *equipment*. Here we find expenditures for goods of a varied sort—lathes, trucks, generators, computers, office typewriters.* The total includes both *new equipment* and *replacement equipment*.

New equipment is obviously a very important means of widening and deepening capital—that is, of promoting growth. But let us take a moment to consider **replacement investment**. Exactly what does it mean to "replace" a given item of equipment? Suppose we have a textile loom that cost $100,000 and that is now on its last legs. Is the loom replaced by spending another $100,000, regardless of what kind of machine the money will buy? What if loom prices have gone up and $100,000 no longer buys a loom of the same capacity? Or suppose that prices have remained steady but that owing to technological advance, $100,000 now buys a loom of double the old capacity?

Such problems make the definition of "replacement" an accountant's headache and an economist's nightmare. At the moment there isn't even a generally accepted estimate of replacement investment. We need not involve ourselves deeper in the question, but we should note the complexities introduced into a seemingly simple matter once we leave the changeless world of stationary flow and enter the world of invention and innovation.

3. Construction—residential

Our next section on the expenditure bar (Figure 12.1) is total *residential construction*, another big growth item. But why do we include this $114 billion in the investment sector when most of it is represented by new houses that householders buy for their own use?

Part of the answer is that most houses are built by business firms, such as contractors and developers, who put up the houses *before* they are sold. Thus the original expenditures involved in building houses typically come from businesses, not from households. Later, when the householder buys a house, it is an existing asset, and his or her expenditure does not pump new incomes into the economy but only repays the contractor who *did* contribute new incomes.

Actually, this is a somewhat arbitrary definition, since, after all, business owns *all* output before consumers buy it. However, another reason for considering residential construction as investment is that, unlike most consumer goods, houses are typically maintained as if they were capital goods. Thus their durability also enters into their classification as investment goods.

Finally, we class housing as investment because residential purchases behave very much like other items of construction. Therefore it simplifies our

---

*But *not* typewriters bought by consumers. Thus the same good can be classified as a consumption item or an investment item, depending on the use to which it is put.

understanding of the forces at work in the economy if we classify residential construction as an investment expenditure rather than as a consumer expenditure.

4. Other construction—plant

Last on the bar, $92 billion of *other construction* is largely made up of the "plant" in "plant and equipment"—factories and stores and private office buildings and warehouses. (It does not, however, include public construction such as roads, dams, harbors, or public buildings, all of which are picked up under government purchases.) It is interesting to note that the building of structures, as represented by the total of residential construction plus other private construction, accounts for over half of all investment expenditures, and this total would be further swelled if public construction were included herein. This tells us that swings in construction expenditure can be a major lever for economic change.

INVESTMENT IN HISTORIC PERSPECTIVE

With this introduction behind us, let us take a look at the flow of investment, not over a single year, but over many years.

In Figure 12.3 several things spring to our attention. Clearly, investment demand is not nearly so smooth and unperturbed a flow of spending as consumption. Note that gross investment in the depths of the Depression virtually disappeared—that we almost failed to *maintain*, much less add to, our stock of wealth. (Net investment was, in fact, a negative figure for several years.) Note also investment was reduced during the war years as private capital formation was deliberately limited through government allocations.

Four important conclusions emerge from this examination of investment spending:

First, as we have many times stressed, investment is a major vehicle for growth. The upward sweep of investment is a basic explanation of our long-run rising GNP.

Second, as we have already seen, investment spending contains a component—net additions to inventory—that is capable of drastic, sudden shifts. This accounts for much of the wavelike movement of the total flow of investment expenditure.

Third, investment spending as a whole is capable of more or less total collapses of a severity and degree that are never to be found in consumption.

Fourth, unlike household spending, investment can fluctuate independently of income. It may rise when GNP is low, perhaps to usher in a boom. It can fall when GNP is high, perhaps to trigger a recession. It is an independent variable in the determination of demand.

The prime example of such a collapse was, of course, the Great Depression. From 1929 to 1933, while consumption fell by 41 percent, investment fell by *91 percent,* as we can see in Figure 12.3. At the bottom of the Great Depression in 1933, it was estimated that one-third of total unemployment was directly associated with the shrinkage in the capital goods industry. Conversely, whereas consumption rose by a little more than half from 1933 to 1940, investment in the same period rose by *nine times.*

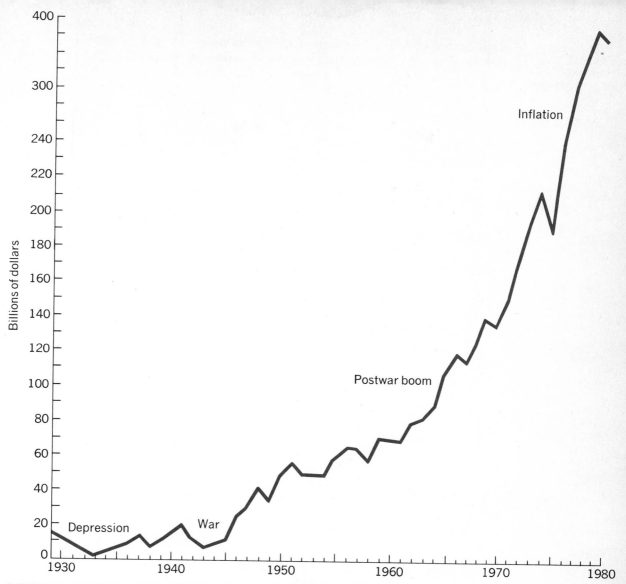

FIGURE 12.3 GROSS PRIVATE DOMESTIC INVESTMENT 1929–1980
It is evident that investment is a much more volatile item than consumption. Look at the collapse in the Great Depression. The World War I trough was different—investment was pushed aside for war spending. Then came the great postwar boom—until the troubled 1970s.

THE MULTIPLIER

We shall look more closely into the reasons for the sensitivity of investment spending. But first a question must surely have occurred to the reader. For all its susceptibility to change, the investment sector is, after all, a fairly small sector. In 1979, total expenditures for gross private domestic investment came to less than one-seventh of GNP, and the normal year-to-year variation in investment spending in the 1960s and 1970s is only about 1 to 2 percent of GNP. To devote so much time to such small fluctuations seems a disproportionate emphasis. How could so small a tail as investment wag so large a dog as GNP?

SNOWBALL EFFECT

The answer lies in a relationship of economic activities known as the *multiplier*. **The multiplier describes the fact that additions to spending (or diminutions in spending) have an impact on income that is greater than the original increase or decrease in spending itself.** In other words, even small increments in spending can *multiply* their effects (whence the name).

It is not difficult to understand the general idea of the multiplier. Suppose that we have an island community whose economy is in a perfect circular flow, unchanging from year to year. Next, let us introduce the stimulus of a new investment expenditure in the form of a stranger who arrives from another island (with a supply of acceptable money) and who proceeds to build a house. This immediately increases the islanders' incomes. In our case, we will assume that the stranger spends $1,000 on wages for construction workers, and we will ignore all other expenditures he may make. (We also make the assumption that these workers were previously unemployed, so that the builder is not merely taking them from some other task.)

Now the construction workers, who have had their incomes increased by $1,000, are very unlikely to sit on this money. As we know from our study of the marginal propensity to consume, they are apt to save some of the increase (and they may have to pay some to the government as income taxes), but the rest they will spend on additional consumption goods. Let us suppose that they save 10 percent and pay taxes of 20 percent on the $1,000 they get. They will then have $700 left over to spend for additional consumer goods and services.

But this is not an end to it. The sellers of these goods and services will now have received $700 over and above their former incomes and they, too, will be certain to spend a considerable amount of their new income. If we assume that their family spending patterns (and their tax brackets) are the same as the construction workers, they will also spend 70 percent of their new incomes, or $490. And now the wheel takes another turn, as still *another* group receives new income and spends a fraction of it.

CONTINUING IMPACT OF RESPENDING

If the newcomer then departed as mysteriously as he came, we would have to describe the economic impact of his investment as constituting a single "bulge" of income that gradually disappeared. The bulge would consist of the original $1,000, the secondary $700, the tertiary $490, and so on. If everyone continued to spend 70 percent of his new income, after ten rounds all that would remain by way of new spending traceable to the original $1,000 would be about $28. Soon, the impact of the new investment on incomes would have virtually disappeared.

But now let us suppose that after our visitor builds his house and leaves, another visitor arrives to build another house. This time, in other words, we assume that the level of investment spending *continues* at the higher level to which it was raised by the first expenditure for a new house. We can see that the second house will set into motion precisely the same repercussive effects as did the first,

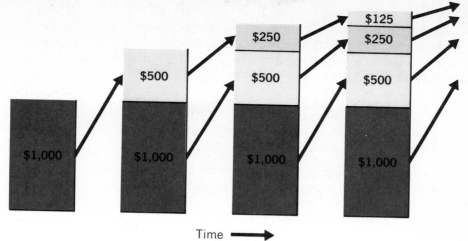

**FIGURE 12.4
THE
MULTIPLIER**

Time ⟶

This flow chart shows how respending creates additional income from one period to the next. This addition to income is called the multiplier. The size of the multiplier is the relation between the original new spending ($1,000) and the total new income created ($2,000). In this case the multiplier is 2.

and that the new series of respendings will be added to the dwindling echoes of the original injection of incomes.

In Figure 12.4, we can trace this effect. The succession of colored bars at the bottom of the graph stands for the continuing injections of $1,000 as new houses are steadily built. (Note that this means the level of new investment is only being maintained, not that it is rising.) Each of these colored bars now generates a series of secondary, tertiary, etc., bars that represent the respending of income after taxes and savings. In our example we have assumed that the respending fraction is 50 percent.

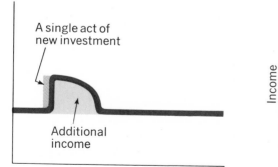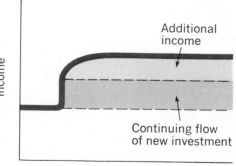

**FIGURE 12.5
ONCE-OVER
AND
CONTINUING
EFFECTS OF
INVESTMENT**

A single act of new spending creates a bulge in income that gradually disappears as successive receivers save part of their receipts and therefore do not respend them. A continuing flow of new spending creates a permanent addition to incomes that is larger than the new investment. Here the gradual retirement of new receipts into saving is offset by pumping out fresh additions to income.

Let us now examine the effects of investment spending in a generalized fashion, without paying attention to specific dollar amounts. In Figure 12.5, we see the effects of a single, *once-and-for-all* investment expenditure (the stranger who came and went), contrasted with the effects of a *continuing* stream of investment.

Our diagrams show us two important things:

1. A single burst of investment creates a bulge of incomes larger than the initial expenditure, but a bulge that disappears.

2. A continuing flow of investment creates a new steady level of income, higher than the investment expenditures themselves.

MARGINAL PROPENSITY TO SAVE

We can understand now that *the multiplier is the numerical relation between the initial new investment and the total increase in income.* If the initial investment is $1,000 and the total addition to income due to the respending of that $1,000 is $3,000, we have a multiplier of 3; if the total addition is $2,000, the multiplier is 2.

What determines how large the multiplier will be? The answer depends entirely on our marginal consumption (or, if you will, our marginal saving) habits —that is, on how much we consume (or save) out of each dollar of additional income that comes to us. Let us follow two cases in Figure 12.6. In the first, we will

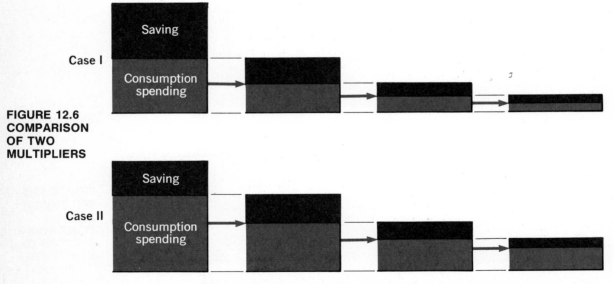

FIGURE 12.6 COMPARISON OF TWO MULTIPLIERS

The graph makes visually apparent the obvious fact that the amount we can respend is determined by the amount we save. Therefore, the lower our savings ratio, the higher the total of our respending. Or vice versa, high marginal propensities to save result in low multipliers.

assume that each recipient spends only one-half of any new income that comes to him, saving the rest. In the second case, he spends three-quarters of it and saves one-quarter.

It is very clear that the amount of income that will be passed along from one receiver to the next will be much larger where the marginal propensity to consume is higher. In fact, we can see that the total amount of new incomes (total amount of boxes below) must be mathematically related to the proportion that is spent each time.

What is this relationship? The arithmetic is easier to figure if we use not the consumption fraction, but the *saving fraction* (the two are, of couse, as intimately related as the first slice of cake and the remaining cake). If we use the saving fraction, the sum of new incomes is obtained by taking the reciprocal of (i.e., inverting, or turning upside down) the fraction we save. Thus, if we save ½ our income, the total amount of new incomes generated by respending will be ½ inverted, or 2 (twice the original increase in income). If we save ¼, it will be the reciprocal of ¼, or 4 times the original change.

BASIC MULTIPLIER FORMULA

We call the fraction of new income that is saved the *marginal propensity to save* (often abbreviated as mps). As we have just seen, this fraction is the complement of an already familiar one, the marginal propensity to consume. If our marginal propensity to consume is 80 percent, our marginal propensity to save must be 20 percent; if our mpc is three-quarters, our mps must be one-quarter. *In brief, mps + mpc ≡ 1.*

Understanding the relationship between the marginal propensity to save and the size of the resulting respending fractions allows us to state a very simple (but very important) formula for the multiplier:

$$\text{change in income} = \text{multiplier} \times \text{change in investment}$$

Since we have just learned that the multiplier is determined by the reciprocal of the marginal propensity to save, we can write:

$$\text{multiplier} = \frac{1}{\text{mps}}$$

If we now use the symbols we are familiar with, plus a Greek letter Δ, delta, that means "change in," we can write the important economic relationship above as follows:

$$\Delta Y = \left(\frac{1}{\text{mps}} \right) \times \Delta I$$

Thus, if our mps is ¼ (meaning, let us not forget, that we save a quarter of increases in income and spend the rest), then an increase in investment of $1 billion will lead to a total increase in incomes of $4 billion

$$\$4 \text{ billion} = 1 / \left(\frac{1}{\frac{1}{4}} \right) \times \$1 \text{ billion}$$

Note that the multiplier is a complex or *double* fraction:

it is $1/(\frac{1}{4})$ and *not* $1/4$.

If the mps is 1/10, $1 billion gives rise to incomes of $10 billion; if the mps is 50 percent, the billion will multiply to $2 billion. And if mps is 1? This means that the entire increase in income is unspent, that our island construction workers tuck away (or find taxed away) their entire newly earned pay. In that case, the multiplier will be 1 also, and the impact of the new investment on the island economy will be no more than the $1,000 earned by the construction workers in the first place.

LEAKAGES

The importance of the size of the marginal savings ratio in determining the effect that additional investment will have on income is thus apparent. Now, however, we must pass from the simple example of our island economy to the more complex behavioral patterns and institutional arrangements of real life. The average propensity to save (the ratio of saving to disposable income) runs around 6 to 7 percent. In recent years, the *marginal* propensity to save (the ratio of additional saving to increases in income) figured over the period of a year has not departed very much from this figure. If this is the case, then, following our analysis, the multiplier would be very high. If mps were even as much as 10 percent of income, a change in investment of $1 billion would bring a $10 billion change in income. If mps were nearer 6 percent—the approximate level of the average propensity to save—a change of $1 billion would bring a swing of over $16 billion. Were this the case, the economy would be subject to the most violent disturbances whenever the level of spending shifted. For example, the $50 billion swing in inventory investment from late 1973 to early 1975 would have produced a sixteenfold fall in GNP—a fall of $800 billion!

Taxes. In fact, however, the impact of the multiplier is greatly reduced because the successive rounds of spending are dampened by factors other than personal saving. One of them we have already introduced in our imaginary island economy. This is the tendency of *taxation* to "mop up" a fraction of income as it passes from hand to hand. This mopping-up effect of taxation is in actuality much larger than that of saving. For every dollar of change in income, federal taxes will take about 30 cents, and state and local taxes another 6 cents.

Business Saving. Another dampener is the tendency of respending to swell *business savings* as well as personal incomes. Of each dollar of new spending, perhaps 10 cents goes into business profits, and this sum is typically saved, at least for a time, rather than immediately respent.

Imports. Still another source of dampening is the tendency of consumers and businesses to increase purchases from abroad as their incomes rise. These rising *imports* divert 3 to 4 percent of new spending to foreign nations and accordingly reduce the successive impact of each round of expenditure.

The Effect of Leakages. All these withdrawals from the responding cycle are called *leakages,* and the total effect of all leakages together (personal savings, business savings, taxes, and imports) is to reduce the overall impact of the multiplier from an impossibly large figure to a very manageable one. In dealing with the multiplier equation ($\Delta Y = 1/\text{mps} \times \Delta I$), we usually interpret mps to mean the total withdrawal from spending due to all leakages. **The combined effect of all leakages brings the actual multiplier in the United States in the 1970s to a little more than 2 over a period of 2 years.**

To be sure—and this is very important—all these leakages *can* return to the income stream. Household saving can be turned into capital formation; business profits can be invested; tax receipts can be disbursed in government spending programs; and purchases from foreign sellers can be returned as purchases *by* foreigners. What is at stake here is the regularity and reliability with which these circuits will be closed. In the case of ordinary income going to a household, we can count with considerable assurance on a "return expenditure" of consumption. In the case of the other recipients of funds, the assurance is much less; hence we count their receipts as money that has leaked out of the expenditure flow, for the time being.

THE DOWNWARD MULTIPLIER

The multiplier, with its important magnifying action, rests at the very center of our understanding of economic fluctuations. Not only does it explain how relatively small stimuli can exert considerable upward pushes, but it also makes much clearer than before how the failure to offset a small savings gap can snowball into a serious fall in income and employment.

For just as additional income is respent to create still further new income, a loss in income will not stop with the affected households. On the contrary, as families lose income, they cut down on their spending, although the behavior pattern of the propensity-to-consume schedule suggests that they will not cut their consumption by as much as their loss in income. Yet each reduction in consumption, large or small, lessens to that extent the income or receipts of some other household or firm.

We have already noted that personal savings alone do not determine the full impact of the multiplier. This is even more fortunate on the way down than on the way up. If the size of the multiplier were solely dependent on the marginal propensity to save, an original fall in spending would result in a catastrophic contraction of consumption through the economy. But the leakages that cushion the upward pressure of the multiplier also cushion its downward effect. As spending falls, business savings (profits) fall, tax receipts dwindle, and the flow of imports declines. We shall discuss this cushioning effect when we look into the government sector.

All of these leakages now work in the direction of mitigating the repercussions of the original fall in spending. The fall in business profits means that less will be saved by business and thus less withdrawn from respending; the decline in taxes means that more money will be left to consumers; and the drop in imports similarly releases additional spending power for the domestic market. Thus, just as the various leakages pulled money away from consumption on the way up, on the way down they lessen their siphoning effect and in this way restore purchasing power to consumers' hands. As a result, in the downward direction as in the upward, the actual impact of the multiplier is about 2, so that a fall in investment of, say, $5 billion will lower GNP by $10 billion.

Even with a reduced figure, we can now understand how a relatively small change in investment can magnify its impact on GNP. If the typical year-to-year change in investment is around $10 billion to $20 billion, a multiplier of 2 will produce a change in GNP of $20 billion to $40 billion, by no means a negligible figure.

THE MULTIPLIER AND INFLATION

Is the multiplier an inflation-breeding process? It is easy to think so, because the very word "multiplier" suggests inflation.

But that is not a correct way of looking at the question. The multiplier itself only describes the outcome of a basic pattern of economic behavior—the fact that we spend part of any additional income we receive. In itself, respending is not inflationary. But two things could make it so:

(1) **If there are no more goods available—if we have reached a ceiling on production—then indeed our efforts to spend more money will only succeed in driving up prices.** Here is really "too much money chasing too few goods." But in that case the inflation-creating condition is the ceiling on production. The effort to use our income for more enjoyments is still perfectly normal.

(2) **If we begin to expect inflation and therefore spend more of our incomes than we ordinarily would, or if we rush to get rid of our income as soon as possible for fear that prices will be higher tomorrow, then indeed our spending pushes us toward inflation.** This kind of panicky spending is a very important perpetuating mechanism for inflation, and we will be considering it more carefully in our chapter devoted to inflation. But even here, it is the scary expectations that are the cause of inflation. The respending itself is a normal part of economic behavior.

THE DEMAND FOR INVESTMENT

Consumption demand, we remember, is essentially directed at the satisfaction of the individual—at providing him with the "utilities" of the goods and services he buys. An increasingly affluent society may not be able to say that consumer expenditure is any longer solely geared to necessity, but at least it obeys the fairly constant promptings of the cultural and social environment, with the result that consumer spending, in the aggregate, fluctuates relatively little, except as income fluctuates.

PROFIT EXPECTATIONS

A quite different set of motivations drives the investment impulse. Whether the investment is for replacement of old capital or for the installation of new capital, the ruling consideration is not apt to be the personal use or satisfaction that the investment yields to the owners of the firm. Instead, the touchstone of investment decisions is *expected profit*.

Note the stress on *expectations*. One firm may be enjoying large profits on its existing plant and equipment at the moment; but if it anticipates no profits from the sale of goods that an *additional* investment would make possible, the firm will make no additions to capital. Another firm may be suffering current losses; but if it anticipates a large profit from the production of a new good, it may launch a considerable capital expenditure. The view is never backward, but always forward.

There is a sound reason for this anticipatory quality of investment decisions. Typically, the capital goods bought by investment expenditures are expected to last for years and to pay for themselves only slowly. In addition, they are often highly specialized. If capital expenditures could be recouped in a few weeks or months, or even in a matter of a year or two, or if capital goods were easily transferred from one use to another, they would not be so risky and their dependence on expectations not so great. But it is characteristic of most capital goods that they *are* durable, with life expectancies of ten or more years, and that they tend to be limited in their alternative uses, or to have no alternative uses at all. You cannot spin cloth in a steel mill or make steel in a cotton mill.

The decision to invest is thus always forward-looking. Even when the stimulus to build is felt in the present, the calculations that determine whether or not an investment will be made necessarily concern the flow of income to the firm in the future. These expectations are inherently much more volatile than the current drives and desires that guide the consumer. Expectations, whether based on guesses or forecasts, are capable of sudden and sharp reversals of a sort rare in consumption spending. Thus in its orientation to the future we find a main cause for the volatility of investment expenditures.

THE DETERMINANTS OF INVESTMENT

We speak of consumption as a function of income because we know that there is a behavioral pattern that relates the flow of consumer spending to household incomes. Can we speak of a similar investment function relating capital spending to corporation incomes?

No such simple function exists. This is because 'the forward-looking nature of investment makes it inherently independent of past influences. Some investment is "induced" by past consumption—inventories, for example, may follow sales—but other investment is "autonomous"—quite independent of consumption. Much investment depends on technology, which is largely unpredictable. And other erratic or unknowable events also bring their effects to bear—the gyrations of the stock market, changes in the inflationary outlook, the ups and downs of foreign relations, and the like.

THE ACCELERATION PRINCIPLE

Nevertheless, investment expenditure is not just a random variable. There are patterns in investment, even though they may be upset by sudden, unforeseen shifts in total investment spending.

One such pattern of considerable importance is called the *acceleration principle*, or sometimes just the accelerator. The name springs from the fact that investment often depends upon the rate of growth of the economy.

Year	Sales (millions)	Existing capital (millions)	Needed capital (2 × sales) (millions)	Replacement investment (millions)	Induced new investment (2 × addition to sales) (millions)	Total investment
1	$100	$200	$200	$20	—	$20
2	120	200	240	20	$40	60
3	130	240	260	20	20	40
4	135	260	270	20	10	30
5	138	270	276	20	6	26
6	140	276	280	20	4	24
7	140	280	280	20	—	20
8	130	280	260	—	—	0
9	130	260	260	20	—	20

TABLE 12.1 A MODEL OF THE ACCELERATOR
The accelerator model shows how investment spending can fall, even though sales are rising. Compare the total amount of investment in the last column with the change in sales in the second column. In the third year sales are up by $10 million. But investment spending is down by $20 million!

Table 12.1 is a model that explains this phenomenon. It shows us an industry whose sales rise for six years, then level off, and finally decline. We assume it has no unused equipment and that its equipment wears out every ten years. Also, we will make the assumption that it requires a capital investment of $2 to produce a flow of output of $1.

Now let us see the accelerator at work.

In our first view of the industry, we find it in equilibrium with sales of, let us say, $100 millions, capital equipment valued at $200 millions, and regular replacement demand of 20 millions, or 10 percent of its stock of equipment. Now we assume that its sales rise to $120 millions. To produce $120 millions of goods, the firm will need (according to our assumptions) $240 millions of capital. This is $40 millions more than it has, so it must order new equipment. Note that its demand for capital goods now shoots from $20 millions to $60 millions: $20 millions for replacement as before, and $40 millions for new investment. Thus investment expenditures *triple,* even though sales have risen but 20 percent!

Now assume that in the next year sales rise further, to $130 millions. How large will our firm's investment demand be? Its replacement demand will not be larger, since its new capital will not wear out for ten years. And the amount of new capital needed to handle its new sales will be only $20 millions, not $40 millions as before. Its total investment demand has *fallen* from $60 millions to $40.

What is the surprising fact here? It is that *we can have an actual fall in induced investment, though sales are still rising!* In fact, as soon as the *rate of increase* of consumption begins to fall, *the absolute amount* of induced investment declines. Thus a slowdown in the rate of improvement in sales can cause an absolute decline in the orders sent to capital goods makers. This helps us to explain how weakness can appear in some branches of the economy while prosperity seems still to be reigning in the market at large. It will play a role when we come to explain the phenomenon of the business cycle.

Now look at what happens to our model in the eighth year, when we assume that sales slip back to 130 millions. Our existing capital (280 millions) will be greater by 20 millions than our needed capital. That year the industry will have no new orders for capital goods and may not even make any replacements, because it can produce all it needs with its old machines. Its orders to capital goods makers will fall to zero, even though its level of sales is 30 percent higher than at the beginning. The next year, however, if sales remain steady, it will again have to replace one of its old machines. Its replacement demand again jumps to 20 millions. No wonder capital goods industries traditionally experience feast or famine years!

There is, in addition, an extremely important point to bear in mind. The accelerator's upward leverage usually takes effect only when an industry is operating at or near capacity. When an industry is not near capacity, it is relatively simple for it to satisfy a larger demand for its goods by raising output on its underutilized equipment. Thus, unlike the multiplier, which yields its effects on output only when we have unemployed resources, the accelerator yields its effects only when we do *not* have unemployed capital.

INTEREST RATES AND COST OF INVESTMENT

There is a second element in the economy that imposes a certain degree of orderliness on investment. This is the influence of interest rates on investment.

Interest rates affect investment in two ways. The first is to change the costs of investment. If businesses must borrow to make capital expenditures, a higher rate of interest makes it more expensive to undertake an investment. For huge firms that target a return of 15 to 20 percent on their investment projects, a change in the interest rate from 10 to 11 percent may be negligible. But for certain kinds of investment—notably utilities and home construction—interest rates constitute an important component of the cost of investment funds. To these firms, the lower the cost of borrowed capital, the more stimulus for investment. The difference in *interest costs* for $1 million borrowed for 20 years at 10 percent (instead of 11 percent) is $200,000, by no means a negligible sum. Since construction is the largest single component of investment, the interest rate therefore becomes an important influence on the value of total capital formation.

INTEREST RATES AS A GUIDE TO DISCOUNTING

A second guide is offered to business not directly seeking to borrow money for investment but debating whether to invest the savings (retained earnings) of the firms. This problem of deciding on investments introduces us to an important idea: the discounting of future income.

Suppose that someone gave you an ironclad promise to pay you $100 a year hence. Would you pay him $100 *now* to get back the same sum 365 days in the future? Certainly not, for in parting with the money you are suffering an *opportunity cost* or a cost that can be measured in terms of the opportunities that your

THE STOCK MARKET AND INVESTMENT

How does the stock market affect business investment? There are three direct effects. One is that the market has traditionally served as a general barometer of the expectations of the business-minded community as a whole. We say "business-minded" rather than "business," because the demand for, and supply of, securities mainly comes from securities dealers, stockbrokers, and the investing public, rather than from nonfinancial business enterprises themselves. When the market is buoyant, it has been a signal to business that the "business climate" is favorable, and the effect on what Keynes called the "animal spirits" of executives has been to encourage them to go ahead with expansion plans. When the market is falling, on the other hand, spirits tend to be dampened, and executives may think twice before embarking on an expansion program in the face of general pessimism.

This traditional relationship is, however, greatly lessened by the growing power of government to influence the trend of economic events. Business once looked to the market as the key signal for the future. Today it looks to Washington. Hence, during the past decade when the stock market has shown wide swings, business investment in plant and equipment has remained basically steady. This reflects the feelings of corporate managers that government policy will keep the economy growing, whatever "the market" may think of events.

A second direct effect of the stock market on investment has to do with the ease of issuing new securities. One of the ways in which investment is financed is through the issuance of new stocks or bonds whose proceeds will purchase plant and equipment. When the market is rising, it is much easier to float a new issue than when prices are falling. This is particularly true for certain businesses—A.T. & T. is a prime example—that depend heavily on stock issues for new capital rather than on retained earnings.

Finally, when the market is very low, companies with large retained earnings may be tempted to buy up other companies, rather than use their funds for capital expenditure. Financial investment, in other words, may take the place of real investment. This helps successful companies grow, but does not directly provide growth for the economy as a whole.

action (to pay $100 now) has foreclosed for you. Had the going rate of interest been 10 percent, for example, you could have loaned your $100 at 10 percent and had $110 at the end of the year. Hence, friendship aside, you are unlikely to lend your money unless you are paid something to compensate you for the opportunities you must give up while you are waiting for your money to return. Another way of saying exactly the same thing is that we arrive at the *present value* of a specified sum in the future by discounting it by some percentage. If the discount rate is 10 percent, the present value of $100 one year in the future is $100 ÷ 110, or approximately $90.90.

DISCOUNTING THE FUTURE

This brings us back to the business that is considering whether or not to make an investment. Suppose it is considering investing $100,000 in a machine that is expected to earn $25,000 a year for 5 years, over and above all expenses, after which it will be worthless. Does this mean that the expected profit on the machine is therefore $25,000—the $125,000 of expected earnings less the $100,000 of original cost? No, it does not, for the expected earnings will have to be discounted by some appropriate percentage to find their present value. Thus the first $25,000 to be earned by the machine must be reduced by some discount rate; and the second $25,000 must be discounted *twice* (just as $100 to be repaid in *two* year's time will have to yield the equivalent of *two* years' worth of interest); the third $25,000, three times, etc.*

Clearly, this process of discounting will cause the present value of the expected future returns of the machine to be less than the sum of the undiscounted returns. If, for example, its returns are discounted at a rate of 10 percent, the business will find that the present value of a five-year flow of $25,000 per annum comes not to $125,000 but to only $94,700. This is *less* than the actual expenditure for the machine ($100,000). Hence, at a discount rate of 10 percent, the business would not undertake the venture.

On the other hand, if it used a discount rate of 5 percent, the present value of the same future flow would be worth (in round numbers) $109,000. In that case, the machine *would* be a worthwhile investment.

MARGINAL EFFICIENCY OF INVESTMENT

What rate should our business use to discount future earnings? Here is where the rate of interest enters the picture. Looking out at the economy, the business manager sees that there is a whole spectrum of interest rates, ranging from very low rates on bonds (usually government bonds) where the element of risk is very small, to high rates on securities of the same maturity (that is, coming due in the same number of years) where the risk is much greater, such as "low-grade" corporate bonds or mortgages. Among this spectrum of rates, there will be a rate at which he or she can borrow—high or low, depending on each one's credit worthiness in the eyes of the banking community. By applying that rate the manager can discover whether the estimated future earning from the venture, properly discounted, is actually profitable or not.

We can see the expected effect of interest rates on investment in Figure 12.7. Suppose that a businessman has a choice among different investment projects from which he anticipates different returns. The technical name for these discounted returns is the **marginal efficiency of investment**. Suppose he ranks those projects, as we have in Figure 12.7, starting with the most profitable (A) and proceeding to the least profitable (G). How far down the list should he go? The rate of interest gives the answer. Let us say that the rate (for projects of comparable risk) is shown by OX. Then all his investment projects whose marginal efficiency is higher than OX (investments A through D) will be profitable, and all

---

*The formula for calculating the present value of a flow of future income that does not change from year to year is:

$$\text{Present value} = \frac{R}{(1 + i)} + \frac{R}{(1 + i)^2} + \ldots + \frac{R}{(1 + i)^n}$$

where R is the annual flow of income, i is the interest rate, and n is the number of years over which the flow will last.

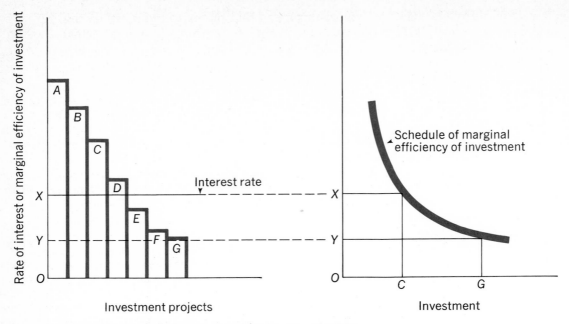

FIGURE 12.7 MARGINAL EFFICIENCY OF CAPITAL
A businessman calculates profitability by discounting the expected returns of various ventures. This gives him the marginal efficiency of those ventures. By comparing these marginal efficiencies with the rate of interest for projects of the same degree of risk, he can tell whether the opportunity cost of putting his money into the venture is worthwhile or not.

those whose marginal efficiency falls below *OX* (*E* through *G*) will be discarded or at least postponed.

Note that if the interest rate falls, more investments will be worthwhile; and that if it rises, fewer will be. As the figure on the right shows in generalized form, a fall in the rate of interest (e.g., from *OX* to *OY*) induces a rise in the quantity of investment (from *OC* to *OG*).

INTEREST AND INVESTMENT

Thus, whether we figure interest as a cost or as a guideline against which we measure the expected returns of a capital investment, we reach the important conclusion that low interest rates should encourage investment spending—or in more formal language, that investment should be inversely related to the rate of interest.

To be sure, the fact that a given investment, such as project *B* above, has a marginal efficiency higher than the interest rate is no guarantee that a business actually will undertake it. Other considerations—perhaps political, perhaps psychological—may deter management, despite its encouraging calculations. But assuredly a business will not carry out a project that yields less than the interest rate, because it can make more profit by lending the money, at the same degree of risk, than by investing it.

Real vs. financial investment

Four main forms of investment expenditure. Inventories as a source of investment instability

Differences of investment and consumption: expectations a key factor

**Investment exerts an upward or downward multiplier. The multiplier is determined by the respending fraction, mpc or its reciprocal mps.
mps ≡ 1–mpc**

Respending in itself is not inflationary

$$\Delta Y = \frac{1}{mps} \times \Delta I$$

**Leakages:
•savings
•imports
•taxes
•business profits—
•lower multiplier to about 2**

The acceleration principle links investment to increases in output. Investment may fall even though output is still rising

Interest rates affect investment through cost

Future income must be discounted to allow for opportunity cost. Interest rates are the guide to whether the marginal efficiency of a given investment is profitable

Low interest rates encourage investment

LOOKING BACK

1. By the term investment, economists usually refer to the use of resources to create new capital, not to using money to buy assets. Investment is crucial as the key to growth.

2. There are four main kinds of investment expenditure: equipment, residential construction, plant, and inventories. Equipment and construction, both for residential and nonresidential purposes, are important for growth. Inventory investment is often the cause of cyclical swings.

3. Investment is in large degree an independent, not a dependent, variable. It is subject to swings or even collapses of a kind unknown to consumption. Above all, investment is keyed to expectations of future profit, and not to past income.

4. Investment exerts a larger effect on GNP than the direct change in investment spending. This is because income created by new investment (or income reduced by a fall in investment) is multiplied. The multiplier depends on the degree to which the original change in investment is respent. This respending fraction is the marginal propensity to consume, or its reciprocal, the marginal propensity to save. Respending is normal, not inflationary. It creates inflation only when there is too little production or when respending becomes panicky.

5. The effect of a change of investment on GNP therefore depends on the mpc or the mps. The simplest way to calculate the multiplier is to use the formula $Y = 1/mps$. Do not forget that mps is itself a fraction: If mps = ¼, then the multiplier is 1 ÷ ¼ = 4.

6. The actual mps is not just determined by our personal savings. Imports, marginal taxes, and business savings also absorb increases in income and therefore lower respending. These are all leakages, which together reduce the actual effect of the multiplier to about 2 over the period of a year.

7. Although investment can be highly unstable, it does have some internal patterns and regularities. One of these is the accelerator or acceleration principle. This is a wave-like pattern that is induced in investment, to the extent that increases in output require ("induce") increases in investment. As output rises, induced investment at first rises faster; then investment may actually fall even though output is still growing.

8. Interest rates also influence investment spending. One obvious effect is that interest is a cost of investment.

9. Interest rates are also a guide to investment profitability. Businessmen discount the expected future earnings of investment, because future income represents an opportunity cost. Interest rates show the returns available for various kinds of risk. A businessman compares the discounted earnings of any project—its marginal efficiency —with the interest rate to see if it is worth the opportunity cost.

10. Whether as a cost, or as a guide to marginal efficiencies, interest rates encourage investment when they go down, discourage it when they go up.

ECONOMIC VOCABULARY

QUESTIONS

1. If you buy a share of stock on the New York Stock Exchange, does that create an equal amount of investment?

2. Why are inventories subject to such sudden shifts?

3. Why do we face the possibility of a large-scale collapse in investment spending but not in consumption spending?

4. Draw a diagram of boxes showing the multiplier effect of $100 expenditure when the marginal propensity to spend is one-tenth. Draw a second diagram showing the effect when the mps is nine-tenths. The larger the savings ratio, the larger or smaller the multiplier?

5. Calculate the impact on income if investment rises by $10 billion and the multiplier is 2. If it is 3. If it is 1.

6. A simple problem: Income is $500 billion. Inventories decline by $5 billion. The multiplier is 2. What is the new level of income?

7. Suppose you had the following leakages: mps, 10 percent; marginal taxation, 20 percent; marginal propensity to import, 5 percent; marginal addition to business saving, 15 percent. What will be the size of the second round of spending, if the first round is $1 billion? What will be the size of the third round? What will be the final total of new spending?

8. Explain the relationship between the marginal propensity to consume and the marginal propensity to save. Why must these two fractions always add up to 1?

9. Complete the following accelerator model, assuming that you need $2 of equipment to produce $1 of output, and that replacement is at 20 percent per year. Check back on page 176 if you need guidance.

Year	Output	Replacement investment	New equipment needed	Total investment
1	100	20	0	—
2	120	—	40	—
3	130	—	—	—
4	135	—	—	—

10. If the rate of interest were 10 percent, what would be the present value of $100 due a year hence? Two years hence? Remember: the first year's discounted value has to be discounted a second time.

AN EXTRA WORD ABOUT
THE EXPORT SECTOR

Before we go on to the problem of public demand, we must mention, if only in passing, a sector we have so far largely overlooked. This is the foreign sector, or more properly the sector of net exports.

If we lived in Europe, South America, or Asia, we could not be so casual in our treatment of foreign trade, for this sector constitutes the very lifeline of many, perhaps even most, countries. Our own highly self-sustained economy in which foreign trade plays only a small quantitative (although a much more important qualitative) role in generating total output is very much the exception rather than the rule.

In part, it is the relatively marginal role played by foreign trade in the American economy that allows us to treat it so cavalierly. But there is also another problem. The forces that enter into the flows of international trade are much more complex than any we have heretofore discussed. Not alone the reactions of American consumers and firms, but those of foreign consumers and firms must be taken into account. Thus comparisons between international price levels, the availability of foreign or domestic goods, credit and monetary controls, exchange rates—a whole host of other such considerations—lie at the very heart of foreign trade. To begin to unravel these interrelationships, one must study international trade as a subject in itself, and that we will defer until Chapter 21. Nevertheless, we should try to understand the main impact of foreign trade on the demand for GNP, even if we cannot yet investigate the forces and institutions of foreign trade as thoroughly as we might like.

IMPACT OF FOREIGN TRADE

We must begin by repeating that our initial overview of the economic system, with its twin streams of consumption and investment, was actually incomplete. It portrayed what we call a "closed" system, an economy with no flows of goods or services from within its borders to other nations or from other nations to itself.

Yet such flows must, of course, be taken into account in computing our national output. Let us therefore look at a chart that shows us the main streams of goods and services that cross our borders. (See Figure 12.8).

First a word of explanation. Exports show the total value of all goods and services we sold to foreigners. Imports show the total value of all goods and services we bought from foreigners. Our bottom line shows the net difference between exports and imports, or the difference between the value of the goods we sold abroad and the value we bought from abroad. This difference is called *net exports,* and it constitutes the net contribution of foreign trade to the demand for GNP.

If we think of it in terms of expenditures, it is not difficult to see what the net contribution is. When exports are sold to foreigners, their expenditures add to American incomes. Imports, on the contrary, are expenditures that we make to other countries (and hence that we do not make at home). If we add the foreign expenditures made here and subtract the domestic expenditures made abroad, we will have left a net figure that will show the contribution (if any) by foreigners to GNP.

THE EXPORT MULTIPLIER

What is the impact of this net expenditure on GNP? It is much the same as net private domestic investment. If we have a rising net export balance, we will have a net increase in spending in the economy.

Conversely, if our net foreign trade balance falls, our demand for GNP will decline, exactly as if the demand for domestic investment fell. Thus, even though we must defer for a while a study of the actual forces at work in international trade, we can quickly include the effects of foreign trade on the level of GNP by considering the net trade balance as a part of our investment demand for output.

One point in particular should be noted. If there is a rise in the net demand generated by foreigners, this will have a *multiplier effect,* exactly as an increase in investment will have. Here is, in fact, our illustrative story of an individual visiting an island (p. 168) come to life. Additional net foreign spending will generate new buying; and decreased net foreign spending will diminish incomes, with a similar train of secondary and tertiary effects. We will look into this problem again when we study the foreign trade difficulties of the United States in Chapter 21.

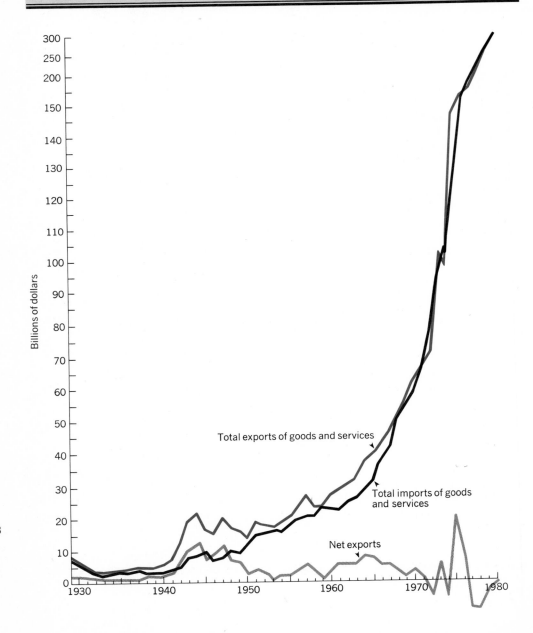

**FIGURE 12.8
EXPORTS,
IMPORTS,
AND NET
EXPORTS**

Chapter

13 GOVERNMENT DEMAND

A LOOK AHEAD

This chapter covers three main ideas:

(1) The way in which the public sector can offset a demand gap. Since the mechanics are exactly the same as the mechanics of the business sector, there will be no difficulty here.

(2) The question of how we finance a government deficit. Because national debts are not at all like the debts of households and businesses, there is something surprising to learn here.

(3) The question of how the government sector can be used to quicken or slow down the flow of GNP.

As we shall see, there are many problems in "demand management."

THE PUBLIC SECTOR

The government sector, taken as a whole, has changed from a very small sector to a very large one. In 1929, total government purchases of goods and services were only half of total private investment spending; in 1979 total government purchases were almost 25 percent *larger* than private investment. In terms of its contributions to GNP, government is now second only to consumption. Thus, the public sector, whose operation we will have to examine closely, has become a major factor in the economy as a whole.

KINDS OF GOVERNMENT SPENDING

Let us begin by learning to distinguish carefully among various aspects of what we call "government spending." As we shall see, it is very easy to get confused between *"expenditures"* and *"purchases"*; between *federal* spending and *total government* spending (which includes the states and localities); and between *war* and *nonwar* spending.

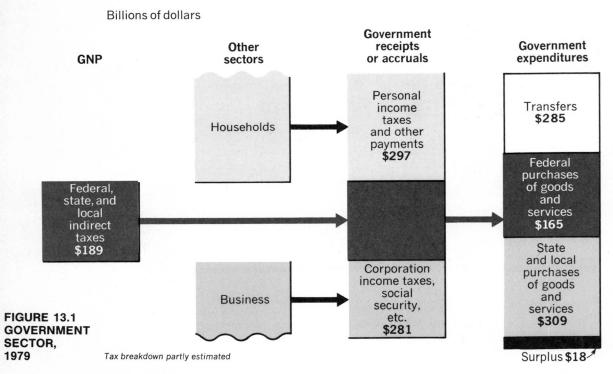

Billions of dollars

**FIGURE 13.1
GOVERNMENT
SECTOR,
1979**

Tax breakdown partly estimated

This familiar flow chart is different in one vital respect from those for consumption and investment. The consumption flow has a normal demand gap. The investment flow has a normal net contribution to demand. But the government flow can have either. It is possible to run the public sector at a surplus or a deficit. That is actually the theme of this chapter.

1. Government expenditures vs. purchases of goods and services

When we speak of government spending, we must take care to specify whether we mean total *expenditures of the government* or *purchases of goods and services.* The difference lies in the category we have called *transfer payments,* payments that are made to redistribute income, not to pay for work or for economic activity.

Transfers are a very important part of government spending. As Figure 13.1 shows, in 1979 the public sector spent $285 billion for transfer purposes. This includes Social Security payments, unemployment insurance, various agricultural and business subsidies, and the like. When we add up all the expenditures of government, including these transfers, the total is over $759 billion, or about one-third of GNP.

However we must remember that transfer payments only rearrange incomes. They do not directly create incomes through new production. Therefore if we want to measure the impact of government spending on GNP, we should exclude transfers. This gives us a total of $474 billion or about 20 percent of GNP.

2. Federal vs. state and local spending

The second distinction we must make is to differentiate between federal and nonfederal spending. If we take the total purchases of goods and services, we should note that $309 billion—just under two-thirds—arises from the expenditures of state and local governments, and only the remaining third from federal spending. Federal spending is larger than state and local only if we include transfers. When these payments are added in, federal spending becomes about a third larger than nonfederal.

It also makes a big difference whether we are speaking of federal or total government when we consider the deficit of the public sector. In Fig. 13.1 we can see a surplus of $18 billion for the public sector as a whole. That year, the federal budget was in deficit to the tune of $11 billion. But the public sector showed a surplus because state and local surpluses outweighed the federal budget enough to change the balance. To complicate things still more, the reason for the state and local surplus was partly the consequence of federal grants to the states. If the federal government had not helped out the states and localities, there would have been a federal surplus and a state and local deficit.

3. Welfare vs. warfare

A last caution has to do with the nature of federal spending. Much of the flow of federal purchases is connected with arms. Two-thirds of federal purchases in 1980 was for defense purposes. Despite the cry of an expanding federal government, Table 13.1 shows that federal purchases of nonwar goods and services are hardly a larger percentage of GNP than in 1940! Then why the outcry? The reason lies in the very marked growth of welfare services, many of them financed by state and local government as well as by federal government. These include health and medical programs, public educa-

Selected years	1929	1933	1940	1950	1960	1970	1976	1977	1978	1979	1980
Federal Purchases	1.4	3.8	6.1	6.5	10.6	9.7	8.1	7.6	7.1	7.0	6.9
Federal Expenditures (Purchases plus transfers)	2.5	7.2	10.0	14.3	18.4	20.8	23.3	22.2	21.6	21.4	22.5

TABLE 13.1 FEDERAL NONDEFENSE PURCHASES AND EXPENDITURES AS PERCENT OF GNP

The proportion of government spending for total purchases is still a small part of GNP. The relation of government expenditures (including transfers) has risen very much faster.

tion and housing, welfare assistance and Social Security. **Total welfare expenditures today come to about 20 percent of GNP, compared with less than 1 percent in 1929.**

TOO MUCH WELFARE?

Is this too high a level? There is no doubt that there exists a very strong anti-government sentiment in many parts of the nation today, evidenced in the tax revolt that has surfaced in a number of states. Much of this anti-government sentiment, it is only fair to point out, has a strong flavor of self-interest. City dwellers do not think that government spends too much on urban problems, but country dwellers do. Country dwellers do not think that government spends too much on agricultural problems, but city dwellers do. Couples with children do not want school expenditures cut, but childless couples do. Older people want higher Social Security benefits, but not younger people.

An economist has no special expertise that enables him to solve these essentially *political* problems. Economists can speak with some knowledge about the effects of various kinds of welfare spending—for example, the effects of unemployment insurance in making it less costly for someone to quit a job—but they cannot really pronounce on whether the effect is good or bad. That is a matter where value judgments come into play. We have set aside Chapter 20 to examine some of the issues in this tangled problem.

ECONOMICS OF THE PUBLIC SECTOR

However one feels about what government *should* do, it is vital to understand what it *does* do. This brings us away from the value-laden, political aspect of government spending to its objective, economic aspect. Economists who disagree sharply about the best government policy for the country can still agree in their understanding of how the public sector works. (Where they do not agree, we'll point out the bone of contention.)

MOTIVATIONS

Here the appropriate place to begin seems to be in the difference in *motivations* that guide public, as contrasted with private, spending. We recall that the motivations for the household sector and the business sector are lodged in the free decisions of their respective units. Householders decide to spend or save their incomes as they wish, and we are able to construct a propensity-to-consume schedule only because there seem to be spending and saving patterns that emerge spontaneously from the householders themselves. Similarly, business firms exercise their own judgments on their capital expenditures, and as a result we have seen the inherent variability of investment decisions.

But when we turn to the expenditures of the public sector, we enter an entirely new area of motivation. It is no longer fixed habit or profit that determines the rate of spending, but *political decision*—that is, the collective will of the people as it is formulated and expressed through their local, state, and federal legislatures and executives.

As we shall soon see, this does not mean that government is therefore an entirely unpredictable economic force. There are regularities and patterns in the government's economic behavior, as there are in other sectors. **Yet the presence of an explicit political will that can direct the income or outgo of the sector as a whole (especially its federal component) gives to the public sector a special significance. This is the only sector whose expenditures and receipts are open to deliberate control. We can exert (through public action) very important influences on the behavior of households and firms. But we cannot directly alter their economic activity in the manner that is open to us with the public sector.**

THE GOVERNMENT AS A BALANCING SECTOR

The basic idea behind modern fiscal policy is simple enough. We have seen that economic recessions have their roots in a failure of the business sector to offset the savings of the economy through sufficient investment. If savings or leakages are larger than intended investment, there will be a gap in the circuit of incomes and expenditures that can cumulate downward, at first by the effect of the multiplier, thereafter, and even more seriously, by further decreases in investment brought about by falling sales and gloomy expectations.

But if a falling GNP is caused by an inadequacy of expenditures in one sector, our analysis suggests an answer. Could not the insufficiency of spending in the business sector be offset by higher spending in another sector, the public sector? Could not the public sector serve as a supplementary avenue for the transfer of savings into expenditure?

As Figure 13.2 shows, a demand gap can indeed be closed by transferring savings to the public sector and spending them. The diagram shows savings in the household sector partly offset by business investment and partly by government spending. It makes clear that at least so far as the mechanics of the economic flow are concerned, the public sector can serve to offset savings or other leakages equally as well as the private sector.

How is the transfer accomplished? It can be done much as business does it, by offering bonds that individuals or institutions may buy with their savings. Unlike business, the government cannot offer stock, for it is not run as a profit-making enterprise. However, government has a source of funds quite different from business; namely, *taxes.* **In effect, government can commandeer purchasing power in a way that business cannot.**

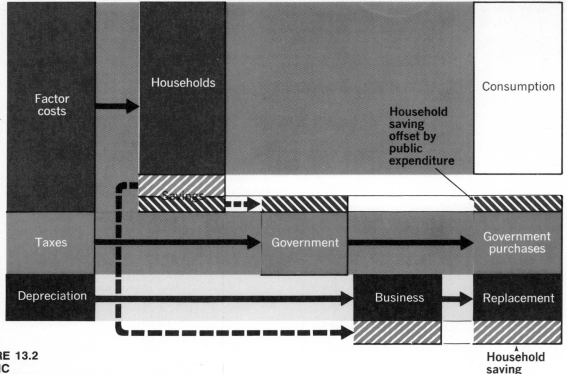

FIGURE 13.2 PUBLIC EXPENDITURE AND THE DEMAND GAP

The "economics" of filling a demand gap by government spending are exactly like those of investment spending. The "politics" are not.

Labels within figure: Factor costs, Households, Consumption, Household saving offset by public expenditure, Savings, Taxes, Government, Government purchases, Depreciation, Business, Replacement, Household saving offset by new investment

DEFICIT SPENDING

But isn't it inflationary when the government borrows money? It certainly can be, but economists of all shades of opinion agree that it need not be: It depends on many factors that we will take up, some in this chapter, some later.

First, however, we must understand exactly what it means for the government to borrow. **Any government that uses its budget as a stabilizing device must be prepared to spend more than it takes in in taxes. On occasion it must purposefully plan a budget in which outgo exceeds income, leaving a negative figure called a** *deficit.*

That raises a problem that alarms and perplexes many people. Like a business or consumer, the government cannot spend money it does not have. Therefore it must *borrow* the needed funds from individuals, firms, or banks in order to cover its deficit. Deficit spending, in other words, means the spending of borrowed money, money derived from the sale of government bonds.

DEFICITS AND LOSSES

Can the government safely run up a deficit? Let us begin to unravel this important but perplexing question by asking another: can a private business afford to run up a deficit?

There is one kind of deficit that a private business *cannot* afford: a deficit that comes from spending more money on current production than it will realize from its sale. This kind of deficit is called a *business loss;* and if losses are severe enough, a business firm will be forced to discontinue its operations.

But there is another kind of deficit, although it is not called by that name, in the operations of a private firm. This is an excess of expenditures over receipts brought about by spending money on *capital assets.* When the American Telephone and Telegraph Company or the Exxon Corporation uses its own savings or those of the public to build a new plant and new equipment, it does not show a loss on its annual statement to stockholders, even though its total expenditures on current costs and on capital may have been greater than sales. Instead, expenditures are divided into two kinds, one relating current costs to current income, and the other relegating expenditures on capital goods to an entirely separate capital account. Instead of calling the excess of expenditures a deficit, they call it investment.*

DEBTS AND ASSETS

Can A.T. & T. or Exxon afford to run deficits of the latter kind indefinitely? The answer is yes! To be sure, after a stated number of years, A.T. & T.'s or Exxon's bonds will come due and must be paid back. Perhaps the companies can do that out of their accumulated earnings. Usually, however, when a bond becomes due, a corporation issues *new* bonds equal in value to the old ones. It then sells the new bonds and uses the new money it raises to pay off its old bondholders.

Many big corporations such as Exxon or A.T. & T. do, in fact, continuously "refund" their bond issues, paying off old bonds with new ones, and never paying back their indebtedness as a whole. A.T. & T., for instance, actually increased its total indebtedness almost ten-fold between 1929 and 1980. Exxon ran up its debt from $170.1 million in 1929 to over $4 billion in 1980. And the credit rating of both companies today is as good as, or better than, it was in 1929.

GOVERNMENT DEFICITS

Can government, like business, borrow "indefinitely"? The question is important enough to warrant a careful answer. Hence, let us begin by comparing government borrowing and business borrowing.

One difference that springs quickly to mind is that businesses borrow in order to acquire productive assets. That is, matching the new claims on the busi-

---

*Investment does not *require* a deficit, since it can be financed out of current profits. But many expanding companies do spend more money on current and capital account than they take in through sales, and thereby incur a deficit for at least a part of their investment.

ness sector is additional real wealth that will provide for larger output. From this additional wealth, business will also receive the income to pay interest on its debt or dividends on its stock. But what of the government? Where are its productive assets?

We have already noted that the government budget includes dams, roads, housing projects, and many other items that might be classified as assets. During the 1960s, federal expenditures for such civil construction projects averaged about $5 billion a year. Thus the total addition to the gross public debt during the 1960s (it rose from roughly $240 billion in 1960 to $301 billion in 1969) could be construed as merely the financial counterpart of the creation of public assets.

Why is it not so considered? Mainly because, as we have seen, the peculiar character of public expenditure leads us to lump together all public spending, regardless of kind. In many European countries, however, public capital expenditures are sharply differentiated from public current expenditures. If we had such a system, the government's deficit on capital account could then be viewed as the public equivalent of business's deficit on capital account. Such a change might considerably improve the rationality of much discussion concerning the government's deficit.

SALES VS. TAXES

But there is still a difference. Private capital enhances the earning capacity of a private business, whereas most public capital, save for such assets as toll roads, does not make money for the public sector. Does this constitute a meaningful distinction?

We can understand, of course, why an individual business insists that its investment must be profitable. The actual money that the business will pay out in the course of making an investment will almost surely not return to the business that spent it. A shirt manufacturer, for instance, who invests in a new factory cannot hope that the builders of that factory will spend all their wages on the firm's shirts. The manufacturer knows that the money spent through investment will soon be dissipated throughout the economy and that even strenuous selling efforts will only recapture part of it.

Not so with a national government, however. Its income does not come from sales but from taxes, and those taxes reflect the general level of income of the country. Thus any and all money that government lays out, just because it enters the general stream of incomes, redounds to the taxing capacity or, we might say, the "earning capacity" of government.

Under today's normal conditions, the government will recover about half or a little more of its expenditure.* But in any event, note that the government does not lose its money in the way that a business does. Whatever goes into the income stream is always *available* to the government as a source of taxes; whereas

---

*We can make a rough estimate of the multiplier effect of additional public expenditure as 2 and of the share of an additional dollar of GNP going to federal taxes as about ⅓ (see p. 172). Thus $1 of public spending will create $2 of GNP, of which 67¢ will go back to the federal government.

whatever goes into the income stream is not necessarily available to any single business as a source of sales.

This reasoning helps us understand why federal finance is different from state and local government finance. An expenditure made by New York City or New York State is apt to be respent in many other areas of the country. Thus taxable incomes in New York will not, in all probability, rise to match local spending. As a result, *state and local governments must look on their finances much as an individual business does.* The power of full fiscal recapture belongs solely to the federal government.

INTERNAL AND EXTERNAL DEBTS

This difference between the limited powers of recoupment of a single firm and the relatively limitless powers of a national government lies at the heart of the basic difference between business and government deficit spending. It helps us understand why the government has a capacity for financial operation that is inherently of a far higher order of magnitude than that of business. We can sum up this fundamental difference in the contrast between the *externality of business debts* and the *internality of national government debts.*

What do we mean by the externality of business debts? We simply mean that business firms owe their debts to someone distinct from themselves—someone over whom they have no control—whether this be bondholders or the bank from which they borrowed. Thus, to service or to pay back its debts, business must transfer funds from its own possession into the possession of outsiders. If this transfer cannot be made, if a business does not have the funds to pay its bondholders or its bank, it will go bankrupt.

The government is in a radically different position. Its bondholders, banks, and other people or institutions to whom it owes its debts belong to the same community as that whence it extracts its receipts. In other words, the government does not have to transfer its funds to an outside group to pay its bonds. It transfers them, instead, from some members of the national community over which it has legal powers (taxpayers) to other members of the *same* community (bondholders). The contrast is much the same as that between a family that owes a debt to another family, and a family in which the husband has borrowed money from his wife; or again between a firm that owes money to another, and a firm in which one branch has borrowed money from another. **Internal debts do not drain the resources of one community into another, but merely redistribute the claims among members of the same community.**

To help bring home the point, imagine that you and your roommate exchange $1,000 IOUs. Each of you now has a $1,000 asset (an IOU from the other person) but each of you also has a $1,000 liability (the IOU each owes the other). The total debt of the room is now $2,000. But is your room richer or poorer, or is any individual in the room richer or poorer? The answer is obviously no. No one is better or worse off than before. And what happens if you now each pay off your IOUs? Once again no one is richer or poorer than before. The same thing is true at the national level. The national debt makes us neither richer nor poorer, since we (as taxpayers) owe it to ourselves (as bondholders).

THE POWER TO PRINT MONEY

Ultimately the federal government has the power to incur an unlimited deficit because it has the power to print money. If a local government such as New York City incurs too much debt, investors lose confidence in the ability of the city to buy back its bonds when they come due. Therefore they will refuse to buy the city bonds and the municipality can go bankrupt.

This cannot happen to the federal government because by constitutional authority it has the power to create money. It could, therefore, simply print up the money needed to buy back its own obligations!

Needless to say, this is a cure that might well be worse than the disease. We hear about "rolling the printing presses" as the worst symptom of inflation. If the government actually began printing money wholesale to buy its own bonds, there would be a flight from the currency—maybe from the country!—and the spectre of a runaway inflation might become a reality. We will discuss printing money again in Chapter 17. But we must recognize that the *unused* power of the printing press still reassures investors that they will never face default on a federal bond. It is odd, isn't it: The power to print money is the most important safeguard for government bonds—as long as it isn't used!

PROBLEMS OF GOVERNMENT SPENDING

We have spent enough time in gaining an understanding of the question of government deficit. It is time to return to the central question of this chapter—using the public sector as a means of keeping the economy moving ahead.

DEFICITS AND INFLATION

Again the pressing question is raised: Isn't government spending inflationary? We are now close enough to an overall understanding of macroeconomics so that we can see why economists agree that the answer is: sometimes yes, sometimes no. The reason is that government spending in itself is really no different from any other kind of spending. The check you receive from the Internal Revenue Service goes into your pocket—and out of it—exactly the same way as does the check you receive from your employer. Somewhat as in the case of the multiplier, we must see that a government *expenditure* in and of itself, whether financed by taxes or borrowing, is no different from a private expenditure which may be financed by selling output or by borrowing money from the public.

Then what could make government spending inflationary? Two things:

1. **If government spending is financed by borrowing from the Federal Reserve system, this may create monetary pressures that have inflationary consequences.** We will have to defer consideration of this until we get to Chapters 17 and 19.

2. **If government spending adds to total national expenditure at a time when there is already too much consumer and business spending, the added flow of public spending will certainly send up prices. Government spending to buy war supplies is a typical example of this.**

Therefore government spending *can* be inflationary in certain cases. But there are also clear cases where it will not be inflationary. If there is a large amount of slack in the economy—unemployed men and women and unused equipment—more expenditure of any kind will be welcome, and prices are not likely to rise appreciably.

OTHER PROBLEMS: REDISTRIBUTION

We will be back to inflation again many times. Here we still want to clear up the economics of the public sector. And that requires us to take brief notice of two other problems that are brought by public spending.

One of these problems is that the people or institutions from whom taxes are collected are not always exactly the same people and institutions to whom interest is paid, so that servicing a government debt often poses problems of *redistribution of income*. For instance, if all government bonds were owned by rich people and if all government taxation were regressive (i.e., proportionately heavier on low incomes), then servicing a government debt would mean transferring income from the poor to the rich. Considerations of equity aside, this would also probably involve distributing income from spenders to savers and would thereby intensify the problem of closing the savings gap.

In addition, a debt that a government owes to foreign citizens is *not* an internal debt. It is exactly like a debt that a corporation owes to an outside public, and it can involve payments that can cripple a nation. Do not forget that the internality of debts applies only to *national* debts held as bonds by members of the same community of people whose incomes contribute to government revenues. About 20 percent of the U.S. debt is held by foreigners.

THE DISCOURAGEMENT OF PRIVATE SPENDING

Finally we must pay heed to one more problem. A rising public debt may cause indirect but nonetheless serious harm if it discourages private investment.

This could be a very real cost of government debts, were such a reaction to be widespread and long-lasting. It may well be (we are not sure) that the long drawn out and never entirely successful recovery from the Great Depression was caused, to a considerable extent, by the adverse psychological impact of government deficit spending on business investment intentions. Business did not understand deficit spending and interpreted it either as the entering wedge of socialism (instead of a crash program to save capitalism) or as a wasteful and harebrained economic scheme. To make matters worse, the amount of the government deficit (at its peak $4 billion), while large enough to frighten the business community, was not big enough to begin to exert an effective leverage on total demand, particularly under conditions of widespread unemployment and financial catastrophe.

Today, however, it is much less likely that deficit spending would be attended by a drop in private spending. A great deal that was new and frightening in thought and practice in the 1930s is today well-understood and tested. World War II was, after all, an immense laboratory demonstration of what public spending could do for GNP. The experience of recent years gives good reason to believe that deficit spending does not cause a significant slowdown in private investment expenditure: There has been no statistical evidence that federal spending has discouraged or **crowded out** private investment.

DEMAND MANAGEMENT

We have spent a lot of time discussing the problems of the public sector. Now we shall familiarize ourselves with the possibilities of using that sector to stabilize, or to spur on, the economy.

PUBLIC PROPENSITIES

We shall start by discovering something surprising about public spending. Despite the fact that it is politically determined, public spending reveals propensities, much like private spending.

The reason for these propensities is that both government income and government outgo are closely tied to private activity. Government receipts are derived in the main from taxes, and taxes—direct or indirect—tend to reflect the trend of business and personal income. If fact, we can generalize about tax payments in much the same fashion as we can about consumption, describing them as a predictable function of GNP. To be sure, this assumes that tax *rates* do not change. But since rates change only infrequently, we can draw up a general schedule that relates tax receipts and the level of GNP. The schedule will show not only that taxes rise as GNP rises, but that they rise *faster* than GNP.

Why faster? Largely because of the progressive structure of the federal income tax. As household and business incomes rise to higher levels, the percentage "bite" of income tax increases. Thus as incomes rise, tax liabilities rise even more. Conversely, the tax bite works downward in the opposite way. As incomes fall, taxes fall even faster, since households or businesses with lowered incomes find themselves in a less steep tax bracket.

PERSONAL DEBTS AND PUBLIC DEBTS

In view of the fact that our national debt today figures out to approximately $2,880 for every man, woman, and child, it is not surprising that we frequently hear appeals to "common sense," telling us how much better we would be without this debt, and how our grandchildren will groan under its weight.

Is this true? We have already discussed the fact that internal debts are different from external debts, but let us press the point home from a different vantage point. Suppose we decided that we would pay off the debt. This would mean that our government bonds would be redeemed for cash. To get the cash, we would have to tax ourselves (unless we wanted to roll the printing presses), so that what we would really be doing would be transferring money from taxpayers to bondholders.

Would that be a net gain for the nation? Consider the typical holder of a government bond—a family, a bank, or a corporation. It now holds the world's safest and most readily sold paper asset from which a regular income is obtained. After our debt is redeemed, our families, banks, and corporations will have two choices: (1) They can hold cash and get *no* income, or (2) they can invest in other securities that are slightly *less* safe. Are these investors better off? As for our grandchildren, it is true that if we pay off the debt they will not have to carry its weight. But to offset that, neither will they be carried by the comfortable government bonds they would otherwise have inherited. They will also be relieved from paying taxes to meet the interest on the debt. Alas, they will be relieved as well of the pleasure of depositing the green Treasury checks for interest payments that used to arrive twice a year.

Government expenditures also show certain propensities, which is to say some government spending is also functionally related to the level of GNP. A number of government programs are directly correlated to the level of economic activity in such a way that spending *decreases* as GNP *increases,* and vice versa. For instance, unemployment benefits are naturally higher when GNP is low or falling. Many payments such as food stamps, aid to dependent children, or various welfare programs are highly sensitive to unemployment: in 1976, for example, when unemployment neared 9 percent, such outlays were $20 billion higher than if unemployment had been 5 percent. So, too, disbursements to farmers under various agricultural programs vary inversely with good and bad crop years.

AUTOMATIC STABILIZERS

All these automatic effects taken together are called the *automatic stabilizers* or the *built-in stabilizers* of the economy. What they add up to is an automatic government counterbalance to the private sector. As GNP falls because private spending is insufficient, taxes decline even faster and public expenditures grow, thereby automatically causing the government sector to offset the private sector to some extent. In similar fashion, as GNP rises, taxes tend to rise even faster and public expenditures decline, thereby causing the government sector to act as a brake.

The public sector therefore acts as an automatic compensator, even without direct action to alter tax or expenditure levels, pumping out more public demand when private demand is slowing, and curbing public demand when private demand is brisk.

How effective are the built-in stabilizers? It is estimated that the increase in transfer payments plus the reduction in taxes offset about 35¢ of each dollar of original decline in spending. Here is how this works. Suppose that private investment were to fall by $10 billion. If there were no stabilizers, household spending might fall by another $10 billion (the multiplier effect), causing a total decline of $20 billion in incomes.

The action of the stabilizers, however, will prevent the full force of this fall. First, the reduction in incomes of both households and firms will lower their tax liabilities. Since taxes take about 35¢ from each dollar, the initial drop of $10 billion in incomes will reduce tax liabilities by about $3.5 billion. Most of this—let us say $3 billion—is likely to be spent. Meanwhile some public expenditures for unemployment insurance and farm payments will rise, pumping out perhaps $1 billion into the consumption sector, all of which we assume to be spent by its recipients.

Thus, the incomes of firms and households, having originally fallen by $10 billion, will be offset by roughly $4 billion—$1 billion in additional transfer incomes and $3 billion in income spent by households because their taxes are lower. As a result, the decline in expenditure will be reduced from $10 billion to about $6 billion (actually $6.5 billion, according to the calculations of the Council of Economic Advisers).

This is certainly an improvement over a situation with no stabilizers. Yet if the drop in investment is not to bring about some fall in GNP, it will have to be *fully* compensated by an equivalent increase in government spending or by a fall in taxes large enough to induce an equivalent amount of private spending. This will require public action more vigorous than that brought about automatically. Indeed, it requires that the government take on a task very different from any we have heretofore studied, the task of *demand management*, or acting as the *deliberate* balancing mechanism of the economy.

FISCAL VS. MONETARY POLICY

It has two basic alternatives: fiscal and monetary policy. We will have to defer a consideration of the second alternative until a later chapter. **Here we will focus on fiscal policy, by which we mean two courses of action:**
  1. increasing or decreasing government spending;
  2. raising or lowering taxes.
We have already looked into the mechanics of the first option in Figure 13.2, where we showed that government expenditure fills a demand gap exactly like private expenditure. It follows that a decrease in government spending will also create a decrease in final demand, just as a drop in the spending of any other sector.

Our diagram did not show the direct effect of tax changes simply because it is difficult to draw such a diagram clearly. But it is not difficult to understand the effect of a tax change. When the government lowers taxes it diminishes the transfer of income from households or firms into the public sector. Households and firms therefore have more income to spend. Conversely, in raising taxes a government withdraws spending power from households and firms. As a result, we can expect that private spending will fall.

FULL EMPLOYMENT BUDGETS

The direct effects of expenditures and taxes are thus easy to picture, and the rule for demand management should be simple: Establish a government budget that will have an expansionary influence when GNP is too low and a restraining influence when it is too high; and balance the budget when GNP is at desired levels.

But this seemingly obvious guideline is not as simple as it looks. Suppose that we are suffering from mild unemployment and the President's advisers accordingly recommend a level of expenditure that, combined with existing tax rates, would produce a small deficit. Isn't this following the proper guide?

The answer is: not necessarily. For if we calculate the flow of tax receipts that the government would be receiving *if we were operating at full employment,* the planned level of expenditure may in fact be so small that it would not even produce a neutral budget, but a deflationary one at the *desired* level of GNP! A glance at Figure 13.3 shows that this can indeed be the case. In 1974, for example, the actual budget was in substantial deficit, as the colored line shows. But if we calculate the budget *at full employment levels* of tax receipts, we find that our flow of expenditure was far too short of the levels needed to spend our receipts *at that level.* As the black line shows, our flows of taxes and expenditures at full employment would have given us a surplus! Therefore the $12 billion deficit was too little to give us the stimulus we needed to reach full employment. A true full-employment budget would have raised expenditures (or cut taxes) to bring the economy up to a high level of operation.

Paradoxically, although this would have required more expenditures or a

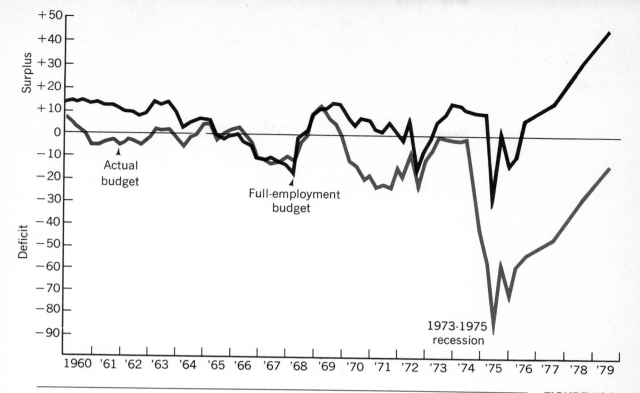

FIGURE 13.3
FULL
EMPLOYMENT
AND ACTUAL
BUDGET
DEFICITS

lower tax rate, the effect at full employment might have been a government budget that was balanced, rather than one in deficit.

In other words, wise fiscal policy—whether of stimulus or restraint—must be figured on a basis of full employment *because that is the only way to get us there.*

TAX CUTS VS. EXPENDITURES

Which of the two direct methods of managing demand—taxes or spending—is preferable? The question basically asks us which we need more: public goods or private goods. But there are a number of technical economic criteria that we must also bear in mind.

First, tax cuts and expenditures tend to favor different groups. Tax cuts benefit those who pay taxes, and expenditures benefit those who receive them. This simple fact reveals a good deal about the political and economic pros and cons of each method. Tax cuts are of little direct benefit to poor families whose incomes are so low that they pay little or no income taxes. Expenditure programs *can* benefit these disadvantaged groups or areas—for example, by slum clearance in specific cities, training programs, or simply higher welfare payments. Expenditure programs can also help special groups, such as military or road contractors, or middle-income families who usually benefit from housing programs.

The difference, then, is that tax programs have a widespread impact, whereas expenditure programs tend to have a concentrated impact: Tax cuts or increases are diffused across the economy, exerting their influences on different income strata, whereas expenditure programs are often concentrated geographically or occupationally. (Some expenditure programs, such as Social Security or medical aid, can have a broad "horizontal effect" as well.)

Second, expenditure programs tend to be more reliable as a means of increasing demand, whereas tax programs tend to be effective in decreasing demand. The reason is clear enough. If the government wishes to increase final demand and chooses to lower taxes, it makes possible a higher level of private spending, but there is no guarantee that firms or households will in fact spend all their tax savings. Indeed, the marginal propensity to consume leads us to be quite certain that firms and households will not spend all their tax reductions, at least for a time. Thus if the government wants to increase demand by say $7 billion, it may have to cut taxes by about $10 billion.

On the other hand, tax increases are a very reliable method of decreasing demand. Individuals or firms *can* "defy" tax increases and maintain their former level of spending by going out and borrowing money or by spending their savings, but it is unlikely they will do so. If the government tries to hold back total demand by cutting its own expenditure programs, however, there is the chance that firms and individuals will undo the government's effort to cut demand by borrowing and spending more themselves.

There is no magic formula that will enable us to declare once and for all what policy is best for demand management. It is often impossible to raise taxes for political reasons, in which case a decrease in expenditures is certainly the next best way to keep total demand from rising too fast. So, too, it may be impossible to push through a program of public expenditure because public opinion or congressional tempers are opposed to spending. In that case, a tax cut is certainly the best available way to keep demand up if the nation is threatened with a recession.*

RESPONSIBILITY OF PUBLIC DEMAND

All these considerations point out how difficult it is to conduct demand management as smoothly in practice as in textbooks. There was a time not too long ago when economists talked rather glibly of "fine-tuning" the economy. That was in the first flush of triumph of the *idea* of managed demand, before the hard realities of full-employment budgets and other problems had been fully faced. Economists are a good deal more modest in their claims these days.

Nevertheless, the basic idea of using the government as a balancing mechanism for the economy remains valid, however difficult it may be to realize the perfect balance in fact. It is valid because the federal sector is the only sector whose operations we can collectively control. There is no way for business to determine how much it should spend as a sector, no way for consumers to concert their activity. More important, even if there were such a way, business and consumer actions might not accord with the needs of the macroeconomy. Only the public sector can act consciously on behalf of the public interest; only the public sector can attempt to reconcile the needs of all groups. However exasperating or inefficient or clumsy public demand management may be, it remains a major accomplishment, both in theory and fact, of twentieth-century economics.

---

*We should add that there is a school of economic thought that holds futile all efforts to steer the economy away from its self-determined track. We will discuss the ideas of this school of "rational expectations" in Chapter 18.

LOOKING BACK

1. The public sector is second in size only to consumption. We must learn to distinguish the sector as defined by purchases—a net contribution to GNP—and as defined by expenditures (purchases plus transfers).

2. The public sector can be used to offset a demand gap exactly as the business sector can. The difference is that the public sector can be deliberately used to manage the economy in a way that the private sector cannot.

3. The public sector typically borrows money to finance its gap-filling expenditures. This creates deficits, or an excess of expenditures over tax receipts. These deficits differ from private debts in two ways. First, the government has the power to capture revenues through taxation, which no business can do. Second, a government debt may be internal—owed by the community to itself. This may create problems of redistribution, but the internality of debt avoids the external drain, or burden, that is imposed on all non-national borrowers.

4. Deficit spending may be, but need not be, inflationary. It is inflationary if financed in an inflationary manner, as we shall later see, or if government spending is increased at a time when the economy is already tight. But deficit spending when the economy is slack will mainly add to output, not to price rises.

5. Although the public sector is an independent variable determined by political decision, it has propensity-like attributes. Because tax receipts rise faster (and fall more slowly) than GNP, and because welfare-type expenditures fall when GNP rises and vice versa, the public sector acts as an automatic stabilizer, exerting an influence against the movement of GNP.

6. There are two basic means of demand management—monetary and fiscal policy. We will study monetary policy shortly. Fiscal policy uses government spending or taxing to influence the level of national economic activity. In the choice between taxes and expenditure, advantages lie on both sides. Higher taxes are a better way to hold back GNP than expenditure cuts; higher expenditures are more directly aimed at needy groups. Expenditure increases are a stronger boost to a weak economy. In figuring the appropriate change needed, tax or expenditure, the authorities must calculate on the basis of a full employment situation.

7. The fiscal management of demand is full of difficulties but it is the only manner in which we can attempt to influence the behavior of GNP.

ECONOMIC VOCABULARY

QUESTIONS

1. What are the main differences between the public and private sectors? Are these differences economic or political?

2. Show in a diagram how increased government spending can offset a demand gap. Can you show how decreased taxation can do the same?

3. Show how the automatic stabilizers might work if we had an increase of investment of $20 billion and the multiplier were two, and if the increase in taxes and the *decrease* public expenditure associated with the rise in investment were $3 billion and $1 billion respectively.

4. If the government is going to go into debt, does it matter whether it spends money for roads or for relief? For education or weapons? Is there a connection between the economic effects of government spending and the welfare effects? How about the various kinds of things we could buy with $10 billion of private investment?

5. Why is the internality of debts so important?

6. Could you explain to a conservative that government spending was (a) safe and (b) not "socialistic"? Or do you think that it is not safe and that it *is* socialistic? All government spending?

AN EXTRA WORD ABOUT

STATE AND LOCAL FINANCES

State and local finances are very sensitive to the condition of the economy. When national output goes down, state and local revenues (in real terms) also decline. Occasionally a state goes up against the national trend, but usually a national slowdown pulls down all state and local revenues. As household incomes fall, state and local income taxes decline. As household spending weakens, sales tax receipts fall. As employment worsens, revenues from payroll taxes fall off. All this results in pressure to cut back state and local budgets. And this, in turn, adds its undertow to the national picture, giving the recession additional force.

One suggested remedy for this built-in weakness of state and local finance is *countercyclical revenue sharing.* This remedy would automatically authorize federal grants-in-aid to state and local governments when times were bad. Such grants would be sufficiently large to maintain state and local spending at the levels they would have reached if the recession had not occurred. This would allow state and local governments to make long-range plans without having to worry about short-run fluctuations in their revenues, and it would also prevent these governments from inadvertently worsening a national recession by cutting back on their own expenditures.

A difficulty in countercyclical revenue sharing lies in different regional growth rates. Incomes and output have been growing faster in the West and South, for example, than in the Midwest or Northeast. This uneven pace has been going on for some years, but has recently been exaggerated by high energy prices. The slower-growing Northeast and Midwest have to use expensive oil, whereas the faster-growing South and West have available to them the relatively cheaper energy source of natural gas.

As a result, the lucky states in high-growth regions may show budget surpluses when the unlucky states in slow-growth regions show deficits. Countercyclical revenue sharing would then have to make the difficult choice of whether or not to seek to equalize differences or to ignore them.

Northeast	.86
Midwest	.76
South	1.14
West	1.20

Source: *National Journal,* June 26, 1976, p. 881.

**TABLE 13.2
RATIO OF
FEDERAL EX-
PENDITURES
TO FEDERAL
TAX COLLEC-
TIONS, 1975**

There is a natural tendency to say "Ignore them," because such differences hardly seem a matter of federal concern. But a second look shows us that the matter is not as simple as this. For the federal government itself is a partial cause of some of these very differences! When we look at federal individual income taxes received and grants-in-aid paid out in different areas, it is clear that the federal government is taking net spending power out of the slow-growing Northeast and Midwest and injecting it in the fast-growing South and West.

Thus the federal government is contributing to the differences in growth rates, although we should stress that this is only one cause of the differences, and certainly not the main one.

What should the federal government do? Beginning with Franklin Roosevelt, it has followed a deliberate policy of trying to equalize regional differentials. TVA is probably the most well-known effort to aid one particular region, but actually nearly all federal programs are structured to give more help to low-income states than to high-income ones. If the South, for example, has been, and still is, favored in federal policy it is because, despite its rapid growth, its average family income remains below that of the Northeast, $15,657 compared to $17,680 in 1978.

Most people favor this federal equalizing role. The question today is whether, and to what degree, the policy should now be extended within states to localities. New York City, for example, lies in the middle of one of the richest regions in the nation, but it is a pocket of serious poverty. If the federal government decides that it wants to help low-income localities, as well as low-income states, how should this be done? By federalizing welfare? By relieving localities of hospital expenses through federal health insurance? By giving federal aid to primary education in low-income cities? These are some of the suggestions that have been put forth. None of them is without problems. But at issue is the basic question whether we want the federal government to play the same role with localities that it has long played with regions. Once that issue is clarified, the problems will begin to take care of themselves.

THE NEW YORK CITY DEBT CRISIS

New York City's 1976 debt crisis was a vivid illustration of how even very large and seemingly rich government institutions *that are not national in scope* have limits to the amount of deficit finance they can safely undertake. Because any resident can leave New York, all the city's debt is potentially external to it.

As Table 13.3 shows, New York City's debt had been building up for a long period. But over most of these years its bonds were rated very highly by various companies, such as Standard and Poor's, that give ratings (risk designations) to private and public bonds. We can also see that the debt build-up accelerated after 1970, partly the consequence of financially imprudent actions on the part of New York City officials, partly the result of the 1974–1975 recession that hit many northeastern cities hard.

To pay its bills, the city had to borrow larger and larger sums at the very time that the federal government had created a very tight situation in the money markets—a "credit crunch"—as part of its efforts to curb inflation. In a tight-money period, everyone has trouble borrowing, and banks and other lenders reexamine their credit applicants to determine who should be first in line and who should be last.

In this reexamination, New York City fared very badly. Its bond ratings suddenly fell. Overnight it became apparent to everyone that its debt and deficit had reached levels that could not be sustained in the long run. As a result, New York suddenly found itself unable to borrow. Not only was no one willing to lend funds to cover its current deficit, which had reached a staggering $700 million for the year 1974, but banks or other lenders would not even lend the city money to finance its outstanding debt. That is, the normal process of rolling over the debt by replacing bonds that had become due with new bonds was impossible.

What were the city's options at this point? All were unpleasant. One was to slash expenditures to the point at which the deficit would be eliminated, and revenues would cover debt repayments. This would have required so drastic a cut in expenditures (something on the order of 25 percent) that city officials

TABLE 13.3
NEW YORK
CITY'S DEBT
($ BILLIONS)

1950	$ 3
1960	6
1970	8
1974	14
1976	16

feared the city could not be safely operated—too few police, firemen, sanitation workers, teachers.

Another option was to raise taxes by the amount needed to cover debt repayment. There were two problems here. First, this course would have required additional taxing powers for the city, which the state legislature was loathe to hand over. Second, city taxes, already among the highest in the nation, would have soared to such astronomical levels that many taxpayers would have voted with their feet, by moving out of the city to the suburbs or to neighboring states.

A third option was to default on debt repayments—simply not to honor the old bonds that came due. Here the difficulties were obvious. A default would still have left the city short of funds to cover its current deficit. And, of course, a default would have terribly damaged its prospects for selling bonds in the future. Once burned, twice shy in the bond market. Then, too, many worried lest a default in New York's bonds might not set off a series of defaults in other municipal bonds, giving rise to a serious panic in the capital markets.

Last was the hope that the federal government would save the situation, and city officials pleaded with the Ford administration to add a federal guarantee to city bonds, thereby assuring their saleability, or for outright federal loans or grants to cover the deficit. But the Ford administration was not eager to rescue the city on easy terms. It felt that the city was itself responsible for much of its financial plight and that a rescue operation for New York could lead to requests from many other hard-pressed cities.

What happened in the end? All options were used to some extent. The city did cut its services. City taxes were raised. Default was technically avoided, but holders of city bonds were forced to exchange their securities for long-term bonds that carried lower interest rates. And the federal government made some necessary loans.

As part of the rescue operation, city finances were placed under the scrutiny of a committee of state, federal, and private representatives who monitor its union contracts and other expenditures, its taxes, and its budgets. Since that time of crisis the city has staggered along, managing to postpone a second crisis, but not really achieving financial solidity. Other cities, such as Cleveland, have experienced similar or even more drastic financial crunches. It is likely that many cities are going to be financially troubled for a long time, unless the federal government relieves them of burdens such as welfare or local hospital costs.

Is it all a cautionary tale, warning us of the profligacy of local governments and the shortsightedness of politicians? To some extent it is because the sins of both commission and omission by various city mayors have been great. But it is not *just* that. While New York, Newark, Detroit, and Cleveland have suffered, Houston, Dallas, and the sun-belt cities in general have prospered. Is this because their politicians are more honest, their government structures more efficient? More likely it is because these cities are the recipients of a movement of labor and capital away from the frost belt to sunnier climes. The eastern cities are located in a region which is experiencing a relative decline. Expenses are high because many of these cities were pioneers in offering social services, but today their revenues are dwindling. They are in for a long season of tribulation unless the federal government acts to mitigate this drift.

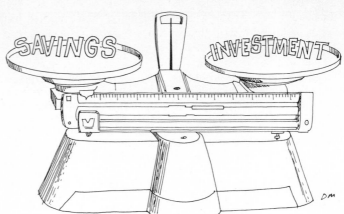

Chapter

14 THE DETERMINATION OF GNP

A LOOK AHEAD

We have gradually assembled the parts of the puzzle. We now have a good idea of the way that the various sectors behave and interact. It remains only to piece them together to get a picture of how GNP is determined. That is what we do in this chapter.

(1) We will clarify the idea of a supply curve for GNP—a curve that will establish the costs of producing a larger or smaller output within our production possibility frontier.

(2) We will add a demand curve for GNP—a curve that will show how much output the sectors will want to buy at different levels of utilization.

(3) Putting the curves together will give us an equilibrium GNP. We will take a look at how this GNP can move upward or downward as the sectors alter their activity.

We have reached the destination toward which we have been traveling for several chapters. We are finally in a position to understand how the forces of supply and demand determine the actual level of GNP that confronts us in daily life—"the state of the economy" that affects our employment prospects, our immediate well-being, our satisfaction or dissatisfaction with the way things are going.

SUPPLY AND DEMAND IN MACRO

As we have begun to see, the short-run level of GNP is determined by the outcome of two opposing tendencies of supply and demand, just as the level of prices and quantities in a marketplace is set by the counterplay of these forces. In fact, **the opposition of supply and demand plays just as central a role in macroeconomics as in microeconomics. The crucial difference is that in macroeconomics we talk of supply and demand in relation to GNP, whereas in microeconomics we speak of them mainly in relation to price.**

THE UTILIZATION OF OUR POTENTIAL

What determines the supply of GNP? For the long run, the answer hinges on the quantity and quality of our inputs, a question we looked into in Chapter 8. These inputs determine the limits of our productive power—the production possibility frontiers that constrain our capacity to produce.

But in the short run our supply of GNP depends on how much of our production potential we actually use. Here we come up against the impossibility of going beyond the production possibility curve. **Therefore it is the degree of utilization of our production capacity—the extent to which we achieve full employment of human and material capital—that determines how close we come to the production frontier.**

What will we use as supply and demand curves to establish where that point will be? The demand curve is easy to imagine—it will be determined by the amount of expenditure the community generates at different levels of employment and utilization. Obviously, the more fully we employ our manpower, the more incomes individuals will have and the more output they will want. We shall shortly see how the demand for output can be represented in graphic form.

But what about the supply of output? Here we want to show how the value of output will change as we use more or less of our available productive power. The supply curve will show how much output costs at different levels of utilization. **The supply curve will therefore relate output and costs, and the demand curve will relate output and expenditure.**

THE SUPPLY CURVE OF INCOME

What does such a supply curve look like? Here we make use of an identity **that we learned in Chapter 9. Incomes and output are always the same. The amount of income made available to the community must rise, dollar for dollar, with the amount of production, because every dollar going into production must become income to some individual or institution.**

Our supply curve must show this identity, and Figure 14.1 makes clear that the resulting curve will be a 45° line. Notice that $OX = OY$, $OX' = OY'$, and so on. Notice also that this supply curve is fixed, in that the relation between in-

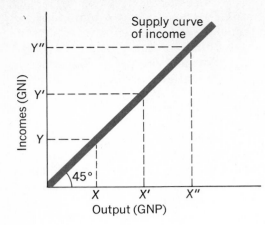

**FIGURE 14.1
SUPPLY
CURVE OF
INCOME**

The supply curve of income makes use of the identity between output ($C+I+G+X$) and income ($F+T+D$). Every unit of output generates incomes that exactly match its costs. This identity gives rise to a 45° line, which lies equidistant between the two axes at all points.

These panels show the amounts of spending that will take place in each sector (and then the three combined) as the degree of utilization increases. Spending rises in the household sector because of the propensity to consume. The accelerator and various governmental "propensities" give a slight positive slope to spending in those sectors as well.

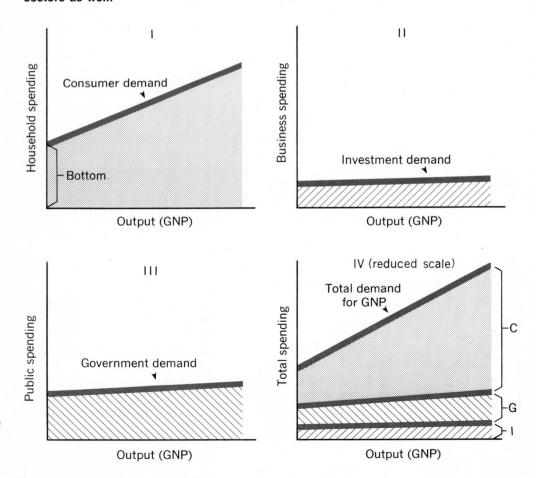

**FIGURE 14.2
THE DEMAND
FOR GNP**

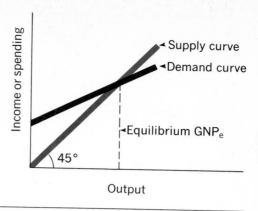

Here the supply curve shows the amount of income associated with different amounts of output. They are identical. The demand curve shows the amount of spending at different levels of output. Where spending equals income we have an equilibrium level of GNP.

FIGURE 14.3 SUPPLY AND DEMAND FOR GNP

comes (GNI) and output (GNP) is always the same—identical. Again, for each dollar that we increase output, we add a dollar to income. Thus the supply of income is identical with the value of output.

DEMAND CURVE FOR GNP

Now what about the demand for GNP? We already know that the demand curve will show us the amount of spending (demand for output) that will be generated by the community as output rises from zero to the full utilization of existing resources.

Of course such a curve will slope upward. In Figure 14.2 we see why this is so. Panels I through IV sum up the demand of consumption, investment, and government. *They show that total spending will rise as output rises: Here is our upward sloping demand curve.*

It now remains only to put the demand and supply curves together, as in Figure 14.3.

This equilibrium shows us the money value of GNP brought about by the flow of demand against supply. It might, for example, indicate that this value of GNP was $1.5 trillion. It does *not* tell us whether $1.5 trillion is a *good* size for GNP, any more than a price of $20 for a commodity tells us whether that is a good or bad price from the viewpint of buyers, producers, or the economy at large. We shall return to this critical point at the end of our chapter.

ANOTHER VIEW OF EQUILIBRIUM

SAVING AND INVESTMENT

Equilibrium is always a complicated subject to master, so let us fix the matter in our minds by going over the problem once more. Suppose that by means of a questionnaire we are going to predict the level of GNP for an island community. To simplify our task, we will ignore government and exports, so that we can concentrate solely on consumption, saving, and investment.

We begin by interrogating the island's business community about their intentions for next year's investment. Now we know that some investment will be induced and that, therefore, investment will partly be a result of the island's

Income	Consumption (In millions)	Saving	Investment
$100	$75	$25	$30
110	80	30	30
120	85	35	30

TABLE 14.1

The interplay of saving and investment reveals the equilibrium output just as schedules of supply and demand show an equilibrium price.

level of income; but again for simplification, we assume that businesses have laid their plans for next year. They tell us they intend to spend $30 million for new housing, plant, equipment, and other capital goods.

Next, our team of pollsters approaches a carefully selected sample of the island's householders and asks them what their consumption and savings plans are for the coming year. Here the answer will be a bit disconcerting. Reflecting on their past experience, our householders will reply: "We can't say for sure. We'd *like* to spend such-and-such an amount and save the rest, but really it depends on what our incomes will be." Our poll, in other words, will have to make inquiries about different possibilities that reflect the island's propensity to consume.

Now we tabulate our results, and find that we have the schedule shown in Table 14.1.

INTERPLAY OF SAVING AND INVESTMENT

If we look at the last two columns of Table 14.1, those for saving and investment, we can see a powerful cross play that will characterize our model economy at different levels of income, for the forces of investment and saving will not be in balance at all levels. At some levels, the propensity to save will outrun the act of purposeful investment; at others, the motivation to save will be less than the investment expenditure made by business firms. In fact, our island model shows that at only one level of income—$110 million—will the saving and investment schedules coincide.

What does it mean when intended savings are greater than the flow of intended investment? It means that people are *trying* to save out of their given incomes a larger amount than business is willing to invest. Now if we think back to the exposition of the economy in a circular flow, it will be clear what the result must be. The economy cannot maintain a closed circuit of income and expenditure if savings are larger than investment. This will simply give rise to a demand gap, the repercussions of which we have already explored.

But a similar lack of equilibrium results if intended savings are less than intended investment expenditure (or if investment spending is greater than the propensity to save). Now business will be pumping out more than enough to offset the savings gap. The additional expenditures, over and above those that compensate for saving, will flow into the economy to create new incomes—and out of those new incomes, new savings.

Income and output will be stable, in other words, only when the flow of intended investment just compensates for the flow of intended saving. Investment and saving thus conduct a tug of war around this pivot point, driving the economy upward when intended investment exceeds the flow of intended saving; down-

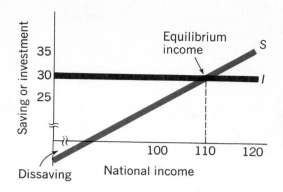

**FIGURE 14.4
SAVING AND
INVESTMENT**

Equilibrium income

Here we simply put into graphic form
the schedules of saving and investment
(or leakages and injection). The
equilibrium point is easy to see.

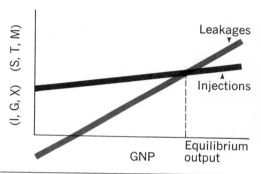

**FIGURE 14.5
LEAKAGES
AND
INJECTIONS**

ward when it fails to offset saving. In Figure 14.4 we show this crosscurrent in
schematic form. Note that as incomes fall very low, householders will *dissave*.

INJECTIONS VS. LEAKAGES

We can easily make our graph more realistic by adding taxes (T) and imports (M) to savings, and exports (X) and government spending to investment.
The vertical axis in Figure 14.5 now shows all *leakages and injections*.

We recall that leakages are any acts, such as savings, increased taxes, profits,
or imports that reduce spending. Similarly, injections are any acts, such as investment or higher government spending or rising exports or even a spontaneous
jump in consumption, that lead to higher spending. And just to introduce another
feature of the real world, we will tilt the injection line upward, on the assumption that induced investment will be an important constituent of total investment.
The leakages curve will not be exactly the same shape as the savings curve, but it
will reflect the general tendency of savings and imports and taxes to rise with
income.

INTENDED AND UNINTENDED S AND I

The careful reader may have noted that we speak of *intended* savings and
intended investment as the critical forces in establishing equilibrium. This is
because there is a formal balance—an identity—between *all* saving and investment (or all leakages and all injections) at every moment in the economy. In the
same way, purchases in any market must exactly equal sales at each and every
moment, but that does not mean the market is in equilibrium at all times.

Economists distinguish between the formal identity between total saving and investment (or between all leakages and all injections) and the active difference between *intended* savings and investment (or *intended* saving, *intended* imports, *intended* business saving, etc., and *intended* additional expenditures of all kinds).

What matters in the determination of GNP are the *actions* people are taking —actions that lead them to try to save or to invest or that make them struggle to get rid of unintended inventories or to build up desired inventories. These are the kinds of activities that will be moving the economy up and down in the never-ending "quest" for its equilibrium point. The fact that at each moment past savings and investment are identical from the viewpoint of the economy's balance sheet is important only insofar as we are economic accountants. As analysts of the course of future GNP, we concentrate on the inequality of future, intended actions.

THE PARADOX OF THRIFT

The fact that income must always move toward the level where the flows of intended saving and investment are equal leads to one of the most startling—and important—paradoxes of economics. **This is the so-called paradox of thrift, a paradox that tells us that the attempt to increase intended saving may, under certain circumstances, lead to a fall in actual saving.**

The paradox is not difficult for us to understand at this stage. An attempt to save, when it is not matched with an equal willingness to invest or to increase government expenditure, will cause a gap in demand. This means that business will not be getting back enough money to cover costs. Hence, production will be curtailed or costs will be slashed, with the result that incomes will fall. As incomes fall, savings will also fall, because the ability to save will be reduced. Thus, by a chain of activities working their influence on income and output, the effort to *increase* savings may end up with an actual *reduction* of savings.

This frustration of individual desires is perhaps the most striking instance of a common situation in economic life, the incompatibility between some kinds of individual behavior and some collective results. An individual farmer, for instance, may produce a larger crop in order to enjoy a bigger income; but if all farmers produce bigger crops, farm prices are apt to fall so heavily that farmers end up with less income. So, too, a single family may wish to save a very large fraction of its income for reasons of financial prudence; but if all families seek to save a great deal of their incomes, the result—unless investment also rises—will be a fall in expenditure and a common failure to realize savings objectives. The paradox of thrift, in other words, teaches us that the freedom of behavior available to a few individuals cannot always be generalized to all individuals.*

---

*The paradox of thrift is actually only a subtle instance of a type of faulty reasoning called the fallacy of composition. The fallacy consists of assuming that what is true of the individual case must also be true of all cases combined. The flaw in reasoning lies in our tendency to overlook "side effects" of individual actions (such as the decrease in spending associated with an individual's attempt to save more, or the increase in supply when a farmer markets his larger crop) which may be negligible in isolation but which are very important in the aggregate.

An increase of injections of *AB* leads to a larger increase in GNP, *XY*. This is a graphic presentation of the multiplier. It is important to understand why *AB* creates *XY*. The reason is that the leakage curve slopes. And why does it slope? Because its slope represents the marginal propensity to save. And *that* is the cause of the multiplier.

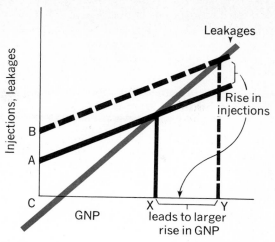

FIGURE 14.6 MULTIPLIER IN GRAPHIC FORM

THE MULTIPLIER

There remains only one part of the jigsaw puzzle to put into place. This is the integration of the *multiplier* into our analysis of the determination of GNP.

We remember that the essential point about the multiplier was that changes in investment, government spending, or exports resulted in larger changes in GNP because the additions to income were respent, creating still more new incomes. Further, we remember that the size of the multiplier effect depended on the marginal propensity to consume, the marginal propensity to tax, and the marginal propensity to buy imports as GNP rises. Now it remains only to show how this basic analytic concept enters into the determination of equilibrium GNP.

Let us begin with the diagram that shows injections and leakages, and let us now draw a new line showing an increase in injections (Figure 14.6). Notice that the increase in GNP is larger than the increase in injections. *This is the multiplier itself in graphic form.*

SLOPE OF THE LEAKAGE CURVE

Both diagrams also show that the relation between the original increase in injections and the resulting increase in GNP depends on the *slope* of the leakage line. Figure 14.7 shows us two different injection-GNP relationships that arise from differing slopes.

Notice how the *same* increase in spending (from *OA* to *OB* on the injections axis) leads to a much smaller increase in panel I GNP (from *OX* to *OY*), where the leakage slope is high, than in panel II (from *OX'* to *OY'*), where the slope is more gradual.

Why is the increase greater when the slope is more gradual? The answer should be obvious. The slope represents the marginal propensity to save, to tax, to import—in short, all the marginal propensities that give rise to leakages. If these propensities are high—if there are high leakages—then the slope of the leakage curve will be high. If it is low, the leakage curve will be flat.

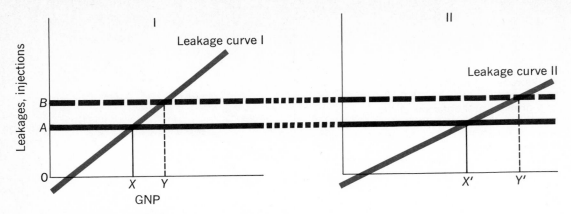

FIGURE 14-7 TWO MULTIPLIERS
Here is another chance to relate the graphics of the multiplier to the underlying behavior that causes the multiplier. The two differently sloped leakage curves generate different multipliers. This is because their different slopes picture different patterns of spending and saving.

A LAST LOOK AT EQUILIBRIUM

Thus we finally understand how GNP reaches an equilibrium position after a change in demand. Here it is well to reiterate, however, that the word "equilibrium" does not imply a static, motionless state. Nor does it mean a desired state. We use the word only to denote the fact that *given* certain behavior patterns, there will be a determinate point to which their interaction will push the level of income; and *so long as the underlying patterns of injections and leakages remain unchanged, the forces they exert will keep income at this level.*

In fact, of course, the flows of spending and saving are continually changing so that the equilibrium level of the economy is constantly shifting, like a Ping-Pong ball suspended in a rising jet of water. Equilibrium can thus be regarded as a target toward which the economy is constantly propelled by the push-pull between leakages and injections. The target may be attained but momentarily before the economy is again impelled to seek a new point of rest. What our diagrams and the underlying analysis explain for us, then, is not a single determinate point at which our economy will in fact settle down, but the *direction* it will go in quest of a resting place as the dynamic forces of the system exert their pressures.

EQUILIBRIUM AND FULL EMPLOYMENT

Like the market for any single good or service, the market for all goods and services will find its equilibrium where the total quantity of goods demanded equals that supplied. But now we must note something of paramount importance. While the economy will automatically move to this equilibrium point, the point need not bring about the full employment of the factors of production, particularly labor. In Figure 14.8, the economy at equilibrium produces a GNP indicated by GNP_e, but as our diagram indicates, this may be well short of the volume of production needed to bring about full employment (GNP_f). Equilibrium

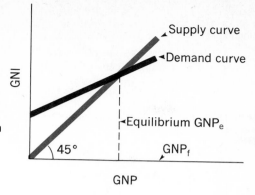

This last, simple-looking graph is perhaps the most important of all. It shows that equilibrium GNP_e may not be full utilization GNP_f—that we may be at rest far behind production possibility.

**FIGURE 14.8
SUPPLY AND
DEMAND FOR
GNP**

can thus occur at any level of capacity utilization. All we can say about it—exactly as in the market for goods and services—is that it is the level toward which the system will move, and from which it will not budge unless the demand curve shifts. It is certainly not necessarily the "right" level in any sense, and it may indeed be a very poor or unsatisfactory level, as during the Great Depression.

The aim of macroeconomic policy making is therefore to raise or lower the demand curve for GNP so that it crosses the supply curve at, or near, full employment or some other desired level of output. As we have already seen, this is an objective that is exceedingly difficult to accomplish; but at least we possess, in the body of macroeconomics itself, the basic intellectual tools needed to understand the nature of the task.

KEY CONCEPTS

Actual output depends on the degree of utilization of human and other resources

Demand for GNP relates spending and output. Supply and GNP relates cost and output

The identity of cost and income means that the supply curve will be a 45° line

Equilibrium GNP is most easily shown as the level of output where S = I, or leakages equal injections

LOOKING BACK

1. The potential output of the economy is determined by its production possibilities. But the amount actually produced depends on how close we can get to the production possibility frontier. This depends on the degree to which we utilize our human and other resources.

2. The degree of utilization depends on the demand and supply for GNP. The demand for GNP is determined by the amounts the sectors will want to buy at different levels of utilization. The supply of GNP will relate the cost of GNP to its level of output.

3. The supply curve of GNP uses the identity between costs and incomes to show that at all levels of utilization, output will generate incomes equal to its cost. The relation of identity between cost and income means that the supply curve of GNP will be a 45° line. Whatever the level of output, the supply of income (or spending power) will be identical with the cost of producing that output.

4. Equilibrium GNP is determined by the interplay of the supply of and demand for GNP. It is most easily depicted in terms of the interaction of the savings and investment, or leakage and injection, schedules. At equilibrium, saving must equal investment, and leakages must equal injections.

Investment or injection
determine the level of
income, via the multiplier.
Attempts to increase S
without increasing income
will fail

5. In the interplay between S and I (or leakages and injections), it is investment (or injections) that play the critical role in establishing the equilibrium level of output. Saving or leakages are dependent, passive variables in the process. Changes in intended investment will lead, via the multiplier, to changes in income that permit the economy to save the amount that matches intended investment. Attempts to save more, without boosting income first, are doomed to failure—the paradox of thrift.

6. An equilibrium GNP may not be a socially satisfactory GNP. The economy may be at rest although it is well behind its production frontiers.

ECONOMIC VOCABULARY

QUESTIONS

1. Suppose an economy turns out to have the following consumption and saving schedule (in billions): (You can fill in the missing numbers.)

income	saving	consumption
$400	$50	$350
450	—	395
—	60	440
550	70	—
600	85	—

Now suppose that firms intend to invest $60 billion. What will be the level of income? If investment rises to $85 billion, what will be the new level of income? What would be the multiplier?

2. Diagram the model above assuming that $I = 60$, then that $I = 85$.

3. Show in the diagram that the multiplier is determined by the slope of the leakage curve. What does this slope represent?

4. Copy diagram 14.3 showing the supply and demand curves that establish where equilibrium GNP will be. Now draw a new, higher demand curve, and drop a perpendicular line to the horizontal axis to show where the new equilibrium GNP will be. Measure the distance showing the rise in the demand for GNP and the distance showing the change in equilibrium GNPs. Can you see that GNP will increase by more than the rise in demand? And that this is simply another way of showing the multipler? And that as in Figure 14.7, the multiplier will depend on the slope of the leakage curve, here depicted as its twin, the marginal propensity to spend?

MONEY

A LOOK AHEAD

With this chapter we open a new section in our macro studies—an investigation into the nature and function of money. It is necessary to begin by learning the definitions and terms that make up the economic vocabulary we will use (as we did with GNP). Much of this chapter consists of an introduction to the meaning of money, which is not just the currency and coins we offhand think of as money.

In addition we shall learn how banks use the money we deposit with them to carry on lending and investing operations. The central process we shall trace is the manner in which banks *create* money through their normal business operations.

We have almost completed our analysis of the major elements of macroeconomics, and soon we can bring our analysis to bear on some major problems of the economy. But first there is a matter that we must integrate into our discussion. This is the role that money plays in fixing or changing the level of GNP, along with the other forces that we have come to know.

Actually, we have been talking about money throughout our exposition. After all, one cannot discuss expenditure without assuming the existence of money. But now we must look behind this unexamined assumption and find out exactly what we mean when we speak of money. This will entail two tasks. In this chapter we shall investigate the question of what money *is*—for money is surely one of the most perplexing inventions of human society. Then in our next chapter, once we have come to understand what currency and gold and bank deposits are and how they come into being, we will look into the effect that money has on our economic operations.

THE SUPPLY OF MONEY

Let us begin by asking "What is money?" Coin and currency are certainly money. But are checks money? Are the deposits from which we draw checks money? Are savings accounts money? Government bonds?

The answer is somewhat arbitrary. Basically, money is anything we can use to make purchases with. But there exists a spectrum of financial instruments that serve this purpose—a continuum that varies in liquidity, or the ease with which it can be used for purchasing. By law, coin and currency are money because they are defined by law as "legal tender": a seller *must* accept them as payment. Checks do not have to be accepted (we have all seen signs in restaurants saying, "WE DO NOT ACCEPT CHECKS"), although in fact checks are overwhelmingly the most prevalent means of payment. In some states checks can be written on savings accounts as well as on checking accounts. On occasion, government bonds are accepted as a means of payment.

Thus, a variety of things can be counted as money. By far the most important general definition is the sum of all cash in the hands of the public plus all demand deposits. This amount is called M1-A by the Federal Reserve, which also keeps track of M1-B (M1-A plus some additional checking accounts at thrift institutions), M-2, M-3 and still further expanded definitions. The distinctions between these definitions are important for the monetary authorities but not for us. We will simply use the letter M to refer to the money supply, meaning cash in the hands of the public plus demand deposits.

CURRENCY

Money, then, is mainly currency and checking accounts. In 1979 for example, M was $382 billion, of which $107 billion was currency in the hands of the public, and $275 billion was the total of checking accounts, or demand deposits, to give them their technical name.

Of the two kinds of money, currency is the form most familiar to us. Yet there is a considerable mystery even about currency. Who determines how much currency there is? How is the supply of coins or bills regulated?

CREDIT CARDS

Money serves as a mechanism for storing potential purchasing power and for actually purchasing goods and services. Since cash and personal checks are the principal means for making these purchases, money has come to be defined as cash outside banks plus checking accounts. But what about credit cards. Shouldn't they be considered money?

Credit cards clearly can be used to make purchases, so that they appear on the surface to have a vital attribute of money. But a moment's reflection shows that in fact they *substitute* for cash or checks in which payment is finally made. The moment you pay your credit card bill, or the moment the credit card company pays the local merchant, the credit card is replaced by standard money. *Thus credit cards play the role of money only to the extent that credit bills are unpaid!*

In this role credit cards are not unique. Any unpaid bill or charge account is like money, in that you are able to purchase goods and services in exchange for your personal IOU. In a sense, each person is able to "print" money to the extent that he can persuade people to accept his IOUs. For most of us, that extent is very limited.

From an economist's point of view, the value of all outstanding trade credit (unpaid bills, unpaid charge accounts, or credit cards) *should* be considered money. It is not included in the official statistics for two reasons. First, it is difficult or impossible to figure how much trade credit is outstanding at any moment. Second, fluctuations in trade credit do not have a big impact on the economy. Ordinarily, the value of trade credit does not vary much, and therefore trade credit does not give rise to substantial changes in the effective money supply.

We often assume that the supply of currency is set by the government that issues it. Yet when we think about it, we realize that the government does not just hand out money, and certainly not coins or bills. When the government pays people, it is nearly always by check.

Then who does fix the amount of currency in circulation? You can answer the question by asking how you yourself determine how much currency you will carry. If you think about it, the answer is that you cash a check when you need more currency than you have, and you put the currency back into your checking account when you have more than you need.

What you do, everyone does. The amount of cash that the public holds at any time is no more and no less than the amount that it *wants* to hold. When it needs more—at Christmas, for instance—the public draws currency by cashing checks on its own checking accounts; and when Christmas is past, shopkeepers (who have received the public's currency) return it to their checking accounts.

Thus the amount of currency we have bears an obvious, important relation to the size of our bank accounts, for we can't write checks for cash if our accounts will not cover them.

Does this mean, then, that the banks have as much currency in their vaults as the total of our checking accounts? No, it does not. But to understand that, let us follow the course of some currency that we deposit in our banks for credit to our accounts.

BOOKKEEPING MONEY

When you put money into a commercial bank,* the bank does not hold that money for you as a pile of specially earmarked bills or as a bundle of checks made out to you from some payer. The bank takes notice of your deposit simply by crediting your account, a bookkeeping page recording your present balance. After the amount of the currency or check has been credited to you, the currency is put away with the bank's general store of vault cash and the checks are sent to the banks from which they came, where they will be charged against the accounts of the people who wrote them.

There is probably no misconception in economics harder to dispel than the idea that banks are warehouses stuffed with money. In point of fact, you might search as hard as you pleased in your bank, but you would find no money that was yours other than a bookkeeping account in your name. This seems like a very unreal form of money; and yet, the fact that you can present a check at the teller's window and convert your bookkeeping account into cash proves that your account must nonetheless be real.

But suppose that you and all the other depositors tried to convert your accounts into cash on the same day. You would then find something shocking. There would not be nearly enough cash in the bank's till to cover the total withdrawals. In 1979 for instance, total demand deposits in the United States amounted to about $275 billion. But the total amount of coin and currency held by the banks was only $11 billion!

At first blush, this seems like a highly dangerous state of affairs. But second thoughts are more reassuring. After all, most of us put money into a bank because we do *not* need it immediately, or because making payments in cash is a nuisance compared with making them by check. Yet, there is always the chance—more than that, the certainty—that some depositors *will* want their money in currency. How much currency will the banks need then? What will be a proper reserve for them to hold?

FEDERAL RESERVE SYSTEM

For many years, the banks themselves decided what reserve ratio constituted a safe proportion of currency to hold against their demand deposits. Today, however, most large banks are members of the Federal Reserve, a central banking system established in 1913 to strengthen the banking activities of the nation. Under the Federal Reserve System, the nation is divided into twelve districts, each with a **Federal Reserve Bank** owned (but not really controlled) by the member banks of its district. In turn, the twelve Reserve Banks are themselves coordinated by a seven-member Federal Reserve Board in Washington. Since the President, with the advice and consent of the Senate, appoints members of the board for fourteen-year terms, they constitute a body that has been purposely established as an independent nonpolitical monetary authority.[†]

---

*A commercial bank is a bank that is empowered by law to offer checking services. It may also have savings accounts.

†The independence of the Federal Reserve is a perennially controversial issue. See "An Extra Word" at the end of Chapter 16.

One of the most important functions of the Federal Reserve Board is to establish reserve ratios for different categories of banks, within limits set by Congress. Historically these reserve ratios have ranged between 13 and 26 percent of demand deposits for city banks, with a somewhat smaller reserve ratio for country banks. Today, reserve ratios are determined by size of bank and by kind of deposit, and they vary between 18 percent for the largest banks and 8 percent for the smallest. The Federal Reserve Board also sets reserve requirements for time deposits (the technical term for savings deposits). These range from 1 to 6 percent, depending on the ease of withdrawal.

THE BANKS' BANK

Yet here is something odd! We noticed that in 1979 the total amount of deposits was $275 billion and that banks' holdings of coin and currency were only $11 billion. This is much less than the 16 percent reserve against deposits established by the Federal Reserve Board. How can this be?

The answer is that cash is not the only reserve a bank holds against deposits. Claims on other banks are also held as its reserve.

What are these claims? Suppose, in your account in Bank A, you deposit a check from someone who has an account in Bank B. Bank A credits your account and then presents the check to Bank B for payment. Bank A does not expect to be paid coin and currency, however. Instead, Bank A and Bank B settle their transaction at still *another* bank where both Bank A and Bank B have their own accounts. These accounts are with the twelve Federal Reserve Banks of the country, where all banks who are members of the Federal Reserve System (and this accounts for banks holding most of the deposits in our banking system) *must* open accounts. Thus at the Federal Reserve Bank, Bank A's account will be credited, and Bank B's account will be debited, in this way moving reserves from one bank to the other.*

The Federal Reserve Banks serve their member banks in exactly the same way as the member banks serve the public. Member banks automatically deposit in their Federal Reserve accounts all checks they get from other banks. As a result, banks are constantly clearing their checks with one another through the Federal Reserve System, because their depositors are constantly writing checks on their own banks payable to someone who banks elsewhere. **Meanwhile, the balance that each bank maintains at the Federal Reserve—that is, the claim it has on other banks—counts, as much as any currency, as part of its reserve against deposits.**

In 1979, therefore, when demand deposits were $275 billion and cash in the banks only $11 billion, we would expect the member banks to have had heavy accounts with the Federal Reserve banks. And so they did—$33 billion in all. Thus, total reserves of the banks were $44 billion ($11 billion in cash plus $30 billion in Federal Reserve accounts), enough to satisfy the legal requirements of the Fed.

---

*When money is put into a bank account, the account is credited; when money is taken out, the account is debited.

FRACTIONAL RESERVES

Thus we see that our banks operate on what is called a *fractional reserve system.* That is, a certain specified fraction of all demand deposits must be kept on hand at all times in cash or at the Fed. The size of the minimum fraction is determined by the Federal Reserve, for reasons of control that we shall shortly learn. It is *not* determined, as we might be tempted to think, to provide a safe backing for our bank deposits. For under *any* fractional system, if *all* depositors decided to draw out their accounts in currency and coin from all banks at the same time, the banks would be unable to meet the demand for cash and would have to close. We call this a "run" on the banking system. Needless to say, runs can be terrifying and destructive economic phenomena.*

Why, then, do we court the risk of runs, however small this risk may be? What is the benefit of a fractional banking system? To answer that, let us look at our bank again.

LOANS AND INVESTMENTS

Suppose its customers have given our bank $1 million in deposits and that the Federal Reserve Board requirements are 20 percent, a simpler figure to work with than the actual one. Then we know that our bank must at all times keep $200,000 either in currency in its own till or in its demand deposit at the Federal Reserve Bank.

But having taken care of that requirement, what does the bank do with the remaining deposits? If it simply lets them sit, either as vault cash or as a deposit at the Federal Reserve, our bank will be very "liquid," but it will have no way of making an income. Unless it charges a very high fee for its checking services, it will have to go out of business.

And yet there is an obvious way for the bank to make an income while performing a valuable service. The bank can use all the cash and check claims it does not need for its reserve to make *loans* to businesses or families or to make financial *investments* in corporate or government bonds. It will thereby not only earn an income, but it will assist the process of business investment and government borrowing. Thus the mechanics of the banking system lead us back to the concerns at the very center of our previous analysis.

INSIDE THE BANKING SYSTEM

Fractional reserves allow banks to lend, or to invest in securities, part of the funds that have been deposited with them. But that is not the only usefulness of the fractional reserve system. It works as well to help enlarge or diminish the supply of investible or loanable funds, as the occasion demands. Let us follow the workings of this process. To make the mechanics of banking clear, we are going to look at the actual books of the bank—in simplified form, of course—so that we can see how the process of lending and investing appears to the banker himself.

---

*A "run" on the banking system is no longer so much of a threat as in the past, because the Federal Reserve could supply its members with vast amounts of cash. We shall learn how, later in this chapter.

ASSETS AND LIABILITIES

We begin by introducing two basic elements of business accounting: *assets* and *liabilities*. Every student at some time or another has seen the balance sheet of a firm, and many have wondered how total assets always equal total liabilities. The reason is very simple. Assets are all the things or claims a business owns. Liabilities are claims against those assets—some of them the claims of creditors, some the claims of owners (called the *net worth* of the business). Since assets show everything that a business owns, and since liabilities show how claims against these self-same things are divided between creditors and owners, it is obvious that the two sides of the balance sheet must always come to exactly the same total. The total of assets and the total of liabilities are an identity.

T ACCOUNTS

Businesses show their financial condition on a *balance sheet* on which all items on the left side represent assets and all those on the right side represent liabilities. By using a simple two-column balance sheet called a "T account" (because it looks like a T), we can follow very clearly what happens to our bank as we deposit money in it or as it makes loans or investment. (See Table 15.1.)

ORIGINAL BANK	
Assets	Liabilities
$1,000,000 (cash and checks)	$1,000,000 (money owed to depositors)
Total $1,000,000	Total $1,000,000

TABLE 15.1

T accounts always balance, because liabilities show claims on assets.

We start off with the example we have just used, in which we open a brand new bank with $1 million in cash and checks on other banks. Accordingly, our first entry in the T account shows the two sides of this transaction. Notice that our bank has gained an asset of $1 million, the cash and checks it now owns, and that it has simultaneously gained $1 million in liabilities, the deposits it *owes* to its depositors (who can withdraw their money).

ORIGINAL BANK			
Assets		Liabilities	
Vault Cash	$100,000	Deposits	$1,000,000
Deposit at Fed	900,000		
Total	$1,000,000	Total	$1,000,000

TABLE 15.2

This is how the T account looks after checks have been cleared through the Federal Reserve. If you will examine some bank balance sheets, you will see these items listed as "Cash and due from banks." This means, of course, cash in their own vaults plus their balance at the Federal Reserve.

As we know, however, our bank will not keep all its newly gained cash and checks in the till. It may hang on to some of the cash, but it will send all the checks it has received, plus any currency that it feels it does not need, to the Fed for deposit in its account there. Table 15.2 shows the resulting T account.

EXCESS RESERVES

Now we recall from our previous discussion that our bank does not want to remain in this very liquid, but very unprofitable, position. According to the law, it must retain only a certain percentage of its deposits in cash or at the Federal Reserve—20 percent in our hypothetical example. All the rest it is free to lend or invest. As things now stand, however, it has $1 million in reserves—$800,000 more than it needs. Hence, let us suppose that it decides to put these *excess reserves* to work by lending that amount to a sound business risk. (Note that banks do not lend the excess reserves themselves. These reserves, cash and deposits at the Fed, remain right where they are. Their function is to tell the banks how much they may loan or invest.)

MAKING A LOAN

Assume now that the Smith Corporation, a well-known firm, comes in for a loan of $800,000. Our bank is happy to lend them that amount. But making a loan does not mean that the bank now pays the company in cash out of its vaults. Rather, *it makes a loan by opening a new checking account for the firm* and by crediting that account with $800,000. (Or if, as is likely, the Smith firm already has an account with the bank, it will simply credit the proceeds of the loan to that account.)

Now our T account shows some interesting changes (see Table 15.3).

There are several things to note about this transaction. First, our bank's reserves (its cash and deposit at the Fed) have not yet changed. The $1 million in reserves are still there.

Second, notice that the Smith Corporation loan counts as a new asset for the bank because the bank now has a legal claim against the company for that amount. (The interest on the loan is not shown in the balance sheet; but when it is paid, it will show up as an addition to the bank's cash.)

Third, deposits have increased by $800,000. Note, however, that this $800,000 was not paid to the Smith firm out of anyone else's account in the bank.

ORIGINAL BANK				
Assets			*Liabilities*	
Cash and at Fed	$1,000,000		Original deposits	$1,000,000
Loan (Smith Corp.)	800,000		New deposit (Smith Corp.)	800,000
Total	**$1,800,000**		**Total**	**$1,800,000**

TABLE 15.3

The bank has used its excess reserves to make a loan. The loan itself is a signed IOU which is a new asset for the bank. The corresponding liability is the new deposit opened in the name of the borrower.

It is a new checking account, one that did not exist before. As a result, the supply of money is also up! More about this shortly.

THE LOAN IS SPENT

Was it safe to open this new account for the company? Well, we might see whether our reserves are now sufficient to cover the Smith Corporation's account as well as the original deposit accounts. A glance reveals that all is well. We still have $1 million in reserves against $1.8 million in deposits. Our reserve ratio is much higher than the 20 percent required by law.

It is so much higher, in fact, that we might be tempted to make another loan to the next customer who requests one, and in that way further increase our earning capacity. But an experienced banker shakes his head. "The Smith Corporation did not take out a loan and agree to pay interest on it just for the pleasure of letting that money sit with you," he explains. "Very shortly, the company will be writing checks on its balance to pay for goods or services; and when it does, you will need every penny of the reserve you now have."

That, indeed, is the case. Within a few days we find that our bank's account at the Federal Reserve Bank has been charged with a check for $800,000 written by the Smith Corporation in favor of the Jones Corporation, which carries its account at another bank. Now we find that our T account has changed dramatically. Look at Table 15.4.

ORIGINAL BANK

Assets		Liabilities	
Cash and at Fed	$ 200,000	Original deposits	$1,000,000
Loan (Smith Corp.)	800,000	Smith Corp. deposits	0
Total	**$1,000,000**	**Total**	**$1,000,000**

SECOND BANK

Assets		Liabilities	
Cash and at Fed	$800,000	Deposit (Jones Corp.)	$800,000
Total	**$800,000**	**Total**	**$800,000**

TABLE 15.4

The borrower uses the loan, and its deposits fall to zero. But the assets (and deposit liabilities) of another bank have risen.

Let us see exactly what has happened. First, the Smith Corporation's check has been charged against our account at the Fed and has reduced it from $900,000 to $100,000. Together with the $100,000 cash in our vault, this gives us $200,000 in reserves.

Second, the Smith Corporation's deposit is entirely gone, although its loan agreement remains with us as an asset.

Now if we refigure our reserves we find that they are just right. We are required to have $200,000 in vault cash or in our Federal Reserve account against our $1 million in deposits. That is exactly the amount we have left. Our bank is now fully "loaned up."

CONTINUING EFFECTS

But the banking *system* is not yet fully loaned up. So far, we have traced what happened only to our bank when the Smith Corporation spent the money in its deposit account. Now we must trace the effect of this action on the deposits and reserves of other banks.

We begin with the bank in which the Jones Corporation deposits the check it has just received from the Smith Corporation. Another look at Table 17.4 will show you that the Jones Corporation's bank now finds itself in exactly the same position as our bank was when we opened it with $1 million in new deposits, except that the addition to this second generation bank is smaller than the addition to the first generation bank.

As we can see, our second generation bank has gained $800,000 in cash and in deposits. Since it needs only 20 percent of this for required reserves, it finds itself with $640,000 excess reserves, which it is now free to use to make loans as investments. Suppose that it extends a loan to the Brown Company and that the Brown Company shortly thereafter spends the proceeds of that loan at the Black Company, which banks at yet a third bank. The two T accounts in Table 15.5 show how the total deposits will now be affected.

SECOND BANK
(after Brown Co. spends the proceeds of its loan)

Assets		Liabilities	
Cash and at Fed	$160,000	Deposits (Jones Corp.)	$800,000
Loan (to Brown Co.)	640,000	Deposits (Brown Co.)	0
Total	**$800,000**	**Total**	**$800,000**

THIRD BANK
(After Black Co. gets the check of Brown Co.)

Assets		Liabilities	
Cash and at Fed	$640,000	Deposit (Black Co.)	$640,000
Total	**$640,000**	**Total**	**$640,000**

TABLE 15.5

Here is a repetition of the same process, as the Second Bank uses its lending capacity to finance Brown Co.

As Figure 15.1 makes clear, the process will not stop here but can continue from one bank to the next as long as any lending power remains. Notice, however, that this lending power gets smaller and smaller and will eventually reach zero.

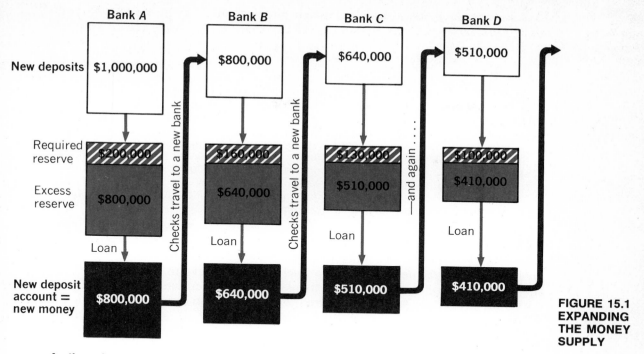

	Bank A	Bank B	Bank C	Bank D
New deposits	$1,000,000	$800,000	$640,000	$510,000
Required reserve	$200,000	$160,000	$130,000	$100,000
Excess reserve	$800,000	$640,000	$510,000	$410,000
	Loan	Loan	Loan	Loan
New deposit account = new money	$800,000	$640,000	$510,000	$410,000

Checks travel to a new bank — and again . . . . .

**FIGURE 15.1
EXPANDING
THE MONEY
SUPPLY**

As the relending process continues, successive banks add to their deposits, and the money supply increases. Note the resemblance to the multiplier process.

EXPANSION OF THE MONEY SUPPLY

If we now look at the bottom of Figure 15.1 we will see something very important. Every time any bank in this chain of transactions has opened an account for a new borrower, *the supply of money has increased.* Remember that the supply of money is the sum of currency outside the banking system (i.e., in our own pockets) plus the total of demand deposits. As our chain of banks kept opening new accounts, it was simultaneously expanding the total check-writing capacity of the economy. Thus, money has materialized, seemingly out of thin air.

Now how can this be? If we tell any banker in the chain that he has "created" money, he will protest vehemently. The loans he made, he will insist, were backed at the time he made them by excess reserves as large as the loan itself. Just as we had $800,000 in excess reserves when we made our initial loan to the Smith Corporation, so every subsequent loan was always backed 100 percent by unused reserves when it was made.

Our bankers are perfectly correct when they tell us that they never, never lend a penny more than they have. Money is not created in the lending process because a banker lends money he doesn't have. **Money is created because you and I generally pay each other by checks that give us claims against each other's bank.** If we constantly cashed the checks we exchanged, no new money would be

MONEY AND DEBT

All this gives us a fresh insight into the question of what money is. We said before that it is whatever we use to make payments. But what do we use? The answer is a surprising one. We use *debts*—specifically, the debts of commercial banks. Deposits are, after all, nothing but the liabilities that banks owe their customers. Furthermore, we can see that one purpose of the banking system is to buy debts from other units in the economy, such as businesses or governments, in exchange for its own debts (which are money). For when a bank opens an account for a business to which it has granted a loan or when it buys a government bond, what else is it doing but accepting a debt that is *not* usable as money, in exchange for its deposit liabilities that *are* usable as money. And why is it that banks create money when they make loans, but you or I do not, when we lend money? Because we all accept bank liabilities (deposits) as money, but we do not accept personal or business IOUs to make payments with.

created. But we do not. We deposit each other's checks in our own bank accounts; and in doing so, we give our banks more reserves than they need against the deposits we have just made. These new excess reserves make it possible for our banks to lend or invest, and thereby to open still more deposit accounts, which in turn lead to new reserves.

LIMITS ON THE EXPANSION

This all sounds a little frightening. Does it mean that the money supply can go on expanding indefinitely from a single new deposit? Wouldn't that be extremely dangerous?

It would of course be very dangerous, but there is no possibility that it can happen. For having understood how the supply of money can expand from an original increase in deposits, we may now understand equally well what keeps an expansion within bounds.

1. Not every loan generates an increase in bank deposits

If our bank had opened a loan account for the Smith Corporation at the same time that another firm had paid off a similar loan, there would have been no original expansion in bank deposits. In that case, the addition of $800,000 to the Smith account would have been exactly balanced by a decline of $800,000 in someone else's account. Even if that decline would have taken place in a different bank, it would still mean that the nation's total of bank deposits would not have risen, and therefore no new money would have been created. Thus, only net additions to loans have an expansionary effect. We will shortly see how such net additions arise in the first place.

2. There is a limit to the rise in money supply from a single increase in deposits

As Figure 15.1 shows, in the chain of deposit expansion each successive bank has a smaller increase in deposits, because each bank has to keep some of its newly gained cash or checks as reserve. Hence the amount of *excess* reserves, against which loans can be made, steadily falls.

Further, we can see that the amount of the total monetary expansion from an original net increase in deposits is governed by the size of the fraction that has to be kept aside each time as reserve. **In fact, we can see that just as with the multiplier, the cumulative effect of an increase in deposits will be determined by the reciprocal of the reserve fraction.** If each bank must keep one-fifth of its increased deposits as reserves, then the cumulative effect of an original increase in deposits, when it has expanded through the system, is five times the original increase. If reserves are one-fourth, the expansion is limited to four times the original increase, and so on.*

3. The monetary expansion process can work in reverse

Suppose that the banking system as a whole suffers a net loss of deposits. Instead of putting $1 million into a bank, the public takes it out in cash. The bank will now have too few reserves and it will have to cut down its loans or sell its investments to gain the reserves it needs. In turn, as borrowers pay off their loans, or as bond buyers pay for their securities, cash will drain from other banks who will now find *their* reserves too small in relation to their deposits. In turn, they will therefore have to sell more investments or curtail still other loans, and this again will squeeze still other banks and reduce their reserves, with the same consequences.

Thus, just as an original expansion in deposits can lead to a multiple expansion, so an original contraction in deposits can lead to a multiple contraction. The size of this contraction is also limited by the reciprocal of the reserve fraction. If banks have to hold a 25 percent reserve, then an original fall of $100,000 in deposits will lead to a total fall of $400,000, assuming that the system was fully loaned up to begin with. If they had to hold a 20 percent reserve, a fall of $100,000 could pyramid to $500,000.

4. The expansion process may not be fully carried through

We have assumed that each bank in the chain always lends out an amount equal to its excess reserve, but this may not be the case. The third or fifth bank along the way may have trouble finding a credit-worthy customer and may decide—for the moment, anyway—to sit on its excess reserves. Or borrowers along the chain may take out cash from some of their new deposits and thereby reduce the banks' reserves and their lending powers. Thus the potential expansion may be only partially realized.

5. The expansion process takes time

Like the multiplier process, the expansion of the money supply encounters many "frictions" in real life. Banks do not instantly expand loans when their reserves

---

*If M is the money supply, D is net new deposits and r is the reserve ratio, then $\Delta M = 1/r \times \Delta D$. Notice that this formula is exactly the same as that for the multiplier.

rise; bank customers do not instantly spend the proceeds of bank loans. The time lags in banking are too variable to enable us to make an estimate of how long it takes for an initial increase in new deposits to work its way through the system, but the time period is surely a matter of months for two or three rounds.

WHY BANKS MUST WORK TOGETHER

There is an interesting problem concealed behind this crisscrossing of deposits that leads to a slowly rising level of the money supply. Suppose that an imaginary island economy was served by a single bank (and let us forget about all complications of international trade, etc.), and this bank, which worked on a 20 percent reserve ratio, was suddenly presented with an extra one million dollars worth of reserves—let us say newly mined pure gold. Our bank could, of course, increase its loans to customers. By how much? *By five million dollars!*

In other words, our island bank, all by itself, could use an increase in its reserves to create a much larger increase in the money supply. It is not difficult to understand why. Any borrower of the new five million, no matter where he spent his money on the island, would only be giving his checks to someone who also banked at the single, solitary bank. The whole five million, in other words, would stay *within* the bank as its deposits, although the identity of those depositors would, of course, shift. Indeed, there is no reason why such a bank should limit its expansion of the money supply to five million. As long as the soundness of the currency was unquestioned, such a bank could create as much money as it wanted through new deposits, since all of those deposits would remain in its own keeping.

The imaginary bank makes it plain why ordinary commercial banks *cannot* expand deposits beyond their excess reserves. Unlike the monopoly bank, they must expect to *lose* their deposits to other banks when their borrowers write checks on their new accounts. As a result they will also lose their reserves, and this can lead to trouble.

OVERLENDING

This situation is important enough to warrant taking a moment to examine. Suppose that in our previous example we had decided to lend the Smith Corporation not $800,000 but $900,000, and suppose as before that the Smith Corporation used the proceeds of that loan to pay the Jones Corporation. Now look at the condition of our bank after the Smith payment has cleared (Table 15.6).

ORIGINAL BANK			
Assets		Liabilities	
Cash and at Fed	$ 100,000	Original deposits	$1,000,000
Loan (Smith Corp.)	900,000	Smith Corp. deposit	0
Total	$1,000,000	Total	$1,000,000

TABLE 15.6

A bank that lends an amount larger than its excess reserve will be in trouble. Its reserves will fall below the level required by law.

Our reserves would now have dropped to 10 percent! Indeed, if we had loaned the company $1,000,000 we would be in danger of insolvency.

Banks are, in fact, very careful not to overlend. If they find that they have inadvertently exceeded their legal reserve requirements, they quickly take remedial action. One way that a bank may repair the situation is by borrowing reserves for a short period (paying interest on them, of course) from another bank that may have a temporary surplus at the Fed; this is called borrowing *federal funds*. Or a bank may quickly sell some of its government bonds and add the proceeds to its reserve account at the Fed. Or again, it may add to its reserves the proceeds of any loans that have come due and deliberately fail to replace these expired loans with new loans. Finally, a bank may borrow reserves directly from its Federal Reserve Bank and pay interest for the loan. We shall shortly look into this method when we talk about the role of the Federal Reserve in regulating the quantity of money.

The main point is clear. A bank is safe in lending only an amount that it can afford to lose to another bank. But of course one bank's loss is another's gain. That is why, by the exchange of checks, the banking system can accomplish the same result as the island monopoly bank, whereas no individual bank can hope to do so.

INVESTMENTS AND INTEREST

If a bank uses its excess reserves to buy securities, does that lead to the same multiplication effect as a bank loan?

It can. When a bank buys government securities, it usually does so from a securities dealer, a professional trader in bonds.* Its check (for $800,000 in our example) drawn on its account at the Federal Reserve will be made out to a dealer, who will deposit it in his bank. As a result, the dealer's bank suddenly finds itself with an $800,000 new deposit. It must keep 20 percent of this as required reserve, but the remainder is excess reserve against which it can make loans or investments as it wishes.

Is there a new deposit, corresponding to that of the borrower? There is: the new deposit of the securities dealer. Note that in his case, as in the case of the borrower, the new deposit on the books of the bank has not been put there by the transfer of money from some other commercial bank. The $800,000 deposit has come into being through the deposit of a check of the Federal Reserve Bank, which is not a commercial bank. Thus it represents a new addition to the deposits of the private banking system.

Let us see this in the T accounts. Table 15.7 shows what our first bank's T account looks like after it has bought its $800,000 in bonds (paying for them with its Federal Reserve checking account).

As we can see, there are no excess reserves here. But look at the bank in which the seller of the government bond has deposited the check he has just received from our bank (Table 15.8). Here there are excess reserves of $640,000 with which additional investments can be made. It is possible for such new deposits, albeit diminishing each time, to remain in the financial circuit for some

---

*The dealer may be only a middleman, who will in turn buy from, or sell to, corporations or individuals. This doesn't change our analysis, however.

ORIGINAL BANK				
Assets			Liabilities	
Cash and at Fed	$ 200,000		Deposits	$1,000,000
Government bonds	800,000			
Total	**$1,000,000**		**Total**	**$1,000,000**

TABLE 15.7

Excess reserves can be used to buy bonds as well as to finance loans.

SECOND BANK				
Assets			Liabilities	
Cash	$800,000		New deposit of bond seller	$800,000
Total	**$800,000**		**Total**	**$800,000**

TABLE 15.8

When the seller of the bond deposits his check, the same money-expanding process will be set into motion.

time, moving from bank to bank as an active business is done in buying government bonds.

YIELDS

Meanwhile, however, the very activity in bidding for government bonds is likely to raise their price and thereby lower their rate of interest.

This is a situation that you will probably be faced with in your personal life, so you should understand it. A bond has a *fixed* rate of return and a stated face value. If it is a 9 percent, $1,000 bond, this means it will pay $90 interest yearly. If the bond now sells on the marketplace for $1,200, the $90 yearly interest will be less than a 9 percent return ($90 is only 7.5 percent of $1,200). If the price should fall to $900, the $90 return will be more than 9 percent ($90 is 10 percent of $900). Thus the *yield* of a bond varies inversely—in the other direction—from its market price.

When the price of government bonds changes, all bond prices tend to change in the same direction. This is because all bonds are competing for investors' funds. If the yield on "governments" falls, investors will switch from governments to other, higher-yielding bonds. But as they bid for these other bonds, the prices of these bonds will rise—and their yields will fall, too!

In this way, a change in yields spreads from one group of bonds to another. A lower rate of interest or a lower yield on government securities is quickly reflected in lower rates or yields for other kinds of bonds. In turn, a lower rate of interest on bonds makes loans to business look more attractive. Thus, sooner or later, excess reserves are apt to be channeled to new loans as well as new investments. Thereafter the deposit-building process follows its familiar course.

LOOKING BACK

1. The supply of money is generally defined as the cash in the possession of the public (not the cash in bank vaults) plus checking deposits, technically known as demand deposits. The total is called M (technically M1–A). Other measures of money include savings accounts and other liquid assets.

2. Banks are required by the Federal Reserve Act to maintain stated proportions of actual cash (in their own vaults) or claims on other banks as reserves against their deposits. These reserves are largely maintained as accounts with one of the twelve Federal Reserve banks of the country. This is called the fractional reserve system. It permits banks to use excess reserves, above the legal requirement, to make loans or investments.

3. When a bank makes a loan against its excess reserve, it opens a deposit in the name of the borrower. That deposit is normally used for business purposes, and thereby becomes a new deposit in some other bank. In turn that bank must keep a legal reserve to cover part of its new deposit, but is free to lend or invest an amount equal to its excess reserve.

4. The successive spending of loans creates additional deposits through the system, acting like a multiplier. These new deposits are additions to the money supply. No single bank on its own would dare to expand the total of deposits, but working together as a system, the member banks can increase this supply to the extent that fractional reserve requirements permit.

5. The money expansion has several limits: Only net loans create new money, not loans that are offset by repayments; expansion is controlled by the reserve fraction, just like the multiplier process; monetary expansion can work in reverse if repayments exceed new loans; the expansion process may not be carried all the way through; and the process takes time.

6. A bank that uses its excess reserve to buy bonds also creates new deposits when the seller of the bond deposits his check. This too can expand the money supply.

7. As bonds are bought and sold, their price changes. Because bonds have fixed interest obligations, a higher or lower price for a bond changes its yield. As bond prices rise, yields fall, and vice versa.

ECONOMIC VOCABULARY

QUESTIONS

1. Why do we not count cash in the tills of commercial banks in the money supply? When you deposit currency in a commercial bank, what happens to it? Can you ask for your particular bills again? If you demanded to see "your" account, what would it be?

2. What determines how much vault cash a bank must hold against its deposits? Would you expect this proportion to change in some seasons, such as Christmas? Do you think it would be the same in worried times as in placid times? In new countries as in old ones?

3. What are excess reserves? Suppose a bank has $500,000 in deposits and that there is a reserve ratio of 30 percent imposed by law. What is its required reserve? Suppose it happens to hold $200,000 in vault cash or at its account at the Fed. What, if any, is its excess reserve?

4. If the bank above wanted to make loans or investments, how much would it be entitled to lend or invest? Suppose its deposits increased by another $50,000. Could it lend or invest this entire amount? Any of it? How much?

5. If a bank lends money, it opens an account in the name of the borrower. Now suppose the borrower draws down his new account. What happens to the reserves of the lending bank? Show this in a T account.

6. Suppose the borrower sends his check for $1,000 to someone who banks at another bank. Describe what happens to the deposits of the second bank. If the reserve ratio is 20 percent, how much new lending or investing can it do?

7. If the reserve ratio is 20 percent, and the original addition to reserves is $1,000, what will be the total potential amount of new money that can be created by the banking system? If the ratio is 25 percent?

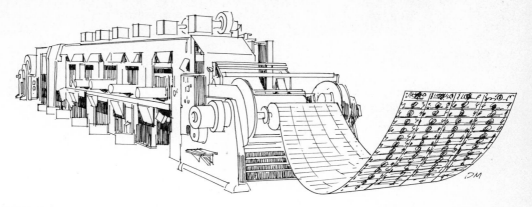

Chapter 16 CONTROLLING THE MONEY SUPPLY

A LOOK AHEAD

In our last chapter we learned what money was and how the money supply could be increased. But we have not yet investigated the methods by which the national government exercises control over the money supply; this we shall do here.

(1) First we look into the workings of the Federal Reserve System, particularly with respect to the three ways in which it can loosen or tighten the monetary strings. The question of how much money the Federal Reserve *should* create is taken up in the next chapter; the material here prepares us to understand it.

(2) Second, we explore a question everyone is curious about: What exactly is the connection between money and gold?

(3) Finally we will trace the process by which money is actually made and distributed. Here we take a look at the printing presses and catch a glimpse of Fort Knox.

We have now seen how a banking system can create money through the creation of excess reserves. But the key to the process is the creation of the *original* excess reserves, for without them the cumulative process will not be set in motion. We remember, for example, that a loan will not result in an increase in the money supply if it is offset by a decline in lending somewhere else in the banking system; neither will the purchase of a bond by one commercial bank if it is only buying a security sold by another. **To get a net addition to loans or investments, however, a banking system—assuming that it is fully loaned up—needs an increase in its reserves.** Where do these extra reserves come from? That is the question we must turn to next.

ROLE OF THE FEDERAL RESERVE

In our example we have already met one source of changes in reserves. When the public needs less currency, and it deposits its extra holdings in the banks, reserves rise, as we have seen. Contrariwise, when the public wants more currency, it depletes the banks' holdings of currency and thereby lowers their reserves. In the latter case, the banks may find that they have insufficient reserves behind their deposits. To get more currency or claims on other banks, they will have to sell securities or reduce their loans. This might put a very severe crimp in the economy. Hence, to allow bank reserves to be regulated by the public's fluctuating demand for cash would seem to be an impossible way to run our monetary system.

But we remember that bank reserves are not mainly currency; in fact, currency is a relatively minor item. Most reserves are the accounts that member banks hold at the Federal Reserve. Hence, if these accounts could somehow be increased or decreased, we could regulate the amount of reserves—and thus the permissible total of deposits—without regard to the public's changing need for cash.

This is precisely what the Federal Reserve System is designed to do. Essentially, the system is set up to regulate the supply of money by raising or lowering the reserves of its member banks. When these reserves are raised, member banks find themselves with excess reserves and are thus in a position to make loans and investments by which the supply of money will increase further. Conversely, when the Federal Reserve lowers the reserves of its member banks, they will no longer be able to make loans and investments, or they may even have to reduce loans or get rid of investments, thereby extinguishing deposit accounts and contracting the supply of money.

MONETARY CONTROL MECHANISMS

How does the Federal Reserve operate? There are three ways.

1. Changing reserve requirements

It was the Federal Reserve itself, we will remember, that originally determined how much in reserves its member banks should hold against their deposits. Hence by changing that reserve requirement for a given level of deposits, it can give its member banks excess reserves or can create a shortage of reserves.

237
CHAPTER 16
CONTROL-
LING THE
MONEY
SUPPLY

This has two effects. First, it immediately changes the lending or investing capacity of all banks. In our imaginary bank we have assumed that reserves were set at 20 percent of deposits. Suppose now that the Federal Reserve determined to lower reserve requirements to 15 percent. It would thereby automatically create extra lending or investing power for our *existing* reserves. Our bank with $1 million in deposits and $200,000 in reserves could now lend or invest an additional $50,000 without any new funds coming in from depositors. On the other hand, if requirements were raised to, say, 30 percent, we would find that our original $200,000 reserve was $100,000 short of requirements, and we would have to curtail lending or investing until we were again in line with requirements.

Second, the new reserve requirements raise or lower the reserve multiplier —expanding or contracting the limits of the flexible money system. Because these new reserve requirements affect *all* banks, changing reserve ratios is a very effective way of freeing or contracting bank credit on a large scale. But it is an instrument that sweeps across the entire banking system in an undiscriminating fashion. It is therefore used only rarely, when the Federal Reserve Board feels that the supply of money is seriously short or dangerously excessive and needs remedy on a countrywide basis.

2. Changing discount rates

A second means of control uses interest rates as the money-controlling device. Recall that member banks that are short on reserves have a special privilege, if they wish to exercise it. They can *borrow* reserve balances from the Federal Reserve Bank itself and add them to their regular reserve account at the bank.

The Federal Reserve Bank, of course, charges interest for lending reserves, and this interest is called the **discount rate**. By raising or lowering this rate, the Federal Reserve can make it attractive or unattractive for member banks to borrow to augment reserves. Thus, in contrast with changing the reserve ratio itself, changing the discount rate is a mild device that allows each bank to decide for itself whether it wishes to increase its reserves. In addition, changes in the discount rate tend to influence the whole structure of interest rates, either tightening or loosening money. When interest rates are high, we have what we call **tight money**. This means not only that borrowers have to pay higher rates, but that banks are stricter and more selective in judging the credit worthiness of business applications for loans. Conversely, when interest rates decline, money is called easy, meaning that it is not only cheaper but literally easier to borrow.

Although changes in the discount rate can be used as a major means of controlling the money supply and are used to control it in some countries, they are not used for this purpose in the U.S. The Federal Reserve Board does not allow banks to borrow whatever they would like at the current discount rate. The discount "window" is a place where a bank can borrow small amounts of money to cover a small deficiency in its reserves, but it is not a place where banks can borrow major amounts of money to expand their lending portfolios. As a result, **the discount rate serves more as a signal of what the Federal Reserve would like to see happen than as an active force in determining the total borrowings of banks.**

3. Open-market operations

Most frequently used, however, is a third technique called open-market operations. This technique permits the Federal Reserve Banks to change the supply of reserves by buying or selling U.S. government bonds on the open market.

How does this work? Let us suppose that the Federal Reserve authorities wish to increase the reserves of member banks. They will begin to buy government securities from dealers in the bond market, and they will pay these dealers with Federal Reserve checks.

Notice something about these checks: *They are not drawn on any commercial bank!* They are drawn on the Federal Reserve Bank itself. The security dealer who sells the bond will, of course, deposit the Federal Reserve's check, as if it

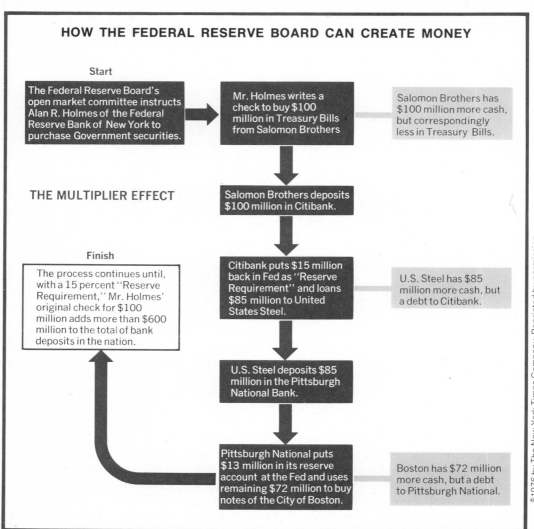

HOW THE FEDERAL RESERVE BOARD CAN CREATE MONEY

Start

The Federal Reserve Board's open market committee instructs Alan R. Holmes of the Federal Reserve Bank of New York to purchase Government securities.

Mr. Holmes writes a check to buy $100 million in Treasury Bills from Salomon Brothers

Salomon Brothers has $100 million more cash, but correspondingly less in Treasury Bills.

THE MULTIPLIER EFFECT

Salomon Brothers deposits $100 million in Citibank.

Finish

The process continues until, with a 15 percent "Reserve Requirement," Mr. Holmes' original check for $100 million adds more than $600 million to the total of bank deposits in the nation.

Citibank puts $15 million back in Fed as "Reserve Requirement" and loans $85 million to United States Steel.

U.S. Steel has $85 million more cash, but a debt to Citibank.

U.S. Steel deposits $85 million in the Pittsburgh National Bank.

Pittsburgh National puts $13 million in its reserve account at the Fed and uses remaining $72 million to buy notes of the City of Boston.

Boston has $72 million more cash, but a debt to Pittsburgh National.

were any other check, in his own commercial bank; and his bank will send the Federal Reserve's check through for credit to its own account, as if it were any other check. *As a result, the dealer's bank will have gained reserves, although no other commercial bank has lost reserves.* On balance, then, the system has more lending and investing capacity than it had before. In fact, it now has *excess* reserves and these, as we have seen, will spread out through the system. **Thus by buying bonds the Federal Reserve has, in fact, deposited money in the accounts of its members, thereby giving them the extra reserves that it set out to create** (see box).

Conversely, if the authorities decide that member banks' reserves are too large, they will sell securities. Now the process works in reverse. Security dealers or other buyers of bonds will send their own checks on their own regular commercial banks to the Federal Reserve in payment for these bonds. This time the Fed will take the checks of its member banks and charge their accounts, thereby reducing their reserves. **Since these checks will not find their way to another commercial bank, the system as a whole will have suffered a diminution of its reserves.** By selling securities, in other words, the Federal Reserve authorities lower the Federal Reserve accounts of member banks, thereby diminishing their reserves. Isn't this, you might ask, really the same thing as raising or lowering the reserve ratio? If the Fed is really just putting money into member bank accounts when it buys bonds and taking money out when it sells them, why does it bother to go through the open market? Why not just tell the member banks that their reserves are larger or smaller?

Analytically, you are entirely right. There are however cogent reasons for working through the bond market. The open-market technique allows banks to *compete* for their share of the excess reserves that are being made available or taken away. Banks that are good at attracting depositors will thereby get extra benefit from an increase in the money supply. Thus, rather than assigning excess reserves by executive fiat, the Fed uses the open market as an allocation device.

In addition, open-market operations allow the Fed to make very small changes in the money supply, whereas changes in reserve requirements would be difficult to adjust in very fine amounts.

ASYMMETRIC CONTROL

How effective are all these powers over the money supply? The Federal Reserve Board's capacity to control money is often compared to our ability to manipulate a string. If the Federal Reserve Board wishes to *reduce* the money supply, it can increase the discount rate or sell bonds. Sooner or later, this tends to be effective. If banks have free or excess reserves, they will not immediately have to reduce their lending portfolios; but eventually, by pulling on the string hard enough, the Fed can force a reduction in bank loans and the money supply.

The Federal Reserve Board's capacity to increase the money supply is not equally great. It can reduce reserve rates and buy bonds, but it cannot *force* banks to make loans if they do not wish to do so. Banks can, if they wish, simply increase their excess reserves. Normally, banks wish to make loans and earn profits; but if risks are high, they may not wish to do so. Such a situation occurred in the Great Depression. Banks piled up vast reserves rather than make loans, since the

239
CHAPTER 16
CONTROL-
LING THE
MONEY
SUPPLY

risk of default was too high to make most loans an attractive economic gamble. In terms of our analogy, the Federal Reserve Board can pull, but it cannot push on its string of controls.

STICKY PRICES

We are almost ready to look into the dynamics of money in our next chapter, but we must examine a question that we have heretofore passed over in silence. We have taken for granted that we need a larger supply of money in order to expand output. But why should we? Why could we not grow just as well if the supply of money were fixed?

Theoretically we could. If we cut prices as we increased output, a given amount of money (or a given amount of expenditure) could cover an indefinitely large real output. Furthermore, as prices fell, workers would be content not to ask for higher wages (or would even accept lower wages), since in real terms they would be just as well or better off.

It is not difficult to spot the flaw in this argument. In the real world, prices of many goods cannot be cut easily. If the price of steel rose and fell as quickly and easily as prices on the stock exchange or if wages went down without a mur-mur of resistance or if rents and other contractual items could be quickly ad-justed, then prices would be flexible and we would not require any enlargement of our money supply to cover a growing real output.

In fact, as we know, prices are extremely "sticky" in the downward direc-tion. Union leaders do not look with approval on wage cuts, even when living costs fall. Contractual prices cannot be quickly adjusted. Many big firms admin-ister their prices and carefully avoid price competition: Note, for example, that the price of many customer items is printed on the package months before the item will be sold.

Thus we can see that a fixed supply of money would put the economy into something of a straitjacket. As output tended to increase, business would need more money to finance production, and consumers would need more money to make their larger expenditures. If business could get more money from the banks, all would be well. But suppose it could not. Then the only way it could get a larger supply of cash would be to persuade someone to lend the money, and persuasion would be in the form of a higher rate of interest. But this rising in-terest rate would discourage other businesses from going ahead with their plans. Hence the would-be-boom would be stopped dead in its tracks by a sheer short-age of spending power.

A flexible money supply obviates this economic suffocation. The fact that banks can create money (provided that they have excess reserves) enables them to take care of businesses that wish to make additional expenditures. The expendi-tures themselves put additional money into the hands of consumers. And the spending of consumers in turn sends the enlarged volume of purchasing power back to business firms to complete the great flow of expenditure and receipt.

HIGH POWERED MONEY AND INFLATION

A flexible money supply rescues the system from suffocation. But does it expose it to the dangers of hyperventilation? Does an expandable money supply threaten us with inflation?

In our next chapter we will directly tackle the relation between the money supply and the level of prices. But we ought to say a preliminary word here. For clearly bank reserves have an inflationary potential in a fractional reserve system, simply by virtue of the fact that they are capable of creating a multiple of themselves. That is why bank reserves are called *high powered money,* and why economists pay careful attention to the volume of reserves when they are considering the extent of the inflationary dangers facing an economy.

But the fact that high powered money *can* become the basis for inflation is not at all the same as saying that inflation is directly caused by high powered money. It merely tells us that the existence of a flexible money supply poses a problem of monetary management—the theme of the chapter to come.

There is, however, a special source of inflationary increases in bank reserves that we should know about. If a nation becomes the recipient of large inflows of foreign gold, as the United States was during the 1930s; or if foreigners put their money in its banks, as has been the case with Germany and Switzerland in modern times, banks will find their deposits rising. Unlike the case in which deposits increase because of central bank action, this rise may take place despite efforts of the central bank to hold down the quantity of high powered money. The remedy for such inflationary inflows of gold and foreign money takes us into the area of international finance, not a subject for this chapter. But we ought to be aware that such problems can arise, and that they may be difficult to cope with.

PAPER MONEY AND GOLD

Finally, let us clear up one last mystery of the monetary system—the mystery of where currency (coin and bills) actually comes from and where it goes. If we examine most of our paper currency, we will find that it has "Federal Reserve Note" on it: That is, it is paper money issued by the Federal Reserve System. We understand, by now, how the public gets these notes: It simply draws them from its checking accounts. When it does so, the commercial banks, finding their supplies of vault cash low, ask their Federal Reserve district banks to ship them as much new cash as they need.

And what does the Federal Reserve Bank do? It takes packets of bills ($1 and $5 and $10) out of its vaults, *where these stacks of printed paper have no monetary significance at all,* charges the requisite amount against its member banks' balances, and ships the cash out by armored truck. So long as these new stacks of bills remain in the member banks' possession, they are still not money! But soon they will pass out to the public, where they will be money. Do not forget, of course, that as a result the public will have that much *less* money left in its checking accounts.

Could this currency-issuing process go on forever? Could the Federal Reserve print as much money as it wanted to? Suppose that the authorities at the Federal Reserve decided to order a trillion dollars worth of bills from the treasury mints. What would happen when those bills arrived at the Federal Reserve Banks? The answer is that they would simply gather dust in their vaults. There would be no way for the Federal Reserve to "issue" its money unless the public wanted cash. And the amount of cash the public could want is always limited by the amount of money in its checking accounts.

241
CHAPTER 16
CONTROL-
LING THE
MONEY
SUPPLY

Thus the spectre of "rolling the printing presses" has to be looked at skeptically. In a nation such as pre-Hitler Germany, where most individuals were paid by cash, not by check, it was easier to get the actual bills into circulation than it would be in a highly developed check money system such as ours. The roads to inflation are many, but the actual printing of money is not likely to be one of them.*

THE GOLD COVER

Are there no limitations on this note-issuing or reserve-creating process? Until 1967 there *were* limitations imposed by Congress, requiring the Federal Reserve to hold gold certificates equal in value to at least 25 percent of all outstanding notes. (Gold certificates are a special kind of paper money issued by the U.S. Treasury and backed 100 percent by gold bullion in Fort Knox.) Prior to 1964 there was a further requirement that the amount of gold certificates also be sufficient to give a 25 percent backing as well to the total amount of member bank deposits held by the Fed. Thus the legal obligation not to go beyond this 25 percent gold cover provided a strict ceiling on the amount of member bank reserves the Federal Reserve system could create or on the amount of notes it could ship at the request of its member banks.

All this presented no problem in, say, 1940, when the total of member bank reserves plus Federal Reserve notes came to only $20 billion, against which we held gold certificates worth almost $22 billion. Trouble began to develop, however, in the 1960s when a soaring GNP was accompanied by a steadily rising volume of both member bank reserves and Federal Reserve notes. By 1964, for example, member bank reserves had grown to $22 billion, and outstanding Reserve notes to nearly $35 billion. At the same time, our gold stock had declined to just over $15 billion. With $57 billion in liabilities ($22 billion in member bank reserves plus $35 billion in notes) and only $15 billion in gold certificates, the 25 percent cover requirement was clearly imperiled.

Congress thereupon removed the cover requirement from member bank reserves, leaving all our gold certificates available as backing for our Federal Reserve notes. But even that did not solve the problem. Currency in circulation contined to rise with a record GNP until it exceeded $40 billion in 1967. Our gold stock meanwhile continued to decline to $12 billion in that year and threatened to fall further. The handwriting on the wall indicated that the 25 percent cover could not long be maintained.

There were basically two ways out. One would have been to change the gold cover requirements from 25 percent to, say, 10 percent. That would have made our gold stock more than adequate to back our paper money (and our member bank deposits, too).

---

*We have all seen pictures of German workers being paid their wages in wheelbarrow loads of marks. The question is this: Why didn't the German authorities simply print paper money with bigger denominations, so that someone who was paid a billion marks a week could get ten 100 million mark notes, not ten thousand 1 million mark notes? The answer is that it takes time to go through the bureaucratic process of ordering a new print run of higher denomination notes. Imagine a young economist at the finance ministry suggesting to his chief that they ought to stock up on billion mark notes to be put into circulation six months hence. His superior would certainly be horrified. "You can't do that," he would protest. "Why, an order for billion mark notes would be—inflationary!"

**243
CHAPTER 16
CONTROL-
LING THE
MONEY
SUPPLY**

GOLDFINGER AT WORK

Some years ago a patriotic women's organization, alarmed lest the Communists had tunneled under the Atlantic, forced an inspection of the gold stock buried at Fort Knox. It proved to be all there. An interesting question arises as to the repercussions, had they found the great vault to be bare. Perhaps we might have followed the famous anthropological example of the island of Yap in the South Seas, where heavy stone cartwheels are the symbol of wealth for the leading families. One such family was particularly remarkable insofar as its cartwheel lay at the bottom of a lagoon, where it had fallen from a canoe. Although it was absolutely irretrievable and even invisible, the family's wealth was considered unimpaired, since everyone knew the stone was there. If the Kentucky depository had been empty, a patriotic declaration by the ladies that the gold really was in Fort Knox might have saved the day for the United States.

The second way was much simpler: *eliminate the gold cover entirely.* With very little fuss, this is what Congress did in 1967.

GOLD AND MONEY

Does the presence or absence of a gold cover make any difference? From the economist's point of view it does not. Gold is a metal with a long and rich history of hypnotic influence, so there is undeniably a psychological usefulness in having gold behind a currency. But unless that currency is 100 percent convertible into gold, *any* money demands an act of faith on the part of its users. If that faith is destroyed, the money becomes valueless; so long as it is unquestioned, the money *is* "as good as gold."

Thus the presence or absence of a gold backing for currency is purely a psychological problem, so far as the value of a domestic currency is concerned. But the point is worth pursuing a little further. Suppose our currency *were* 100 percent convertible into gold—suppose, in fact, that we used only gold coins as currency. Would that improve the operation of our economy?

A moment's reflection should reveal that it would not. We would still have to cope with a very difficult problem that our bank deposit money handles rather easily. This is the problem of how we could increase the supply of money or diminish it, as the needs of the economy changed. With gold coins as money, we would either have a frozen stock of money (with consequences that we shall trace in the next chapter), or our supply of money would be at the mercy of our luck in goldmining or the currents of international trade that funneled gold into our hands or took it away. And incidentally, a gold currency would not obviate inflation, as many countries have discovered when the vagaries of international trade or a fortuitous discovery of gold mines increased their holdings of gold faster than their actual output.

MONEY AND BELIEF

How, then, do we explain the world-wide rush to buy gold—a rush that has raised the dollar price of gold from $35 an ounce—its official price as late as 1971 —to over $800 an ounce in 1979, before it fell again to half that level.

Once again, the economist offers no rational explanation for such a phenomenon. There is nothing in gold itself that possesses more value than silver, uranium, land, or labor. Indeed, judged strictly as a source of usable values, gold is rather low on the spectrum of human requirements. **The sole reason why people want gold—rich people and poor people, sophisticated people and ignorant ones—is that gold has been for centuries a metal capable of catching and holding our fancy, and in troubled times it is natural enough that we turn to this enduring symbol of wealth as the best bet for preserving our purchasing power in the future.**

Will gold in fact remain valuable forever? And if so, how valuable? There is absolutely no way to answer such a question.

As we cautioned at the outset, money is a highly sophisticated and curious invention. At one time or another nearly everything imaginable has served as the magic symbol of money: whales' teeth, shells, feathers, bark, furs, blankets, butter, tobacco, leather, copper, silver, gold, and (in the most advanced nations) pieces of paper with pictures on them, or simply numbers on a computer printout. In fact, anything is usable as money, provided that there is a natural or enforceable scarcity of it, so that men can usually come into its possession only through carefully designated ways. Behind all the symbols, however, rests the central requirement of faith. **Money serves its indispensable purposes as long as we believe in it. It ceases to function the moment we do not. Money has well been called "the promises men live by."**

But the creation of money and the control over its supply is still only half the question. We have yet to trace how our money supply influences the flow of output itself—or to put it differently, how the elaborate institutions through which men promise to honor one another's work and property affect the amount of work they do and the amount of new wealth they accumulate. This is the subject to which our next chapter will be devoted.

KEY CONCEPTS

The Federal Reserve is the source of most of the net increases (or decreases) in deposits

Three methods of changing the money supply:
1. Raising or lowering reserve requirements. This is a powerful but undiscriminating weapon

2. Changing discount rates signals a policy of tighter or easier money

LOOKING BACK

1. The volume of demand deposits can only increase if there is an increase in deposits that is not matched by a decrease elsewhere. This net increase in deposits and reserves mainly comes from the Federal Reserve system. In the same way the money supply will only contract if a fall in deposits at one bank is not balanced by a rise elsewhere. Again, the Federal Reserve is the source of such net decreases.

2. The Fed has three methods by which it can change the net total of deposits. The first is by changing the reserve requirement. This directly freezes or frees a portion of the reserves of each bank and also changes the deposit multiplier. This is a potent means of bringing about large changes in money supply but it exerts its effect across the board in an undiscriminating fashion.

3. Second, the Federal Reserve can change discount rates—the rate at which member banks can borrow. This action not only directly encourages or discourages member bank borrowing, but is widely regarded as a signal to the financial world that the Fed is eager to make money tight or easier.

3. Open market operations are an important week-to-week means of control. When the Fed buys government bonds it creates net deposits; selling bonds reduces total deposits

4. Third and most important in week-to-week activities are open market operations. These operations are the buying and selling of government bonds conducted by the New York Federal Reserve Bank in the bond market. When the Fed buys bonds it pays for them by its own check. This check, when deposited in a bank, creates a new deposit that is not gained from another bank. It is a net increase in money supply. Selling a bond withdraws deposits in the same way. Open market operations enable banks to compete for their share of the new deposits that will be created.

Asymmetric controls makes it easier to tighten than to expand loans and investments

5. The controls over the money supply are not evenly balanced, but asymmetric. It is easier for the Reserve to pull on the string and reduce lending or investing capacity than to push on the string and assure an increase in loans or investments.

A flexible money system is necessary for an economy with sticky prices

6. The flexible monetary system is necessary because prices are sticky. This is the consequence of long-term contracts, wage agreements, and similar institutional rigidities that make it impossible for prices to fall so that a fixed money supply could finance a growing volume of real output.

High powered money has an inflationary potential

7. Bank reserves are high powered money which creates an inflationary potential. This is a challenge for monetary management.

Paper money has no gold backing. It only passes into use when the public converts its demand deposits into cash

8. Printed money is not actually money until it passes into the hands of the public. The amount depends on the public's demand for cash and the size of its checking accounts. There is no longer a gold cover behind printed money.

Gold is valuable because of its long symbolic importance

9. Gold has long held a special place in the human imagination and this accounts for its value. There is no way of knowing whether gold will continue to hold that special place.

ECONOMIC VOCABULARY

QUESTIONS

1. Suppose that a bank has $1 million in deposits, $100,000 in reserves, and is fully loaned up. Now suppose the Federal Reserve System lowers reserve requirements from 15 percent to 10 percent. What happens to the lending capacity of the bank? What happens to the deposit multiplier?

2. The Federal Reserve Banks buy $100 million in U.S. Treasury notes on the open market. How do they pay for these notes? What happens to the checks? Do they affect the reserves of member banks? Will buying bonds increase or decrease the money supply?

3. Now explain what happens when the Fed sells Treasury notes. Who buys them? How do they pay for them? Where do the checks go? How does payment affect the accounts of member banks at their Federal Reserve bank?

4. Why do you think gold has held such a prestigious place in people's minds?

5. Explain why monetary policy is a better instrument for slowing down an economy than for revving it up. Is this still true if we include inflation as part of revving up? Why is real output more difficult to attain than high prices?

247
CHAPTER 16
CONTROL-
LING THE
MONEY
SUPPLY

AN EXTRA WORD ABOUT
INDEPENDENCE OF THE FED

The Federal Reserve Board is run by 7 governors, each appointed to a 14-year term by the President with the approval of Congress. The governors of the Federal Reserve System cannot be removed during their terms of office except for wrongdoing. Thus, although fiscal policy is located in the executive and legislative branches of the government, monetary policy is vested in an independent board.

There were two initial justifications for this institutional arrangement. The first was that monetary policies were necessarily subject to quick changes. Second, it was felt that monetary policies ought to be insulated from the political process.

Are these reasons still valid? Some economists think so; others, including ourselves, think not. To take the first argument: It is true that Congress cannot be expected to operate an efficient open-market system on a daily basis. But this is not an argument for divorcing the responsibility for such operations from the *executive* branch. In most of the world's governments, Central Banks (the equivalent of the Fed) are located within the executive establishment, usually as a part of the Treasury or Finance ministries or departments. These banks have no trouble making quick decisions. Moreover, even if Congress could not be expected to approve of every jiggle in monetary measures, there is no reason why it could not endorse or direct the major thrust of monetary strategy toward an expansionary or a contractive general objective.

The argument about "insulation" depends on one's view of democracy, where values once again reign supreme. There is a curious inconsistency, however, in trying to insulate only monetary policies, not fiscal policies. Why should we trust the democratic mechanism to establish expenditures and taxes, but not the supply of money?

As in most institutional debates, dramatic changes are unlikely, although we seem to be moving in a more democratic direction in our monetary management. Congress now expects to be briefed every quarter on the Fed's monetary targets for the following year. There are also bills pending in Congress to integrate the Fed more fully by altering the tenure of the Chairman to be concomitant with that of the President; or to require the Fed to issue an economic report directly after the President's Economic Report, stating what differences, if any, lie between them, and justifying the Fed's course of action if it differs from that of the administration.

Meanwhile, a high degree of integration exists in fact, although not in law. More and more, the Fed bows to public pressure or to pressure from the administration. This is hardly surprising. As we shall see in our next chapter, we live at a time when the importance of money in the economy is more highly regarded than it used to be. The idea of an independent Fed does not sit so well in an era when we think of the Fed as bearing a prime responsibility for our economic well-being. Having created the Federal Reserve Board in the first place, Congress can alter it, as it wishes; and it undoubtedly would alter it, were the Fed to risk a direct confrontation with congressional or presidential economic objectives. The more important money management becomes, the more powerful are the pressures to place it within, not outside the main political mechanisms of the nation.

Chapter
17 MONEY AND THE MACRO SYSTEM

A LOOK AHEAD

In our preceding chapter, we found out something of what money is and how it comes into being. Now we must turn to the much more complicated question of how money works.

(1) What happens when the banks create or destroy deposits?

(2) Can we directly raise or lower incomes by altering the quantity of money?

(3) Can we control inflation or recession by using the monetary management powers of the Federal Reserve System?

These extremely important questions will be the focus of discussion in this chapter.

THE QUANTITY THEORY OF MONEY

249

**CHAPTER 17
MONEY
AND THE
MACRO
SYSTEM**

QUANTITY EQUATION

One relation between money and economic activity must have occurred to us. It is that the quantity of money must have something to do with *prices*. Does it not stand to reason that if we increase the supply of money, prices will go up, and that if we decrease the amount of money, prices will fall?

Something very much like this belief lies behind one of the most famous equations (really identities) in economics. The equation looks like this:

$$MV \equiv PT$$

where

$M =$ *quantity of money* (currency outside banks plus demand deposits)
$V =$ *velocity of circulation,* or the number of times per period or per year that an average dollar changes hands
$P =$ *the general level of prices,* or a price index
$T =$ *the number of transactions made in the economy* in a year, or a measure of physical output

If we think about this equation, its meaning is not hard to grasp. What the quantity equation says is that the amount of *expenditure* (M times V, or the quantity of money times the frequency of its use) equals the amount of *receipts* (P times T, or the price of an average sale times the number of sales). Naturally, this is an identity. In fact, it is our old familiar circular flow. What all factors of production receive (PT) must equal what all factors of production spend (MV).

Just as our GNP identities are true at every moment, so are the quantity theory of money identities true at every instant. They merely look at the circular flow from a different vantage point. And just as our GNP identities yielded useful economic insights when we began to inquire into the functional relationships within those identities, so the quantity theory can also shed light on economic activity if we can find functional relationships concealed within its self-evident "truth."

ASSUMPTIONS OF THE QUANTITY THEORY

To move from identities to functional relationships, we need to make assumptions that lend themselves to investigation and evidence. In the case of the GNP $\equiv C + G + I + X$ identity, for instance, we made a critical assumption about the propensity to consume, which led to the multiplier and to predictive statements about the influence of injections on GNP. In the case of $MV \equiv PT$, we need another assumption. What will it be?

The crucial assumptions made by the economists who first formulated the quantity theory were two: (1) The velocity of money—the number of times an average dollar was used per year—*was constant;* and (2) transactions (sales) *were always at a full-employment level.* If these assumptions were true, it followed that the price level was a simple function of the supply of money:

$$P = \frac{V}{T} \cdot M$$

$$P = kM$$

where k was a constant defined by V/T.

If the money supply went up, prices went up; if the quantity of money went down, prices went down. Since the government controlled the money supply, it could easily regulate the price level.

TESTING THE QUANTITY THEORY

Is this causal relation true? Can we directly manipulate the price level by changing the size of our stock of money?

The original inventors of the quantity equation, over half a century ago, thought this was indeed the case. And of course it *would* be the case if everything else in the equation held steady while we moved the quantity of money up or down. In other words, if the velocity of circulation, V, and the number of transactions, T, were fixed, changes in M would have to operate directly on P.

Can we test the validity of this assumption? There is an easy way to do so. Figure 17.1 shows us changes in the supply of money compared with changes in the level of prices.

A glance at Figure 17.1 answers our question. Between 1929 and 1979 the supply of money in the United States increased over eleven-fold, while prices rose only a little more than four-fold. Clearly, something *must* have happened to

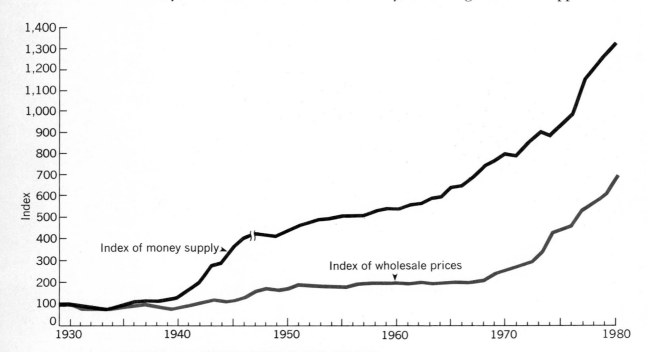

FIGURE 17.1 MONEY SUPPLY AND PRICES
Money supply has risen faster than price levels, proof that there is
no iron linkage between *M* and *P*. *V* and *T* must be taken into account.

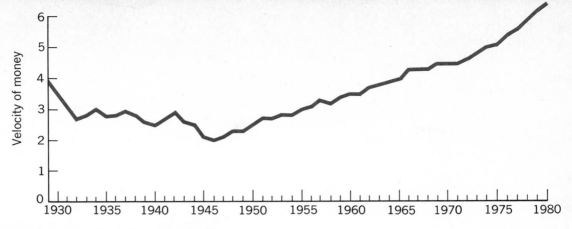

FIGURE 17.2 VELOCITY OF MONEY
**Velocity is an important source of change. The quicker we spend
money, the more dollars we send chasing after goods.**

V or to *T* to prevent the eleven-fold increase in *M* from bringing about a similar increase in *P*. Let us see what those changes were.

CHANGES IN *V*

Figure 17.2 gives us a first clue as to what is wrong with a purely mechanical interpretation of the quantity theory. In it we show how many times an average dollar was used to help pay for each year's output.* We derive this number by dividing the total expenditure for each year's output (which is, of course, the familiar figure for GNP) by the actual supply of money—currency plus checking accounts—for each year. As the chart shows, the velocity of money fell by 50 percent between 1929 and 1946, only to rise above the 1929 level over the postwar years.

We shall return later to an inquiry into why people spend money less or more quickly, but it is clear beyond question that they do. This has two important implications for our study of money. First, it gives a very cogent reason why we cannot apply the quantity theory in a mechanical way, asserting that an increase in the supply of money will *always* raise prices. For if people choose to spend the increased quantity of money more slowly, its impact on the quantity of goods may not change at all, whereas if they spend the same quantity of money more rapidly, prices can rise without any change in *M*.

Second and more clearly than we have seen, the variability of *V* reveals that money itself can be a destabilizing force—destabilizing because it enables us to do two things that would be impossible in a pure barter economy. We can:

1. Delay between receiving and expending our rewards for economic effort.
2. Spend more or less than our receipts by drawing on, or adding to, our cash balances.

---

*Note that final output is not quite the same as *T*, which embraces *all* transactions, including those for intermediate goods. But if we define *T* so that it includes only *transactions that enter into final output*, *PT* becomes a measure of gross national product. In the same way, we can count only those expenditures that enter into GNP when we calculate *MV*. It does no violence to the idea of the quantity theory to apply it only to final output, and it makes statistical computation far simpler.

Classical economists used to speak of money as a "veil," implying that it did not itself play an active role in influencing the behavior of the economic players. But we can see that the ability of those players to vary the rate of their expenditure—to hang onto their money longer or to get rid of it more rapidly than usual—makes money much more than a veil. Money (or rather, people's wish to hold or to spend money) becomes an independent source of change in a complex economic society. **To put it differently, the use of money introduces an independent element of uncertainty into the circular flow.** *

CHANGES IN *T*

Now we must turn to a last and perhaps most important reason why we cannot relate the supply of money to the price level in a mechanical fashion. This reason lies in the role played by *T*; that is, by the volume of output.

Just as the early quantity theorists thought of *V* as essentially unvarying, so they thought of *T* as a relatively fixed term in the quantity equation. In the minds of nearly all economic theorists before the Depression, output was always assumed to be as large as the available resources and the willingness of the factors of production would permit. While everyone was aware that there might be minor variations from this state of full output, virtually no one thought they would be of sufficient importance to matter. **Hence the quantity theory implicitly assumed full employment or full output as the normal condition of the economy.** With such an assumption, it was easy to picture *T* as an unimportant term in the equation and to focus the full effect of changes in money on *P*.

The trauma of the Great Depression effectively removed the comfortable assumption that the economy naturally tended to full employment and output. At the bottom of the Depression, real output had fallen by 30 percent. Aside from what the Depression taught us in other ways, it made unmistakably clear that changes in the volume of output (and employment) were of crucial importance in the overall economic picture, and that the economy does *not* naturally gravitate to full employment levels.

A MODERN QUANTITY THEORY?

It is clear, then, that the old-fashioned quantity theorists were mistaken. (For an explanation of *why* they erred, see the box on p. 253.)

Does this mean that there is *no* relation between the quantity of money and the rate of inflation? Certainly no one would go that far. There is not the faintest doubt that we could create a terrific inflation by recklessly increasing the money supply, or that we would bring inflation to a stop (along with the whole economy) by ruthlessly pulling on the string of monetary control.

The problem is whether we can find a functional relationship that will enable us to predict, with tolerable accuracy, the effects of ordinary increases or decreases in *M* on *P*. This would mean replacing the assumption of a fixed *V* with a variable *V* related in some fashion to other elements in the system, and

---

*Technically, the standard economic definition of money is that it is both a means of exchange and a store of value. It is the latter characteristic that makes money a potentially disturbing influence.

253
**CHAPTER 17
MONEY
AND THE
MACRO
SYSTEM**

WHY THE OLD QUANTITY THEORISTS ERRED

Modern economists can easily show that the velocity of money is not constant and that the volume of transactions (GNP) is not always at full employment. But it should not be thought that the originators of the quantity theory were stupid or too lazy to look up the basic data. Most of the numbers on which economists now rely were simply not in existence then. The national income, for example, was not calculated until the early 1930s, and the GNP was not "invented" until the early 1940s. You cannot calculate the velocity of money unless you know the national income or the gross national product.

Neither did the original quantity theorists have accurate measures of unemployment or capacity utilization. They used the only method available to them: direct observation of the world, a method that is notoriously inaccurate when one's view is much smaller than "the world." The idea of mass involuntary unemployment required the idea of an equilibrium output that would be less than a full-employment output, an idea completely foreign to pre-Keynesian thought.

it would also require finding a way of relating increases in MV to T as well as to P.

There has been a very active search for such precise relationships, but so far none have been found. Therefore we do not yet have a new quantity equation—a way of predicting how much P will change as we change M, or of foretelling how a given change in MV will be split between P and T. Until we find such functional relationships, a new quantity theory remains a hope, not an achievement.

OUTPUT AND PRICES

How does our modern emphasis on the variability of output and employment fit into the overall question of money and prices? The answer is very simple, but very important. We have come to see that the effect of more money on prices cannot be determined unless we also take into account the effect of spending on the volume of transactions or output.

It is not difficult to grasp the point. Let us picture an increase in spending, perhaps initiated by a business launching a new investment program or by the government inaugurating a new public works project. These new expenditures will be received by many other entrepreneurs as the multiplier mechanism spreads the new spending through the economy. But now we come to the key question. What will entrepreneurs do as their receipts increase?

It is at this point that the question of output enters. For if factories or stores are operating *at less than full capacity*, and if there is an *employable supply of labor available*, the result of their new receipts is almost certain to be an increase in output. That is, employers will take advantage of the rise in demand to produce and sell more goods and services. They may also try to raise prices and increase their profits further; but *if their industries are reasonably competitive, it is doubtful that prices can be raised very much*. Other firms with idle plants will simply undercut them and take their business away. An example is provided

MAXIMUM VS. FULL EMPLOYMENT

What is "full" employment? Presumably government spending is guided by the objectives of the Employment Act of 1946, which declares the attainment of "maximum employment" to be a central economic objective of the government.

But what is maximum employment? Does it mean zero unemployment? This would mean that no one could quit his job even to look for a better one. Or consider the problem of inflation. Zero unemployment would probably mean extremely high rates of inflation, for reasons we will look into more carefully later. Hence no one claims that full employment is maximum employment in the sense of an absence of *any* unemployment whatsoever.

But this opens the question of how much *unemployment* is accepted as consistent with maximum employment. Under Presidents Kennedy and Johnson, the permissible unemployment rate was 4 percent. Under Presidents Nixon, Ford, and Carter the permissible unemployment rate rose to a range of 4.5 to 5 or even 6 percent, largely because inflation had worsened. Hence the meaning of full employment is open to the discretion of the economic authorities, and their policies may vary from one period to another.

by the period 1934 through 1940 when output increased by 50 percent while prices rose by less than 5 percent. The reason, of course, lay in the great amount of unemployed resources, making it easy to expand output without price increases.

FULL EMPLOYMENT VS. UNDEREMPLOYMENT

This is a very important finding for macroeconomics, for it helps us see that policies that make sense in one economic situation make no sense in another. This is particularly the case with policies that promote spending of any kind—public spending or private spending, spending out of earned income or deficit spending. If an economy is suffering from large numbers of unemployed workers and from large amounts of underutilized capacity, it *must* spend more if it is to move back to its production frontiers. As we have learned in Chapter 9, expenditure is the necessary precondition for output. Unless we spend more, we are doomed to remain permanently underemployed.

But spending more will not bring us more output if we are at, or close to, the production frontier. Then more spending—for consumption or investment, for private use or public use—can only send prices higher, with little or no effect on the volume of output.

Until recently, this distinction between the beneficial effects of expenditure when unemployment was high, and the bad effects of expenditure when unemployment was low, was a central premise of modern macroeconomics. Today, the distinction is not so sharp as it once was, for we seem to have moved into a condition in which spending sends up prices even though we are certainly not in a state of full employment or utilization. This is a problem that we will study more closely in Chapter 19, which is devoted to the dilemmas of modern inflation.

MONEY AND EXPENDITURE

255
CHAPTER 17
MONEY
AND THE
MACRO
SYSTEM

We have almost lost sight of our subject, which is not yet inflation but how money affects GNP. And here there is an important point. How does an increased supply of money get into GNP? People who have not studied economics often discuss changes in the money supply as if the government put money into circulation, mailing out dollar bills to taxpayers. The actual connection between an increase in M and an increase in MV is much more complex. Let us look into it.

1. The transactions demand for money

From our previous chapter we know the immediate results of an increased supply of money, whether brought about by open-market operations or a change in reserve ratios. **The effect in both cases is a rise in the lendable or investible reserves of banks.** *Ceteris paribus,* **this will lead to a fall in interest rates as banks compete with one another in lending their additional unused reserves to firms or individuals.**

As interest rates decline, **some firms and individuals will be tempted to increase their borrowings.** It becomes cheaper to take out a mortgage, to buy a car on an installment loan, to finance inventories. Thus, as we would expect, the demand curve for spending money, like that for most commodities, slopes downward. As money gets cheaper, people want to buy (borrow) more of it. To put it differently, the lower the price of money, the larger the quantity demanded. We speak of this demand curve for money to be used for expenditure as the *transactions demand for money.*

2. Financial demand

But there is also another, quite separate source of the demand for money. This is the demand for money for *financial purposes,* to be held by individuals or corporations as part of their assets.

What happens to the demand for money for financial purposes as its price goes down? Financial demand also increases, although for different reasons. When interest rates are high, individuals and firms tend to keep their wealth as fully invested as possible, in order to earn the high return that is available. But when interest rates fall, the opportunity cost of keeping money idle is much less. If you are an investor with a portfolio of $10,000, and the rate of interest is 10 percent, you give up $1,000 a year if you are very liquid (i.e., all in cash), whereas if the interest rate is only 6 percent, your opportunity cost for liquidity falls to $600.

LIQUIDITY PREFERENCE

Economists call this increased willingness to be in cash as interest rates fall *liquidity preference.* The motives behind liquidity preferences are complex— partly speculative, partly precautionary. With low opportunity costs for holding money, we can afford to hold cash for any good investment or consumption opportunity that happens to come along. Similarly, it is cheaper to hold more money to protect ourselves against any unexpected emergencies.

In this way, both the speculative and precautionary motives make us more and more willing or eager to be in cash when interest rates are low, and less and less willing when rates are higher. Thus the financial demand for cash, like the transactions demand, is a downward sloping demand curve.

If we now put together the transactions and the financial demands for money and add the supply curve of money—the actual stock of money available—the result looks like Figure 17.3.

Our diagram shows us that at interest rate *OA*, there will be *OX* amount of money demanded for transactions purposes and *OY* amount demanded for li-

PRECAUTIONARY AND SPECULATIVE DEMAND

Both the precautionary and the speculative demand for money can be illustrated in the problem of buying or selling bonds. Most bonds are a promise to pay a certain stated amount of interest and to repay the principal at some fixed date. To simplify things, forget the repayment for a moment and focus on the interest. Suppose that you paid $1,000 for a perpetual bond that had a "coupon"—an interest return—of $100 per year with no date of repayment. And suppose that you wanted to sell that bond. What would it be worth?

The answer depends wholly on the current market rate of interest for bonds of equal risk. Suppose that this rate of interest were 10 percent. Your bond would then still be worth $1,000, because the coupon would yield the buyer of the bond 10 percent on his money. But suppose that interest rates had risen to 20 percent. You would now find that your bond was only worth $500. A buyer can go into the market and purchase other bonds that will give him a 20 percent yield on his money. Therefore he will pay you only $500 for your bond, because your $100 coupon is 20 percent of $500. If you want to sell your bond, that is the price you will have to accept.

On the other hand, if interest rates have fallen to 5 percent, you can get $2,000 for your bond, for you can show the buyer that your $100 coupon will give him the going market return of 5

percent at a price of $2,000. (If you were to buy a *new* $1,000 bond at the going 5 percent interest rates, it would carry a coupon of only $50.)

These calculations also show that it can be very profitable at times to hold money. When interest rates are rising, bond prices are falling. Therefore, the longer you wait before you buy, the bigger will be your chances for a capital gain if interest rates turn around and go the other way. This means that we tend to get "liquid" whenever we think that interest rates are below normal levels and bonds are too high; and that we tend to get out of money and into bonds whenever we think that interest rates are above normal levels, and therefore bonds are cheap. The trick, of course, is being right about the course of interest rates before everyone else.

Actual operations in the bond market are complicated, because we must take into account not only interest rates but the time left until a bond becomes mature (i.e., is repaid). The closer it is to maturity, the less its price will depart from its face value or principal. Nonetheless, very great gains and losses can be made in bonds that have some years to go before maturity. Even the most conservative bonds, such as government bonds, will swing in price as our speculative and precautionary impulses incline us now toward liquidity, now toward a fully invested position.

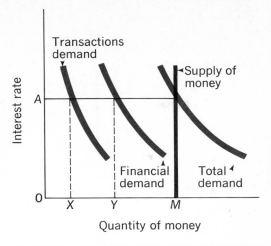

The demand for money has a negative slope, whether we want money to spend or to hold as a liquid investment: The lower interest rates fall, the more money we will seek. The supply of money, as we can see, is a fixed quantity in the short run.

**FIGURE 17.3
TRANSAC-
TIONS AND
FINANCIAL
DEMANDS
FOR MONEY**

quidity purposes. The total demand for money will be OM ($= OX + OY$), which is just equal to the total supply.

CHANGING THE SUPPLY OF MONEY

Let us suppose that the monetary authorities reduce the supply of money. We show this in Figure 17.4. Now we have a curious situation. The supply of money has declined from OM to OM'. But notice that the demand curve for money shows that firms and individuals want to hold OM at the given rate of interest OA. *Yet they cannot hold amount* OM, *because the monetary authorities have cut the supply to* OM'. What will happen?

The answer is very neat. As bank reserves fall, banks will tighten money— raise lending rates and screen loan applications more carefully. Therefore in-

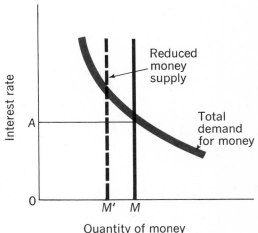

The Fed reduces the money supply from *OM* to *OM'*. *OA* is no longer a price for money that will clear the market. Now see Figure 17.5.

**FIGURE 17.4
REDUCING
THE SUPPLY
OF MONEY**

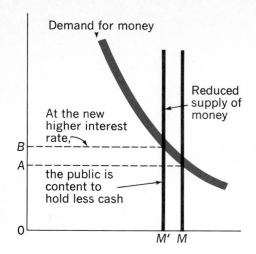

FIGURE 17.5 DETERMINATION OF NEW EQUILIBRIUM

Demand for money

Reduced supply of money

At the new higher interest rate,

B

A

the public is content to hold less cash

0

M' M

When the quantity of money shrinks, the public will try to acquire money by selling bonds. As they do so, bond yields rise. As yields rise, the demand for money falls. The market now finds a new clearing price (*OB*) for its smaller quantity of *OM'*.

dividuals and firms will be competing for a reduced supply of loans and will bid more for them. At the same time, individuals and firms will feel the pinch of reduced supplies of cash and will try to get more money to fulfill their liquidity desires. The easiest way to get more money is to sell securities, to get out of bonds and into cash. Note, however, that selling securities does not create a single additional dollar of money. It simply transfers money from one holder to another. But it does change the rate of interest. As bonds are sold, their price falls; and as the price of bonds falls, the interest yield on bonds rises.

Our next diagram (Figure 17.5) shows what happens. As interest rates rise, the public is content to hold a smaller quantity of money. Hence a new interest rate, *OB*, will emerge, at which the public is *willing* to hold the money that

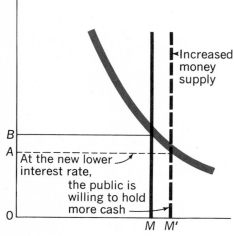

FIGURE 17.6 INCREASING THE SUPPLY OF MONEY

Increased money supply

B

A

At the new lower interest rate,

the public is willing to hold more cash

0

M M'

Here is the opposite story. The Fed increases *M* to *OM'*. Individuals do not want more money at the old price (*OB*). They use the new supply of money to buy bonds. Bond prices rise, yields fall. At a lower interest rate (*OA*) the public will be willing to hold *OM'*.

there *is to hold*. The attempt to become more liquid ceases and a new equilibrium interest rate prevails.

Suppose the authorities had increased the supply of money. In that case, individuals and firms would be holding more money than they wanted at the going rate of interest. They would try to get out of money into bonds, sending bond prices up and yields down. Simultaneously, banks would find themselves with extra reserves and would compete with one another for loans, also driving interest rates down. As interest rates fell, firms and individuals would be content to hold more money either for transactions or liquidity purposes until a new equilibrium was again established. Figure 17.6 shows the process at work.

DETERMINATION OF INTEREST RATES

This gives us the final link in our argument. We have seen that interest rates determine whether we wish to hold larger or smaller balances, either for transactions or financial (liquidity) purposes. But what determines the interest rate itself?

The Federal Reserve can, of course, raise or lower the discount rate, and big banks from time to time can announce a new "prime rate"—the rate at which they will lend to their best customers. But neither the Fed nor the biggest bank could make a rate "stick" if there were no bidders for money at that level, or conversely, if everyone converged on the bank for a loan. Although rates are announced by the monetary authorities or by big banks, they must accord with the forces of the marketplace if they are to hold steady. And we can now see that the forces of the marketplace are summed up in the interplay of supply and demand that we have been discussing.

Our demand for money is made up of our transactions demand curve and our financial (liquidity) demand curve. The supply of money is given to us by the monetary authorities. The price of money—interest—is therefore determined by the demand for, and supply of, money, exactly as the price of any commodity is determined by the demand and supply for it.

MONEY AND EXPENDITURE

What our analysis enables us to see, however, is that once the interest rate is determined, it will affect the use to which we put a given supply of money. Now we begin to understand the full answer to the question of how changes in the supply of money affect GNP (and prices). Let us review the argument one last time.

1. Suppose that the monetary authorities want to increase the supply of money. They will lower reserve ratios or buy government bonds on the open market.

2. Banks will find that they have larger reserves. They will compete with one another and lower lending rates.

3. Individuals and firms will also find that they have larger cash balances than they want at the going rate of interest. They will try to get rid of their extra cash by buying bonds, thereby sending bond yields down.

4. As interest rates fall, both as a result of bank competition and rising bond prices, the new, larger supply of money will find its way into use. *Part of it will*

259
CHAPTER 17
MONEY
AND THE
MACRO
SYSTEM

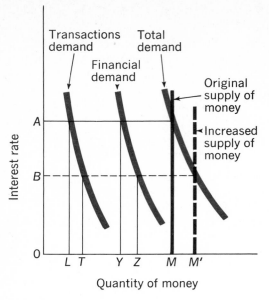

**FIGURE 17.7
USING MONEY
FOR TWO
PURPOSES**

This is exactly the same situation as that shown in Figure 19.6, but here we show how the increased supply of money is divided between transactions (LT) and financial uses (YZ).

be used for additional transactions purposes, as individuals and firms take advantage of cheaper money and increase their borrowings. Part of it will be used for larger financial balances, as the public's desire for liquidity grows with falling interest rates.

We can see the process very clearly in Figure 17.7. We begin with OM money supply and a rate of interest OA. As we can see, OL amount of money is held for liquidity purposes, and OY for transactions purposes. Now the stock of money is increased to OM'. The interest rate falls, for the reasons we now understand, until it reaches OB. At the new interest rate, liquidity balances have increased to OT, and transactions balances to OZ.

Exactly the same process would take place in reverse if the stock of money were decreased from OM' to OM. Can you see that the decreased supply of money will result partly in smaller transactions balances and partly in smaller liquidity balances? Do you understand that it is the higher rate of interest that causes the public to hold these smaller balances?

MONETARISM

In recent years much controversy has been generated by a new approach to money management called *monetarism*, an approach originally advanced by Nobel Laureate Milton Friedman. Monetarism has three interesting propositions:

1. **Increases or decreases in the supply of money affect spending directly, not just indirectly via their effects on the rate of interest**

Monetarists believe this to be the case because they hold that the public has a strong propensity to keep a fixed proportion of its income in liquid form, and will therefore spend any "excess" cash that is thrust upon it: If you find that your bank account is unexpectedly large, you will tend to buy something rather than hold the cash.

2.   **Only monetary policy can influence the course of GNP**

Monetarists hold that increases in public expenditure only displace, or **crowd out,** private expenditure. Therefore fiscal policy comes to naught, except to shift resources from private to public purposes. Fiscal policy cannot increase the level of GNP because an increase in public spending will be offset by a decrease in private spending.

3.   **There is a natural tendency to stability in the economy**

Monetarism strongly espouses the belief that the market mechanism is a powerful and efficient regulator of economic activity, and that left to itself it will steer the economy on a steady, high employment course. Moreover, most efforts to alter this course, by correcting for minor dips and swings for example, only aggravate small instabilities and make them into big ones. In fact, Professor Friedman holds that the depth and persistence of the Great Depression was entirely the consequence of the erroneous policies followed by the Federal Reserve during the 1930s.

This does not mean that the government should follow no policy. On the contrary, Friedman urges that a steady automatic increase in the money supply, geared to increases in productivity, would be the best way of urging and assisting the natural processes of expansion. He seeks an unvarying growth in money, not a varying one—a growth determined by rules, not by decisions.

Are the monetarists right? We do not really know. A great deal of interest has been stirred up by their bold and provocative ideas, and without doubt economists have become more interested in, and concerned about, money as a result of Friedman's work. But the matter is not yet settled scientifically. It is not easy to demonstrate that a crowding out effect actually takes place. It is not by any means clear that the Depression would have ended sooner had the Federal Reserve not followed its probably wrong-headed policies.

We are not going to pass judgment on monetarism here. Rather, in our next chapter we will return to the question as part of a larger issue—the issue of how much control we are able to exert over our path of economic growth.

THE ART OF MONETARY MANAGEMENT

Whether the monetarists are finally shown to be correct or not, we do not today have anything like a steady or automatic increase in money supply. On the contrary, the members of the Federal Reserve Boards meet regularly to discuss what changes in monetary policy seem advisable—whether money should be tightened or loosened, and what means should be used to reach their targets. Thus the art of money management is very much with us.

Why "art"? Is not the task of the monetary authority very clear? By increasing the supply of money, it pushes down interest rates and encourages expenditure. Hence all it has to do is to regulate the quantity of money to maintain a level of spending that will keep us at a high, but not too high, level of employment.

SHIFTING LIQUIDITY PREFERENCES

Unfortunately, things are not that simple. Suppose that the Fed is concerned about an acceleration of inflation and decides to tighten money to hold back the pressure on prices. But suppose that at the same time the public's liquidity preferences are going down because they too expect higher prices and want to spend their dollars "while they're still good."

The result may be a shift that frustrates the intentions of the Fed. In Figure 17.8 we can see that the Fed has reduced *M*, obviously in the hope of sending interest rates up from *OA* to *OB*. But the public has meanwhile shifted its demand curve to the left so that interest rates remain unchanged.

Shifts such as these that make the demand for money change in the "wrong" way (from the Reserve's point of view) enormously complicate the money management task.

CREDIT CRUNCHES

Suppose now that the monetary authorities are convinced that the brakes have to be applied swiftly and firmly to the money supply. They know from past experience that they may create a *credit crunch*. When the brakes are slammed on, not all parts of the economy suffer alike. Mortgage loans, for example, may be very hard to get. Little customers are much more likely to get turned down by the banks than big customers.

This uneven reduction in lending was very marked in the crunch of 1974. While residential and state and municipal borrowing declined by 24 percent, corporate borrowing rose by 114 percent. Even these figures understate the differences among sectors of the economy. Large corporations were not only able to gain more domestic loans than small business or local governments, but they also had access to international money markets. Thus to some extent they were exempt from the control of domestic monetary authorities. Many large firms, for instance, borrowed in West Germany to make investments in the United States.

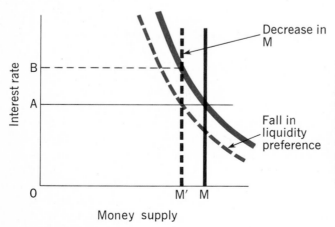

FIGURE 17.8
A SHIFT IN
LIQUIDITY
PREFERENCE

The Fed cuts the money supply from *OM* to *OM'*. It hopes to raise interest rates from *OA* to *OB*; and it would —if liquidity preferences were unchanged. But the downward shift in the demand curve for money frustrates the Fed. Interest rates remain at *OA*.

But even large corporations can run into trouble during credit crunches. In the 1968 crunch the Chrysler Corporation almost collapsed. And the Penn Central did collapse. **Such disasters together with the uneven effects of a crunch, place a limit on monetary policies. Very stringent restraints seem both institutionally and politically impossible.** After the 1969–1970 credit crunch, efforts were made to develop financial intermediaries that would lend to the sectors most severely hurt and thus spread the effects of monetary policies more evenly across the economy. During the 1974 recession, however, these intermediaries proved to be ineffective. A painful credit crunch occurred despite these new institutions. Will we have another bad crunch as we enter the 1980s? There are some signs that we will in housing and other industries especially hard hit by high interest rates.

263
CHAPTER 17
MONEY
AND THE
MACRO
SYSTEM

A CONTINUING PROBLEM

All these problems help us understand why money management is an art, not a science. Much depends on the "feel" of the economy, on experience, on mature judgment. There is very little that can be reduced to a pat formula.

Could money management become a science? Only if we were to adopt a monetarist position and abandon all efforts to intervene in the economy, trusting entirely to the effects of a steady, unvarying, automatic growth in the money supply. In our next chapter we will look into this question further, for it is one of the central issues of our day.

KEY CONCEPTS

Originally the quantity theory was formulated as $MV = PT$, where P and T were taken as fixed. We know that they are not

Modern quantity theory seeks a way of relating V to M, and MV to both P and T

More spending should not send up prices when unemployment is high. This is less true in an inflationary economy

Money supply affects expenditure two ways. As interest rates fall, more is borrowed for ordinary spending

LOOKING BACK

1. The quantity theory, in its original formulation, directly related increases in M, the stock of money, to increases in P, the price level. The formula for the theory was $MV = PT$, where V, velocity, and T, transactions (output) were assumed to be unchanging.

2. Empirical evidence, not available at the time of the original formulation, has made it clear that V and T are both variables, not constants. This is particularly the case with T, which can no longer always be assumed to tend to full utilization levels.

3. A modern quantity theory would relate V to M, and would divide the effects of MV between P and T. No such reliable formulation has yet been achieved.

4. As a general rule, increases in spending will generate additional output, with or without price increases, as long as there is large unused capacity in the labor and capital markets. But additional spending, private or public, will generate only price rises and no more output as we reach full employment. This distinction is somewhat blurred in today's inflationary economy.

5. Increases (or decreases) in the money supply affect expenditure in two different ways. The demand for money for ordinary transactional purposes is negatively sloped, like most demand curves. As interest rates fall, individuals and businesses borrow more money for transaction motives.

The demand for money for liquidity purposes also increases as interest rates fall

6. A second source of demand on the money supply is for financial purposes. As interest rates fall the opportunity cost of liquidity also falls. Accordingly, individuals sell bonds to get into cash. This demand curve is known as liquidity preference. Changes in the supply of money are therefore partly absorbed by changes in transaction balances and partly by changes in liquidity balances.

When the Fed changes the stock of M, individuals find themselves holding more money, or less money, than desired. They will buy or sell bonds, and in so doing will change yields. Thus the rate of interest is set by S and D for money

7. By changing the stock of money, the authorities create more or less money than the public wants to hold at existing interest rates. The public will buy bonds to get out of money or sell them to get into cash. Buying and selling will not change the amount of money, but it will change bond yields. Thus interest rates are determined by the supply and demand for money.

Monetarism has 3 basic tenets:
(1) Changes in the quantity of money directly affect spending
(2) Public spending crowds out private, so that only monetary policy can alter GNP
(3) The best monetary policy is steady, automatic, unchanging growth

8. Monetarism is a theory that suggests that changes in the supply of money affect spending directly, even without changing interest rates, because individuals tend to spend excess cash. The monetarist position also holds that the system responds only to monetary, not fiscal, policy. This is because monetarists believe that public spending displaces or crowds out private spending, leaving total GNP largely unaffected in size. And last, monetarism holds the system to be inherently stable, and blames monetary policy for destabilizing it. The best monetary policy would be a steady automatic increase in M, geared to productivity.

Money management is an art. Liquidity shifts and potential credit squeezes limit its effectiveness

9. Monetary management is an art, not a science. Shifts in liquidity preference and potential credit crunches, among other problems, can frustrate or limit the effectiveness of monetary policy.

ECONOMIC VOCABULARY

QUESTIONS

1. Why is the quantity equation a truism? Why is the interpretation of the quantity equation that M affects P not a truism?

2. If employment is full, what will be the effects of an increase in private investment on prices and output, supposing that everything else stays the same?

3. In what way can an increase in excess reserves affect V or T? Is there any certainty that an increase in reserves will lead to an increase in V or T?

4. Suppose that you had $1,000 in the bank. Would you be more willing to invest it if you could earn 5 percent or 8 percent? What factors could make you change your mind about investing all or any part at, say, 8 percent? Could you imagine conditions that would make you unwilling to invest even at 10 percent? Other conditions that would lead you to invest your whole cash balance at, say, 3 percent?

5. Suppose that the going rate of interest is 7 percent and that the monetary authorities want to curb expenditures and act to reduce the quantity of money. What will the effect be in terms of the public's feeling of liquidity? What will the public do if it feels short of cash? Will it buy or sell securities? What would this do to their price? What would thereupon happen to the rate of interest? To investment expenditures?

6. Suppose that the monetary and fiscal authorities want to encourage economic expansion. What are the general measures that each should take? What problems might changing liquidity preference interpose?

7. Do you unconsciously keep a "liquidity balance" among your assets? Suppose that your cash balance rose. Would you be tempted to spend more?

8. Show in a diagram how a decrease in the supply of money will be reflected in lower transactions balances and in lower financial balances. What is the mechanism that changes these balances?

9. Do you understand (a) how the rate of interest is determined; (b) how it affects our willingness to hold cash? Is this in any way different from the mechanism by which the price of shoes is determined or the way in which the price of shoes affects our willingness to buy them?

Chapter

18 GROWTH AND ITS PROBLEMS

A LOOK AHEAD

Here we reach the final chapter of our basic macro studies, returning to the issue with which we began: economic growth. There are three main problems discussed in the pages to follow.

(1) The first is an investigation into the characteristics and possible causes of the business cycle.

(2) The second is the matter of trying to reach our maximum potential growth.

(3) The third is the complex question: Can we improve our growth rate?; can we intervene effectively in the macro system? We shall look into arguments on both sides of the matter before summing up the problem as we see it.

From the very first pages of our study of macroeconomics, growth has been at the center of our focus. Now, in this final chapter on that subject, we must return explicitly to the problem, adding to our previous knowledge and reflecting on issues that we have not yet had an opportunity to explore in depth.

UNEVEN GROWTH

Let us begin by investigating an aspect of growth that we have heretofore ignored. It is the uneven pace at which the historic trajectory of growth proceeds. If you will take a moment to look back at the chart of national growth on p. 30, you will notice its long, almost uninterrupted upward slope; or again, a glance at p. 33 will show the same thing.

SHORT VS. LONG RUN

But these long-run charts, on which only very large movements are visible, conceal from our view another aspect of the growth process that is of very great

1895–1896	− 2.5%	1900–1901	+ 11.5%
1896–1897	+ 9.4	1901–1902	+ 1.0
1897–1898	+ 2.3	1902–1903	+ 4.9
1898–1899	+ 9.1	1903–1904	− 1.2
1899–1900	+ 2.7	1904–1905	+ 7.4

**TABLE 18.1
U.S. RATES
OF GROWTH
1895–1905**

Source: *Long-Term Economic Growth* (U.S. Dept of Commerce, 1966), p. 107.

importance. In any short-run period, the long-run consistency fades from view and the economy is marked by sharp ups and downs in the growth in output.

Take the years 1895 to 1905, very smooth-looking on the chart on p. 33. As Table 18.1 reveals, those years were, in fact, anything but steady.

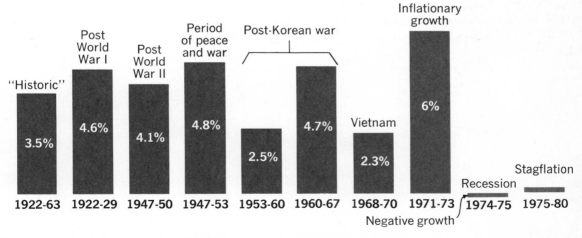

FIGURE 18.1 SHORT-TERM VARIATIONS IN THE RATE OF GROWTH
Except in periods of real recession, such as 1974–75 or 1979–80, the economy always shows growth. But the rate of growth varies considerably, as we can see.

Or examine a more recent period, not year by year, but in groups of years. As we can see in Figure 18.1 the rate of growth has varied greatly over the last fifty years. At times, such as the 1974–1975 recession, the economy has even shown negative rates of growth. These episodes may show up only as small dips in the graph of our long-term advance, but they have meant suffering and deprivation for millions of persons who were robbed of work or income as a consequence of these dips.

BUSINESS CYCLES

This sequence of ups and downs, periods of growth followed by doldrums, introduces us to the question of business cycles. For if we inspect the profile of the long ascent carefully, we can see that its entire length is marked with irregular tremors or peaks and valleys. Indeed, the more closely we examine year-to-year figures, the more of these tremors and deviations we discover, until the problem becomes one of selection: Which vibrations shall we consider significant and which shall we discard as uninteresting.

The problem of sorting out the important fluctuations in output (or in statistics of prices or employment) is a difficult one. Economists have actually detected dozens of cycles of different lengths and amplitudes. Cycles vary from the very short rhythms of expansion and contraction that can be found, for example, in patterns of inventory accumulation and decumulation, to large background pulsations of 17 or 18 years in the housing industry. Possibly (the evidence is

FIGURE 18.2 THE BUSINESS CYCLE

This chart, prepared by the Cleveland Trust Company, vividly shows our swings. Note that the swings lie around a base line called "long-term trend." That is actually an upward tilting line reflecting our long-term growth rate of 1.5 percent per capita.

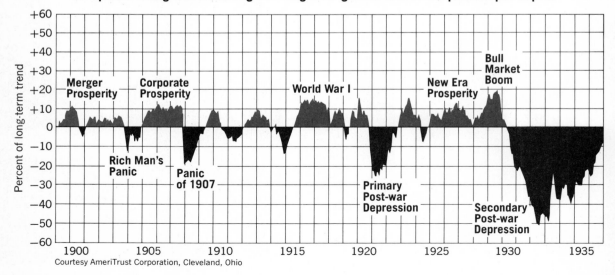

Courtesy AmeriTrust Corporation, Cleveland, Ohio

unclear) there are swings of 40 to 50 years in the path of capitalist development as a whole, called Kondratief cycles after their Russian discoverer.

Generally, however, when we speak of the business cycle we refer to a wavelike movement that lasts, on the average, about 7 to 11 years. In Figure 18.2 this major oscillation of the American economy stands forth very clearly, for the chartist has eliminated the underlying tilt of growth, so that the profile of economic performance looks like a cross section at sea level rather than a cut through a long incline.

STYLIZED CYCLES

In a general way we are all familiar with the meaning of business cycles, for the alternation of "boom and bust" or prosperity and recession (a polite name for a mild depression) is part of everyday parlance. It will help us study cycles, however, if we learn to speak of them with a standard terminology—**peak, contraction, trough, recovery.** We can do this by taking the cycles from actual history, superimposing them, and drawing the general profile of the stylized cycle that emerges. It looks like Figure 18.3. This model of a typical cycle enables us to speak of the length of a business cycle as the period from one peak to the next or from trough to trough. If we fail to measure from *similar* points on two or more cycles, we can easily get a distorted picture of short-term growth—for instance, one that begins at the upper turning point of one cycle and measures to the trough of the next. Much of the political charge and countercharge about growth rates can be clarified if we examine the starting and terminating dates used by each side.

FIGURE 18.2 (continued)

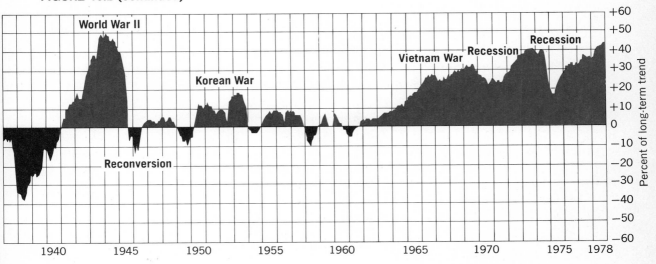

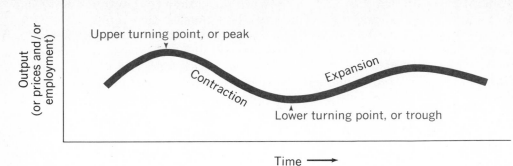

**FIGURE 18.3
THE STYLIZED
CYCLE**

An idealized cycle serves to give us standard nomenclature, so that we can compare two or more cycles.

CAUSES OF CYCLES

What lies behind this more or less regular alternation of good and bad times?

Innumerable theories, none of them entirely satisfactory, have been advanced to explain the business cycle. A common business explanation is that waves of optimism in the world of affairs alternate with waves of pessimism—a statement that may be true enough, but that seems to describe the sequence of events rather than to explain it. Hence economists have tried to find the underlying cyclical mechanism in firmer stuff than an alternation of moods. One famous late-nineteenth-century economist, W. S. Jevons, for example, explained business cycles as the consequence of sunspots—perhaps not as occult a theory as it might seem, since Jevons believed that the sunspots caused weather cycles that caused crop cycles that caused business cycles! The trouble was that subsequent investigation showed that the periodicity of sunspots was sufficiently different from that of rainfall cycles to make the connection impossible.

Other economists have turned to causes closer to home: to variations in the rate of gold mining (with its effects on the money supply); to fluctuations in the rate of invention; to the regular recurrence of war; and to yet other factors. There is no doubt that many of these events can induce a business expansion or contraction. The persistent problem, however, is that not one of the so-called underlying causes itself displays an inherent cyclicality—much less one with a periodicity of 7 to 11 years.

THE MULTIPLIER-ACCELERATOR CYCLE

Then how do we explain cycles? **Economists no longer seek a single explanation of the phenomenon in an exogenous (external) cyclical force. Rather, they tend to see cycles as our own eye first saw them on the growth curve—as variations in the rate of growth that tend to be induced by the dynamics of growth itself.**

We can gain considerable insight into this uneven pace of growth if we combine our knowledge of the multiplier and the accelerator—the latter, we recall, showing us the investment induced by the growth of output.

Boom and bust. Let us, then, assume that some stimulus such as an important industry-building invention, has begun to increase investment expenditures. We can easily see how such an initial impetus can generate a cumulative and self-feeding boom. As the multiplier and accelerator interact, the first burst of investment stimulates additional consumption, the additional consumption induces more investment, and this in turn reinvigorates consumption. Meanwhile, this process of mutal stimulation serves to lift business expectations and to encourage still further expansionary spending. Inventories are built up in anticipation of larger sales. Prices firm up, and the stock market rises. Optimism reigns. A boom is on.

What happens to end such a boom? There are many possible reasons why it may peter out or come to an abrupt halt. It may simply be that the new industry will get built and thereafter an important stimulus to investment will be lacking. Or even before it is completed, wages and prices may have begun to rise as full employment is neared, and the climate of expectations may become wary. ("What goes up must come down," is an old adage in business, too.) Meanwhile, perhaps tight money will choke off spending plans or make new projects appear unprofitable.

Or investment may begin to decline because consumption, although still rising, is no longer rising at the earlier *rate* (the acceleration principle in action). We have already noticed that the action of the accelerator, all by itself, could give rise to wavelike movements in total expenditure (see p. 176). The accelerator, of course, never works all by itself, but it can exert its upward and downward pressures within the flux of economic forces and in this way give rise to an underlying cyclical impetus.

Contraction and recovery. It is impossible to know in advance what particular cause will retard spending—a credit shortage, a very tight labor market, a saturation of demand for a key industry's products (such as automobiles). But it is all too easy to see how a hesitation in spending can turn into a general contraction. Perhaps warned by a falling stock market, perhaps by a slowdown in sales or an end to rising profits, business begins to cut back. Whatever the initial motivation, what follows thereafter is much like the preceding expansion, only in reverse. The multiplier mechanism now breeds smaller rather than larger incomes. Downward revisions of expectations reduce rather than enhance the attractiveness of investment projects. As consumption decreases, unemployment begins to rise. Inventories are worked off. Bankruptcies become more common. We experience all the economic and social problems of a recession.

But just as there is a natural ceiling to a boom, so there is a more or less natural floor to recessions. The fall in inventories, for example, will eventually come to an end, for even in the severest recessions, merchants and manufacturers must have *some* goods on their shelves and so must eventually begin stocking up. The decline in expenditures will lead to easy money, and the slack in output will tend to a lower level of costs; and both of these factors will encourage new investment projects. Meanwhile, the countercyclical effects of government fiscal policy will slowly make their effects known. Sooner or later, in other words, expenditures will cease falling, and the economy will tend to bottom out.

GOVERNMENT-CAUSED CYCLES

We have spoken about business cycles as if they were initially triggered by a spontaneous rise in investment or by a natural cessation of investment. But our acquaintance with the relative sizes of the components of GNP should make us wary of placing the blame for recessions solely on industry. More and more, as government has become a major source of spending, cycles have resulted from variations in the rate of government spending, not business spending. Cycles these days, more often than not, are made in Washington.

Take the six recessions (periods of decline in real GNP lasting at least six months) since World War II. Every one of them can be traced to changes in government budgetary policies. The first four recessions—in 1949, 1954, 1957–1958, and 1960–1961—resulted from changes in the military budget. In each case, the federal government curtailed its rate of military expenditure without taking compensatory action by increasing expenditure elsewhere or by cutting taxes. The result in each instance was a slackening in the rate of growth.

The 1969–1970, the 1974–1975, and the 1980 recessions are even more interesting. They represent cases in which the federal government deliberately created a recession through fiscal and monetary policies aimed at slowing down the economy. The purpose, as we know, was to dampen inflation. The result was to reverse the trend of growth. Thus it is no longer possible, as it once was, to discuss business cycles as if they were purely the outcome of the market process.

There is no doubt that the market mechanism has produced cycles in the past, and would continue to produce them if the government were miraculously removed from the economy. But given the size of the public sector these days, we need to look first to changes in government spending as the initiating source of a cycle.

POTENTIAL GROWTH

Can we curb the business cycle? We shall see. But the idea of a fluctuation-free path of growth directs our attention once again to the long historic trajectory with which we began our study of growth. If we multiply the rise in our year-to-year hours of labor input by an index of the rising productivity of that labor, we can easily derive a curve showing our *potential output over time.* The question is therefore how much of that potential output we do in fact produce.

Through much of the 1950s and 1960s, potential output ran well ahead of the output we actually achieved. Figure 18.4 shows that between 1974 and 1979 the amount of lost output represented by this gap came to the staggering sum of $310 billion. In 1979 we could have added another $30 billion to GNP—$136 per person—if we had brought unemployment down from the actual level of 5.8 percent to 5.1 percent, the level now used to calculate potential GNP. In the recession year of 1980 the loss was far greater still.

REASONS FOR SLOW GROWTH

Why have we fallen so far short of our potential growth? There are two reasons. The first is that we have deliberately pursued policies of tight money and fiscal restraint, hoping to hold down the rate of inflation. That is a problem to

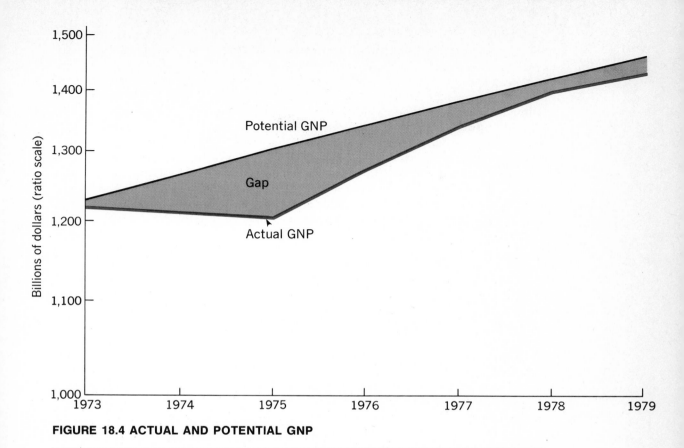

FIGURE 18.4 ACTUAL AND POTENTIAL GNP

---

which we will return shortly, when we ask whether we could make up this short-fall by different economic policies.

But there is a second, more long-run, reason for our disappointing performance. It is that our productivity has been dropping for some years. In the period 1973–1978, industrial productivity rose about 4 percent per year in West Germany, about 5 percent per year in Japan—but only one percent annually in the United States. This drop in productivity actually became negative during 1979, when output per manhour in the nonfarm private business sector *fell* for a brief period at an annual rate of 2.3 percent. If that decrease continued, the Joint Economic Committee of Congress warned, Americans would suffer a drastic decline in real living standards.*

---

*Our international position has already worsened because of the long relative fall in our productivity. We are no longer the nation with the world's highest standard of living, but the nation with the fifth highest standard, outranked by Switzerland, Denmark, West Germany, and Sweden, with Japan only 7 percent behind. Such international comparisons are always treacherous because tastes and styles differ so much among countries. But the basic fact that American living standards are now shared—or bettered—abroad is indisputable.

Why has our productivity fallen? The long-term reasons are fairly clear. We have been devoting a smaller fraction of our GNP to new plant and equipment than have our major economic competitors. Over the last decade, our investment has been roughly 10 percent of GNP. West Germany's rate has been 15 percent; Japan's 20 percent. In addition, our R & D expenditures have not only fallen, but may have been aimed less advantageously than those of our competitors. Mounting concern over the environment has dictated costly antipollution expenditures which add to cost but not to measured output. Finally, we have a much larger military establishment than any other Western nation. Over a quarter of our national R & D effort goes for military purposes, compared with 7 percent for West Germany and 4 percent for Japan.* A strong defense establishment may be a national necessity, but it exacts a price in slower growth. It takes a while before these causes exert their effects, but eventually they pull down our rate of production per manhour. That is the condition from which we are suffering today.

RECENT POOR PERFORMANCE

The reasons for our recent precipitous decline into negative productivity rates is something else, however. Here one main cause is simply the poor performance of the economy itself. When the rate of utilization sags, we do not typically lay off managers, research departments, salesmen, maintenance staff and the like, even though we may not be able to use their potential inputs fully. The result is a drop in productivity because there is a lot of unused manpower per unit of output. Conversely, when we move out of recession, productivity runs ahead of the economy because we can greatly increase production for a while without adding much to overhead.

Probably 30 percent of our productivity slowdown stems from this factor. Another 20 percent comes from a changing mix of our outputs. In the U.S. there are large differences in productivity among industries. In 1978 an hour of work produced not quite $6 worth of output in services (valued at 1972 prices), $8.70 in manufacturing, and $11.56 in agriculture. With so wide a range, shifts in our composition of output will have significant effects on our average productivity. And after 1972, such a shift occurred. Output grew largely in the low productivity service sectors rather than in high productivity areas like electronics or agriculture.

Another 30 percent of our decline in growth can be traced to problems in specific industries—mining, construction and utilities. Utilities have suffered because of high fuel prices which have lead to sluggish growth and resulting sluggish productivity. Mining is an industry beset with health and safety problems which affect its working force and the environment. We are now moving more rapidly than in the past to remedy these problems, but falling productivity is one of the prices we must pay. Construction has also been a very poor performer on the productivity scale. Perhaps this is only because its output is diffi-

---

*B. Depalme and others, *Science and Technology in the New Socioeconomic Context*, OECD, Paris, 1980 (forthcoming).

cult to measure. Perhaps it is because we are building fewer large-scale projects where efficiency is high and more small ones where it is lower. Perhaps it is because zoning and other laws make building more expensive.

That accounts for 80 percent of our productivity decline. The source of the remaining 20 percent remains a mystery.

RAISING THE GROWTH RATE

Obviously there is no quick fix to our productivity problem. But it is equally obvious that there are policies that would gradually, if not immediately, improve our annual rate of potential growth. There is no doubt that measures to increase our rate of capital formation will sooner or later yield more output per manhour. So will efforts to raise, or to direct more skillfully, our R & D expenditures. So will policies to assist industries such as mining to modernize their operations, or policies to enable other unproductive industries, such as textiles, to "disinvest" —shrink back their size.

But such policies are easier to devise than to implement. Raising investment expenditures in industry may mean cutting them back elsewhere—for example in urban renewal. Is that what we want to do? Spurring investment will probably necessitate higher corporate profits, which many will oppose. Allowing unproductive industries to fade away will impose heavy burdens on their employees who will fight with all their power to prevent their livelihoods from also fading away. Relaxing environmental protection standards will boost productivity—but at what social cost?

Thus problems abound. Nonetheless, with all the difficulties, no one disputes that it is within our national capacity to raise the rate of long-term growth by improving the quality and quantity of our key inputs. **Finally, we ought to bear in mind that there is often a trade-off between efficiency and equity**—a point stressed by Arthur Okun, former Chairman of the Council of Economic Advisers. Policies that encourage growth may do so at the expense of well-being: We would certainly grow faster if we transferred all insurance workers into factories. Assuming that *they* wouldn't mind the switch, would we welcome a world without insurance? How about a world of highly efficient houses, all built with cookie-cutter duplication? A world of high output per mine worker, but also high accident rates and high pollution? Productivity is very important, but it is not the only thing that is very important.

THE SHORT RUN

Recall, however, that much of the recent decline in productivity is the result of our disappointing economic performance rather than the cause of it. To accelerate our short-run growth rate, we have to move up to the production frontier rather than move the frontier further out. And here the question becomes more complex and more interesting. For economists are by no means unanimous that we can change our degree of utilization by using the conventional measures we have learned about—expansive fiscal policies or increases in the money supply. We remember that the monetarists have even asserted that the efforts of the Federal Reserve to intervene in the market typically make things worse, not better!

Thus we find ourselves today in the midst of a debate over the efficacy of intervention. Can we significantly improve our rate of growth? Let us first examine the arguments against, then those in favor, and finally try to strike a balance.

ARGUMENTS AGAINST INTERVENTION

Why do some economists feel that the conventional ways of improving our performance are futile? There are three reasons:

1. TIME LAGS

One cogent argument is the problem of time lags. The argument is very simple and entirely true. It takes time to collect data. It takes time to interpret data. It takes time to convince people who look at data that the situation has—or has not—changed. It takes time to devise a new policy. It takes time to implement a policy by action. It takes time for the new policy—expenditure, taxes, interest rates, or whatever—to exert its effect.

Various estimates have been made of some of these time lags. Table 18.2 shows an estimate for a Federal Reserve stimulus:

TABLE 18.2 ESTIMATED TIME LAGS

Type of lag	Estimated length (months)
data	2.0
recognition	2.0
legislative	0.5
transmission	1.0
effectiveness	8.5

Source: Robert Gordon, *Macroeconomics* (Boston: Little Brown, 1978), p. 471.

The disconcerting result of this lag is that by the time the remedy has arrived on the scene, the illness may have changed. Indeed, there is even the possibility that the underlying situation will have markedly changed and that the remedy will only make the problem worse.

2. RATIONAL EXPECTATIONS

A second argument against the effectiveness of intervention is called the theory of rational expectations. Essentially it claims that government intervention cannot change the outcome of a market economy, because the market will have already anticipated government action and will have taken steps that will nullify it.

We have already seen such nullifying actions when we noted that shifts in liquidity preferences could offset Federal Reserve intentions (see page 261). Now we must add the possibility that investors or market participants will deliberately change their behavior because they expect that the government will undertake a certain policy. We all read the newspapers and magazines, watch TV and hear radio. We all know, long before the event, that the government is considering raising or lowering taxes, tightening or loosening money. Will we not, then, pursue our best economic advantage by taking these expectations into account as we plan our economic activity?

Suppose, for example, that investors read about pressure on the Federal Reserve to increase the money supply and lower interest rates. Will not a rational investor buy bonds immediately, in order to sell them at a profit when yields fall? In that case, when the Fed actually does increase the money supply, there is no change in interest rates because the change has already occurred in anticipation of government policy!

What the theory of rational expectations tells us is that well-informed mass action can make it very difficult for the government to bring about a desired economic change in any area of the economy. According to the theory it will be as difficult or impossible to change the level of employment as to change the level of spending because the actors on the marketplace will always manage to attain their objectives. In fact, government intervention is likely to bring about undesired changes. Take the well known case of the banker who makes a public statement assuring his depositors that their money is safe. Perhaps it *was* safe before he made the pronouncement, but his words instill anxiety and the next thing you know there is a run on his bank. In the same way, a highly placed administration official can assure the American public that there will be plenty of gasoline, but his very assurance may stir up enough anxiety so that the next day we find lines at the gas pumps.

Such perversely self-fulfilling prophecies are an example of rational expectations. Each person is driven to maximize his or her self-interest in a market system —indeed, that is how the system gets its energy. **But that very driving force, coupled with a continuous search for as much information as possible, makes it very difficult to force the market to yield a solution different from its natural, spontaneous outcome. What the theorists of rational expectations are telling us is that the market mechanism is a much more powerful, self-steering process than interventionists tend to believe.**

3. NATURAL STABILITY AND MOMENTUM

We have already encountered the third main argument of the noninterventionists when we looked into monetarism. The contention is that the economy is essentially a stable, growing process, and that efforts to alter its course are likely to destabilize or depress, not steady or strengthen its inherent momentum.

At bottom, this view also rests on the dynamics of the maximizing, competitive process. In the view of the noninterventionists the constant tendency of all markets is to seek equilibria—prices that will clear the quantities offered and sought. So, too, the noninterventionists emphasize the tendency of the market process as a whole to express the main elements within it—the search for work, the incentive for profit, the level of skill and industrial technique. **These real forces, they believe, will determine the degree of utilization that prevails, and efforts to change that level cannot produce lasting effects because they cannot change the underlying drives and technical realities of our situation.**

One important instance of this emphasis on the natural stability of the system involves the crowding out phenomenon we mentioned in our last chapter. The noninterventionists believe that the amount of investment in the nation will be limited to the amount of saving it can generate—that is, the resources it can divert from consumption. When the government absorbs some of those savings into the public sector, whether by taxing them or by attracting them into public bond issues, it lowers the availability of savings for the private sector. There will be a shift of national effort from the production of private goods to the production of public goods, but there will not be any more growth because added public expenditure will be offset by lowered private spending.

NONINTERVENTIONIST POLICY

What sort of government policy do the noninterventionists advocate? They all agree that we can improve our long-run growth potential by adopting measures that will improve the quantity and quality of inputs. Therefore noninterventionists advocate encouragement to investment and R & D, for instance, by changing the tax laws to promote saving and profit-making. Needless to say, their opponents accuse them of pursuing highly interventionist policies in the name of noninterventionism!

Second, noninterventionists believe in encouraging the natural stability and expansiveness of the economy by establishing automatic increases in the money supply, as we have previously discussed. And that is essentially all. Noninterventionists would balance the full employment budget. They would eliminate all Federal Reserve policies to raise or lower reserve ratios or discount rates, or to act in the open market, with the possible exception of policies needed to cope with international pressures on the dollar, a matter we discuss in Chapter 21, "Defending the Dollar."

Thus in place of an active fiscal and monetary policy, noninterventionists advocate a firm but unchanging monetary policy. We have tried to improve the economy, they claim, but we have not succeeded. Now it is time to let it manage itself.

ARGUMENTS FOR INTERVENTION

There is, of course another side to the story. Here is the problem as the interventionists see it:

1. THE POWER OF PREDICTION

Interventionists do not fault their opponents when they call attention to the problem of time lags and the mischief they can cause. They claim, however, that the record of *short-run* predictions is good enough so that we should be able to circumvent what has been a source of trouble in the past. During the 1970s, according to economist Robert J. Gordon, "Forecasters have been able to predict accurately a year in advance the direction of most changes in unemployment, even though they failed badly in predicting the magnitude of the increase in unemployment following the 1973–74 supply shock episode."*

Interventionists know that policy decisions got us into as much trouble as they got us out of during the past decade or so; but they believe that it would be foolish to abandon all efforts to ward off, or to correct, poor economic performance on that account. Most monetary policy lags are about a year in length.

---

*Robert J. Gordon, *Macroeconomics* (Boston: Little, Brown & Co., 1978) p. 476.

Interventionists now think we can make reliable forecasts for such periods, so that policy decisions will work their eventual effects in the direction we want them to, and not against it.

279
CHAPTER 18
GROWTH
AND ITS
PROBLEMS

2. REMEDYING IMPERFECT MARKETS

We recall that a second major plank in the noninterventionist platform was that markets tended to frustrate the intentions of government policy makers because market participants always beat them to the punch. But this theory is clearly only valid for markets where there exists a great deal of information and mobility. That is emphatically not the case with many of the market processes into which government seeks to intervene.

Take as an instance the difference between the financial market and the labor market. The financial market is a quivering network of information. You can prove that by going into any brokerage house and finding out what the going price is for any of two or three thousand securities. If you wish to buy those securities you can always do so by bidding a fraction more than the market, and you can always sell by offering them at a fraction less. Compare the labor market. If you walk into an employment office, you will have difficulty learning about the price or quantity of employment available outside your city, or outside a few standard trades or professions. If you offer your skills for sale at a fraction less than the going rate, the chances are very great that this price advantage will not suffice to get you a job.

In such imperfect markets, which make up a great deal of the economy, it makes no sense to apply a theory of rational expectations. The participants in the labor market do not behave in the same way as those in the financial markets. Therefore the market for employment does not maximize in the same manner as the market for capital funds. The government can improve employment and the degree of utilization, argue the interventionists, because nothing like a network of information or mobility exists.

3. THE DANGER OF INSTABILITY

Third, the interventionists stress the instability, not the inherent steadiness, of the private sector. They do not argue with the noninterventionists that capitalism is a dynamic system always seeking to grow, or that its market mechanism is a powerful force for clearing its supplies and demands (with the caution, noted above, that not all markets work the way the noninterventionists claim). Their own position centers on two major claims.

First, they point to the historic record of boom and bust that marked the course of capitalism long before the existence of government as an intervening force. In the 1890s for instance, we had a depression in which almost a fifth of the labor force was thrown out of work. That kind of instability, the interventionists assert, is the consequence of capitalism's dynamism: New industries are built up and peak out; booms develop momentum and slide to a halt; external shocks such as war or natural disaster shake it out of its routines. Moreover, the interventionists go on to claim, the instability of the system is much greater—and much more dangerous—in an economy of giant businesses than in one of shopkeepers and local handicrafts. The economy of the nineteenth century, they say, was stable as a pile of sand is stable even when it receives a blow. The late twentieth-century system is unstable as a great tower of blocks, each block a giant company, would be unstable if it were to receive a similar blow.

Second, the interventionists argue that we no longer have the social or political option of not intervening. In the great depressions of the past the public accepted a passive government response because it was generally believed that government had no right (as well as no capacity) to deal with economic misfortunes. That point of view is now as dead as the dodo, interventionists insist. When growth slows down or inflation speeds up, the public cry is that government should "do something." To be told that doing nothing is the best response to economic trouble is an idea that no Western electorate would accept, and that no Western government would propose. Therefore an interventionist response is forced on us, the activists say, and the attitude of those who advocate noninterventionism is simply irresponsible.

THE UPSHOT OF THE ARGUMENT

Is it possible to sum up the pros and cons of this complex argument? Perhaps we can suggest two conclusions that award some recognition to each side and that present the issue as we see it.

1. **Unquestionably we are going to pursue interventionist economic policies, both in the short and the long run**

The last argument of the interventionists seems to us irrefutable. It is no longer imaginable that any modern government would take a passive stance toward such problems as inflation, unemployment, energy, productivity, and a dozen similar issues. Many of these problems can be addressed in different ways, and in Part 4, we discuss what some of these alternative policies might be. But there is no doubt in our minds that some form of active policy will be followed.

2. **Our policy determinations will be seriously hampered by the kinds of problems raised by the noninterventionists.**

Thus we are going to try to improve our short-run economic performance. But how well will we succeed in doing so? The objections raised by the noninterventionists suggest that efforts to accelerate or decelerate, redirect or guide the economy will be much more difficult than we have thought in the past. It was not so very long ago that economists spoke of "fine tuning" the economy as if it were a vast hi-fi set that could be regulated with precision by turning the knobs labeled "fiscal policy" and "monetary policy." We now know that this cannot be done. Some knobs are stuck; others turn without much affecting the quantity or quality of sound; still others seem to set up feedback that distorts the results we seek.

But this is not to say that we cannot regulate the economy at all. Our own belief is that we can intervene to our collective benefit, provided that we have realistic expectations of what it lies within our power to do. Modern industrial economies are very complex systems and we should not expect that we can fiddle with them like radios. But some success is better than none—and some success seems possible. That takes us, however, to the arena of public policy and the array of giant problems confronting us there; to this matter we devote all of Part 4.

KEY CONCEPTS

The business cycle exhibits the fluctuating rhythm of economic growth

The 7- to 11-year cycle is analyzed in terms of a multiplier-accelerator interaction, often triggered by government action

Potential growth focuses attention on the output that full employment would yield. Actual growth has fallen seriously short of this in recent years

Growth and productivity have lagged because of low investment and R & D, shifts to less productive occupations, and the inefficiency of recessions

Growth can almost surely be aided by long-term policies to boost investment and R & D

Can short-term growth be affected by fiscal and monetary policy? Noninterventionists say no because of the problems of time lags, rational expectations, and the natural stability of the system

Interventionists place their faith in short-run forecasts, in the inapplicability of rational expectations to markets such as the labor market, and in the belief that instability is politically intolerable

LOOKING BACK

1. Growth is not an even process, but is marked by fluctuations that we designate as a business cycle. There are many kinds of cycle, of varying periodicities (durations). We speak of their phases as four: upper turning point or peak, contraction, lower turning point or trough, and expansion.

2. No entirely satisfactory explanation has been found for the 7- to 11-year periodicity of the principal business cycle. Economists analyze the alternation of boom and bust mainly in terms of the interaction of the multiplier and accelerator. The cause of the cyclical pattern lies as much in government action as in the spontaneous behavior of the business economy.

3. The attention of economists today is focused less on cycles than on the difference between potential and actual growth. Potential growth is the trend of output that would result from the continuous full employment of the labor force. Actual growth is the value of GNP in fact produced. In recent years there has been a serious growth gap.

4. The growth gap is attributed to a slowdown in productivity, and to anti-inflation measures that have curbed economic activity. Productivity in the U.S. has been falling for a decade. The reasons are numerous: relatively low investment, low R & D expenditures, nonproductive expenses such as the installation of pollution controls, shifts in occupations, and the tendency to build up overhead costs during recession. In addition, certain important industries have been beset with performance problems.

5. Raising the growth rate involves long- and short-run policies. Most economists would agree that long-run institutional changes, such as increasing R & D, or raising the investment rate, would assist growth.

6. There are divergent views as to whether growth can be boosted in the short run by fiscal and monetary policy. The noninterventionists argue that such policies have little effect for three reasons: (1) Time lags make proper timing difficult or impossible: (2) rational expectations lead to frustration of government plans because the market anticipates such plans or sidesteps them; and (3) there is a natural stability and momentum to the economy that government policies cannot change.

7. Interventionists argue that time lags can be offset by reasonably dependable short-run forecasting; that rational expectations only work in near-perfect markets such as finance, not in the labor market where employment is immediately affected; and that the history of capitalism shows a great deal of instability. They argue, moreover, that in modern times it is not politically feasible for government to stand aside.

8. Our own belief is that interventionism is a fact of life, but that the effective implementation of policy will be more difficult than was once believed for the reasons raised by the interventionists.

ECONOMIC VOCABULARY

QUESTIONS

1. Explain how the interaction of the multiplier and the accelerator can give rise to cycles. Why does not such a multiplier-accelerator interaction shed light on the question of periodicity? Have you any ideas as to why the typical cycle is 8–10 years long? Suppose that capital goods tended to wear out in this period of time: Would this give rise to a cycle if their replacement were bunched in time?

2. Try to get hold of a time series, such as a short of stock market prices or GNP over the last 20 years. Can you spot a cyclical pattern at all? How do you think you would go about locating such a cycle?

3. What are the sources of growth for potential GNP? Explain how potential GNP is a kind of production possibility curve through time.

4. Can you suggest ways in which we might empirically investigate the reasons for the decline in growth? Suppose that your city was lagging in employment and prosperity, and that you were asked to determine why. How would you try to discover whether part of the reason was a relative decline in local productivity?

5. If you follow the newspapers, how long do you think it takes you, on the average, to spot a trend—say in the performance of a baseball team? How long does it take you to change your mind that a trend you thought you had identified was in fact incorrect? If you were going to change the performance of a team, how far ahead would you have to forecast its results to compensate for the time lags involved in spotting trends and in changing your mind?

6. Have you ever changed your actual economic behavior to achieve a result you wanted, *before* some anticipated government action made that impossible? If you felt that rationing were coming, would you stock up on gasoline? Would you buy diamonds if you believed that diamond purchases would be declared illegal in the future? Would you change your college program if you had reason to believe that government was going to change the training requirements for various professions?

7. What is your own appraisal of the willingness of the public to accept economic reversals without calling for government to "do something"? Do you think it is less tolerant of inaction in the case of inflation or unemployment?

4 The Major Economic Challenges

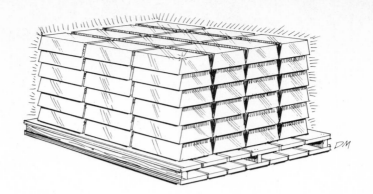

Chapter

19 INFLATION

This chapter brings us to the very frontiers of economic knowledge—and ignorance. Inflation is not a problem that is fully understood, therefore it is our own view that is presented here rather than one that is generally accepted, for no such consensus exists.

Three aspects of the inflationary problem will be dealt with here.

(1) Costs. Some costs of inflation are imaginary. Some are threats. Some are real.

(2) Explanations. We shall try to present a cogent argument as to why inflation exists and how it perpetuates itself.

(3) Remedies. There is no sure way of turning off inflation, but we shall examine a number of policies representing a wide spectrum of opinion.

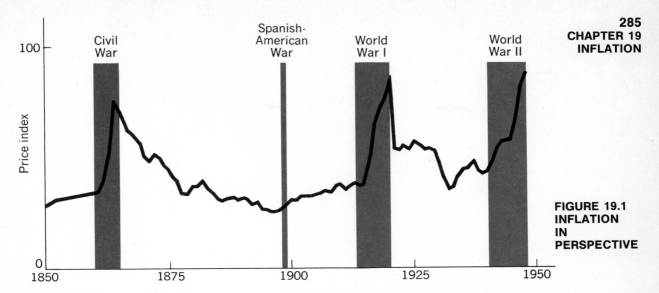

FIGURE 19.1
INFLATION
IN
PERSPECTIVE

Looking back in history, inflation is a chronic consequence of war. But in the past it was always short-lived.

INFLATION IN RETROSPECT

Inflation is both a very old problem and a very new one. If we look back over history, we discover many inflationary periods. Diocletian tried (in vain) to curb a Roman inflation in the fourth century A.D. Between 1150 and 1325, the cost of living in medieval Europe rose fourfold. Between 1520 and 1650, prices doubled and quadrupled, largely as a result of gold pouring into Europe from the newly opened mines of the New World. In the years following the Civil War, the South experienced a ferocious inflation. And during World War I, prices in the United States rose 100 percent.

Let us focus more closely on the U.S. experience up to 1950 (Figure 19.1). Two things should be noted about this chart. **First, major wars are regularly accompanied by inflation.** The reasons are obvious enough. War greatly increases the volume of public expenditure, but governments do not curb private spending by an equal amount through taxation. Invariably, wars are financed largely by borrowing; and the total amount of spending, public and private, rises rapidly. Meanwhile, the amount of goods available to households is cut back to make room for war production. The result fits the classic description of inflation: Too much money chasing too few goods.

Second, U.S. inflations have always been relatively short-lived in the past. Notice that prices fell during the long period 1866 to 1900, and again from 1925 to 1933. The hundred-year trend, although generally tilted upward, is marked with long valleys as well as sharp peaks.

RECENT INFLATIONARY EXPERIENCE: STAGFLATION

Now examine Figure 19.2, which shows the record of U.S. price changes since 1950. Once again we notice that the outbreak of war has brought price

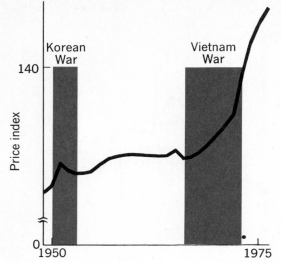

**FIGURE 19.2
WHOLESALE
PRICES
SINCE 1950**

**After World War II, the pattern
changed. Inflation has become
chronic and persistent.**

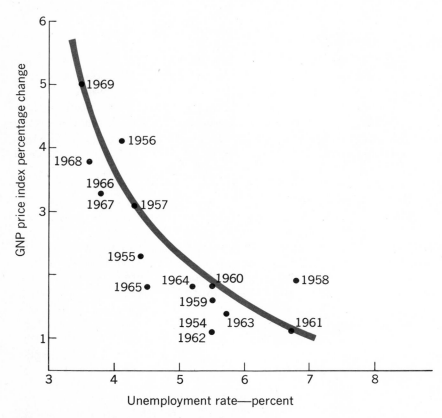

**FIGURE 19.3
UNEMPLOY-
MENT
INFLATION
RELATION**

Until 1969 the Phillips curve looked very clear.

rises, albeit relatively small ones. But in a vital way, contemporary experience differs from that of the past. Peaks of inflationary rises have not been followed by long, gradual declines. Instead, inflation seems to have become a chronic element in the economic situation.

Moreover, the inflation has not only been chronic and persistent, but it has been accompanied by considerable levels of unemployment. We will be looking into unemployment more carefully in our next chapter, but we should note that our rising level of inflation has been accompanied by a rising level of unemployment. In the period 1960–1965, for instance, the rate of inflation averaged 1.6 percent and the average level of unemployment, 5.5 percent. In the years 1975–1979, inflation has jumped to 7.5 percent, and unemployment has also risen, to an average of 7.0 percent.

The presence, side by side, of inflation and unemployment has come as a new puzzle for economists. Economists have always known that inflation was almost inevitable for a system that was bumping up against the boundaries of its production possibilities curve. **But it was widely believed that inflation would go away if we retreated from those boundaries and accepted even a modest amount of unemployment. Now we know that that is not the case. Recession and inflation can exist together in a condition that has become known as** *stagflation*—stagnation plus inflation. Explaining stagflation is the central challenge to economic theory today. Remedying it is the central challenge to economic policy.

THE DISAPPEARING PHILLIPS CURVE

A good way to understand the problem of modern stagflation is to examine what has happened to the most widely accepted recent explanation of inflation, known as the Phillips Curve. Back in 1958 the British economist A. W. Phillips called attention to what then seemed like a very clear-cut and important relationship. This was the correlation between the rate of inflation and the rate of unemployment. The Phillips Curve displaying that relationship for the years through 1969 is shown in Figure 19.3. As you can see, there seems to be a strong correlation—the lower unemployment was, the higher was inflation.

The trouble began as we entered the 1970s. For it became apparent that the relation between unemployment and inflation at least within normal ranges of unemployment was not what we thought. In Figure 19.4 we see the relationship plotted through 1980. There is no longer a predictable association between a given rate of unemployment and its accompanying rate of inflation. Look particularly at the shaded rectangle that covers an unemployment range from about 4.5 percent to 8.5 percent. Inflation rates since 1970 have varied from barely more than 3 percent to over 10 percent—in the early part of 1980 (not shown on the chart) they reached almost 20 percent!

THE COSTS OF STAGFLATION

We will want to look carefully into the reasons behind, and the mechanisms of, this urgent challenge. But first we must take a careful measure of the problem itself. How serious is inflation? What costs does it impose? How costly is the "stag" part of stagflation?

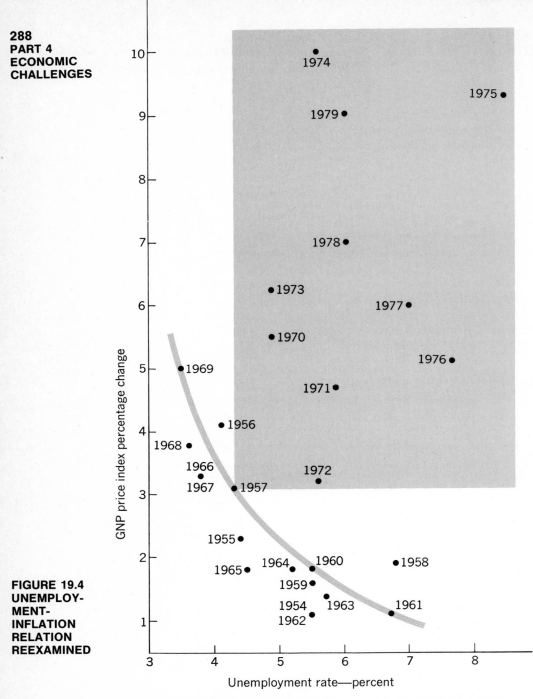

**FIGURE 19.4
UNEMPLOY-
MENT-
INFLATION
RELATION
REEXAMINED**

Recent experience makes it clear that there is no reliable unemploy-
ment-inflation relation within the "normal" range of unemployment.

There are real dangers imposed by inflation and certainly there are real costs in stagflation. But there are also imaginary consequences, and we had better clear our heads of those so that we can pay attention to the real problems.

Inflation and Money Illusion. One of the imaginary costs of inflation is that it has been eating away at our real standard of living. This is simply untrue. From 1969 to 1979, real per capita disposable income—income after inflation and taxes and population growth—was up by about 28 percent, as Table 19.1 shows.

	Current Dollars	1972 Dollars
1969	3,111	3,515
1970	3,348	3,619
1971	3,588	3,714
1972	3,837	3,837
1973	4,285	4,062
1974	4,646	3,973
1975	5,088	4,025
1976	5,504	4,144
1977	6,009	4,285
1978	6,672	4,449
1979	7,279	4,515

Despite inflation, real incomes per capita have risen. The rate of real growth has been about 1.3 percent per year.

**TABLE 19.1
PER CAPITA
DISPOSABLE
PERSONAL
INCOME**

Thus the average American is better off, not worse off, than he or she was 8 to 10 years ago—and much better off than he or she was 20 years ago.

Then why the widespread belief that our living standards are declining? Probably the answer is a phenomenon that economists call the money illusion. This is our tendency to measure our real well-being by the number of dollars we get—not by their purchasing power. Money illusion brings very sharp psychological costs in a period of inflation because our real incomes lag far behind our money incomes. Take the period 1969–1979 again. Over those years our money incomes rose by over 134 percent. That is, the number of dollars in the average pay envelope in 1979 was easily double the number in 1969. But the increase in purchasing power of those 1979 dollars was only about 28 percent, much less than the increase in their number. Thus we had the illusion that our real incomes had doubled, whereas in fact they had only risen by about a quarter.

Imagine that someone agreed to give you a present of $134 tomorrow morning along with the morning papers. When you opened the envelope, there was only $28 in it. Actually, you are $28 better off than before; but you had expected to be $134 better off. Are you glad or mad? Do you feel lifted up or let down? It is the same in the economic world. If we had experienced a real gain of $100 over the past decade, we would all be very content. But that would have been far, far beyond the limits of our production possibility frontier.

Inflation and Social Perceptions. Another reason for our general feeling of a falling income standard is that inflation turns many personal problems into social problems. In a market system some individuals are always winners and others are losers, either absolutely or by comparison. When there is no inflation, people take these changing positions as part of the economic game, as part of "life." In an inflationary period, however, everyone has a rising *money* income. Those who are losers are those whose income rises less rapidly than the rate of inflation. In a world without inflation, such persons would blame their economic plight on bad luck or on bad judgment or on any number of other factors. Except during a great depression, they would not blame their misfortune on "the system."

During inflation, however, because losers are still receiving money increases —although perhaps not enough to stay abreast of the cost of living—they tend to blame inflation for a condition that may not be the consequence of inflation at all. College professors may blame inflation for their falling real incomes when the real trouble lies in the oversupply of Ph.D.s. Factory workers blame inflation for their very real pinch when the problem is that the rise in female workers and in part-time employment has been cutting into the work week, and thereby lowering weekly wages, even though hourly rates go up.

Inflation as a Zero Sum Game. The confused perceptions that arise during an inflationary period tend to blind us to a very important difference between recessions and inflations. In recessionary times, incomes fall. Unemployed individuals above all suffer real losses in purchasing power. Moreover there is no social gain to be offset against their loss. The purchasing power given up by an unemployed family does not appear in anyone else's pocket.

Not so during inflation. Here, the decline in purchasing power of one unlucky individual or group of individuals is *always* offset by a rise in the purchasing power of some other person or group. *That is because every rise in prices always creates a rise in incomes.* Perhaps the gainer is a strategically placed group of workers whose higher wages are the other side of higher prices. Perhaps it is a group of businessmen for whom higher prices will mean higher profits. But higher prices always mean higher incomes for someone in the system.

Thus inflation is a zero sum game—a game of redistribution in which you win what I lose, or vice versa. Recessions, on the other hand, are not zero sum, but negative sum: Losses incurred by some individuals will not be transferred to others as income.

In analyzing the costs of inflation, therefore, we always have to look for winners and losers. From 1970 to 1980, our real GNP grew by $324 billion in 1972 dollars. Someone had to be receiving that larger real income. Who was it? Just the very rich? The oil companies? The municipal workers? The answer is: All of us. We can see this if we look at the distribution of income among the poor, working class, middle class, and upper class. If any one of those groups had gained a major share of our growth in GNP, income distribution would have changed. But a look at Table 19.2 shows that it has not.

	1970	1978
The poor (bottom 20 percent)	5.4	5.2
Working class (next 40 percent)	29.8	29.1
Middle class (next 35 percent)	49.2	50.0
Upper class (top 5 percent)	15.6	15.6

TABLE 19.2 SHARES OF INCOME BY FAMILY, 1970 AND 1978

Despite inflation, income shares are almost unchanged.

Hidden Winners and Losers. Of course, there have been some social groups whose well-being has changed over the last years, but those changes have not always accorded with our expectations about inflation. It has always been held, for example, that the worst losers in any inflation would be fixed income receivers. But the single most important class of fixed income receivers in the United States —the recipients of Social Security—have been winners, not losers. This is because Congress has periodically hiked up Social Security benefits ahead of living costs and has now tied those benefits to the cost of living index. From 1970 to 1980, the average elderly family slightly improved its position relative to that of the average family in the nation as a whole!

Striking losers in the last ten years have been stockholders, most of whom are to be found in the upper class. Just as conventional wisdom led us to expect that all pensioners would suffer during an inflation, so it was commonly believed that stockholders would benefit from, or would at least stay abreast of, inflation. Because stocks represented shares of companies whose assets would be rising in value as a result of inflation, they were thought to be a "hedge" against inflation.

That is not how things have turned out. Over the last ten years prices have roughly doubled. The stock market has remained essentially unchanged. This means that the purchasing power of a portfolio made up of average stocks has had its value cut in half! That is about as bad as the fall experienced during the Great Depression!*

It is possible, further, that inflation has exerted its impact painfully on lower- and working-class families even though the distribution of income is roughly unchanged. This is because inflation has been particularly marked in four categories of goods: food, energy, shelter, and medical care. The price of these four necessities has been rising almost 50 percent faster than the price of non-necessities, and the proportion of household budgets going for necessities is markedly greater among the poor and working classes than among the middle and upper classes.[1]

Thus there are certainly real impacts of inflation both on the poor and on the rich. Our analysis shows, however, that we must be very careful in assessing its impact. There has not been an overall deterioration of well-being, even though it *feels* that way. Certain groups have been more severely hit than others; some groups are actually worse off than they were in 1975. For most of us, however, two decades of inflation have brought real, although largely unnoticed, improvements in real living standards.

THE REAL THREATS OF INFLATION

Does this mean we have been worrying needlessly about inflation? That is certainly not our opinion. Even if Americans judged the problem wrongly

---

*Why have stocks not been a hedge against inflation? There seem to be two reasons. First, interest rates are much higher than dividend rates, so that many investors prefer to put their wealth into short-term bonds rather than stocks. Second, investors are simply gloomy about the future, mainly because of inflation. Rightly or wrongly, many think that a share of IBM is a less solid store of value than a bar of gold.

[1]Leslie Ellen Nulty, *Understanding the New Inflation: The Importance of the Basic Necessities,* Exploratory Project for Economic Alternatives, Washington, 1977; also Nulty, *Challenge* Jan.—Feb., 1979.

because of money illusion or the deceptive impact of inflation, there are ample reasons to place it at the top of the nation's agenda of problems. Specifically, there are four reasons to worry about inflation: the first three are threats and the fourth is an actual cost.

1. Inflation holds out the threat of running away

One of the most disturbing aspects of inflation has been its tendency to accelerate. From 1950 to 1965, for example, the average rate of inflation in the United States was 2 percent per year. During the last half of the 1960s, that rate had picked up to 4 percent. In the first five years of the decade of the 1970s it reached 6 percent. From 1976 to 1980 the rate first declined and then (in 1979) reached 9 percent. In early 1980 it zoomed further, and for a time threatened to reach 20 percent.

This pattern of irregularly accelerating inflation can be discovered in most parts of the world. In the 10 leading industrial nations the price level rose by about 2.5 percent a year during the 1950s; by not quite 3.5 percent a year in the 1960s; by over 9 percent in the 1970s. We can see this irregularly upward-tending pattern in Figure 19.5.

The reason for this acceleration will become clearer shortly when we study the mechanisms of inflation. Undoubtedly, however, inflation holds the *threat* of "running away"—of quickening its pace until finally the value of money drops to zero and we have a complete social and economic collapse. Even though actual runaway inflations (or hyperinflations) have been very rare, and in all cases the consequence of previous military or social disasters, the spectre of such a possibility is profoundly unsettling. This is probably the main reason we perceive inflation to be a danger: It is not so much for what it is, but for what it might become.

2. Inflation threatens the value of monetary assets

Closely associated with the threat of a runaway economy is the threat of eroding assets. Inflation eats away at the value of monetary assets such as savings accounts, insurance policies, government bonds, and the like. Moreover, as we have seen, it has also badly eroded the value of stocks, although this may change if the stock market begins to take a brighter view of the future.

The threat of inflation is that it could wipe out the money assets of the middle and upper classes, as runaway inflations in the past have done. To date, however, most families with monetary assets seem to have stayed even with inflation, using their higher money incomes to add to their savings accounts or insurance policies. For example, during the years 1970–1980, the value of savings accounts has risen from $194 to $670 billion, more than enough to allow for inflation. Insurance policies in force have risen from $1,400 to $3,300 billion. Nevertheless, the fear of losing all their monetary assets is acutely experienced by families who hold them, and it is not a threat to be dismissed.

The value of some assets typically rises during inflations. Land is one of these; works of art; antiques—whatever is scarce and deemed to be of lasting value. Some of these investments work out very well, others do not: The land you buy may turn out to be in the wrong place; the picture may be by an artist whose reputation fails. Most significant of all the hedges against inflation is gold, the magical metal. Economists have always pointed out that the value of gold is only magical, and that it is not intrinsically a source of value and true hedge against inflation. So far, economists have been wrong and gold has soared during the inflationary era. How high can it go? The answer lies with your estimate as to how stubborn or persistent are people's beliefs; if the past is any guide, they are very stubborn and very persistent indeed.

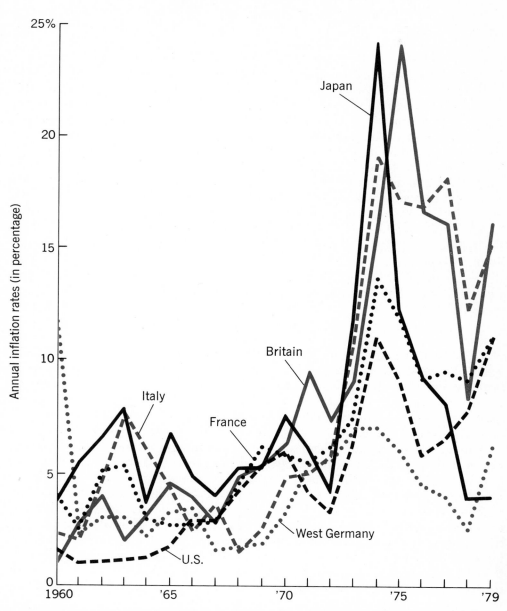

**FIGURE 19.5
WORLDWIDE
INFLATION:
SELECTED
COUNTRIES**

Inflation has been a worldwide accelerating phenomenon in which U.S. experience was rather favorable until the end of the 70s.

3.   Inflation threatens financial instability

Inflation brings serious distortions into the nation's credit structure. One of the most troublesome consequences of inflation is the way it affects the relationship between businesses and banks. In inflationary times it is always advantageous to borrow money, because dollars will be cheaper and more plentiful when it comes time to repay the loan. Therefore businesses seek to borrow funds—but banks are loath to lend, for exactly the same reasons.

Two results follow. First, interest rates go ever higher to compensate banks for the falling value of the dollars they will receive. This puts a serious crimp in many kinds of investment spending, such as construction. Second, banks refuse to lend for more than short periods of time. The result is that business has to take on short-term loans at high interest rates. As short-term debt piles up, the system becomes vulnerable to any untoward event that will prevent the regular refinancing of debt. If a bank or a municipality encounters trouble, the whole financial community becomes endangered. Thus New York City's threatened bankruptcy in 1976 brought fears of a general credit collapse. The liquidity of the banking system—its ability to absorb a loss without resorting to panicky measures to raise cash—becomes a matter of general concern, rather than a matter taken for granted. Thus the threat of large-scale financial instability is another very good reason to worry about inflation.

4.   Inflation inhibits us from trying to reach potential growth

The real cost of inflation is very clear: It prevents us from trying to use all of our productive power for fear that we may tip an acceptable degree of inflation into an unacceptable or outright dangerous one. Thus the real cost of inflation is the unemployment that it thrusts upon us—not only the unemployment that stems from high interest rates and lessened investment, but the unemployment that governments deliberately tolerate or encourage in order to prevent inflation from getting worse, or in the hope of making it better.

Unlike the imagined cost of inflation—the feeling that our living standards are declining—there is nothing imaginary about the cost of unemployment. A person who is without work suffers a real fall in income and a great deal of damage to his or her sense of personal worth. The production that is foregone because of a recession is foregone forever. There is no way ever of enjoying the goods that we do not produce.

The costs of unemployment are important enough for us to devote our entire next chapter to them. But we should recognize that these costs, however large, do not seem as significant to the American people as the costs or threats of inflation, however exaggerated. The reason is easily understood. The costs of unemployment are borne by a small minority of the population and, as we shall see, a minority without much political voice. But the effects of inflation are felt by everyone. Thus it is not surprising that all over the world, the need to hold back inflation has been regarded by governments as being of much greater urgency than the need to remedy unemployment. Governments and electorates alike are ready to accept more unemployment in exchange for less inflation; they are not ready to accept more inflation in exchange for less unemployment.

At the end of this chapter we will discuss various means of trying to hold back inflation. Let us conclude this discussion by emphasizing that stagnation, directly caused by inflation itself or brought about by efforts to stem inflation, is by far the most serious of the actual costs that inflation brings. Indeed, in our opinion, stagnation can be justified only if there is no other way of preventing inflation from running away or from giving rise to the kind of political panic that a chronic inflation threatens to introduce.

EXPLAINING INFLATION

Certainly, then, we want to curb inflation; but in order to do so we must first understand what causes it. Here we encounter a difficulty. There is no general consensus among economists as to the causes or even the mechanisms of inflation comparable to the consensus that exists about many other kinds of problems. What follows, therefore, we loudly and clearly state, is *our* diagnosis of the nature of the inflationary phenomenon. It is to be thought about, and perhaps argued with. We hope that it will shed light; we cannot promise total illumination.

BASIC MARKET INSTABILITY

Our argument begins with a simple but essential fact. It is that market systems are easily disturbed. Wars, changes in political regimes, resource changes, new technologies, shifts in demand, all disturb the equilibrium of the market system as stones cast ripples in a pond.

These unsettling events have caused different kinds of disturbances at different periods in capitalism's political and economic development. For economists, the most important of these disturbances has been the tendency of the market system to develop instabilities in production and prices and employment. We have already encountered these instabilities in the form of business cycles, or tendencies to recession, or in the inflationary propensities of recent years.

It may not seem important to begin from a stress on this deepseated and long visible characteristic of the market system. But once we place instability at stage center, we can see that a pressing question must be answered: **Why does instability in our times result in rising prices rather than in mass unemployment?** To take a specific instance, why did the shock of higher oil prices in 1973 touch off a new wave of inflation? A comparable shock a hundred years earlier—say a sudden fourfold increase in coal prices—would almost certainly have caused a massive depression. What has happened between that day and this to alter the way in which the market system responds to shocks?

PUBLIC BARRIERS AGAINST DEPRESSION

It is not difficult to answer the question. Profound changes have occurred within the social and economic structure of capitalism throughout the world. Of these changes, the most significant for our purposes is the emergence of large and powerful public sectors. In all Western capitalisms these sectors pump out from 30 to 50 percent of all expenditures, providing a floor of economic stability that did not exist before.

This floor does not prevent the arrival of recessions. The market system continues to be vulnerable to shocks and changes as always before. The difference

is that a market system with a core of public spending does not move from recession into depression. The downward effect on production or employment is limited. Cumulative, bottomless depressions are changed to limited, although persisting, recessions.

In addition, the emplacement of the new public sector has greatly increased the political responsibility of governments for the overall macro performance of their economies. That is why central banks cannot carry out the restrictive monetary policies that might bring inflation to a halt. Central banks can and do pull on the string to tighten money. But when they pull too hard, the economy begins to choke. No government can afford to carry out so severe an economic program. The string is therefore quickly relaxed—and inflation goes on its way.

INCREASED PRIVATE RIGIDITY

Related to, but nonetheless distinct from, the rise of the public sector, we can see another vast change when we compare capitalism today and yesterday. This is the much greater rigidity we find in its private sector—that is, the much greater degree of organization and control that marks the structure of business power and labor power.

We have already noted that one of the most striking differences between modern inflations and those of the past is that in former days, inflationary peaks were followed by long deflationary periods when prices fell. Why did they fall? One reason is that it was not unusual, in the nineteenth and early twentieth centuries, for large companies to announce across-the-board wage cuts when times were bad. In addition, prices declined as a result of technological advances and as the consequence of sporadic price wars that would break out among industrial competitors.

Most of that seems a part of the past beyond recall. Technology continues to lower costs, but this has been offset by a "ratchet tendency" shown by wages and prices since World War II. A ratchet tendency means that prices and wages go up, but they rarely or never come down. This characteristic is due to the increasing presence of concentrated big industry, to stronger trade unions, and to a business climate in which wage cuts and price wars are no longer regarded as legitimate economic policies. These rigidities have also added to our inflationary propensities.

OTHER BACKGROUND REASONS

There are still other changes that have made today's system more inflation-prone than the system of a hundred, or even fifty, years ago. We are a more service-oriented, less goods-oriented, economy and productivity rises less rapidly in services than in goods. We are more affluent and much less willing to abide meekly by traditional pecking orders in society. These changes tilt the system toward inflation.

Our inflationary experience can also be traced to specific shocks and blows. It received its first impetus from the boost to spending that resulted from the Vietnam War. A powerful stimulus to inflation in other countries resulted from the manner in which the United States used its strategic position during the 1960s to "export" inflation to other nations through its international economic policies. And by no means least has been the effect of "oil shock," first in 1973 when the

Organization of Petroleum Exporting Countries (OPEC) raised petroleum prices from $3 to $11, and then again in 1979 when oil prices jumped from $13 to $28 in the wake of Iran's revolution. In contrast to the inflation-inducing effects of spending, called **demand-pull**, boosts to inflation from wage increases or increases in oil prices are called **cost-push**.

TRANSMITTING INFLATION BY INDEXING

Here we must again pause to reflect. We have suggested that a jump in coal prices in 1870, comparable to oil shock in our time, would probably have had a different effect: Many industries would have had to shut down; steel production would have been dealt a tremendous blow; in all likelihood a great depression would have begun.

Why did the cost-push of higher oil prices result in inflation and not in depression? We have already pointed to background reasons in the presence of a firm government sector and in the more rigid wage and price structure of industry. Now we must pay heed to an equally important transmission mechanism that has made inflation contagious. This is the presence of automatic price-boosters in the economy in the form of arrangements to change various kinds of payment to stay even with the cost of living. Such arrangements are called *indexing*. A few pages back we saw that Congress has indexed Social Security payments so that the checks sent to retired people automatically rise as the cost of living rises. The same kind of indexing arrangements now affect wages and salaries in much of the private sector, or protect industrial purchasers of many commodities. Most people who work expect to get cost-of-living increases whether or not they have worked harder or better.

Indexing changes the way the economy works in profound ways. Higher prices do not serve as a deterrent in an indexed economy as they would in a nonindexed one. Inflation would be self-limiting if prices rose and incomes stayed constant, but indexing means that incomes stay more or less even with prices, as we have already seen. While this may prevent much social hardship, it also tends to make inflation a self-perpetuating process.

Thus when oil shock came, the cost of living was pushed sharply upward and for a moment everyone felt the pinch. Personal savings dropped in 1974 as prices jumped. Then, after a little time, cost of living allowances (COLAs) began to take effect and soon incomes had been given a compensatory boost.

EXPECTATIONS

Along with the boost in incomes came another inflation-transmitting change. Our expectations changed. We began to expect a worsening, not an easing, of prices in the future. Unlike the old days when the prevailing belief was that "What goes up must come down," in an indexed economy we tend to believe that "What goes up will continue to go up."

Expectations are a major transmission mechanism for inflation because inflations, like depressions, have psychological as well as actual causes and self-perpetuating mechanisms. The trigger for depressions in the past has usually been a failure of private investment, whether because of credit shortages, or overbuilding, or threats of war and the like. Once a depression began, however, it continued largely because a psychological factor was lacking—"confidence," it was called during the Great Depression. In the absence of confidence, the rate of investment spending remained depressed.

Whether cost-pushed or demand-pulled, an inflationary boost has a psychological perpetuating mechanism, similar to the lack of confidence that weighs on investment spending during depressions. The mechanism is that of expectations. **Inflation leads individuals to expect more inflation, in part because of indexing. They build those expectations into wage demands, into pricing policies, into household spending behavior. Expectations thus feed on, and justify, themselves. Inflations cannot be stopped until inflationary expectations end.**

CONTROLLING INFLATION

Can we stop inflation? Of course we can. The problem is to stop it with measures that are politically acceptable. Here is a roster of anti-inflationary measures, beginning with very mild ones that probably won't work (but might!) and ending with very severe ones that almost surely would work (but at great cost).

1.   **Balancing the Federal Budget**

One of the most commonly heard quick-cure measures for inflation is that we should balance the federal budget, if necessary by a Constitutional Amendment. Would that stop inflation?

The answer depends very much on how we would balance the budget. For example, if expenditures had been maintained at existing levels, and individual income taxes had been raised by about 5 percent, the federal deficit for 1979 ($11 billion) would have been eliminated. The effect of higher taxes would have served as a downward shock. Inflation might have moderated or even stopped. The question is: Who would have voted for the higher taxes?

Alternatively, tax levels could have been maintained or even cut and federal spending might have been slashed. But where would it have been slashed? About a quarter of all federal expenditures in 1979 went for defense. Few politicians wish to cut defense spending. Roughly half of all spending went for health and income security. There was perhaps room for trimming here, but Social Security and Medicare payments together accounted for over 75 percent of this outlay. Cutting these outlays would not have been politically popular. Another 10 percent of spending went to pay interest on the federal debt: Legally that could not be cut.

That left about $100 billion—a fifth of all federal spending. Of that $100 billion, $75 billion went to states and localities as grants-in-aid. If that item had been eliminated from the budget, the federal government would have shown a substantial surplus in 1979. But state and local governments would have gone deeply into deficit.

Thus when we consider trying to stop inflation by cutting back on federal expenditures, we must look into total public expenditures—federal, state, and local—not just federal spending. In 1979, total public spending was in surplus to the amount of $14 billion, or 0.6 percent of GNP. There was no deficit to eliminate.

To review: We could use cuts in federal spending to give a sharp downward impetus to the economy. The difficulty is finding the areas in which to do it. As

far as the federal deficit is concerned, remember that its deficit may be offset by surpluses in state and local governments.

2. Using tight money to slow inflation down

Tight money is probably the most widely used anti-inflationary policy in capitalist economies today. Does it work? Partly. Tight money has succeeded in reducing the rate of growth, and *perhaps* this has mitigated the rate of inflation. In addition, tight money may hold down inflationary expectations—although some critics claim that very high interest rates, which result from tight money, serve to spur on inflationary expectations!

The problem with tight money is that it leads to on-again, off-again economic policies, often called "stop-go." When prices begin to rise too fast, the money supply is tightened to curb spending. Governments may also trim their budgets. Wage and price guidelines are often announced.

For a time, these stop measures succeed. But then pressures mount in the opposite direction. High interest rates cut into home building. A slowdown in investment causes unemployment to rise. Tight government budgets mean that programs with important constituencies have to be cut back; army bases are closed; social assistance programs abandoned. Business and labor chafe under guidelines. Hence pressures mount for a relaxation. The red light changes to green. The money supply goes up again; investment is encouraged; public spending resumes its former upward trend; guidelines are quietly abandoned. Before long the expected happens: Prices begin to move ahead too rapidly once more, and the pendulum starts its swing in the opposite direction.

3. Downward price shocks

A third approach is to try to break the inflation chain by deliberately causing downward price shocks to offset upward shocks such as oil hikes or very rapid wage increases. How could this be done? One method is to deregulate certain industries and to allow the forces of competition to reduce prices there: The airline industry is a recent example of such a program. Another method is to cut back on taxes that have direct impact on costs: Instead of raising Social Security taxes (which affect employers' costs) or cutting income taxes (which doesn't reduce the cost of living index), the government could concentrate on cutting taxes that bear directly on the cost of living, such as excise and sales taxes.

In addition, government programs that boost prices could be abandoned. The postal service could be opened up to private competition. Agricultural subsidies could be junked. The subsidy paid the merchant marine could go, along with protectionist measures that hold up prices in steel, textiles, shoes, and other commodities. Efforts could be made to break bottlenecks in certain industries such as health care and to eliminate the payment of medical costs by "third parties" (insurance companies).

Such programs could have a very substantial impact on the cost of living. But the problems they present are apparent. Opposing most such cuts is an interest group—the farmers, the companies and labor unions in exposed industries, the comfortably regulated industries that do not want more competition.

4.   A major recession

No one doubts that we could stop inflation dead in its tracks by taking really serious measures, such as bringing money expansion to a halt. If we were to stop the growth in the money supply completely, inflation would come to an end, probably fairly rapidly.

The difficulty is that such a monetary strait-jacket would impose very large economic costs. Here we have the example of West Germany and Switzerland to go by. Both these countries have deliberately introduced the kind of major recession that is sometimes advocated. In 1978, for example, industrial employment in West Germany was 12 percent lower than in 1972. In Switzerland it was 10 percent lower. As a result inflation rates in these countries were among the lowest in the world.

Why do we not follow their example? The reason is that the unemployment in Switzerland and West Germany was almost entirely imposed on their foreign workers, who were simply sent back to their native countries—mainly Italy and Yugoslavia, Turkey and Spain. **Scaled up to an economy of our size, the Swiss alone rounded up 10 million workers and sent them home. Which 10 million American workers would we send where? In fact, equivalent cut-backs in the United States would create unemployment rates approaching 30 percent.**

Such a policy would very likely stop inflation dead in its tracks. But the economy would also come to a full stop. What social and political consequences would follow from such a return to conditions of the 1930s cannot be foreseen; few are willing to find out.

5.   Voluntary Controls

Another approach is to impose voluntary controls on wages and prices, often in the form of guidelines that suggest limits for acceptable wage and price increases, especially for major industries.

The idea behind guidelines is clear and correct. If everyone would agree to limit his or her increase in income to 5 percent, instead of 8 or 10 percent, the inflation rate would promptly drop and *no one would be any worse off!* Unfortunately, unless everyone cooperates the scheme will not work, and the temptations to cheat are enormous. Think about the situation at a football game. It helps everyone to see the game if all remain seated, and no one sees better if all stand up. But if everyone does stay seated, the few individuals who stand get the best views; whereas if everyone stands, the few who agree to sit down get the worst views!

For exactly the same reasons, voluntary controls have not worked well. Therefore a number of proposals have been devised to make adherence to a voluntary program profitable as well as patriotic. Among these are the TIP (Tax Incentive Plan) plans that call for tax penalties against big companies that agree to wage settlements in excess of guideline rates. The tax penalties are intended to provide incentives for employers to resist such wage increases at the bargaining table; and if all companies agree to hold the line, then no labor union will be disadvantaged.

TIP plans might work. The difficulty they present is administrative, not economic. They call for a degree of supervision and intervention on the part of government that is certain to create bureaucracy and to generate friction. That difficulty may well be worth the price, however, if milder measures fail to arrest the inflationary trend.

6.   Mandatory Controls

Last on the list are compulsory controls, possibly of a permanent or stand-by kind, that would be imposed over prices and wages, at least in the big business sector. Such controls are similar to those that would be instantly imposed if war broke out and we faced the prospect of an astronomical inflation.

The difference is that wartime controls work fairly well for two reasons. First, a spirit of patriotism helps enfore them. Second, the overriding necessity of mounting an effective war effort removes all the usual hesitations about the limits of intervention. If controls result in insufficient investment, the government itself builds (or subsidizes) the necessary new plant and equipment. If wage controls reduce labor supplies, government can draft citizens or "freeze" them in their jobs. In peacetime these advantages are not likely to be present. No war-like patriotic spirit exists; indeed the prevailing attitude may well be to find ways of evading controls. And public opinion inhibits the government intervention that might be needed to overcome the problem to which controls would give rise. In addition, controls are onerous. Detailed norms must be written and enforced. In the Korean War we needed 18,000 price and wage inspectors to make the system work. Perhaps the computer can replace some of these inspectors, but not all of them. There is no such thing as wage and price control without a large bureaucracy.

Thus the objection to mandatory controls is two-fold. They are certain to cause a great deal of public irritation. And they will pose an endless series of difficult questions in deciding how prices should be adjusted as our economy changes, grows, and faces new challenges. On the other hand, controls have one major benefit. More surely than any other measure, they will stop the inflationary spiral. If other measures fail, therefore, and if inflation accelerates and public concern mounts, we may yet be forced to resort to this last and most painful policy.

A LAST LOOK

Is there a hope of stopping inflation without controls? The basic problem is that we cannot stop inflation unless we lower some individuals' money incomes. That is simply a matter of definitions, not of economics. Which individuals should they be? Can we devise a method of sharing the cut-back? If we really share it alike, there would be no costs, and we would be rid of the frightening experience of an economy running out of control—or under full controls.

That is about all that an economist can venture to say. The cure for inflation is persuading and educating people to adopt sharing policies that will bring inflation to a painless halt. Failing that, it is to devise policies that will impose the cost of stopping inflation on one group or another in a manner acceptable to the country at large. The difficulty, then, is that the challenge of inflation is not essentially economic. It is political. It involves the distribution and redistribution of gains and losses, the selection of winners and losers. The challenge of inflation is ultimately a challenge to our ability to solve that political problem.

LOOKING BACK

1. Unlike inflations in the past, contemporary inflation has persisted beyond the end of war and despite the presence of unemployment. Hence it is called stagflation—stagnation combined with inflation.

2. Stagflation is reflected in the disappearing Phillips curve. It used to be thought that inflation and unemployment were trade-offs—that an increase in unemployment was accompanied by a decrease in inflation rates. During the 1970s that relation largely disappeared.

3. Inflation has imaginary as well as real costs. One imaginary cost is that it has undermined our standard of living. This is largely the result of money illusion—the disappointment of not enjoying anything like the full value of our increased money incomes. Another cause is that we tend to blame inflation for economic difficulties that may not be based in inflation at all.

4. Inflation is a redistributive process, a zero sum game. Actually, it has not significantly redistributed money incomes among the main classes of income receivers. There have, however, been some winners and losers. Social Security recipients have gained. Owners of stocks have lost. Families in the lower brackets whose expenditures are concentrated on necessities—food, shelter, energy, health—may have been more painfully hit because necessities have risen more than non-necessities.

5. Inflation poses very serious threats. One of these is the threat that it will accelerate faster and faster into a runaway inflation. A second is the associated threat that the value of money assets will be reduced to zero. A third is the threat of widespread financial instability.

6. In addition to threats, inflation has a real cost. Through the effect of inflated interest rates on investment and through its effect on government policies, it retards growth and creates stagnation. The costs of stagnation are real, but borne by a minority. The costs and threats of inflation are diffuse and felt by all. Therefore inflation is felt to be more serious than unemployment.

7. Inflation, in our belief, stems from the instability of capitalist economic systems. This instability no longer creates cumulative depressions, due to the intervention of the government sector. Increased institutional rigidity also limits downward price adjustments. In this new situation shocks to the economy create only mild recessions; and upward tendencies in costs, transmitted by indexing, result in inflationary expectations.

Anti-inflation measures include:
· **balanced budgets**
· **tight money**
· **downward shocks**
· **major recessions**
· **voluntary controls**
· **mandatory controls**

8. There is a spectrum of measures to control inflation, none guaranteed to succeed. Balancing the budget imposes the need for stiff taxes or slashed spending, both hard to achieve. Also the total government budget, not just the federal budget, must be balanced. Tight money is largely ineffectual, leading to stop-go policies. Downward price shocks would be hard to implement. A major recession carries huge political and social repercussions. Voluntary controls do not

work well, although TIP policies might help them work. Mandatory permanent controls are a last fall-back, if needed to break the inflationary spiral.

The political challenge

9. Ultimately, inflation poses a political challenge—either to find a means of sharing the diminution in money income that must accompany any slowdown in inflation, or to select winners and losers from the public.

ECONOMIC VOCABULARY

Stagflation   285
Phillips curve   287
Money illusion   289

Zero sum game   290
Ratchet effect   296
Indexing   297
Cost-push   297

Demand-pull   297
Stop-go policies   299
TIP plans   300

QUESTIONS

1. Do you believe that some inflationary costs are only imaginary? Everyone knows that meat prices have soared. Here are data on beef consumption per capita for 1960, 1965, 1970, and 1975:

	1960	1965	1970	1975
Beef (lbs. per capita)	85.1	99.5	113.7	120.1

Does this make a conclusive case, one way or the other? How about other foods? How would you decide whether there had really been a falling-off in living standards since 1960?

2. Can you give an instance of money illusion from your own experience? How about your parents harping on how much less things cost in their day? Did they necessarily cost less as a percentage of their incomes in those days?

3. Which among many kinds of assets do you consider the most inflation proof? Depression proof? Why? If you had to hold your total fortune in gold or in a collection of industrial stocks for the next 25 years, which would you choose?

4. What kind of event might give rise to a hyperinflation in the U.S.? If such a catastrophe occurred, what policies would you advocate?

5. Is war always inflationary, even if financed by taxes? Is government spending always inflationary? Never inflationary? If the federal government balanced its budget, but the states incurred deficits by selling bonds, would that necessarily be inflationary?

6. How would you try to reckon the costs of inflation versus those of unemployment?

7. Would you be willing to be unemployed, if you were assured that that would keep down the cost of living by some small amount? Would you be willing to designate some one else to lose his or her job, if it could be shown that this would reduce inflation by a perceptible amount?

8. How do you think people should decide whether severe measures, such as a major recession or mandatory controls, are worth their cost?

Chapter
20
UNEMPLOYMENT

A LOOK AHEAD

The other side of the coin of inflation, these days, is unemployment; this chapter is designed to tell us something about its causes, its nature, and its cures.

Three main lessons stand out in the pages ahead.

(1) There is an extreme variation in unemployment rates. If the unemployed are our "inflation fighters," they are chosen, as we shall see, in a highly biased fashion.

(2) Unemployment is not just the difference between the labor force and those at work. The idea of participation rates and an elastic labor force gives new meaning to the idea of joblessness.

(3) There are cures for unemployment. They are essentially two: more demand, and a better fit between demand and supply.

At the very end, a hard question: Is unemployment an integral part of capitalism? Perhaps it is, but certainly not to the extent that we have experienced it in recent years.

Ask American citizens what is their *second* most worrisome economic problem and you will likely get agreement that it is unemployment. Unlike inflation, however, unemployment has not been high on the public's complaints for ten years. This is because large-scale unemployment is a fairly recent problem, the consequence of the economic recession of 1973–1975 and the downturn starting in 1980.

RECESSIONS AND UNEMPLOYMENT

Because unemployment and recession are so closely linked, we had better begin by asking: What is a recession? The answer is very simple. **A recession is a drop in the gross national product that lasts for at least 6 months.** The word *depression* is used to refer to a severe drop in GNP, but there is no generally accepted definition of when a recession becomes a depression. People generally call a downturn a recession if their neighbor is unemployed, but a depression if they are unemployed.

Although recessions always bring unemployment, we can suffer from unemployment even without recession if our growth is too slow. Until recently our productivity has increased by about 3 percent and our labor force by about 1 percent (on the average). This means that each year we have the ability to turn out about 4 percent more goods. **Unless our GNP grows by at least that rate, we will not be able to keep up with our rising productivity capacity. The consequence is that there will be unsold goods and workers who are let go or not rehired.**

Let us trace exactly what happens when GNP falls or lags. The pace of business activity slows down. There is less demand for consumer goods and services, less demand for plant and equipment and other business items. Some businesses fire people, other businesses hire fewer new workers. Because our labor force is steadily growing as our population swells, even a small decrease in the willingness to take on new workers spells a sharp rise in unemployment for certain groups, such as young people. When a recession really deepens, as in 1980, it is not just the young who cannot find work, but experienced workers find themselves thrown out of work, as Figure 20.1 shows.

THE UNEMPLOYED AS INFLATION FIGHTERS

Unemployment is a problem that has to be judged differently from the way we judge inflation. Rising prices affect everyone, although some kinds of wage earners or profit-receivers gain while others lose. Unemployment, however, is a sharply focused economic ill.

When we state that 8 percent of the labor force is unemployed, this does not mean that every worker is laid off for 8 percent of the year. It means that some workers are unemployed for long periods of time. Over 50 percent of the total number of weeks of unemployment is typically borne by individuals who are unemployed for more than half a year. Almost half of those who suffer long spells of unemployment end up not with a job, but by withdrawing from the labor force.

The point is that unemployment is a capricious, as well as an uncertain means of fighting inflation. We draft our "inflation fighters" mainly from the age group 16–24, where unemployment rates are three times those of adults. Females are 38 percent more likely to be subject to the anti-inflation draft than males;

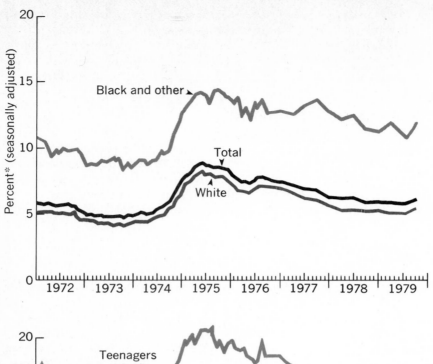

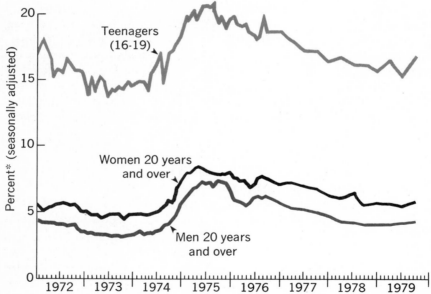

Unemployment as percent of civilian labor force in group specified.
Source: Department of Labor

FIGURE 20.1 IMPACT OF RECESSION ON EMPLOYMENT
This table shows two things: (1) racial minorities, women (mostly part-time workers), and teenagers always experience higher unemployment rates than white older males, and (2) when recession hits, all groups suffer, including the core of white experienced workers.

Year	Unemployed (thousands)	Percent of civilian labor force
1929	1,550	3.2
1933	12,830	24.9
1940	8,120	14.6
1944	670	1.2
1960–65 av.	4,100	5.5
1965–70 av.	3,117	3.9
1971	4,993	5.9
1972	4,840	5.6
1973	4,304	4.9
1974	5,076	5.6
1975	7,530	8.5
1976	7,288	7.7
1977	6,855	7.0
1978	6,047	6.0
1979	5,944	5.8

Unemployment reached its worst level in 1933. But it was still very severe up to World War II. The record throughout the 1970s has been poor.

TABLE 20.1 UNEMPLOY-MENT IN THE U.S.

Hispanics are 75 percent more likely to be called up than whites. These groups share two characteristics: They tend to be relatively unskilled, and they tend to lack political clout.

As we would expect, the group with the lowest unemployment rate is the group of prime-age white males. There are both economic and political reasons why these are the last to be fired in a recession. Yet, if we want our inflation fighters to come from groups whose wage rates are most significant in setting the national pattern, this is the very group from whom we should be recruiting our soldier. Our point, of course, is not to urge higher unemployment rates for anyone. It is only to emphasize that unemployment, as an anti-inflation measure, is neither efficient nor equitable. Worse, as we have already seen, it may not be effective.

SEVERITY OF UNEMPLOYMENT

How serious is unemployment as a national economic problem? Table 20.1 shows us the record of the past few years and gives us the data for earlier, benchmark years to serve as a point of comparison.

The terrible percentages of the Depression years speak for themselves. At the very depth of the Depression, a quarter of the work force was jobless at a time when unemployment insurance and welfare was largely nonexistent. Note, too, that massive unemployment persisted until 1940. Only the advent of World War II finally brought unemployment below 1929 levels.

The record of the 1960s and 1970s is mixed. During the early 1960s, unemployment was at a level considered to be uncomfortably high—roughly between 5 and 6 percent of the labor force. This percentage dropped in the second half of the decade, partly as a consequence of higher spending on armaments.

It is the record of the 1970s that is disturbing. First we watched the number of unemployed soar to over 8 million in May 1975. Then we saw unemployment rates approach 9 percent of the labor force, a rate more serious than any recession in this century, barring only the 1933–40 collapse.

	1978		1978		1978
Males	5.2%	Females	7.2%	Hispanics	9.1%
White Males	4.5	White Females	6.2	16–19	20.6
16–19	13.5	16–19	14.4	Males 20+	6.3
20–24	7.6	20–24	8.3	Females 20+	9.8
25–54	3.0	25–54	4.9		
55–64	2.6	55–64	3.0		
65 & up	3.9	65 & up	3.7		
Black Males	10.9	Black Females	13.1	Total:	6.0
16–19	34.4	16–19	38.4		
20–24	20.0	20–24	21.3		
25–54	6.6	25–54	8.7		
55–64	4.4	55–64	5.1		
65 & up	7.1	65 & up	5.0		

**TABLE 20.2
STRUCTURE
OF UNEM-
PLOYMENT**

**In 1978, the national unemployment rate was 6 percent.
This table shows how that average figure conceals very
much higher rates among certain groups.**

THE DIFFERENTIAL IMPACT OF UNEMPLOYMENT

By the end of the 1970s, the unemployment rate was down to around 6 percent, and some economists argued that this was close to "full" employment for the nation. Their argument was based on the fact that unemployment among the prime-age white group had dropped to under 3.5 percent. By mid 1980, however, unemployment rates were once again moving up towards 1975 levels.

There is no reason to hold that unemployment rates cannot be reduced well below that, as we shall see at the end of this chapter. But if we were to accept 6 percent as full employment, we would be accepting a much higher rate of unemployment for some groups in the population. We have already looked at the unequal odds facing our inflation-fighters. Perhaps we should add that unemployment rates for black teenagers, corrected for those who have dropped out of the system—who are not at school, not at work, and not trying to get work—reveal unemployment rates of up to *90 percent* in central city slums!

Table 20.2 shows us the tremendous spread in the incidence of unemployment, disregarding the pathology of the slum. Notice that black males bear twice the impact of unemployment that white males do, black females double the impact of white females; and all females 50 percent more impact than all males. The table bears study and thought.

MEASURING UNEMPLOYMENT

Before we proceed to policies designed to remedy unemployment we ought to look more carefully into the manner in which we measure it. The statistics of unemployment are gathered by a household-to-household survey conducted each month by the Bureau of the Census among a carefully selected sample. An unemployed person is thereupon defined not merely as a person without a job—for perhaps such a person does not *want* a job—but as someone who is actively seek-

THE GHETTO SKILL MIX

A sad example of the lack of fit between the skills demanded by employers and those possessed by the labor force is to be found in the ghetto, where typically the labor force is badly undertrained. A study by the First National City Bank explored this situation in New York City.

As we can see, in only one category—unskilled service—was the prospective demand for labor roughly in line with the skills available. This meant a reasonable employment prospect for maids, restaurant workers, bellhops, and the like—among the lowest-paid occupations in the nation. As for the common laborer, who comprised over half the "skill pool" of the New York ghetto, his outlook was bleak indeed— less than one percent of new jobs would open in that area. Conversely, for the widest job market in the city—the white-collar trades that offer two-thirds of the new jobs—the ghetto could offer only one-seventh of its residents as adequately trained. These extreme disproportions still apply to the situation in New York and many other slum-ridden cities. If these figures have any meaning, it is that ghetto poverty is here to stay, short of a herculean effort to rescue the trapped ghetto resident.

	Occupational distribution of ghetto unemployed, 1968	Estimated job openings, 1965– 1975
White collar	13.6%	65.7%
Craftsmen	2.8	7.4
Operatives	14.7	7.7
Unskilled personal service	16.6	18.6
Laborers	52.3	0.6

ing work but is unable to find it. Since, however, the number of people who will be seeking work will rise in good times and fall in bad times, figures for any given period must be viewed with caution.

As employment opportunities drop, unemployment will not rise by an equivalent amount. Some of those looking for work when job opportunities are plentiful will withdraw from the labor force and become part of *hidden unemployment*. When job opportunities expand, these hidden unemployed will reenter the labor force, so that unemployment will not fall as fast as employment rises. Thus the ups and downs in the measured unemployment rate reflect the state of the economy, but the swings are not as large as they would be if the term "unemployment" measured the hidden unemployed.

THE ELASTIC LABOR FORCE

This gives rise to a curious and important result. Measured unemployment is not simply the difference between the number of people working and a fixed labor force. It is the difference between the number working and an elastic, changeable labor force.

The result of measuring unemployment is seemingly paradoxical. It is that employment and unemployment can both rise and fall at the same time, as workers (mainly youths and women) enter the labor market in good times, or as they withdraw in discouragement in bad times. Table 20.3 shows us this parallel rise in both the number working and the number without work. Look at the change between 1973 and 1974.

TABLE 20.3 SHORT-RUN CHANGES IN THE LABOR FORCE (MILLIONS)	1973	1974	1975	1976	1977	1978	1979
Number in civilian labor force	88.7	91.0	92.6	94.8	97.4	100.4	102.9
Civilian employment	84.4	85.9	84.8	87.5	90.5	94.4	106.9
Unemployment	4.3	5.1	7.8	7.3	7.0	6.0	5.8

Notice that employment and unemployment can *both* rise, as in the period 1973–1974. This is because the labor force is not a fixed, but a variable, reservoir.

PARTICIPATION RATES

We call this elasticity of the labor force its *short-run participation rate.* This differs from long-run participation rates, which mark historical changes in the ratios of men and women in the labor force, or in the proportions of the young and the old at work. Here we see that short-run changes play a significant role in determining the meaning of the phenomenon we call unemployment. The average number of hours worked per week also varies with good and bad times because employees can or cannot get overtime work or can or cannot "moonlight" (take on a second job).

These considerations mean that economists do not judge the severity of a given unemployment rate just by the percentage of the jobless. They also look to participation rates and hours of work. Relatively low participation rates and a fall in average hours worked per week indicate that the impact of a given unemployment rate is more serious than it appears to be.

CAUSES AND CURES

What causes unemployment and what will cure it? We have already more than once studied the principal reason for joblessness—a lack of sufficient aggregate demand. For reasons that we understand very well, when total spending declines, employers let workers go. Thus the first cause of unemployment lies in too little demand, and the first cure lies in restoring demand to a full employment level.

LEVEL OF DEMAND

This is only the first step in our analysis, however, for we must recognize that a level of demand adequate to produce full or high employment in one year will not be adequate the next. First, there is a normal growth of the labor force as a consequence of population growth. This growth may accelerate if an unusually large number of young people, products of an earlier baby boom, are leaving school. In the 1960s there was a flood of such young entrants; now, fortunately, the flood has ebbed (see box, p. 312).

Second, even if there were no increase in the labor force, we experience a normal growth in productivity as the consequence of adding capital equipment, of improving our techniques of production, and of increasing our stock of skill and knowledge. This year-to-year increase in per capita productivity averages 3 percent. Therefore, unless GNP grows by at least that amount, there will not be enough demand to absorb the output of the given labor force. **Thus we need a growth of GNP equal to the increase in the labor force, plus the increase in productivity, to insure a constant rate of employment.**

But suppose that we have too much unemployment and want to grow fast enough to absorb it? Now comes an important twist that results from the elasticity of the labor force. As employment grows, more people enter the labor force, and hours lengthen. This means that we have to increase the level of GNP enough to absorb the original unemployed, plus the addition to the labor force that results from higher participation rates and more hours worked.

The difficulty with revving up GNP to eliminate unemployment is that we rapidly run into inflationary bottlenecks, once unemployment reaches the 5 to 6 percent level. This brings us to familiar terrain, where we must fight out the battle between unemployment and inflation. **We know how to reduce unemployment by raising aggregate demand, but we do not know how to do so without creating unacceptable levels of inflation.**

AUTOMATION UNEMPLOYMENT

Aggregate demand—or rather the lack of it—is the prime cause of unemployment. A subsidiary cause is automation, which may create unemployment or make difficult its cure even if the level of national spending is high.

Automation joblessness, caused by the introduction of machines, is a problem that vexes and worries us, partly because it is real, partly because we do not understand it very well. Technology can be a source of job creation, especially when it brings whole new industries into being. But machines can also displace people from established jobs—and may not create new industries to absorb them.

Looking back over the history of the United States, it seems as if machines steadily pushed people out of the agricultural sector, through the factory, and into the office. Fifty years ago it took almost 40 percent of the work force to feed us; today it takes only 3 percent. The proportion of the labor force that works in manufacturing has been falling very slowly over the last 50 years. It is the service employments that have burgeoned, employing 65 percent of our labor force today compared with 25 percent in 1900.

Modern technology is more and more oriented to service work, the computer being the prime example. Will computer technology displace people from service jobs, or will it expand the role of services and make new jobs? We do not yet know.

STRUCTURAL UNEMPLOYMENT

If automation did bring about unemployment, could we not take care of it through demand management? The question opens up an aspect of the unemployment problem that we have not yet studied. **Unemployment is not solely a matter of people losing jobs, but of people not being able to find new jobs. We can have unemployment that results from a lack of skills or from a mismatch between existing skills and required skills or because workers looking for jobs do not have the characteristics (such as literacy, or ethnic backgrounds, or education) that employers want.**

This kind of unemployment is called *structural unemployment.* Because it is lodged so strongly in specific attributes of the individual, it resists the "easy" cure of higher aggregate demand. Business may be better for an employer, but he may prefer to pay his existing work force overtime, rather than take on a new labor force that does not meet his specifications.

THE IMPORTANCE OF BEING THE RIGHT AGE

A special kind of unemployment arises because the age composition of the labor force changes, sometimes flooding the market with young untrained workers, sometimes with older workers. Take the group aged 14 to 24. This includes those who are finishing their educations as well as those who have finished and are entering the work force. The "cohort" as a whole increased in numbers by roughly 8 to 10 percent from decade to decade in the period 1890 to 1960.

Then in the 1960s an explosion occurred. The so-called baby boom in the years immediately following World War II began to enter these age ranks. In the decade of the 1960s, the 14-to-24-year-old group increased by 52 *percent*. In the 1970s it increased by a customary 11 percent; in the 1980s it will *decline* by 8 percent. We can confidently predict these changes, because the members of this age group are already born.

Beginning in mid 1980s, however, the rate of growth of the labor force will be very slow, except for women. Job prospects should then be very bright.

The remedy for structural unemployment is more difficult than for general lack-of-demand unemployment. New skills or new attributes (such as punctuality) are needed by the "structurally" unemployed, and these are expensive to impart. The Job Corps program of the 1960s, for example, found that it cost about $10,000 to $12,000 to make an unemployed person—often a member of a ghetto group—acceptable to employers. Society was not willing to pay so large a fee, and employers also resisted (or asked large subsidies for) programs to hire and train "unemployables."

The high cost of retraining or of imparting desired work characteristics is one reason why structural unemployment is a difficult problem. Perhaps even more difficult is the question: For what jobs shall the unemployed be trained? **Unless we very clearly know the shape of future demand, the risk is that a retraining program will prepare workers for jobs that may no longer exist when the workers are ready for them.** And unless the *level* of future demand is high, even a foresighted program will not effectively solve the unemployment problem.

One solution to this problem would be to create a program aimed at creating permanent jobs in specific areas of the public sector, such as the repair, maintenance, and beautification of our inner cities, or the care of the aged. Once again, however, we encounter public resistance. The use of the government as the "employer of last resort" is a potentially powerful weapon for the alleviation of unemployment, but it is a departure that does not yet have the wholehearted endorsement of the public.

UNEMPLOYMENT AND SOCIAL INSURANCE

Next we must glance at a new problem, one that is not yet well researched or understood. This is the possibility that the existence of easily available, relatively high unemployment insurance benefits helps to generate unemployment, especially among low-paid workers.

Unemployment compensation in the United States differs widely among the states. In general, it provides for payment of one-half of an unemployed person's income, up to some maximum weekly benefit. Actual weekly benefits range from $99 in Washington, D.C. to $48 in Mississippi. There is also a limit on how many weeks' unemployment compensation can be claimed. Usually 20 weeks can be collected, although that was temporarily upped to 65 weeks by federal legislation during the 1975–1976 recession.

However, many individuals, such as new entrants into the labor force or employees of government and nonprofit institutions are not eligible for any benefits at all. If a person is not eligible or has exhausted his or her benefits, there is welfare, which also varies from state to state in terms of benefits and eligibility.

Unemployment compensation has been one of the most important social changes of the last 50 years. For what was so frightening about the Great Depression was not merely its terrific rate of joblessness; it was that this economic failure had no social remedy. An unemployed family was literally without any recourse, except its own savings or whatever charity or relief a municipality might provide. The unemployed in the 1930s did not receive unemployment insurance checks. They waited in line at soup kitchens.

Nevertheless, there may well be a cost for the social floor that unemployment insurance has placed under our feet. The cost is that unemployment insurance, because it is not taxable, greatly reduces the incentive to stick to a job. Professor Martin Feldstein has pointed out that the opportunity cost of unemployment is not the comparison of a worker's earnings and his or her unemployment compensation check; it is a comparison of the *after-tax* earnings with that check. The difference may be small. Feldstein believes that our present system encourages unemployment by making it "profitable" to get fired—at least for young or part-time workers. He suggests that we can alleviate the situation by making unemployment benefits taxable.

It is possible that Feldstein is correct in his analysis. Improvements in the equity and the cost of unemployment insurance may be useful reforms. They will not, however, cure the major causes of unemployment itself.

FRICTIONAL UNEMPLOYMENT

We should not leave this discussion of the causes of unemployment without mentioning the normal unemployment that occurs when workers voluntarily leave one job in search of a better one. This kind of unemployment is actually a source of benefit for the economy, because it is one of the ways in which productivity is enhanced, as workers move from declining industries to growing ones.

Nonetheless, we can increase the efficiency of this productivity-promoting flow of labor by reducing the period of "frictional" unemployment as much as possible. The most frequently suggested means of doing so is to provide a nationwide employment service that would make job information available to job searchers, so that a carpenter, wishing to leave an area where work was slow, would know what areas were booming; or a secretary who felt there was no room for promotion in a sluggish business would have available a roster of many other possibilities.

Want ads are a partial, but incomplete, kind of employment service. A full-scale national information service would provide much more complete information; and a full national commitment to minimizing frictional unemployment would even help defray the costs of relocating. Sweden and some other European countries run such labor exchanges, but we have yet to establish one in the United States.

CAPITALISM AND UNEMPLOYMENT

This is by no means a full discussion of all the causes of, or cures for, unemployment. We have, for example, ignored the problem of wage policy, although it must be obvious that unemployment can be generated if unions succeed in pushing up wage rates for certain jobs above the jobs' marginal productivity. And we have paid no heed to the long-run remedy for unemployment played by lengthening the years of schooling, lowering the age of retirement, liberalizing vacation policies, and other changes in social institutions.

But we have covered enough to enable us to draw up a preliminary report on the performance of the economy as a generator of employment. As we saw, when we first examined the data for the 1960s and 1970s, that report is not good. Unemployment has ranged from 3.5 percent in the war-boom years to nearly 9 percent in the 1975 recession. Some of this was frictional unemployment—perhaps 2 to 3 percent of the labor force. All the rest was structural unemployment or the unemployment that resulted from inadequate levels of aggregate demand.

"RESERVE ARMY OF THE UNEMPLOYED"

Is this a consequence of the inherent sluggishness of a capitalist system incapable of attaining high levels of employment except under armaments spending?

Marxists have argued that this is the case and have pointed to the very large workless bottom layer of the American economy. First there are the officially acknowledged unemployed—6 million in 1979. Then there are the underemployed, those who want full-time work but can get only part-time. These are another 4 million. Then there are 1 million who are not looking for work because they think they cannot find it. This gives us a very large "reserve army of the unemployed," to use Karl Marx's term for the jobless whose presence, he argued, served to keep down the wages of those who were employed. Really full employment, a Marxist would claim, would raise wages so high that profits—and capitalism—would disappear.

This is not an analysis to be lightly brushed aside. In Europe, for example, a similar "reserve army" has been created by importing cheap labor from Greece, Spain, Yugoslavia, and Turkey to man the great factories of the continent. When times are bad, many of these "guest workers" are forced to return to their countries of origin; so that the European nations, in fact, export some of their unemployed, as we saw in our last chapter.

U.S. VS. EUROPEAN PERFORMANCE

It may well be, in other words, that some unemployment above the frictional level is needed to prevent wages from squeezing out profits or sending prices skyhigh. Leaders in many countries speak candidly of the need to keep labor "in line," and unemployment is openly acknowledged to be a disciplinary force toward that end. Some degree of unemployment may indeed be inseparable from the operation of a capitalist system.

But what degree? It is also clear that the levels of unemployment that have been generated and tolerated in the United States are not necessary. In Western Europe until very recently, the levels of unemployment have for long periods

Country	Highest	Lowest	Average
United States	6.7%	3.5%	4.9%
Canada	7.1	3.9	5.4
Japan	1.7	1.1	1.3
France	3.0	1.6	2.3
West Germany	2.1	0.3	0.8
Italy	4.3	2.7	3.6
United Kingdom	5.3	1.2	3.2
Sweden	2.7	1.2	1.9

TABLE 20.4 UNEMPLOY-MENT RATES 1960–1974

Source: *The Nordic Economic Outlook,* June 1975.

been far below that of the United States, as Table 20.4 shows—a record of years in which European nations were not "exporting" unemployment but were enjoying a strong boom.

European nations have generally gone much further than we have in providing labor exchanges or in seeking to remedy structural unemployment, and they have been willing to accept a higher level of inflation as a lesser evil than a high level of unemployment.

What is lacking in our nation, to date, is a willingness to place employment at the very head of all the benefits that we expect from an economy, a willingness to bend every effort to achieve the right to work for all. We may still not wholly eliminate structural or aggregate demand employment, but then at least we could not be faulted for having failed to try.

KEY CONCEPTS

The main cause of unemployment is recession

Unemployment "fighters" are mainly recruited from youth, women, and nonwhites

Unemployment has ranged from 5 to 9 percent during the 1970s

Participation rates vary, so that employment and unemployment may rise and fall together

We need a 3½ percent increase in GNP to lower unemployment by 1 point

LOOKING BACK

1. The primary causes of unemployment are recessions or depressions.

2. Unemployment has a different impact than has inflation. The effect of inflation is diffused; the effect of unemployment is concentrated. If the unemployed are our "inflation fighters," they are drafted very unevenly, mainly from young workers, women, and nonwhites. These are the groups whose wage rates have least effect on the national wage pattern.

3. The severity of unemployment during the 1970s has ranged from 5 to nearly 9 percent. This is a poor showing. Moreover, the differential impact is very high among certain groups.

4. Unemployment is measured by the inability of a person who is searching for work to find a job. Therefore the question of searching is important in determining who is, and is not, "participating" in the labor force. Because participation rates drop in recessions as discouraged workers withdraw, it is often the case that unemployment and employment both rise or both fall, rather than moving in opposite directions.

5. The main remedy for unemployment is increasing the level of aggregate demand. The main problem is the risk of accelerating inflation. Because of population growth and normal increases in

productivity, we must increase GNP by about 2½ percent a year just to maintain an even level of employment, and we must increase GNP by 3½ percent to lower the unemployment rate by 1 percent.

Technological unemployment and structural unemployment are different causes for joblessness. They may be combatted by public employment

6. Technology can also create unemployment, displacing labor by machinery as in agriculture. We do not know if the recent burst of computer technology (automation) will have a net labor displacing effect or not. Similar to technological unemployment is structural unemployment, resulting from a mismatch of skills and employers' needs. One remedy for this general kind of unemployment may be public sector employment, using the government as employer of last resort.

Unemployment insurance may magnify unemployment

7. Unemployment insurance is a very important cushion for the unemployed. It is possible, however, that unemployment benefits, because they are tax free, serve to encourage unemployment.

Unemployment may serve a purpose in keeping capitalism going, but European experience shows that unemployment can be reduced far below American levels

8. Unemployment was regarded by Karl Marx as the "reserve army" of capitalism, necessary to keep its wage level down. Recent experience using unemployment to fight inflation bears some resemblance to this. Nonetheless, European experience shows that capitalism can run for long periods with much lower unemployment rates than we have suffered.

ECONOMIC VOCABULARY

QUESTIONS

1. Unemployment rates among the black population in many cities today are worse than during the Great Depression years. What steps do you think should be taken?

2. Do you believe there exists general support for large public employment programs? Why or why not?

3. Do you think the computer on net balance has created jobs? How would you go about researching this question?

4. How much inflation would you yourself accept to lower unemployment by one half? How much inflation do you think the public would accept?

5. Why is frictional unemployment useful but not structural unemployment? If frictional unemployment is useful, why try to reduce it?

6. Explain why we need a rising GNP to maintain a constant level of employment. Would this be true if we had zero population growth but rising productivity? Zero productivity growth but rising population? If we have both, will the target be constant employment or constant unemployment? Or constant unemployment rates?

7. Marx believed that capitalism would not work unless it had a "reserve army" of unemployed to keep wages in check. Do you think that this idea can be scientifically proved true or false? How would you propose going about doing so? If you decide there is *no* way of proving or disproving the idea, why does it continue to be such an important concept in a Marxian view of capitalism?

Chapter

21 DEFENDING THE DOLLAR

A LOOK AHEAD

Our focus shifts from problems at home to problems in the international arena. For several years we have heard about the falling dollar and the need to defend it. This chapter

(1) clarifies what we mean when we say that the dollar is falling, and explains how a nation can ''defend'' its currency;

(2) teaches us the basic elements of international exchange;

(3) gives us a view of the impact on our domestic well-being of international economic trends and our efforts to cope with them.

Foreign trade and international finance used to be subjects that Americans could afford to be ignorant about. In nearly all economic textbooks, including our own, they were reserved for a special section at the end, and it was generally understood that if an instructor had to sacrifice any part of the course because of insufficient time, international economics was the part to go.

That has changed, and changed dramatically, within a very few years. The former invulnerability of the American economy from foreign goings-on has come to an end. The American dollar, once the Rock of Gibraltar in a stormy world, has taken a terrible battering. Millions of American citizens are now directly affected by America's international economic position; all of us are indirectly affected by it. In a word, international economics has become a part of economics with which every student should be familiar.

THE FALLING DOLLAR

The new situation has come home to most of us through headlines that have announced for some years that the dollar is "falling." Sometimes the headlines tell us that gold is soaring, or that the yen or the mark or the Swiss franc have hit new highs. All these phrases mean the same thing—but what is that thing?

THE FOREIGN VALUE OF THE DOLLAR

When the dollar falls in the international money markets, it does not mean that a dollar will buy fewer American goods. That is a very important point to bear in mind. Our dollars fall in domestic value as inflation raises prices, but it is entirely possible for inflation to cheapen the dollar at home—at least for a time—but not cause it to fall on the foreign money markets. Vice versa, it is possible for the dollar to fall abroad but to remain unchanged in its buying power at home.

When we speak of the dollar falling in foreign trade, it means only one thing: A dollar will buy less foreign money—German marks, French or Swiss francs, Swedish krona, or whatever. As a result, it becomes more expensive to buy foreign goods and services.

THE RATE OF EXCHANGE

Suppose, for example, that you enjoy French wine. French wine is sold by its producers for francs, the currency in which French producers pay their bills and want their receipts. Let us suppose that they price their wine at 20 francs the bottle.

How much would 20 franc wine cost in America? The answer depends on the rate at which we can exchange dollars for francs—that is, it depends on the price of francs. We discover this price by going to banks, who are the main dealers in foreign currencies of all kinds, and inquiring what the dollar-franc *exchange rate* is. Let us say we are told it is five francs to the dollar. To buy a bottle of French wine, then, (ignoring transportation, insurance, and other costs) will cost us $4.00 (20 francs ÷ 5 = $4.00).

Now suppose that the dollar "falls." This means that the dollar becomes cheaper on the market for foreign money. It follows, of course, that francs will become dearer in terms of dollars. Instead of getting five francs for a dollar, we now get only four. Meanwhile, the price of wine hasn't changed—it still costs

20 francs. But it now costs us $5.00, not $4.00, to purchase 20 francs. A falling dollar therefore raises the price of foreign goods in terms of American money.

Conversely, a rising exchange rate would cheapen them. Let us imagine that we were contemplating a trip to Germany. We inquire into the prices of German hotels, German meals, and the like, and we are told that we can do it comfortably for (let us say) 100 marks per day. "How much is that in American money?" we ask. The answer depends, of course, on the exchange rate. Suppose the rate is three marks to the dollar. Then 100 marks would be the equivalent of $33 a day. But if the dollar happened to be rising, we could be in for a pleasant surprise. Perhaps by the time we were ready to leave, it would have risen to four marks to the dollar. It still costs 100 marks a day to travel in Germany, but we can now buy 100 marks for only $25 dollars.

We must remember, however, that international economics must always be viewed from both sides of the ocean. When the dollar rises, foreign goods or services become less expensive for us. But for a German, just the opposite is true. A German tourist coming to America might be told that he should allow $50 a day for expenses. "How much will that cost me in marks?" he asks his bank. The answer, again, hangs on the exchange rate. If it costs only three marks to buy a dollar, it will obviously be cheaper for the German tourist than if it costs four marks. Notice that this is exactly the opposite of the American tourist's position.

THE DOLLAR CRISIS

International economics has entered our consciousness because we have been reading about the falling dollar. We know now that this means that the price of dollars, on the market for foreign currencies, must have been dropping. Therefore the price of other currencies must have been rising. It does not, however, mean that the price of *all* foreign currencies is higher than a few years ago. Table 21.1 shows the exchange rate of six foreign currencies against the dollar in 1975 and in early 1980.

	1975	1980 (March)	% Change
German mark	$ .41	.57	+ 39
Japanese yen	.034	.042	+ 23
Swiss franc	.39	.62	+ 59
U.K. pound	2.22	2.25	+ 1
Canadian dollar	.98	.85	− 13
Italian lira	.015	.012	− 20

TABLE 21.1 PRICE OF FOREIGN CURRENCY IN U.S. $

Changes in the exchange rate 1975–1980 took the form of higher prices for most, but not all, currencies.

As the table shows, a German mark cost 39 percent more over the period. But notice that an Italian lira cost 20 percent less! Why, then, do we say that the dollar has fallen, when it has actually risen against some currencies? The answer is that it fell against those currencies for which we had the greatest need. We do very little business in Paraguay, for example, so that it matters little how many Paraguayan guaranis we get for a dollar. We do a great deal of business with Germany and Japan, both as buyers and sellers, and so it matters a great deal what happens to those currencies.

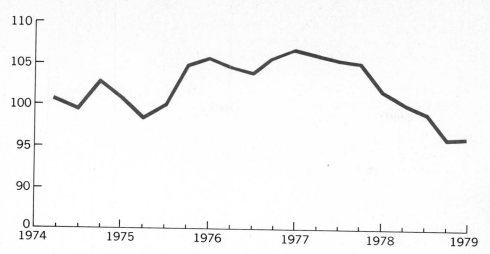

FIGURE 21.1
THE TRADE-
WEIGHTED
DOLLAR

The value of the trade-weighted dollar has dropped.

When we say that the dollar has fallen, we measure it against a "basket" of foreign currencies, in which different currencies are included according to their degree of commercial use. We call this *a trade-weighted dollar.* Over the last five years, the trade-weighted dollar has fallen by about 14 percent. Most of the fall took place rather precipitously during the early part of 1979, as Figure 21.1 shows.

THE MARKET FOR DOLLARS

Why did the dollar fall? As with all price changes, our first task is to look at the supply and demand situation. And that requires us to investigate the nature of the market for dollars and other currencies.

Here we can best begin by mentally grouping all the kinds of dealings in which dollars and other currencies change hands into two basic markets. One is the market for currencies to carry on current transactions. The other is the market for currencies to carry on capital transactions. You will have no trouble following the story if you bear these two markets in mind.

1. Current Transactions

The first market in which currencies are bought and sold is that in which the current transactions between firms, individuals, or governments are carried out. Here *the demand for dollars* comes from such groups as foreigners who want to import U.S. goods and services, and who must acquire dollars to purchase them; or from foreign tourists who need dollars to travel in the U.S.; or from foreign governments who must buy dollars to maintain embassies or consulates in America; or from firms abroad (American or foreign) that want to send dividends or profits to the United States in dollars. All these kinds of transactions require that holders of marks or francs or yen offer their currencies on the foreign exchange market in order to buy U.S. dollars.

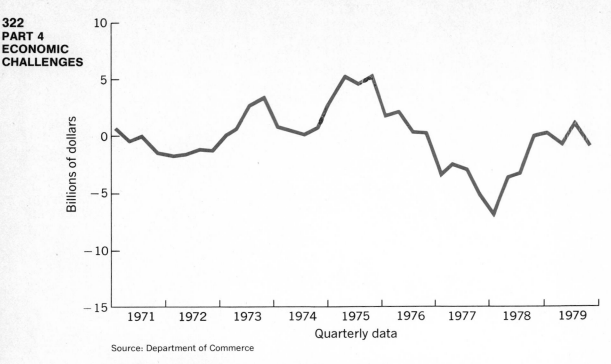

Source: Department of Commerce

FIGURE 21.2 BALANCE ON CURRENT ACCOUNT 1971–1979
**The balance on current account sums up all the supplies and demands for dollars
needed for trade, travel, remittances of profits, government expenses, and the like.
Until roughly 1968, the market for current account always showed a favorable balance. This is no longer the case.**

And, of course, there are similar groups of Americans who *supply dollars*
to the foreign exchange market for exactly the opposite reasons. Here we find
American importers who want to bring in Japanese cameras and must offer
dollars in order to acquire the yen to make their purchases; American or foreign
firms that are sending dividends or profits earned in the U.S. to a foreign branch
or headquarters; Americans or foreign residents who sell dollars in order to buy
lire or drachmas or krona to send money to friends or relatives abroad; or the
American government which uses dollars to buy foreign currencies to pay diplo-
matic living expenses or to make military expenditures abroad.

Balance on Current Account. Taken all together, these supplies and demands
for dollars establish what we call our balance on current account. As Figure 21.2
shows, this balance took a substantial fall after 1970, followed by a sharp rise
and then another fall. That is, the graph shows that up to 1968 foreigners were
buying more dollars for all the various purposes of current transactions than
Americans were selling dollars for those purposes; whereas since the 1970s, the
balance has largely gone the other way.

What was the reason for this sharp adverse change in our current balance of payments? Figure 21.3 shows that it was mainly the result of a dramatic fall in our *merchandise balance of trade*. This is a submarket within the larger flow of all current transactions in which we pay heed only to those dollars supplied and demanded to finance imports and exports of merchandise.

Notice that until 1971 the United States had a small positive balance on merchandise account. This meant that we were selling more goods and services abroad, measured in dollars, than the dollar value of the goods and services we were buying there.

What has happened since then to turn the balance from black to red? The answer in part is the OPEC oil crisis which resulted in a sharp rise in the number of dollars we had to supply to buy oil abroad. In 1972 our oil bill was $5 billion. In 1974 it was $27 billion. By 1979 it had grown to $90 billion.

But oil shock was not the only reason for the falling merchandise balance. The United States has experienced a long gradual decline in its competitive position vis-à-vis the other industrial nations of the West, a decline attributable in considerable part to laggard American productivity. In addition, a number of other developments have tilted the merchandise balance away from America—the international agricultural situation, the respective inflation rates of the U.S. and its main competitors, and still other factors.

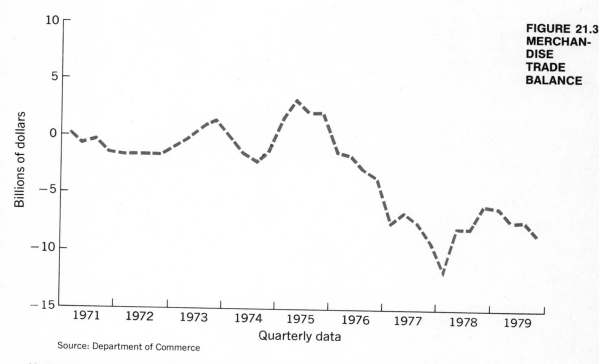

FIGURE 21.3
MERCHAN-
DISE
TRADE
BALANCE

Source: Department of Commerce

Until 1971, we always sold more merchandise abroad than we bought. Many factors have since eroded that comfortable position: laggard productivity, inflation, oil.

We cannot here analyze all the reasons for the decline of the American merchandise balance. It is enough to see that this is one major reason why the supply of dollars, needed for imports, came to exceed the demand for dollars, needed by foreigners to purchase American exports. When the quantity of any commodity supplied exceeds the quantity demanded, its price drops. The dollar was no exception. It fell.

2. The market for capital

But the market for current transactions is not the only arena in which the supply and demand for dollars establish a price for dollars against other currencies. A second, quite separate market, arises to accommodate the need for dollars and other currencies to finance capital transactions, not current ones. Here are such items as building or buying plant and equipment in another country, or buying the bonds or stocks issued within another nation.

The first of these capital flows is called *direct investment*. It arises from the efforts of American firms (mainly multinationals) to expand their ownership of plants and equipment abroad, and from the corresponding efforts of foreign companies to do the same thing here. In 1978, U.S. firms invested over $17 billion in foreign production facilities, ranging from oil refineries to supermarkets, while foreign companies bought or built direct investments worth $6 billion here. Subsequently in 1979 the supply and demand for direct investment funds also pushed down the price of dollars.

The second part of the capital market is made up of American or foreign individuals or firms who want to add to their overseas portfolio investments of stocks and bonds. Here we have Americans who buy stock in a Swedish firm or who buy German government bonds, and foreign investors who buy General Motors stock or U.S. Treasury bonds. In 1979, the balance on **portfolio account** was also against the U.S.

Balance on Capital Account. Adding direct and portfolio investment together, we have a total of $30 billion more dollars being supplied in 1979 than were demanded. This too pushed the supply curve of dollars to the right and contributed to its drop in price.

Why have we had such large capital outflows? Part of the answer is that American multinational corporations have grown faster than their counterparts here. We have heard much in recent years about an "invasion" of Arab money into American markets, but it has clearly not been nearly as large as the continuing "invasion" of American money abroad. Between 1970 and 1978, U.S. direct investment abroad climbed from $76 billion to $168 billion, while foreign direct investment here only rose from $13 to $40 billion.

The negative flow on portfolio account arises from two main stimuli. One of them is that until recently European interest rates have been higher than American rates. Holders of large liquid balances, such as the treasurers of multinationals or wealthy private investors, "park" their money where the return is greatest. Thus short-term money has sought out the highest return—and the dollar has weakened as a consequence. Second, many private investors invest in the stock markets of different countries. The U.S. stock market has made an indifferent showing over the last decade compared with some of Europe's or Japan's stock exchanges. This too has led to a larger supply of dollars than demand for them.

Speculative Demand. One more very important influence bears on the capital markets for foreign exchange. This is the price of foreign exchange that investors expect to receive in the future. If you think that the German mark will rise against the dollar, you can make money by buying German currency before it appreciates. Thus there is a constant flow of "hot" money from country to country as private investors or multinationals move their funds around, hoping to buy cheap and sell dear. A great deal of this speculative ebb and flow has also gone against the United States, because investors have felt that the United States was irresolute in the "defense" of the dollar, and that therefore the dollar would weaken. Of course, by selling dollars, and buying marks or yen or whatever, speculators have helped that very expectation to come true.

PROBLEMS OF A FALLING DOLLAR

We have just mentioned the defense of the falling dollar and we must soon turn our full attention to that subject which is the theme of our chapter. But before we consider means, we had better think about ends. What are we defending the dollar against? What difference does it make to Americans whether one dollar is worth two marks or three? What difference does it make if the dollar—whatever its exchange rate—is declining to a lower rate?

ARE CHEAP OR DEAR DOLLARS BETTER?

Let us consider the first part of the question. Does it matter how many yen, francs, or pounds a dollar exchanges for?

Like so many economic questions, this has a complicated answer. For the exchange value of a currency affects different individuals or groups or regions in different ways. Suppose that the dollar is cheap. Obviously this is good for anyone who wants to buy a U.S. good or service, using foreign money. It makes travel in the U.S. inexpensive for foreigners. It makes American exports attractive. It makes American stocks or physical plant tempting to foreign investors. All this redounds to the benefit of U.S. exporters or hotel keepers or stockbrokers or owners who want to sell to foreigners.

On the other hand, a cheap dollar penalizes other groups. An American traveling abroad finds prices terribly high. An American importer finds that foreign wines, cameras, cars, sweaters are expensive—and so do his customers. American firms, thinking of investing abroad, are deterred by the high price of foreign exchange. All this is bad for American tourists, consumers, and multinationals.

Is there any reason for giving preference to those groups who benefit from the cheap dollar over other groups who benefit from expensive dollars? From the point of view of our national well-being, there is no particular reason to favor one over another. Is it better for a million consumers to buy cameras cheaper, or for 100,000 steel workers to have higher incomes? There is no cut and dried answer.

FINDING A BALANCING RATE

How, then, does a nation determine the right rate for its exchange, when cheap rates help some groups and expensive rates help others? The answer is that a nation tries to discover the rate that will roughly balance out all the supplies and all the demands for its currency, so that it has a stable, "equilibrium" relationship between its own currency and those of other nations.

Consider what happens if country A does not have such an equilibrium relationship. If the rate is too high, there will be a stimulus for country A to buy imports and a deterrent to its exports. The result will be unemployment in its export industries and as a consequence of the multiplier, unemployment elsewhere. Perhaps the most famous case of an overvalued currency was that of England following World War I, when Winston Churchill, then Chancellor of the Exchequer, tried to establish an exchange rate of £1 = $5. At that rate the demand for pounds was far less than the supply, and English exports went into a tailspin, dragging the economy down with them. England suffered a severe depression until its exchange rate was finally reduced to about $4.00.

An undervalued exchange rate also brings problems. Now there is an incentive for foreigners to buy the cheap exports or assets of country A. Foreign money will flow into A's banks, raising the money supply. (Foreign deposits increase M because the new deposits do not come from another domestic bank.) As the money supply increases, inflationary pressures also increase. Country A will suffer from rising prices.

Thus we can present the problem of exchange rates that are too high or too low in this fashion:

Undervalued (too low) exchange rates lead to inflation.
Overvalued (too high) exchange rates lead to unemployment.

EFFECTS OF A FALLING DOLLAR

Defending the dollar, then, means finding an exchange rate that will roughly balance our total supplies and demands for foreign exchange for transactions purposes and capital flows. The fact that the dollar has been falling means that we have not yet found such a rate. The verdict of the marketplace is that the dollar is too high. We know this is the verdict because the demand for dollars vis-à-vis marks and francs and other strong currency has been steadily less than its supplies.

What happens when the dollar falls? Clearly we move from the dangers of an overvalued currency toward those of an undervalued one. That is, a falling dollar spurs our exports and helps employment. It also makes imports more expensive. Alas, in our inflation-prone economy, this results not just in fewer imports, but in another fillip to the price level. Oil prices go up because of the falling exchange rate, along with the price of Hondas and TV sets, coffee and tea.

The net effect of a falling dollar is therefore measured, in part, by the benefit we ascribe to expanding employment minus the cost we assign to higher inflation. As we have seen so often, most people place a higher priority on inflation than on unemployment. We welcome the boost to exports but put more emphasis on the boost to the cost of living.

THE THREAT OF A FALLING DOLLAR

Unfortunately that is not an end to the problems caused by a falling dollar. For in addition to its real costs and benefits, a falling dollar imposes a large overhanging threat. In the end it is this threat, more than the actual effect on employment or prices, that makes the problem of defending the dollar so important and so difficult.

The threat is that the falling dollar will induce a serious crisis in the economy. To many people, especially in business and finance, the news of a falling dollar conveys ominous implications about the state of the U.S. economy. Bankers worry lest international depositors switch funds from U.S. banks to foreign banks, straining the liquidity of the American financial system. Americans who own stocks and bonds worry that the dollar is weak, and begin to sell. A falling stock market and a slumping dollar can cause some corporations to rein in their capital expenditures. These actions in themselves may be sufficient to bring about a genuine financial panic and a fall in GNP.

There is still another repercussion. The government watches these developments with distress and seeks to prevent such a panic. It tries to defend the dollar in various ways including raising interest rates to attract foreign funds and cutting spending to show its determination to stop inflation. **And so the fear of a crisis induces government policy that will bring on a recession. A falling dollar can thereby lead to a falling economy.**

WAYS OF DEFENDING THE DOLLAR

Can we prevent the dollar from falling? Of course we can. Do we want to? That is not so easy to answer, for we shall see that defending the dollar is a difficult course whose benefits may not outweigh costs.

TARIFFS, QUOTAS, AND THE LIKE

One way of defending the dollar is simplicity itself: Take measures to prevent the flow of imports from rising. Anything that will turn the balance of merchandise payments in our favor will unquestionably alter the supply/demand situation and strengthen the dollar.

Is this a sound policy? The answer is not simple. There are certain kinds of imports that we would like to diminish not merely to defend the dollar, but to strengthen the nation. For instance, if we can substitute domestic energy (such as solar or coal) for imported oil, or if we can cut down on oil imports by conservation measures, the United States will gain a much needed measure of strategic independence as well as helping the dollar.

If, however, we cut down imports by blocking cheap shoes, textiles, or steel from abroad, we are simply protecting inefficient industries at home, penalizing Americans by depriving them of the right to buy shoes, textiles, or steel as cheaply as they otherwise might. We can sharpen the point by imagining that our tariff wall was sky high. Then no goods would come into the United States. Would that be good for America?

On the other hand, imports cost jobs. Even if we compensate the workers in threatened industries, or help relocate them, or retrain them, some will not make the transition and will remain unemployed. There is a real human cost to competition—from abroad or home—that should not be lost to sight.

In sum, defending the dollar by choking off imports is probably a short-sighted policy, with the signal exception of seeking to reduce our dependence on foreign oil. What about helping our exports? Many countries have tried to help *their* exports by giving subsidies of various kinds to their producers, so that they could sell their wares abroad cheaply. We have subsidized some exports by underwriting our merchant marine, by arranging for special deals on U.S. arms sales to foreign nations, and by foreign aid policies that have permitted us to sell large amounts of farm products abroad.

As with imports, it is not possible to give black and white answers about the wisdom of defending the dollar by export assistance. It may be in the national interest to sell $8 billion of arms on easy terms, or to export $1 billion of food-stuffs to the underdeveloped nations under Public Law 480, but these policies should be judged on their own merits. The fact that they help defend the dollar is not, and should not be, a controlling consideration.

RESTRICTIONS ON INVESTMENT

Policies to help exports or to hinder imports affect the balance of payments on current account. But there is also the market for foreign exchange for capital purposes. Can we defend the dollar by intervening in that market?

We recall that there are two basic kinds of transaction in the capital market, direct investment (purchasing plant, equipment, and other assets abroad), and portfolio investment (buying stocks or bonds). We can, of course, defend the dollar by simply passing a law preventing United States companies from acquiring foreign assets. The difficulties here are twofold. The first is that any interference with the free movement of capital tends to lower the efficiency of the market system. We have been reluctant to abridge the right of corporations to invest their funds wherever they can yield the highest return, whether at home or abroad.

Second, the stream of profits from our overseas investments constitutes one of the strongest supports for the dollar. In 1979, for example, there was a demand for $66 billion as the earnings of our foreign-located plants were sent back to the U.S. Against that flow was $34 billion leaving the country as the earnings of foreign companies sent to their various home nations. In this international flow of repatriated earnings, the U.S. is clearly a big gainer. Any restriction on the outflow of direct investment will sooner or later diminish this source of dollar earnings.

INTEREST RATES

A second way of defending the dollar in the capital markets is to seek to attract portfolio investment or short-run capital into the United States. This can be done by raising interest rates to bid for the pool of funds that "shops" in the world's money markets.

We have already seen the problem with this method of defending the dollar. Raising interest rates in order to increase the flow of money into the United States exerts the same effect on the economy as raising interest rates for any other reason. Investment is discouraged. Spending slackens. The economy slows down. The price of defending the dollar is therefore to expose the economy to further unemployment.

THE DOLLAR AND INFLATION

We begin to see that there is a connection between the falling dollar on the international exchange and the falling dollar in terms of purchasing power. Policies to defend the dollar abroad are closely linked to policies to defend it at home. That is, the measures needed to bring about a stable supply-demand situation with respect to the international value of the dollar are closely related to measures needed to bring about a stable supply-demand for dollars and goods at home. Fighting the fall in the dollar is therefore much like fighting inflation, with all its familiar difficulties. If we clamped down on all growth in the United States, for example, and allowed a really large rise in unemployment, we would stop or greatly slow down inflation and simultaneously rescue the dollar. The recession at home would cut deeply into imports and that would redress the balance on current account. The fall in profits would discourage U.S. investment abroad. And a sharp rise in interest rates would tempt speculative and short-term funds into American banks and bonds.

All this, however, comes with a very substantial price tag. We have seen that political realities make it very difficult to consider an all-out recession as a cure for inflation. Even more surely, the American public would not tolerate a deep depression as a cure for the falling dollar, an ailment that mystifies most people. Instead, the cry would likely go up for stiff import quotas or for restrictions on the foreign investments of American companies—policies that also impose costs on our economy, but not such visible costs as a recession.

CENTRAL BANKS

There is still another way of arresting the fall of the dollar. It is to use the resources of our Federal Reserve System to support the dollar.

How can the Federal Reserve support the dollar? It does so by buying dollars. But it would do no good for the Federal Reserve to buy dollars at home, using its deposit-creating powers. This would just increase the money supply. Rather, the Fed must support the dollar by buying dollars with foreign currencies!

The Federal Reserve can do this because it holds supplies of foreign currency—yen, marks, francs, and pounds, as well as gold certificates and other international assets. Thus when the Fed defends the dollar it does so by entering the exchange market as if it were a Swiss, a German, or a Frenchman. It simply offers the currencies of these nations, asking dollars in return.

DIRTY FLOATING

All central banks in all nations including the Federal Reserve, operate in the foreign exchange markets, supporting or depressing the price of their currency against foreign currencies. In using their buying and selling powers, the central banks are not permitting the price of their currencies to be set just by the forces of supply and demand, but by "dirty floating"—free market price plus or minus the demand of the central banks.

This means that the ability of the Federal Reserve—or any other central bank—to intervene in the market is limited by the supplies of foreign currencies or gold or other international assets it has on hand. Take gold. In mid-1979, U.S. gold reserves totaled about 267 million ounces, worth (at over $400 per ounce) well over $100 billion. The Federal Reserve could, if the government so directed, use all of that gold to support the dollar. If it did, undoubtedly the price of the dollar would rise substantially; but would it stay at its new higher price when the gold had been used up? Not unless the basic forces of supply and demand had been permanently affected by the rescue operation—a doubtful assumption.

Curiously enough, a government is always able to lower the price of its currency because it can easily sell unlimited quantities of dollars on the foreign exchange market. But its power to buy its own currency is inherently limited. It can step in to stem a speculative rout, but it is unlikely that it can much affect a falling price trend that emerges from the current and capital flows of the world.

THE VIEW FROM ABROAD

Actually it is not only Americans who are eager to stop the dollar from falling; foreigners are also eager to have stable exchange rates. Consider how the situation looks to them as the dollar weakens. The price of American-make goods keeps steadily declining. Conversely, the price of their own goods becomes ever more expensive in America. Thus, just as there is an outcry in America against the falling dollar, so there is an outcry abroad. Therefore, just as the Federal Reserve may step in to defend the dollar by selling its supplies of foreign currency, foreign banks may also find it in their interest to defend the dollar by selling their own currencies and buying dollars. Much time at international financial conferences is devoted to efforts to work out a coordinated defense of the dollar (and sometimes other currencies) by the joint action of several key central banks. What is always the bone of contention at such conferences is the proper exchange relation. Countries that depend on exports want their currency to be cheap in the world markets; countries that depend on imports want their own money to be dear, so that it will buy a larger amount of other currencies.

THE DOLLAR AS A WORLD CURRENCY

We can see that defending a currency is not only a difficult policy to devise, but a difficult policy to define. But we have left out of consideration a matter of much importance for the United States. It is that the dollar is not merely the currency of this country; the dollar has become a world currency. It is the currency in which many central banks hold much of their own international reserves. Japan, for example, holds billions of U.S. dollars as part of its foreign exchange wealth, along with gold and other major currencies. In addition, there are at least $300 billion U.S. dollars (some estimates run much higher) in European bank deposits. These foreign-located dollars, some owned by European individuals and companies, some by American, are called **Eurodollars.** They are one of the means by which the world carries on its vast international business.

The presence of these enormous quantities of dollars held as the reserves of other countries, or as the monetary medium of the world, adds further importance to the need for a stable dollar. When the dollar falls, it imperils the international value of foreign reserves and foreign deposits, and there is always the risk that central banks or corporations will rush to dump their dollars before a further fall occurs. Once again we have the danger of a self-fulfilling speculative disaster. So the dollar has to be defended to secure international economic stability even more urgently than to secure purely American interests.

NEW INTERNATIONAL CURRENCIES

How can the dollar be defended against a worldwide assault—or simply against worldwide nervousness? One possible way is for the dollar to be replaced by other monetary units as the world's reserve currency. To some extent this is slowly happening as other strong currencies, such as German marks and Swiss francs, are gaining the place formerly occupied by U.S. dollars. Alongside the $300 billion American Eurodollars, there are perhaps as much as $100 billion worth of Euromarks, and there are other smaller international reserves denominated in Swiss francs, in yen, and in other currencies.

A second means of taking the strain off the dollar is the rise in the price of gold. In 1979, the supply of gold in the official reserves of various nations was down slightly in physical quantity from 1971—from 1 billion ounces to 931 million ounces. (The difference, plus the gold production of the intervening years, was now owned by private individuals). But the value of the 931 million ounces, with gold selling at over $400 an ounce, was far larger than formerly. The value of the world's official gold reserves in late 1979 had soared to over $500 billion. Thus gold was worth, in value, more than half the total reserves of all the world's central banks. Without ever having decided to do so, say the champions of gold, the world is returning to a gold standard. If it does, the role of the dollar will be much less critical.

SDRs

No one can foretell what will happen to the future price of gold. Therefore let us consider one final way of relieving the dollar of its international burden. This is the gradual adoption of a wholly new money standard invented by the International Monetary Fund (IMF), a part of the World Bank set up under the auspices of the United Nations. This new monetary unit is called an SDR, Special Drawing Right. It is a kind of "paper gold"—an internationally recognized currency available only to central banks, and linked by the International Monetary Fund authorities to gold and to other main currencies.

SDRs are now held by all the major countries of the world in addition to gold and to supplies of each other's currencies. But SDRs have the special advantage of being issued under international control. There is no way that the world can deliberately bring about an increase in the quantity or value of gold. There is no way that the world can change the value or the amounts of dollars or marks or francs available as international reserves. But the nations of the world can agree to augment the value of SDRs, and by using these to settle international payments in place of dollars, they can gradually relieve the dollar of the task of being the world's principal currency, with all the risks attached thereto.

A LAST LOOK

This is nothing like a full survey of the complicated field of international finance. But the main outlines of the problem are perhaps clear by now. **Defend-**

ing the dollar really means locating the American economy in the world economy in such a way that its flows of trade and investment roughly balance out. When they do not balance out, this means that one or both of the main foreign exchange markets is out of kilter. Putting it back into balance ultimately means bringing American production into better adjustment with world production. In turn that means changing the fortunes of American working people and managers—for better and worse—to accord with the economic realities of distant countries and strange peoples. That has long been one of the most difficult problems humanity has faced, as the sad history of international jealousy and war testifies. Defending the dollar successfully means taking steps to make the American economy a partner, not an enemy, in the world economy.

KEY CONCEPTS

A falling dollar in international trade means that dollars buy less foreign currency, not less domestic goods. When the dollar falls, the exchange rate falls for Americans, rises for foreigners

The fall in the dollar means that the demand for dollars is less than their supply in two markets—current account and capital transactions

Lagging exports and booming oil imports have created an adverse balance on current account

The balance on capital account has also been unfavorable due to heavy foreign investment and speculation

Cheap dollars boost exports and aid producers; expensive dollars boost imports and aid consumers. The best rate equilibrates supplies and demands for exchange

Exchange rates below equilibrium create export surpluses with inflationary repercussions. Rates below equilibrium give import surpluses and unemployment

The falling dollar has brought a stimulus to inflation and a threat of financial crisis

LOOKING BACK

1. A falling dollar has a different meaning in international trade than in a domestic economy. Domestically, a falling dollar means that dollars buy less because of inflation. Abroad, falling dollars means that each dollar buys less foreign currency. The dollar can fall abroad even if we do not have inflation at home, and vice versa. A falling dollar means that the exchange rate falls. From a foreigner's view, when the dollar falls, his own currency rises.

2. The fall in the American dollar means that its exchange rate with major trading partners has declined. We can analyze this decline in terms of supply and demand in two markets—current account and capital transactions.

3. The supply/demand situation has moved against America in the current account market because our exports have lagged for various reasons, while our imports, especially oil, have soared. Therefore the balance on current account has shown an excess of supply over demand, pushing down the price of dollars.

4. The market for capital is dominated by money seeking long-term investment in foreign plant, or looking for long- or short-term foreign financial investments. Heavy American investing abroad has also weakened the dollar exchange rate. In addition, pressure on the dollar has come from speculators who sold dollars expecting to buy them back cheaply after they fell.

5. Cheap dollars promote exports but make imports expensive; a high exchange rate has just the opposite effect. Thus cheap dollars benefit producers, and expensive ones help consumers. There is no "best" exchange rate except the one that balances all supplies and demand—an equilibrium rate.

6. An exchange rate that is below equilibrium and is prevented from rising will produce a surplus in foreign exchange as the value of exports exceeds imports. This may have inflationary results from the rise in money supply. A rate that is above equilibrium will result in an import surplus and may bring unemployment.

7. The falling dollar has made imports more expensive and thereby spurred inflation, especially through the impact of higher oil prices. It has also led to severe speculation and the threat of a financial crisis.

This has prompted the Federal Reserve to raise interest rates, with adverse effects on employment.

Defending the dollar by helping exports or hindering imports is a generally poor policy

8. We can try to defend the dollar by measures to help the balance on current account. These include tariffs, import quotas, or steps to promote U.S. exports. There may be valid arguments for each of these policies, but there are also considerable costs associated with them. They are not policies to be lightly adopted just to strengthen the dollar.

Defending the dollar on capital markets threatens our investment income and risks recession

9. Defending the dollar on the capital markets is also difficult. Choking off the flow of American dollars into foreign investment sooner or later costs us the dividend income we would get from these investments. And defending the dollar by higher interest rates means fighting the foreign imbalance by domestic recession.

Central banks try to keep exchange rates stable by intervening—"dirty floating"

10. The reason that supply and demand do not automatically yield equilibrium rates is that central banks intervene to prevent unwanted currency fluctuations. This is called "dirty floating".

The dollar has suffered as a world currency. Higher gold prices and SDRs may reduce world pressure

11. The dollar has been a target for selling because it has become a world currency. The rise in gold prices and the increasing use of SDRs may take some of the pressure off the dollar.

ECONOMIC VOCABULARY

QUESTIONS

1. If the rate of exchange falls, does this make traveling abroad cheaper or dearer? Does it make imports more or less attractive to a U.S. buyer? Is an American investor more or less liable to buy a German bond if the price of a German mark is 30¢ or 50¢?

2. Explain how a fall in the exchange rate of the dollar against francs must be exactly the same as a rise in the exchange rate of the franc against dollars.

3. If the dollar were absolutely free to rise and fall in price, the way prices do on a freely competitive market, would there ever be a balance of payments problem? Show how there is an exact analogy between "shortages" and "surpluses" and positive or negative balances of payment. What is the factor that prevents the dollar from floating freely to an equilibrium price?

4. What is better for a nation's real standard of living—low-priced foreign goods, or identical high-priced domestic goods? Suppose that the imported goods mean that domestic workers lose jobs. Does that change your conclusion? Is there a conflict between the interest of producers and consumers? How can it best be resolved?

5. How would you try to estimate the relative costs and benefits of defending the dollar or letting it fall? Can these be figured in hard and fast terms? How important are political, as compared to economic, considerations?

Chapter

22 THE UNDER-DEVELOPED WORLD

A LOOK AHEAD

The great majority of mankind lives under economic conditions very different from those of modern industrial capitalism. This chapter examines the conditions of under-development—the economic situation of nations exposed to the pressures and pulls of the modern world, but very far removed from it in terms of their way of life. Two problems will command our attention in this chapter.

(1) We will gain some understanding of the economic causes for underdevelopment and the economic steps that may be taken to overcome it.

(2) We must learn about the social and political aspects of underdevelopment, for economics by itself is inadequate to give us an appreciation of this major problem in world politics and history.

Why are the underdeveloped nations so pitiably poor?* Only a half-century ago it was common to attribute their backwardness to geographic or climatic causes. The underdeveloped nations were poor, it was thought, either because the climate was too debilitating or because natural resources were lacking. Sometimes it was just said that the natives were too childlike or racially too inferior to improve their lot.

Bad climates may have had adverse effects. Yet, many hot areas have shown a capacity for sustained economic growth (for example, the Queensland areas of Australia), and we have come to recognize that a number of underdeveloped areas, such as Argentina and Korea, have completely temperate climates. So, too, we now regard the lack of resources in many areas more as a *symptom* of underdevelopment than a cause—which is to say that in many underdeveloped areas, resources have not yet been *looked for*. Libya, for instance, which used to be written off as a totally barren nation, has been discovered to be a huge reservoir of oil. Finally, little is heard today about native childishness or inherent inferiority. (Perhaps we remember how the wealthy classes in Europe similarly characterized the poor not too many centuries ago.) Climate and geography and cultural unpreparedness unquestionably constitute obstacles to rapid economic growth—and in some areas of the globe, very serious obstacles—but there are few economists who would look to these disadvantages as the main causes of economic backwardness.

Why then are these societies so poor?

The answer is that these are poor societies because they are *traditional* societies—that is, societies which have developed neither the mechanisms of effective command nor of the market by which they might launch into a sustained process of economic growth. Indeed, as we examine them further we shall have the feeling that we are encountering in the present the anachronistic counterparts of the static societies of antiquity.

Why did they remain traditional societies? Why, for instance, did Byzantium, which was economically so advanced in contrast with the Crusaders' Europe, fall into decline? Why did China, with so many natural advantages, not develop into a dynamic economic society? There are no fully satisfactory answers. Perhaps the absence of economic progress elsewhere on the globe forces us to look upon our Western experience not as the paradigm and standard for historic development, but as a very special case in which various activating factors met in an environment peculiarly favorable for the emergence of a new economic style in history. The problem is one into which we cannot go more deeply in this book. At any rate, it is today an academic question. The dominant reality of our times is that the backward areas are now striving desperately to enter the mainstream of economic progress with the West. Let us examine further their chances for doing so.

CONDITIONS OF BACKWARDNESS

Every people, to exist, must first feed itself; there is a rough sequence to the order of demands in human society. But to go beyond existence, it must achieve a certain level of efficiency in agriculture, so that its efforts can be turned in

*For a graphic view of this poverty, see "An Extra Word" at the conclusion of this chapter.

SNAPSHOTS OF UNDERDEVELOPMENT

DAMASCUS: In famine years the children of the poor examine the droppings of horses to extract morsels of undigested oats.

CALCUTTA: 250,000 people have no home whatsoever; they live, eat, defecate, mate, and die in the streets.

HONG KONG: Large numbers of families live in floating villages that tourists like to photograph. A family of six, eight, or ten occupies a home approximately the size of a rowboat.

CALI, COLOMBIA: When the rains come, the river rises and the sewers run through the homes of the poor.

HYDERABAD: Child labor employed in sealing the ends of cheap bracelets is paid eight cents per *gross* of bracelets.

KATMANDU, NEPAL: Life expectancy is between 35 and 40 years. Tuberculosis is chronic. One hears people coughing themselves to death at night.

NEW DELHI: "Oh, sir! Someone has dropped ice cream on your shoes! I will clean them." The tourist finds himself propped against a building, with two boys, each shining one shoe. "Oh, sir! Your laces are frayed. See, they break! I will sell you a new pair." The tourist buys the new pair. As he leaves, an Old India Hand says to him: "Have to watch those little beggars. Fling mud on your shoes." These are the tactics which poverty generates.

other directions. What is tragically characteristic of the underdeveloped areas is that this first corner of economic progress has not yet been turned.

Consider the situation of that all-important crop of the East, rice. Table 22.1 shows the difference between the productivity of rice fields in the main Asiatic countries and those of the United States, Australia, and Japan.

What is true of rice can be duplicated in most other crops.° It is a disconcerting fact that the backward peasant nations that depend desperately on their capacity to grow food cannot even compete in these main products with the advanced countries: Louisiana rice undersells Philippine rice, California oranges are not only better but cheaper than Indonesian oranges.

TABLE 22.1
RICE
PRODUCTION
1975

	(100 kilograms per hectare)
U.S.	51.0
Australia	51.2
Japan	61.9
India	18.3
Indonesia	26.9
Thailand	17.1
Philippines	17.6
China	32.4

A vivid example of what "low productivity" means.

*Table 22.1 shows only the productive differentials of equal *areas* of land. When we consider that a single American farmer tends up to a hundred times as large an acreage as a peasant in an underdeveloped area, the difference of output *per man* would be much more striking. The "Green Revolution" (discussed near the end of the chapter) has improved the situation, but we do not yet have the data we need to determine outputs for the new rice strains. Despite the improvement, a vast gulf still separates U.S. agricultural productivity from that of the underdeveloped nations.

Why is agriculture so unproductive? One apparent reason is that the typical unit of agricultural production in the underdeveloped lands is far too small to permit efficient farming. "Postage stamp cultivation" marks the pattern of farming throughout most of Asia and a good deal of Africa and South America. John Gunther, reporting the situation in India over a generation ago, described it vividly. It has not changed materially since that time.

> There is no primogeniture in India as a rule, and when the peasant dies his land is subdivided among all his sons with the result that most holdings are infinitesimally small. In one district in the Punjab, following fragmentation through generations, 584 owners cultivate no less than 16,000 fields; in another, 12,800 acres are split into actually 63,000 holdings. Three-quarters of the holdings in India as a whole are under ten acres. In many parts of India the average holding is less than an acre.[1]

In part, this terrible situation is the result of divisive inheritance practices which Gunther mentions. In part, it is due to landlord systems which drain away the surplus from peasants' land; in part, to the pressure of too many people on too little soil. There are many causes, with one result: Agriculture suffers from a devastatingly low productivity brought about by grotesque man/land ratios.

These are, however, only the first links in a chain of causes for low agricultural productivity. Another consequence of these tiny plots is an inability to apply sufficient capital to the land. Mechanical binders and reapers, tractors and trucks are not only impossible to use efficiently in such tiny spaces, but they are costly beyond the reach of the subsistence farmer. Even fertilizer is too expensive: In much of Asia, animal dung is used to provide free fuel rather than returned to the soil to enrich it.

This paralyzing lack of capital is by no means confined to agriculture. It pervades the entire range of an underdeveloped economy. The whole industrial landscape of a Western economy is missing: No factories, no power lines, no machines, no paved roads meet the eye for mile upon mile as one travels through an underdeveloped continent. Indeed, to a pitiable extent, an underdeveloped land is one in which human and animal muscle power provide the energy with which production is carried on. In India in 1953, for instance, 65 percent of the total amount of productive energy in the nation was the product of straining man and beast. The amount of usable electrical power generated in *all of India* would not have sufficed to light up New York City. Of course, progress has been made since. But in 1975, energy consumption in India averaged 221 kg per capita (coal equivalent). By way of contrast, in Ireland it averaged 3,097 kg; in Canada, 9,880.

SOCIAL INERTIA

A lack of agricultural and industrial capital is not the only reason for low productivity. As we would expect in traditional societies, an endemic cause of low per capita output lies in prevailing social attitudes. Typically, the people of an underdeveloped economy have not *learned* the "economic" attitudes that foster rapid industrialization. Instead of technology-conscious farmers, they are tradition-bound peasants. Instead of disciplined workers, they are reluctant and

---

[1] *Inside Asia* (New York: Harper, 1939), p. 385.

untrained laborers. Instead of production-minded business people, they are trading-oriented merchants.

For example, in the 1960s Alvin Hansen reported from his observations in India:

> Agricultural practices are controlled by custom and tradition. A villager is fearful of science. For many villagers, insecticide is taboo because all life is sacred. A new and improved seed is suspect. To try it is a gamble. Fertilizers, for example, are indeed a risk. . . . To adopt these untried methods might be to risk failure. And failure could mean starvation.

In similar vein, a UNESCO report told us:

> In the least developed areas, the worker's attitude toward labour may entirely lack time perspective, let alone the concept of productive investment. For example, the day labourer in a rural area on his way to work, who finds a fish in the net he placed in the river the night before, is observed to return home, his needs being met. . . .

An equally crippling attitude is evinced by the upper classes, who look with scorn or disdain upon business or production-oriented careers, or who see in economic change a threat to their station in society. More than a decade ago, UNESCO reported that of the many students from the underdeveloped lands studying in the United States—the majority of whom come from the more privileged classes—only 4 percent were studying a problem fundamental to all their nations: agriculture. This has not changed over time.

All these attitudes give rise to a *social inertia* that poses a tremendous hurdle to economic development. A suspicious peasantry, fearful of change that might jeopardize the slim margin yielding them life, a work force unused to the rhythms of industrial production, a privileged class not interested in social change, all these are part of the obdurate handicaps to be overcome by an underdeveloped nation.

FURTHER PROBLEMS: POPULATION GROWTH

In these problem areas, the underdeveloped economy resembles the pre-market economies of antiquity. But in addition to this, the underdeveloped lands often face an obstacle with which the economies of antiquity did *not* have to cope; a crushing rate of population increase that threatens to nullify their efforts to emerge from backward conditions.

Only a few figures are needed to make the point. Let us begin with our southern neighbor, Mexico. If Mexican population continues to grow at current rates, Mexico's population will rise from 67 million in 1979 to 600 million in only 70 years. If birth rates fall in accordance with the most optimistic estimates, Mexican population will still be a staggering 300 million in 70 years. Or take the Caribbean and Central American area. In some thirty years, at present growth rates, that small part of the globe will outnumber the entire population of the United States. South America, now 5 percent less populous than we, will be 200 percent larger than our present population. India could then number a billion souls.

We have already seen one result of the relentless proliferation of people in the fragmentation of landholdings. But the problem goes beyond mere fragmentation. Eugene Black, formerly president of the International Bank for Reconstruction and Development (the World Bank) has written that in India a population equivalent to that of all Great Britain has been squeezed out of any landholding whatsoever—even though it still dwells in rural areas. Consequently, population pressure generates massive and widespread rural poverty, pushing inhabitants from the countryside into the already overcrowded cities. Five hundred families a day move into Jakarta from the surrounding Javanese countryside, where population has reached the fantastic figure of 1,100 per square mile.

Even these tragic repercussions of population growth are but side effects. The main problem is that population growth adds more mouths almost as fast as the underdeveloped nations manage to add more food. They cancel out much economic progress by literally eating up the small surpluses that might serve as a springboard for faster future growth.

Ironically, this population explosion in the underdeveloped countries is a fairly recent phenomenon, attributable largely to the incursion of Western medicine and public health into the low-income areas. Prior to World War II, the poorer countries held their population growth in check because death rates were nearly as high as birth rates. With insecticides and antibiotics, death rates have plunged dramatically. In Ceylon, for example, death rates dropped 40 percent in one year following the adoption of malaria control and other health measures. As death rates dropped in the underdeveloped areas, birth rates, for many reasons, continued high, despite efforts to introduce birth control. In the backward lands, children are not only a source of prestige and of household labor for the peasant family, but also the only possible source of "social security" for old age. The childless older couple could very well starve. As parents or grandparents, they are at least assured of a roof over their heads.

THE POPULATION OUTLOOK

Is there a solution to this problem? The mood of demographers has swung between despair and cautious hope over the past decades. New birth control methods have, from time to time, offered the chance for dramatic breakthroughs. Poor birth control programs have repeatedly dashed these hopes.

Today a mood of cautious optimism is to be found among most demographers. This is because the most recent figures show a truly significant drop in the birthrates of the underdeveloped world—the first large scale drop on record. Although their populations are still rising, because births outnumber deaths, it is now imaginable that within another generation the population flood will have been tamed. **Demographers hope that population in the underdeveloped world will stabilize by the middle of the next century. It has already stabilized in the developed world.**

An important warning has to be sounded along with the optimism. For many poor nations, the population problem will not be solved just because birth control is now a worldwide reality. A peasant family that has only four children is still adding to population growth, even if not as seriously as when it had ten children; many poor nations will be pushed to the very brink of survival during the next two or three decades because of an inability to match mouths with food. Thus as a long-term problem, population is less of a concern than it was. As a short-term problem it continues high on the list of the world's ills.

NINETEENTH-CENTURY IMPERIALISM

This gives us a brief introduction to underdevelopment as it exists today. Before we turn to the problem of how this condition can be remedied, we must inquire into one more question. Why did not the market society, with all its economic dynamism, spread into the backward areas?

The answer is that the active economies of the European and American worlds *did* make contact with the underdeveloped regions, beginning with the great exploratory and commercial voyages of the fifteenth and sixteenth centuries. Until the nineteenth century, unfortunately, that contact was little more than mere adventure and plunder. And then, starting in the first half of that century and gaining momentum until World War I, came that scramble for territory we call the Age of Imperialism.

What was this imperialism? It was, in retrospect, a compound of many things: militarism, jingoism, a search for markets and for sources of cheap raw materials to feed growing industrial enterprises. Insofar as the colonial areas were concerned, however, the first impact of imperialism was not solely that of exploitation. On the contrary, the incursion of Western empires into the backward areas brought some advantages. It injected the heavy doses of industrial capital: rail lines, mines, plantation equipment. It brought law and order, often into areas in which the most despotic personal rule had previously been the order of the day. It introduced the ideas of the West, including, most importantly, the idea of freedom, which was eventually to rouse the backward nations against the invading West itself.

Yet if imperialism brought these positive and stimulating influences, it also exerted a peculiarly deforming impulse on the underdeveloped—indeed, then, totally undeveloped—economies of the East and South. In the eyes of the imperialist nations, the colonies were not areas to be brought along in balanced development, but essentially immense supply dumps to be attached to the mother country's industrial economy. Malaya became a vast tin mine; Indonesia, a huge tea and rubber plantation; Arabia, an oil field. In other words, economic development was steadily pushed in a direction that most benefited the imperial nations, not the underdeveloped countries themselves.

The result today is that the typical underdeveloped nation has a badly lopsided economy, unable to supply itself with a wide variety of goods. It is thereby thrust into the international market with its one basic commodity. For instance, in South America we find that Columbia is dependent on coffee for three-quarters of its exports; Chile, on copper for two-thirds of its foreign earnings; Honduras, on bananas for half of its foreign earnings. On the surface, this looks like a healthy specialization of trade. We shall shortly see why it may not be.

Economic lopsidedness was one unhappy consequence of imperialism. No less important for the future course of development in the colonial areas is a second decisive influence of the West: its failure to achieve political and psychological relationships of mutual respect with its colonial peoples. In part, this was no doubt traceable to an often frankly exploitative economic attitude, in which the colonials were relegated to second-class jobs with third-class pay, while a handful of Western whites formed an insulated and highly paid managerial clique. But it ran deeper than that. A terrible color line, a callous indifference to colonial aspirations, a patronizing and sometimes contemptuous view of "the natives" runs all through the history of imperialism. It has left as a bitter heritage not only an identification of capitalism with its worst practices, but a political and social wariness toward the West, a wariness that deeply affects the general orientation of the developing areas.

IMPERIALISM TODAY

What about imperialism today? Certainly it has changed. The naked land grabs are in the past, when imperialism often meant only the acquisition of territory that would look good on a map. In the past, also, are the seizures of raw materials on the unfair terms characteristic of mineral empires built in the late nineteenth century. Less prominent are attitudes of racial superiority, so infuriating to peoples whose culture was often of far greater delicacy and discrimination than that of the West.

Thus, the nature of this imperialism is now changing, partly under the pressures exerted by a restive Third World, partly as a result of developments within the advanced nations themselves. Imperialism today refers, as much as anything else, to the exposure of traditional societies to the full blast of the powerful market forces emanating from the capitalist core of industrial societies—a blast that often violently upsets traditional societies as they are pulled, willy nilly, into the world market.

Curiously enough, this raises questions that reverse to some extent the older problems of imperialism. For example, the rise of the multinational corporation puts the relationship of advanced and backward countries in a new light. The fear of being drawn into the world market on disadvantageous terms, and of being subordinated to the dictates of foreign enterprises, continues to mobilize sentiment against imperialism in the underdeveloped world. At the same time, the backward nations also want some of the things the multinationals offer. Big multinationals pay higher wages, keep more honest books, provide better working conditions and fancier career opportunities, and bring in more technological expertise than do the domestic enterprises of the host nation.

The result is that the problem of imperialism in our day has taken an unexpected turn. On the economic side of the question, the danger now is as much that the big companies will bypass the backward nations as that they will dominate them.

Meanwhile, the political element of imperialism seems to be diminishing. The erstwhile capitalist empires of Germany, Belgium, Netherlands, England, Portugal, have disappeared. What is left is a strong effort on the part of the United States to preserve its ideological and political influence, particularly in Latin America and Southeast Asia, but the debacle of the American Vietnam policy indicates that the prospects for a successful policy of this kind are limited, at best.

THE ENGINEERING OF DEVELOPMENT

Up to this point we have concentrated our attention mainly on the background of underdevelopment. Now we must ask a more forward-looking, more technically "economic" question: How can an underdeveloped nation emerge from its poverty?

From what we have learned, we know the basic answer to this question. To grow, an underdeveloped economy must build capital.

But how is a starving country able to build capital? When 80 percent of a country is scrabbling on the land for a bare subsistence, how can it divert its energies to building dams and roads, ditches and houses, railroad embankments and factories that, however indispensable for progress tomorrow, cannot be eaten today? If our postage-stamp farmers were to halt work on their tiny unproductive plots and go to work on a great project like, say, the Aswan Dam, who would feed them? Whence would come the necessary food to sustain these capital workers?

BUILDING CAPITAL FROM SAVED LABOR

At first glance the situation seems hopeless. Still, when we look again at the underdeveloped lands, the prospect is not entirely bleak. In the first place, these economies have unemployed factors. In the second place, we find that a large number of the peasants who till the fields are not feeding themselves. They are also, in a sense, taking food from one another's mouths.

As we have seen, the crowding of peasants on the land in these areas has resulted in a diminution of agricultural productivity far below that of the advanced countries. Hence the abundance of peasants working in the fields obscures the fact that *a smaller number of peasants, with little more equipment—perhaps even with no more equipment—could raise a total output just as large.* By raising the productivity of the tillers of the soil, a work force can be made available for the building of roads and dams, while this transfer to capital building need not result in a diminution of agricultural output.

SAVING OUTPUT

This rationalization of agriculture is not the only requirement for growth. When agricultural productivity is enhanced by the creation of larger farms (or by improved techniques on existing farms), part of the ensuing larger output per person must be saved. In other words, peasants who remain on the soil cannot enjoy their enhanced productivity by raising their standard of living and eating up all their larger crops. Instead, the gain in output per cultivator must be siphoned off the farm. It must be saved by the peasant cultivators and shared with their formerly unproductive cousins, nephews, sons, and daughters who are now at work on capital-building projects. We do not expect hungry peasants to do this voluntarily. Rather, by taxation or exaction, the government of an underdeveloped land must arrange for this indispensable transfer. Thus in the early stages of a *successful* development program there is apt to be no visible rise in the individual peasants' food *consumption*, although there must be a rise in their food *production*. What is apt to be visible is a more or less efficient—and sometimes harsh—mechanism for assuring that some portion of this newly added productivity is not consumed on the farm but is made available to support the capital-building worker. This is a problem that caused the Russian planners much trouble in the early days of Soviet industrialization.

What we have just outlined is not, let us emphasize, a formula for immediate action. In many underdeveloped lands, as we have seen, the countryside already crawls with unemployment, and to create, overnight, a large and efficient farming operation would create an intolerable social situation. We should think of the process we have just outlined as a long-term blueprint which covers the course of development over many years. It shows us that the process of development takes the form of a huge internal migration from agricultural pursuits, where labor is wasted, to industrial and other pursuits, where it can yield a net contribution to the nation's progress.

PROBLEM OF EQUIPMENT

Capital building is not just a matter of freeing hands and providing them with food. Peasant labor may construct roads, but it cannot, with its bare hands, build the trucks to run over the roads. It may throw up dams, but it cannot fashion the generators and power lines through which a dam can produce energy. In other words, what is needed to engineer the great ascent is not just a pool of labor. It is also a vast array of industrial equipment.

How is this equipment obtained? In an industrialized economy, by expanding the machine-tool (the capital equipment building) subsector. But an underdeveloped economy does not have a capital-equipment building sector and cannot take the time to create one. Consequently, **in the first stages of industrialization, before the nucleus of a self-contained industrial sector has been laid down, a backward nation must obtain its equipment from abroad.**

This it can do in one of three ways. (1) It can buy the equipment from an industrialized nation by the normal process of *foreign trade.* Libya, for example, can sell its oil and use the foreign currency it receives to purchase abroad the tractors, lathes, and industrial equipment it needs. (2) It can receive the equipment by *foreign investment* when a corporation in an advanced nation chooses to build in a backward area. This is the route by which the United States got much of its capital from Britain during the nineteenth century, and it is the means by which the underdeveloped nations themselves received capital during their colonial days. (3) It may receive the foreign exchange needed to buy industrial equipment as a result of a grant or a loan from another nation or from a United Nations agency such as the World Bank. That is, it can buy industrial equipment with *foreign aid.*

(1) FOREIGN TRADE

Of these three avenues of industrialization, the most important is foreign trade. In 1974 the underdeveloped nations earned just over $100 billion from exports. By no means all of this was available for new capital goods, however. About $60 billion was needed for food and vital raw materials. Some $10 billion was needed to pay interest on foreign debts. This left $30 billion for *all* manufactures, from pharmaceuticals and Mercedes Benzes to lathes, tractors, and jet aircraft.

A problem that has plagued the underdeveloped world in seeking to increase its trade earnings is that their lopsided economies have typically made them sellers of raw materials on the world market.

As sellers of raw commodities—usually only one raw commodity—they face a highly inelastic demand for their goods. Like the American farmer, when they produce a bumper crop, prices tend to fall precipitously and demand does not rise proportionately. At the same time, the industrial materials they buy in exchange tend to be firm or to rise in price over the years.

Terms of trade. Thus the terms of trade—the actual *quid pro quo* of goods received against goods offered—have usually moved against the poorer nations, who have given more and more coffee for the same amount of machinery. In 1957 and 1958, when commodity prices took a particularly bad tumble, the poor nations actually lost more in purchasing power than the total amount of all foreign aid they received. In effect, they subsidized the advanced nations! As another example, it has been estimated that falling prices cost the African nations more, in the first two decades since World War II, than all foreign funds given, loaned, or invested there.

It is possible—we do not yet know—that tightening markets in resources may now reverse this trend. The last few years have seen enormous sums flowing into the coffers of Middle Eastern governments, many of whom may become lenders, not borrowers, on the international capital markets. If the world resource picture worsens, the underdeveloped countries may find themselves the beneficiaries of inelastic demand curves, and the developed nations may be the ones complaining about the terms of world trade.

Third and fourth worlds. In fact, the example of OPEC (the Organization of Petroleum Exporting Countries) has raised the possibility that the underdeveloped world must now be considered as consisting of at least two subworlds. One consists of those nations with low per capita GNPs that possess the raw material resources, or in some cases the organizational skills, to give promise of a potential fairly rapid rise in per capita incomes. Mexico, with its huge oil deposits is such a country; Brazil, another; Venezuela, a third.

Contrasting with this third world is a fourth, made up of those nations that seem at present to offer little or no hope for rapid growth. Bangladesh, Burma,

---

HUMAN CAPITAL AGAIN

An allied problem of no less importance arises from the lack of technical training on which industrialization critically depends. At the lowest level, this is evidenced by appalling rates of illiteracy (up to 80 or 90 percent) which makes it impossible, for instance, to print instructions on a machine or a product and expect them to be followed. And at a more advanced level, the lack of expert training becomes an even more pinching bottleneck. Before Nigeria's destructive civil war, United Nations economists figured that Nigeria alone would need some 20,000 top-level administrators, executives, technicians, etc., and twice as many subordinates over the next 10 years. On a world-wide scale, this implies a need for at least 700,000 top-level personnel and 1,400,000 second-level assistants. Not 1 percent of these skilled personnel exists today in the poor countries, and to "produce" them will be a task of staggering difficulty. Yet, without them it is often impossible to translate development plans into actuality.

Egypt, Ethiopia, India, and Pakistan are among these least hopeful nations whose aggregate population is well over one billion.

Even among many third world nations (except for the oil producers), foreign exchange reserves are still very scarce, and the effort to increase them by exports is intense. One way that has commanded more and more attention is through the development of *commodity stabilization agreements*, not dissimilar to the programs that have long supported American farm prices. Recently, the Western nations have recognized the need for some such device if the underdeveloped countries are to be able to plan ahead with any assurance of stability.

Another possibility lies in the prospect of encouraging diversified exports from the underdeveloped nations—handicrafts, light manufactures, and others. The difficulty here is that these exports may compete with the domestic industry of the advanced nations: witness the problems of the American textile industry in the face of textile shipments from Hong Kong. No doubt a large source of potential earnings lies along this path, and it is likely to rise as the advanced nations gradually allow the backward countries more equal access to their own markets.

(2) FOREIGN INVESTMENT

A second main avenue of capital accumulation for the backward nations is foreign investment. Indeed, before World War II, this was *the* source of their industrial wealth. Today, however, it is a much diminished avenue of assistance. The former capital-exporting nations are no longer eager to invest private funds in areas over which they have lost control and in which they fear to lose any new investments thay might make. For reasons that we have discussed, many of the poorer nations view Western capitalism with ambivalence. They need capital, technology, and expertise; but the arrival of a branch of a powerful corporation run by faraway headquarters looks to them like another form of the domination they have just escaped. As a result, foreign investment is often hampered by restrictive legislation in the underdeveloped nations, even though it is badly needed.

In 1975, $21 billion of private capital was invested in the developing countries, but nearly all of it went to the higher income nations. Probably not much more than $3 billion went overseas as foreign investment into the poorest fourth world nations.

Another difficulty is that Western corporations partially offset the growth-producing effects of their investments by draining profits out of the country. In the period 1950–1965, for example, the flow of income remitted from Latin America to the United States was $11.3 billion, three times larger than the flow of new capital into Latin America. In 1978, income of $4.5 billion was transmitted to the United States, and only $3.7 billion was sent back to Latin America. This pattern of economic flow should not be misinterpreted as implying that foreign investment is a negative influence: The plant and equipment that the West has sent abroad remains in the underdeveloped world, where it continues to enhance the productivity of labor, or perhaps to generate exports. But the *earnings* on this capital are not typically plowed back into still more capital goods, so that their potential growth-producing effect is far from realized.

THE GREEN REVOLUTION

In the critical life-and-death race between mushrooming populations and recalcitrant nature, hopes have been buoyed by the Green Revolution, the name given to efforts to discover high-yielding strains of rice and wheat. Working in field laboratories in Mexico and elsewhere, scientists of the Rockefeller Institute have developed a number of promising new varieties, including the famous IR-8 rice. Some of these new varieties allow two and even three crops to be grown where formerly only one was harvested.

The Green Revolution has been a considerable scientific triumph, but its impact on development has been less spectacular. For one thing, the new strains require vast amounts of fertilizer and water, both in short supply in those areas of the world where present yields are lowest. Second, because the seeds require complementary inputs of fertilizers or tube-well irrigation ditches, the new grains are mainly introduced by the richer peasants. In lands where transportation facilities are lacking, their bumper crops may not find a ready market, and local prices may fall, to the despair of the poor peasant whose output has not risen. Thus the Green Revolution may actually contribute to the poverty of the lowest classes.

These social repercussions, coupled with the vast costs needed to introduce the new seeds on a wide basis, have tempered the first rosy expectations of the food scientists. Nonetheless, the Green Revolution is vital in enabling the world to buy a little precious time while birth control efforts and new production and distribution techniques are worked out.

(3) FOREIGN AID

These considerations enable us to understand the special importance that attaches to the third channel of capital accumulation: foreign aid. Surprisingly, perhaps, in the light of the attention it attracts, foreign aid is not a very large figure. International assistance, from *all* individual nations and from the UN and its agencies, ran at a rate of about $6 billion per year throughout the 1960s and rose to $14 billion only after the OPEC nations devoted considerable sums from their oil earnings for development purposes.

Even $14 billion is an insignificant figure compared with the total GNP of the underdeveloped world. But it is a sizeable fraction—perhaps as much as 15 percent—of the gross investment of South Asia, and more than that in poorest Africa.

In addition, foreign aid plays a number of subsidiary roles not performed by private investment. It is the source of much technical assistance, which allows the underdeveloped countries to overcome handicaps imposed by their lack of skilled personnel. Aid also provides food, often desperately needed in times of crop failure—the United States food program has been a major source of famine relief to Asia and Africa. In addition, foreign aid is sometimes given in "soft" loans repayable in the currency of the developing nation rather than in scarce hard currencies. Such loans are unobtainable from private lenders.

All these forms of international assistance make possible the accumulation of industrial capital much faster than could be accomplished solely as a result of the backward lands' export efforts or their ability to attract foreign private capital.* To be sure, an increase in foreign earnings or in private capital imports would have equally powerful effects on growth. But we have seen the difficulties in the way of rapidly increasing the receipts from these sources. For the near future, foreign aid represents the most effective channel for *quickly* raising the amount of industrial capital which the underdeveloped nations must obtain.

ECONOMIC POSSIBILITIES FOR GROWTH

Against these handicaps, can the underdeveloped nations grow? Can the terrible conditions of poverty be relegated to the past? Economic analysis allows us to ask these questions systematically, for growth depends on the interplay of three variables.

1.   The rate of investment that an underdeveloped nation can generate

As we know, this depends on the proportion of current effort that it can devote to capital-creating activity. In turn, the rate of saving, the success in attracting foreign capital, the volume of foreign aid—all add to this critical fraction of effort on which growth hinges. The *rate of investment* is the driving force of growth.

2.   Productivity of the new capital

The saving that goes into new capital eventually results in higher output. But not all capital boosts output by an equal amount. A million-dollar steel mill, for example, will have an impact on GNP very different from that of a million-dollar investment in schools. In the short run, the mill may yield a higher return of output per unit of capital investment; in the long run, the school may have the edge. But in any event, the effect on output will depend not merely on the amount of investment, but on the **marginal capital/output ratio** of the particular form of investment chosen.

3.   Population growth

Here as we know, is the negative factor. If growth is to be achieved, **output must rise faster than population.** Otherwise, per capita output will be falling or static, despite seemingly large rates of overall growth.

CAPITAL/OUTPUT RATIO

With these basic variables, is growth a possibility for the backward lands? We can see that if investment were 10 percent of GNP and if each dollar of new investment gave rise to a third of a dollar of additional output, a 10 percent rate of capital formation would yield a 3.3 percent rate of growth of output (10 percent × one-third). This is about equal to population growth rates in the nations with the highest rates of population increase.

The trouble is that most of the backward nations, especially in the fourth world, have investment rates that are closer to 5 than to 10 percent of GNP. In that case, even with a marginal capital/output ratio of one-half, growth rates

---

*Note "make possible." There is some disturbing evidence that foreign aid may displace domestic saving, so that an underdeveloped country receiving aid may relax its own efforts to generate capital. Much depends on the political will of the recipient country.

would not be enough to begin a sustained climb against a population growth of 2.5 percent (5 percent × ½ = 2.5 percent). And this gloomy calculation is made gloomier still when we confront the fact that the labor force is rising faster than the population as a whole, as vast numbers of children become vast numbers of workers. In the 1970s in Latin America it was estimated that at least *25 percent* of the working-age population was unemployed. In the decade since then, unemployment as a percent of the labor force seems to have increased in virtually every underdeveloped country.

THE RANGE OF PERFORMANCE

No one can confront these realities and fail to be impressed with the harshness of the outlook for the underdeveloped world. Overall, the 140 third and fourth world countries have barely made perceptible progress during the last fifteen years of unprecedented developmental effort. Indeed, the World Bank, looking back recently on the period 1960–1974, discovered to its dismay that 40 percent of the populations of these countries, despite statistics that seemed to indicate growth, remained in a condition of "absolute poverty."[2]

To be sure, there are important exceptions to this generally disappointing performance. The OPEC nations, as we have noted, are forging ahead on their oil revenues, and some of them now have very high growth rates. So, too, a number of non-OPEC nations have succeeded in mobilizing foreign and domestic capital and national and international entrepreneurship to create extremely impressive growth records, as Table 22.2 shows.

TABLE 22.2 SELECTED GROWTH RATES, GNP PER CAPITA, 1960–1974

	Percent
Singapore	7.6
Republic of Korea	7.3
Hong Kong	6.6
Taiwan	6.5
Puerto Rico	5.3
Brazil	6.3

Some underdeveloped countries have shown an impressive growth rate.

Source: Jameson and Wilbur, op. cit.

SOCIAL STRESSES

Unfortunately, that is not an end to the story. Even the most successful economic development imposes enormous strains on society. This is because the process of dynamic change, especially under the aegis of a market system, does not lift all sectors or classes equally. On the contrary, it favors some and disfavors others, sometimes actually depressing their standard of well-being, at other times merely exposing them to the sense of being unfairly left behind. The skyscrapers that symbolize development in so many surging nations are often within the sight of persons who must still live in mud huts, and the new factories are just around the corner from artisans' stalls. In fact, the artisans may now be exposed

[2]Gerald Meier, ed., *Leading Issues in Economic Development* (N.Y.: Oxford University Press, 1979) pp. 1, 5, 395. See also Kenneth Jameson and Charles K. Wilbur, *Economic Directions in Development* (Notre Dame: Univ. of Notre Dame Press, 1979), pp. 188, 189.

to the blast of competition from goods made in those factories, and the dwellers in those mud huts are exposed to the unsettling influence of a way of life that they never knew existed.

Thus economic development typically brings discontent. The gulf between rich and poor widens; resentments and fears sharpen. The revolution in Iran, once thought to be a paragon of successful development, reveals how unstable can be the social situation in an economically prosperous society—an instability that is very likely present in many booming Middle Eastern nations, as well as in some of the fast-growing Asian and Latin American success stories.

THE POLITICAL SIDE

These considerations enable us to understand how social tensions and economic standards can rise at the same time. And this prospect, in turn, enables us to appreciate the fearful demands on political leadership, which must provide impetus, inspiration, and, if necessary, discipline to keep the great ascent in motion. The stresses of the early industrial revolution in England, with its widening chasm between proletariat and capitalist, are not to be forgotten when we project the likely course of affairs in the developing nations.

In the politically immature and labile areas of the underdeveloped world, this exercise of leadership typically assumes the form of "strong-man" government. In large part, this is only the perpetuation of age-old tendencies in these areas; but in the special environment of development, a new source of encouragement for dictatorial government arises from the exigencies of the economic process itself. Powerful, even ruthless government may be needed, not only to begin the development process, but to cope with the strains of a *successful* development program.

It is not surprising, then, that the political map reveals the presence of authoritarian governments in many developing nations today. The communist areas aside, we find more or less authoritarian rule in Egypt, Pakistan, Burma, South Korea, Indonesia, and a succession of South American juntas. From country to country, the severity and ideological coloring of these governments varies. Yet in all of them we find that the problems of economic development provide a significant rationale for the tightening of political control. At least in the arduous early stages of growth, some form of political command seems as integral to economic development as the accumulation of capital itself. As we try to interpret the headlines we may be reading over the coming years, it would be well to bear these considerations in mind.

KEY CONCEPTS

The conditions of underdevelopment are a complex amalgam of tradition, low productivity, social inertia, and population pressure

LOOKING BACK

1. Underdeveloped nations are traditional societies. Typically they evidence extremely low rates of growth, poor productivity, and considerable social inertia. In addition, their problems are often compounded by high rates of population growth. This last problem is now less threatening for the long run, but it is still a major short-run hurdle.

Imperialism has been a common shaping experience of the underdeveloped countries. Imperialism today still exposes traditional societies to world market forces

2. The underdeveloped countries have all had experience with imperialism. In the nineteenth century this was a combination of economic exploitation, military conquest, and socio-political intolerance. In our own time, it is mainly evidenced in the exposure of the backward lands to the ruthless forces of the world market. This is a two-sided process, for the multinationals also bring benefits of technology and efficiency.

Development is a capital-building process

3. The development process hinges on building capital. This can be done by economizing on the labor used for agriculture and directing it to capital projects. But the rise in agricultural productivity must be used to support those working on capital projects, not for the higher consumption of agricultural workers.

Capital equipment cannot be generated by shifting labor from agriculture. The main source is foreign trade

4. Not all capital can be accumulated by saving agricultural labor and redirecting it to capital-building projects. Equipment of various sorts must also be acquired. The main avenue of acquisition is foreign trade. Until recently the terms of trade have been adverse for most underdeveloped lands; the rise of OPEC has changed that, at least for the oil-producing countries.

Private foreign investment, mainly through multinationals, brings productivity but imposes a drain in foreign exchange

5. Private foreign investment is a second source of capital and technology. Here we encounter the complex problems posed by the relations of the underdeveloped lands and the multinationals. The repatriation of profits means that foreign investment creates a foreign exchange problem for the backward countries although foreign investment enhances productivity.

The UN remains an important source of aid

6. International aid, both bilateral and through the United Nations, remains a very important source of capital, technology, and relief.

Development is a function of investment and its productivity—divided by population growth

7. The rate of economic growth depends on the amount of investment, its productivity (the capital/output ratio), and on population growth, a negative factor.

Social and political strains are inseparable from development

8. Social and political stress is inseparable from economic change. Development is likely to give rise to strong-man governments to cope with those stresses.

ECONOMIC VOCABULARY

Imperialism   340   Terms of trade   344   Captial/output ratio   346

QUESTIONS

1. In what ways do you think underdeveloped countries are different from the American Colonies in the mid-1600s? Think of literacy, attitudes toward work and thrift, and other such factors. What about the relationship to more advanced nations in each case?

2. Why do you think it is so difficult to change social attitudes at the lowest levels of society? At the upper levels? Are there different reasons for social inertia at different stations in society?

3. Many economists have suggested that all advanced nations should give about 1 percent of their GNP for foreign aid. In the U.S., that would mean a foreign aid appropriation of $25 billion. We now appropriate about $3 billion. Do you think it would be practicable to suggest a 1 percent levy? How would the country feel about such a program?

4. What are the main variables in determining whether or not growth will be self-sustaining? If net investment were 8 percent of GNP and the capital/output ratio were ¼, could a nation grow if its rate of population increase were 2¼ percent? What changes could initiate growth?

5. What do you think is the likelihood of the appearance of strong-arm governments in the underdeveloped world? For the emergence of capitalist economies? Socialist ones? Is it possible to make predictions or judgments in these matters that do not accord with your personal preferences?

AN EXTRA WORD ABOUT
UNDERDEVELOPMENT

It is difficult to compress the problem of underdevelopment into one chapter; it deserves book-length treatment. But here is a small array of charts and tables* that will give you more perspective on underdevelopment. We have presented them without comment, because they speak for themselves. They will repay a few minutes of your time now by giving you food for many hours of reflection afterward.

TABLE 22.3
POPULATIONS
HAVING
INSUFFICIENT
PROTEIN/
ENERGY
SUPPLY, 1970

	Total population (millions)	Population with insufficient protein/energy supply	
		Millions	Percent
Developed countries*	1,072	28	3
Developing countries†	1,755	434	25
Latin America	284	36	13
Africa	279	67	24
Near East	171	30	18
Far East	1,021	301	30
World†	2,827	462	16

Note: The table is based on the daily per capita supply of grams of protein and kilocalories contained in the food locally available.
*Europe, North America, U.S.S.R., and Japan.
†Excluding Asian centrally planned economies.

FIGURE 22.1
PER CAPITA
GNPs, 1973

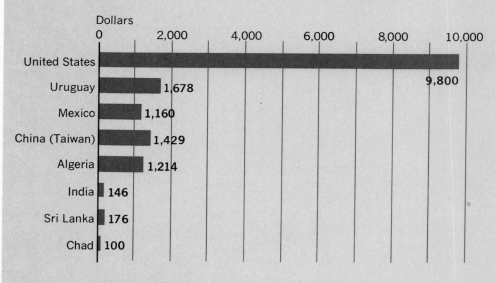

*From Overseas Development Council, *The U.S. and World Development* (New York: Praeger, 1976).

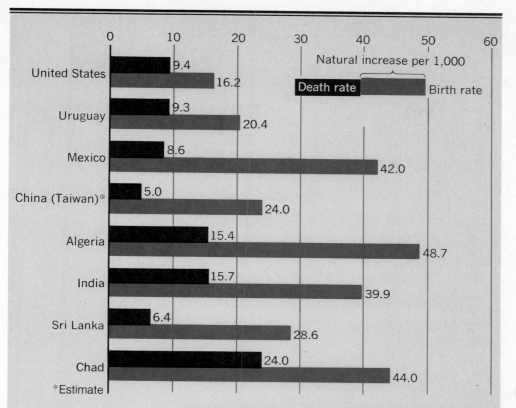

FIGURE 22.2

Death and birth rates per 1,000 (1970–1975 average).

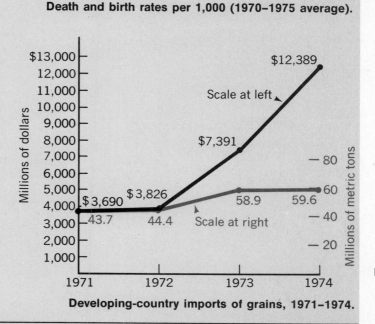

FIGURE 22.3

Developing-country imports of grains, 1971–1974.

FIGURE 22.4
LITERACY
(PERCENT-
AGES)
1974

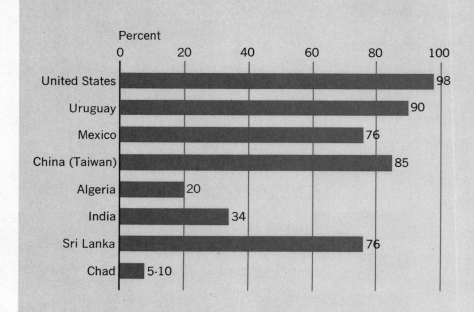

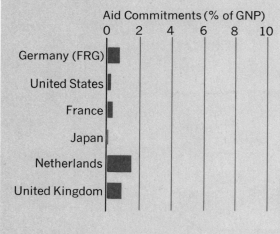

FIGURE 22.5

Per capita aid commitments made by developed countries, 1978.

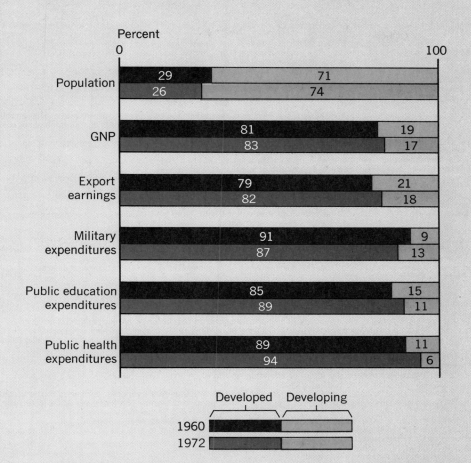

FIGURE 22.6

Relative shares of selected resources and expenditures of developed and developing countries, 1972 (percentages).

GLOSSARY

Accelerator effect. The effect—sometimes stimulating, sometimes depressing—exerted on investment by changes in consumption expenditure.

Appreciation of exchange. A rise in the ability of one nation's currency to buy the currency of another nation.

Average propensity to consume. The relation between consumption and income, C/Y. It differs from the marginal propensity $\Delta C/\Delta Y$ because the latter is concerned only with spending out of marginal incomes.

Average propensity to save. The relation between saving and income s/y. It differs from the marginal propensity $\Delta S/\Delta Y$ because the latter is concerned only with saving out of marginal income.

Automatic stabilizers. Institutional provisions that result in automatic stimulation of the economy in recession times and dampening of it in boom times. The countercyclical flows of unemployment insurance or farm subsidies, and the effect on consumption of the graduated income tax are key elements in these stabilizers.

Balance of payments. A set of accounts that records transactions between two countries. See balance on current and captial accounts.

Balance on capital account. The net sum of demands and supplies for foreign exchange for all items on capital account, mainly direct and portfolio investment.

Balance on current account. The net sum of demands for and supplies of foreign exchange for all items on current account, mainly merchandise exports and imports and similar transactions.

Bonds. Obligations issued by private or public institutions with fixed dates of repayment and stated interest rates or coupons. See yields.

Budget. The amount of spending power possessed by an economic actor.

Business cycles. The more or less regular recurrence of recession and prosperity. Some cycles (usually in inventories) may be of 2–3 years' duration, others (in GNP) typically of 7–11 years' length.

Capital. All means of production that have been produced by man. Also often used to refer to a financial sum of wealth.

Capital goods. Final output used for production, not consumption. See *Investment*.

Capitalism. An economic system in which privately owned means of production—land, labor and capital—are coordinated mainly by a market system.

Capital/output ratio. Relationship between the values of the capital stock and the flow of output of a firm industry, or nation. Marginal capital/output ratios relate increases in output to increases in the capital stock.

Circular flow. The continuous circuit of spending, from households to firms and from firms back to households.

Claims. Legal rights on income or wealth.

Competition. The vying of buyers and sellers in a marketplace. Competition has two aspects: (1) the contest of buyers against sellers, (2) the mutual rivalry of sellers against sellers and buyers against buyers.

Constraints. Barriers or boundaries to behavior.

Consumption. Use of output for purposes of private enjoyment.

Cost push. An explanation of inflation that stresses increases in factor prices such as higher real wages, or the increase in cost of resources or other inputs. (See *Demand pull*.)

Crowding out. The effect of government borrowing on the ability of the private sector to obtain funds on the loan markets.

Deficit spending. Spending that is financed not by current tax receipts but by borrowing, or by drawing on past reserves.

Demand. Willingness and ability to buy. Demand is a schedule that relates the quantities demanded with differing prices. See also Quantity demanded.

Demand gap. The shortfall in demand that arises when the spending of the combined sectors is not enough to maintain a given level of GNP, or a necessary rate of growth of GNP.

Demand pull. An explanation of inflation that stresses the effect of spending on the price level. Demand pull is usually focussed on the effects of government or business spending. (See *Cost push*.)

Dependent variables. Quantities whose value is determined by the value of another "independent" variable, contained in the equation.

Depreciation. The decline in the value of capital goods over time. The term is also used to designate the funds set aside to replace the worn-out capital.

Depreciation of exchange. A fall in the ability of one nation's currency to buy the currency of a foreign nation.

Devaluation. A policy deliberately intended to cheapen the exchange value of a currency in order to encourage exports. (Technically, devaluation means cheapening one's currency in terms of gold.)

Direct investment. Investment in plant and equipment, as contrasted with financial investment.

Direct taxes. Taxes levied by local, state or federal governments on incomes.

Dirty floating. Intervention by central banks in foreign exchange markets to raise or lower the exchange rate of their own currencies.

Discounting. Application of an interest rate to calculate the present value of a sum of money expected to be received or held in the future. At a rate of discount of 10 percent, $100 a year hence is worth $90 today.

Discount rate. The term applied to the interest rate charged by the Federal Reserve banks or loans made to their member banks.

Disinvestment. A failure to create investment equal to the wear and tear on existing capital. Disinvestment means a diminution of capital wealth.

Disposable personal income. Factor earnings plus transfers less direct taxes. Disposable personal income therefore defines aggregate household spending power.

Dissaving. Expenditure that exceeds income. Dissaving requires that a dissaver use past savings, or borrowing, to finance the additional expenditure.

Distribution. The process of allocating output or income among the population. Also used to refer to the results of this process, for example when we say that "income distribution is very unequal."

Endogenous. Influences internal to a system. The rise in income that results from the multiplier effect is endogenous to the determination of GNP.

Entrepreneur. The person whose economic task is to direct the enterprise. His or her main task is to choose the proper scale, to make the best combination of factors, and to establish the best level of output. The entrepreneur may or may not own the enterprise, and therefore may or may not receive profits.

Equations. Mathematical statements usually involving dependent and independent variables in a functional relationship.

Equilibrium. A self-correcting and self-perpetuating level of prices or economic activity. Equilibrium prices equate quantities demanded and supplied, and thereby "clear" markets. Equilibrium flows of output, such as GNP, balance opposing tendencies of savings and investment to create a self-perpetuating flow.

Equity. Ownership, usually stock ownership.

Eurodollars. Supplies of dollars held by foreign or American banks in Europe.

Ex ante. The view looking forward. Ex ante refers to economic activity that has not yet taken place. Ex ante quantities or values may therefore differ from ex post figures, after the event.

Excess reserves. Bank reserves (cash or deposits at the Federal Reserve) over the required amount.

Exchange rate. The price of foreign currencies in terms of one's own currency.

Exogenous. Influences originating outside the system. An exogenous influence on GNP would be a change in the weather, or a war.

Ex post. The view looking backwards. Ex post refers to economic activity that has already happened. (See *Ex-ante.*)

External debts. Debts owed by members of one community, usually a nation, to another community or nation. (See *Internal Debts.*)

Factor of production. The name given to the main kinds of inputs, land, labor and capital in a market society.

Federal Reserve Banks. One of the 12 federally created central banks. Commercial banks may become members of the Federal Reserve System, but are not themselves Federal Reserve Banks.

Federal Reserve System. The formal institution of central banking in the United States, structured around 12 Reserve Banks and governed by a Board of Governors.

Final goods. Goods that have reached the end of the production process. Typically these are of four kinds: consumption goods, investment or capital goods, government or public goods, and exports.

Fiscal policy. Government efforts to control the level of employment or prices by spending and taxing, rather than by monetary policy.

Fixed exchange rates. Exchange relationships between currencies fixed by government agreement and maintained by the action of central banks.

Foreign exchange. Supplies of foreign currencies held by the banks or government of any nation.

Fractional reserves. The legal permission to hold reserves equal to less than 100 percent of bank deposits. Fractional reserves multiply the effect of new deposits on the money supply.

Full employment budgets. Calculation of the impact on GNP of government receipts and expenditure flows assuming that receipts and expenditures are at the levels corresponding to full employment.

Functional relationships. Relationships in which the value of one variable is determined by another.

GNP (gross national product). The dollar value of the final output of the economy for a fixed period, usually a year. GNP is the sum of consumption, gross domestic investment, government purchases and net exports.

Gross investment. The use of resources to create capital, whether as an addition to existing wealth or as a replacement for worn-out capital.

Gross national income. The sum of factor incomes, tax receipts, and depreciation accruals. GNI is always identical with GNP.

Growth. Increase in output. (See *Nominal growth* and *Real growth*).

High powered money. Reserves in commercial banks that can increase the money supply. (See *Fractional reserves.*)

Imperialism. Domination by a highly developed, powerful nation. Specifically used to describe the penetration of capitalist nations into the underdeveloped world.

Independent variables. Quantities whose value is determined independently—that is, outside the equation.

Indexing. Adjustment of nominal payments in accordance with a price index.

Indirect taxes. Taxes levied by local, state, or federal government on the value of output. Cigarette or gas taxes are instances of indirect taxes.

Inflation. A process in which prices in nearly all markets display a chronic upward tendency.

Injections. Any expenditures that raise the flow of income. The main injections are net investment, deficit spending, an excess of exports over imports, or a consumer spending wave, financed by drawing on past saving or on credit.

Interest. The price of the factor capital.

Intermediate goods. Goods or services that enter into final goods. For example, wheat is an intermediate good entering into bread.

Internal debts. Debts owned by members of a community, usually a nation, to one another.

Intersectoral offsets. Spending by one sector, usually business or government, used to offset the insufficient spending of another sector.

Inventories. Goods or raw materials that have been produced but not yet sold to final purchasers. All increases in inventories are counted in the national accounts as net investment.

Investment. The act of building capital. (See *Real vs. financial investment.*)

Invisible Hand. A famous phrase used by Adam Smith to indicate that individuals who followed their private self-interest would in fact fulfill a larger purpose (''as if guided by an Invisible Hand'').

Leakages. Channels through which additional income is diverted from respending by households. The four main leakages are: private saving, business profits, taxes, and imports.

Liquidity. Condition of having immediately spendable resources, such as cash or very easily saleable securities, such as very short-term government notes.

Liquidity preference. The differing proportions of one's wealth that one seeks to hold in liquid form at differing interest rates. High interest rates impose high opportunity costs on holding cash. Therefore, usually we prefer to be less liquid when we can use our cash to earn high interest. Conversely, we seek more liquidity when the opportunity cost is low. Risk also plays an important part in determining our willingness to be liquid or illiquid.

Macroeconomics. That portion of economics concerned with large scale movements of the economy, such as growth or decline, inflation or deflation.

Marginal. Additional, incremental, (plus or minus.)

Marginal efficiency of investment. The value of the expected returns of new investment discounted to the present.

Marginal propensity to consume. The relation between additional income and additional spending: $\Delta C/\Delta Y$. (See *Average propensity to consume.*)

Marginal propensity to save. The relation between additional income and additional saving: $\Delta S/\Delta Y$. (See *Average propensity to save.*)

Maximizing. The driving force of economic activity described as the pursuit of the largest possible amount of pleasurable wealth.

Mixed economies. Economies that combine attributes of capitalism, such as private property and market mechanisms with elements of socialism, in particular welfare structures and some degree of government control over economic activity.

Monetarism. The body of theory that stresses the importance of the quantity of money in determining the rate of inflation and the level of activity.

Money illusion. The tendency to base economic behavior on nominal rather than real prices.

Money supply. There are many ways of calculating the money supply. Perhaps the most common is cash held by the public, plus demand deposits at commercial banks. This is designated $M1_A$. (We have called this M in our text.) Various other definitions ($M1_B$, M2, M3) expand the basic definition by adding various other liquid assets.

Multinational corporations. Corporations that derive a substantial proportion of their income of sales from overseas production, as contrasted with exports.

Multiplier-accelerator. The joint interaction of the multiplier effect, which creates additional income from an injection, and the accelerator effect which creates additional investment from a rise in consumption.

Multiplier effect. The tendency of injections to create increases in income larger than the original injections. The multiplier effect results from the marginal propensity to consume.

National income. The toal amount of factor incomes earned over a period of time. National income does not include transfer payments.

Net investment. The use of money or resources to create additional capital goods.

Net national product. Gross national product minus depreciation. Net national product is also national income (factor earnings) plus the value of indirect taxes.

Nominal growth. Increase in output measured in current dollars, without allowance for changes in the purchasing power of dollars. If we compare the GNPs of two years, without deflating the dollar amounts, we are comparing nominal growth.

Nominal values. The values or prices of objects in current terms with no adjustment for changes in the value of the monetary unit.

Open market operations. The buying and selling of government bonds by the Federal Reserve, as a means of expanding or contracting the reserves of commercial banks.

Participation rate. The proportion of the population of working age that is actively seeking work.

Per capita GNP. Gross national product divided by the population.

Phillips curve. The presumed statistical correlation between unemployment and inflation first pointed out by A. W. Phillips.

Portfolio investment. Financial investment, as opposed to real investment in plant and equipment.

Price index. A statistical measure of price levels in which one year is chosen as a base, and the other years expressed as a percentage of that base.

Production. The use of labor and resources to create utilities.

Production-possibility curve. A graphic depiction of the total outputs available to a society. Production-possibility curves are usually bowed outward because of the law of increasing cost.

Production-possibility frontier. The outer limit of production possibilities as we move resources from one use to another. (See *Production-possibility curves.*)

Productivity. A measure of output per unit of input over a given period of time, such as yearly or hourly output per worker or per machine.

Propensity to consume. The relation between consumption and income: C/Y. (See also *Marginal propensity to consume.*)

Propensity to save. The relation between saving and income: S/Y. (See also *Marginal Propensity to Consume.*)

Purchasing power. The ability to buy.

Quantity theory. The theory that relates the level of prices to the quantity of money, on the assumption that velocity of money remains constant.

Rational expectations. The tendency of markets to foresee and anticipate actions intended to alter market outcomes.

Rationality. The assumption that men can intelligently adapt their actions (means) to their purposes (ends).

Real growth. Increases in output corrected for changes in the purchasing power of the currency.

Real vs. financial investment. Real investment is the act of devoting resources to capital formation. Financial investment denotes the purchase of equities, claims or other instruments that channel personal savings into banks or businesses.

Reserve requirement. The proportion of deposits that must be kept in vault cash or at a Federal Reserve Bank. Reserve requirements are set by the Board of Governors of the Federal Reserve System.

Reserves. Deposits that may not be loaned or invested. Reserves must be held in cash or at a Federal Reserve Bank.

Saving. The act of not using income for consumption. Saving is a financial act when we put money in a bank, but its real meaning is to relinquish a claim on resources.

Schedule. A list of different values of a variable, such as quantities or prices.

SDRs. Special Drawing Rights, an international reserve currency unit created by the International Monetary Fund (IMF), an agency of the United Nations.

Sector. A division of the economy with common characteristics. Usually we speak of the public and the private sector; of the consumption, investment, and government sectors; or of the agricultural, industrial, and service sectors.

Stagflation. An economic condition of simultaneous inflation and stagnation—that is, rising prices and inadequate growth.

Stocks. Legal instruments of ownership in corporations.

Stop-go policies. Alternations of restrictive and stimulative fiscal and monetary measures.

Tight money. A condition, associated with restrictive monetary policy, that makes it difficult for borrowers to obtain bank loans.

Trade-off. An exchange relationship denoting how much of A is needed to obtain a unit of B.

Transactions demand. The amount of cash we need to carry on normal economic transactions. At higher levels of economic activity there is normally a higher demand for transactions balances, for such purposes as meeting payrolls,or financing ordinary expenditures.

Transfers. Any payment from one person or institution to another made for purposes other than to remunerate work. Social security is a transfer payment; so is the payment of an allowance to a minor, or a charity payment.

Unemployment. Inability to find work at the going wage level.

Utility. Pleasure or wellbeing.

Velocity of circulation. The number of times a unit of currency is used during a period of time, usually a year. The velocity of circulation is calculated by dividing output (GNP) by the money supply.

Wealth. Production that yields utilities.

Yields. The income paid by a bond compared with its market value. A bond issued at a price of $1,000 with a ten percent "coupon rate" ($100 of interest payable annually) will have a yield of 20 percent if the bond can be bought on the market at $500. It will have a 10 percent yield if its price is the original issue price. Its yield will fall to 5 percent if the market price of the bond rises to $2,000.

Zero sum game. A contest in which every gain is matched by an exactly equivalent loss.

INDEX

RELATED BOOKS

THE MAKING OF ECONOMIC SOCIETY. 6th ed.
by Robert L. Heilbroner
The basic elements of economic thought
in the context of history.

UNDERSTANDING MICROECONOMICS. 5th ed.
by Robert L. Heilbroner and
Lester C. Thurow
An analytical probing of the inner structure of our economic behavior and
misbehavior.

Robert L. Heilbroner

Photo by
Waring Abbott

Lester C. Thurow

Robert Heilbroner is the author of *The Worldly Philosophers,* surely the most celebrated exposition of economic thought written in our time. Lester Thurow is the author of *The Zero Sum Society,* one of the most influential and best-selling economic statements in recent years. In this book, and in *Understanding Microeconomics,* Heilbroner and Thurow have pooled their talents for clarity, relevance, and intellectual stimulation. Students will find that these books make economics come alive; instructors will find that they make the subject teachable. Here is a new edition of an already classic series, specially oriented to the problems of the 1980s.

0-13-936559